FROM À LA CARTE TO ZUCCHINI

Other books by this author

Letters of Norman Lindsay (with R.G. Howarth)
Dear Robertson: Letters to an Australian Publisher (paperback edition *George Robertson: A Publishing Life in Letters*)
When Was That?: Chronology of Australia (paperback edition *What Happened When: A Chronology of Australia from 1788*)
An Illustrated Treasury of Australian Epic Journeys
One of the First and One of the Finest: Beatrice Davis, Book Editor
The Book of Quotations (with Robert I. Fitzhenry)

FROM À LA CARTE TO ZUCCHINI

An A to Z of Food and Cooking

Anthony Barker

ALLEN & UNWIN

Illustrations by Anna Warren

Cover design by Seymour Designs
Cover photograph by Robyn Latimer

First published 1995
Allen & Unwin Pty Ltd
9 Atchison Street, St Leonards, NSW 2065 Australia

National Library of Australia
Cataloguing-in-Publication entry:

From à la carte to zucchini: an a to z of food and cooking.

ISBN 1 86373 989 0.

1. Cookery—Encyclopedias. 2. Food—Encyclopedias.
I. Barker, A. W. (Anthony Wilhelm), 1930– . II. Title.

641

Set in 10/11pt Times by DOCUPRO, Sydney
Printed by Southwood Press, Sydney

10 9 8 7 6 5 4 3 2 1

Contents

Preface

First, a confession: I am not a cook. I am a book editor who has edited a number of cookbooks over the years, and in doing so I have had to find out a good deal about the techniques of preparing and cooking food, the terms used in cookery, and the ingredients that make up the dishes we eat at table. It has not always been straightforward. To my surprise I found that food authorities often disagreed with one another. I also discovered there were terms that had different meanings in different contexts (not the least the Australian context), terms that looked alike but had different meanings, and terms that were quite different but had much the same meaning. It occurred to me that a reference book would be useful to clarify these matters and also act as a glossary of cookery terms, a dictionary of ingredients in common use in Australia today, and a guide to the selection, preparation, and cooking of food.

Cookery writers have to assume their readers have a certain knowledge of cooking; otherwise they would be forever interrupting themselves to explain terms, procedures, and ingredients, which would be irritating to those readers who didn't need to be told. But there are people new to cooking who don't know what to do when the recipe says 'bake blind', 'deglaze the pan', 'julienne the carrots', or 'reduce the liquid by half'. They are probably confused, as I was, about pâté and pâte, pesto and pistou, pimento and pimiento, ragoût and ragù, tortellini and tortelloni. They may wonder if there is any difference between blanch and parboil, pan-fry and sauté, and what goes to make up a bouquet garni. Even experienced cooks and food lovers could be excused for being unfamiliar with some of the new foods being produced in Australia or imported here—tropical fruits, Asian vegetables, exotic herbs and spices, farmed fish, seafood, and game—and some of the dishes from the cuisines of India, South-East Asia, Latin America, North Africa, and the Middle East, which are becoming increasingly popular as the population becomes increasingly multicultural.

To cover everything, if that were possible when changes are occurring all the time, the book would have to be of encyclopaedic proportions, and that was not practicable for this reference book series. A selection had to be made of the most used and useful subjects. What I did was compile a list of entries from word lists I had kept while editing cookbooks, from glossaries and indexes of the books I used as reference, and from the subjects that came up most often in articles appearing in the daily and weekly press and on radio and television food programs. I am indebted to writers such as Meryl Constance, John Newton, Stephanie Alexander, Maggie Beer, Jill Dupleix, Gay Bilson, Tony Bilson, Tess Mallos, Molly O'Neill, Anabel Dean, Guy Griffin, and others writing in the

Sydney Morning Herald's 'Good Living' supplement and 'Good Weekend' magazine, Cherry Ripe and Diane Holuigue in the *Weekend Australian*, and Alan Saunders of the ABC's 'Food Program' not only for providing me with subject headings but for much information on those subjects which I was able to glean from their articles and programs. They formed part of a range of sources from which I gathered information to write each entry. Books used for reference are listed at the end of this book.

Acknowledgements are due also to the organisations and individuals who responded helpfully to my requests for information: the Australian Meat and Live-Stock Corporation, who also gave me permission to reprint material from their publication *Easy Ways: Cooking with Beef and Lamb*; the National Food Authority for providing the list of approved food additives; the National Heart Foundation of Australia; the Australian Pork Corporation; the New South Wales Department of Agriculture; the Queensland Fruit and Vegetable Growers; the Potato Research Station, Department of Agriculture and Rural Affairs, Healesville, Vic.; the Ricegrowers Co-operative Limited, Leeton, NSW; Olsson's and Pacific Salt Pty Ltd, Adelaide, SA; Annie Foord and Ken Harada of the New South Wales Fish Marketing Authority; Sue Dodd of the Sydney Market Authority; Dr John Paxton, Curator of Fishes at the Australian Museum; Marcel Bouvier, Greg Barca, and John Best of Beecroft Butchery, Beecroft, NSW; and Frank Martelli and the staff of Martelli's Fruit Market, West Epping, NSW.

As well, I would like to acknowledge the help of friends who lent me books and provided me with information and advice. I am especially grateful to Barbara Beckett who made available to me, over a long period, several books from her extensive food library and who generously let me have information from her own research and offered enthusiastic encouragement. Gerry Eltis, too, provided books and suggested avenues of research. I am grateful to Kim Wilson, who directed my attention to Harold McGee's fascinating book *On Food and Cooking*. And I would not have been able to manage without the help of my wife, Joyce, an enthusiastic and knowledgeable cook, who answered my interminable questions patiently, who found many things I was looking for through her intimate knowledge of the contents of her own sizeable collection of cookbooks, and who supplied me with down-to-earth information on cookery gained from preparing incomparable meals daily for the past forty years.

How to use this book

The headword or phrase is printed in **bold type**, capitalised only when it would be printed with an initial capital within a sentence.

Variant spellings and expanded versions of the headword are separated by oblique strokes (e.g., **cardamom / cardamum / cardamon; artichoke / globe artichoke**). The first spelling is usually the preferred one.

Translations of foreign headwords and the foreign equivalents of English headwords, if included, are set in brackets (e.g., **Chinese broccoli (gai laan)**).

On numerous occasions similar, contrasting, or confused terms are treated together; these are separated by commas (e.g., **bake, casserole**, stew; **comfit, confit; macerate, marinate, marinade**), and cross-references are included at the alphabetical place of the other terms in the group.

Cross-references are indicated by printing the word or phrase referred to in SMALL CAPITALS (e.g., 'see also PASTA'; 'The sauce is served with MUSSELS and also with SWEETBREADS and other OFFAL'). They have been included where it seemed useful to let the reader know of the entry's existence or to direct the reader to that entry for further information.

On several occasions in this book a cooking instruction states that the food in question should be cooked in boiling salted water. For those on a salt-reduced diet, the food may be cooked in plain boiling water.

A

à la carte. According to the menu on which each item is priced individually, not as part of a set meal.

à la grecque. Cooked in olive oil with coriander seeds and other seasonings and served cold. Usually applied to vegetables, particularly mushrooms and artichokes.

à la king. Served in a rich cream sauce sometimes flavoured with sherry or Madeira. Chicken à la King is the most famous dish of this kind. It is made with chicken, fresh mushrooms, capsicums and egg yolks in the cream sauce, served on toast triangles or in heated pastry cases.

à la mode. Literally 'in the mode' or 'according to fashion'; *of* something is usually implied or expressed—for example, Tripes à la Mode de Caen' (see TRIPE). Boeuf à la Mode is larded beef braised in wine with carrots, herbs and seasonings, and calves' feet; it can be served hot, or cold in its own jelly. In the United States, *à la mode* means served with ice-cream.

à la poulette. Having a sauce thickened with egg yolks, cream, and lemon to taste. The sauce is served with MUSSELS and also with SWEETBREADS and other OFFAL.

à la reine. A term used to describe an elegant and delicate dish, often made with chicken and a rich cream sauce. The most famous is Potage à la Reine—soup made of puréed chicken breasts combined with egg yolks, heavy cream, and seasonings.

abalone. Also known as muttonfish, the abalone is a marine mollusc with a single shell and a broad, muscular foot with which it clings to rocks. Found mainly in South Australia and Tasmania, abalone has long been a delicacy throughout Asia, and almost all the abalone harvested, or farmed, in Australia is exported. It is therefore expensive to buy. As well as being sold live, abalone is available frozen (cooked and uncooked, in shell or shucked), in cans, and dried.

   The traditional way of treating fresh abalone is to gut and trim it, pound the meat flat to tenderise it as you would a very tough steak, and then grill, barbecue, or braise it for a long time. However, if it is well trimmed and sliced thinly, the meat can be sautéed in less than a minute, when it will be tender and ready to eat; if overcooked, it will toughen.

abiu. Also known as abi and caimo, the abiu is a bright yellow, elliptical to round fruit, 5–10 centimetres across, with shiny thick skin and gelatinous, translucent white flesh. Native to South America, abius are grown in Australia and available most of the year, especially from December to June.

Allow the fruit to ripen at room temperature away from direct sunlight. When ripe, it is soft and the flesh has a sweet, caramel flavour.

To eat an abiu, peel off the skin, remove the seed or seeds, then slice the flesh or cut it into cubes or segments. It may be eaten as it is or used in salads or fruit salads. It may also be puréed and used in drinks, sorbets, and sauces. Abius are an excellent source of vitamin C.

achiote / achuete. Other names for ANNATTO.

acidulated water. Cold water to which vinegar (preferably white wine vinegar), lemon juice, or lime juice has been added, in the proportion of about 1 tablespoon of vinegar or juice to half a litre of water. It is used to prevent cut fruits and vegetables from discolouring and to purify BRAINS and SWEETBREADS.

additives are used in processed foods to restore or improve taste or appearance, to improve keeping quality or stability, to preserve food when this is the most practical way of extending its storage life, and to provide for special dietary needs, such as replacing sugar with an artificial sweetener. In Australia, food labels must list all ingredients in descending order of proportion by weight except water, which may be listed last. Additives listed by their class names, such as 'colour', 'preservative', or 'emulsifier' must also be identified by an individual name or code number, so that anyone who wishes to avoid a specific additive, perhaps because of an allergic reaction to it, can make a choice. The Australian numbering system is based on a system operating internationally. Listed below are the code numbers for food additives approved by the National Food Standards Council as at December 1994. Vitamins and minerals added to food to supplement the diet are not classed as additives unless they perform an additional function—for example, vitamin C (ascorbic acid) used as an antioxidant.

FOOD ADDITIVES IN NUMERICAL ORDER

(function in brackets)

100	Curcumin or Turmeric *(colouring)*	124	Ponceau 4R *(colouring)*	150	Caramel *(colouring)*
101	Riboflavin *(colouring)*	127	Erythrosine* *(colouring)*	151	Brilliant black BN *(colouring)*
102	Tartrazine *(colouring)*	129	Allura red AC *(colouring)*	153	Carbon black *(colouring)*
103	Alkanet *(colouring)*	132	Indigotine *(colouring)*	155	Brown HT *(colouring)*
104	Quinoline yellow *(colouring)*	133	Brilliant blue FCF *(colouring)*	160a	β-Carotene *(colouring)*
110	Sunset yellow FCF *(colouring)*	140	Chlorophyll *(colouring)*	160	β-apo-8' Carotenoic acid methyl ester *(colouring)*
120	Carmines or Cochineal *(colouring)*	141	Chlorophyll-copper complex, chlorophyllin copper complex, sodium and potassium salts *(colouring)*	160b	Annatto extracts *(colouring)*
122	Azorubine *(colouring)*				
123	Amaranth *(colouring)*	142	Food green S *(colouring)*	160e	β-apo-8' Carotenal *(colouring)*

160f	β-apo-8' Carotenoic acid methyl or ethyl ester *(colouring)*	249	Potassium nitrite *(preservative, colour fixative)*	311	Octyl gallate *(antioxidant)*
161	Xanthophylls *(colouring)*	250	Sodium nitrite *(preservative, colour fixative))*	312	Dodecyl gallate *(antioxidant)*
162	Beet red *(colouring)*	251	Sodium nitrate *(preservative, colour fixative)*	315	Erythorbic acid *(antioxidant)*
163	Anthocyanins *(colouring)*	252	Potassium nitrate *(preservative, colour fixative)*	316	Sodium erythorbate *(antioxidant)*
170	Calcium carbonate† *(mineral salt, colouring)*	260	Acetic acid, glacial *(food acid)*	319	*tert*-Butylhydro-quinone *(antioxidant)*

160f   β-apo-8' Carotenoic
       acid methyl or ethyl
       ester
       (colouring)
161   Xanthophylls
       (colouring)
162   Beet red
       (colouring)
163   Anthocyanins
       (colouring)
170   Calcium carbonate†
       *(mineral salt,
       colouring)*
171   Titanium dioxide
       (colouring)
172   Iron oxide (black,
       red, yellow)
       (colouring)
181   Tannic acid
       (colouring)
200   Sorbic acid
       (preservative)
201   Sodium sorbate
       (preservative)
202   Potassium sorbate
       (preservative)
203   Calcium sorbate
       (preservative)
210   Benzoic acid
       (preservative)
211   Sodium benzoate
       (preservative)
212   Potassium benzoate
       (preservative)
213   Calcium benzoate
       (preservative)
216   Propylparaben
       (preservative)
218   Methylparaben
       (preservative)
220   Sulphur dioxide
       (preservative)
221   Sodium sulphite
       (preservative)
222   Sodium bisulphite
       (preservative)
223   Sodium
       metabisulphite
       *(preservative, flour
       treatment agent)*
224   Potassium
       metabisulphite
       (preservative)
225   Potassium sulphite
       (preservative)
228   Potassium bisulphite
       (preservative)
234   Nisin
       (preservative)
235   Natamycin
       (mould inhibitor)

249   Potassium nitrite
       *(preservative, colour
       fixative)*
250   Sodium nitrite
       *(preservative, colour
       fixative))*
251   Sodium nitrate
       *(preservative, colour
       fixative)*
252   Potassium nitrate
       *(preservative, colour
       fixative)*
260   Acetic acid, glacial
       (food acid)
261   Potassium acetate
       (food acid)
262   Sodium diacetate
       *(food acid, acidity
       regulator)*
263   Calcium acetate
       (food acid)
264   Ammonium acetate
       (food acid)
270   Lactic acid
       (food acid)
280   Propionic acid
       (preservative)
281   Sodium propionate
       (preservative)
282   Calcium propionate
       (preservative)
283   Potassium propionate
       (preservative)
290   Carbon dioxide
       (propellant)
296   Malic acid
       (food acid)
297   Fumaric acid
       (food acid)
300   Ascorbic acid
       *(antioxidant, flour
       treatment agent)*
301   Sodium ascorbate
       (antioxidant)
302   Calcium ascorbate
       (antioxidant)
303   Potassium ascorbate
       (antioxidant)
304   Ascorbyl palmitate
       (antioxidant)
306   Tocopherols
       concentrate, mixed
       (antioxidant)
307   dl-α-Tocopherol
       (antioxidant)
308   γ-Tocopherol
       (antioxidant)
309   δ-Tocopherol
       (antioxidant)
310   Propyl gallate
       (antioxidant)

311   Octyl gallate
       (antioxidant)
312   Dodecyl gallate
       (antioxidant)
315   Erythorbic acid
       (antioxidant)
316   Sodium erythorbate
       (antioxidant)
319   *tert*-Butylhydro-
       quinone
       (antioxidant)
320   Butylated
       hydroxyanisole
       (antioxidant)
321   Butylated
       hydroxytoluene
       (antioxidant)
322   Lecithin
       *(antioxidant,
       emulsifier)*
325   Sodium lactate
       (food acid)
326   Potassium lactate
       (food acid)
327   Calcium lactate
       (food acid)
328   Ammonium lactate
       (food acid)
329   Magnesium lactate
       *(acidity regulator,
       flour treatment agent)*
330   Citric acid
       (food acid)
331   Sodium citrates
       (food acid)
332   Potassium citrates
       (food acid)
333   Calcium citrates
       (food acid)
334   Tartaric acid
       (food acid)
335   Sodium tartrates
       (food acid)
336   Potassium tartrates
       (food acid)
337   Potassium sodium
       tartrate
       (food acid)
338   Phosphoric acid
       (food acid)
339   Sodium phosphates
       (mineral salt)
340   Potassium
       phosphates†
       (mineral salt)
341   Calcium phosphates†
       *(mineral salt, flour
       treatment agent)*
342   Ammonium
       phosphates†
       (mineral salt)

343 **Magnesium phosphates†** *(mineral salt)*

349 **Ammonium malate** *(food acid)*

350 **DL-Sodium malates** *(food acid)*

351 **Potassium malates** *(food acid)*

352 **DL-Calcium malates** *(food acid)*

353 **Metatartaric acid** *(food acid)*

354 **Calcium tartrate** *(food acid)*

355 **Adipic acid** *(food acid)*

357 **Potassium adipate** *(food acid)*

365 **Sodium fumarate** *(food acid)*

366 **Potassium fumarate** *(food acid)*

367 **Calcium fumarate** *(food acid)*

368 **Ammonium fumarate** *(food acid)*

375 **Niacin** *(colour retention agent)*

380 **Ammonium citrates** *(food acid)*

381 **Ferric ammonium citrate** *(food acid)*

385 **Calcium disodium ethyl-enediaminetetraacetate** *(sequestrant, preservative)*

400 **Alginic acid** *(thickener and vegetable gum)*

401 **Sodium alginate** *(thickener and vegetable gum)*

402 **Potassium alginate** *(thickener and vegetable gum)*

403 **Ammonium alginate** *(thickener and vegetable gum)*

404 **Calcium alginate** *(thickener and vegetable gum)*

405 **Propylene glycol alginate** *(thickener and vegetable gum)*

406 **Agar** *(thickener and vegetable gum)*

407 **Carrageenan** *(thickener and vegetable gum)*

409 **Arabinogalactan** *(vegetable gum)*

410 **Locust bean gum** *(thickener and vegetable gum)*

412 **Guar gum** *(thickener and vegetable gum)*

413 **Tragacanth** *(thickener and vegetable gum)*

414 **Acacia** *(thickener and vegetable gum)*

415 **Xanthan gum** *(thickener and vegetable gum)*

416 **Karaya gum** *(thickener and vegetable gum)*

420 **Sorbitol** *(artificial sweetening substance, humectant)*

421 **Mannitol** *(artificial sweetening substance, humectant)*

422 **Glycerin** *(humectant)*

433 **Polysorbate 80** *(emulsifier)*

435 **Polysorbate 60** *(emulsifier)*

436 **Polysorbate 65** *(emulsifier)*

440 **Pectin** *(vegetable gum)*

442 **Ammonium salts of phosphatidic acid** *(emulsifier)*

444 **Sucrose acetate isobutyrate** *(emulsifier, stabiliser)*

450 **Sodium and potassium pyrophosphate†** *(mineral salt)*

451 **Sodium and potassium tripolyphosphates†** *(mineral salt)*

452 **Sodium and potassium metaphosphates, polymeta-phosphates and polyphosphates†** *(mineral salt)*

460 **Cellulose, microcrystalline or powdered** *(anti-caking agent)*

461 **Methylcellulose** *(thickener and vegetable gum)*

464 **Hydroxypropyl methylcellulose** *(thickener and vegetable gum)*

465 **Methyl ethyl cellulose** *(thickener and vegetable gum)*

466 **Sodium carboxymethyl-cellulose** *(thickener and vegetable gum)*

470 **Magnesium stearate** *(emulsifier, stabiliser)*

471 **Mono- and di-glycerides of fatty acids** *(emulsifier)*

472a **Acetic and fatty acid esters of glycerol** *(emulsifier)*

472b **Lactic and fatty acid esters of glycerol** *(emulsifier)*

472c **Citric and fatty acid esters of glycerol** *(emulsifier)*

472d **Tartaric and fatty acid esters of glycerol** *(emulsifier)*

472e **Diacetyltartaric and fatty acid esters of glycerol** *(emulsifier)*

473 **Sucrose esters of fatty acids** *(emulsifier)*

475 **Polyglycerol esters of fatty acids** *(emulsifier)*

476 **Polyglycerol esters of interesterified ricinoleic acid** *(emulsifier)*

477 **Propylene glycol mono- and di-esters** *(emulsifier)*

480 **Dioctyl sodium sulphosuccinate** *(emulsifier)*

481 **Sodium oleyl or stearoyl lactylate** *(emulsifier, stabiliser)*

482 **Calcium oleyl or stearoyl lactylate**
(emulsifier, stabiliser)

491 **Sorbitan monostearate**
(emulsifier)

492 **Sorbitan tristearate**
(emulsifier)

500 **Sodium carbonates**
(mineral salt)

501 **Potassium carbonates†**
(mineral salt)

503 **Ammonium carbonates†**
(mineral salt)

504 **Magnesium carbonate†**
(anti-caking agent, mineral salt)

507 **Hydrochloric acid**
(acidity regulator)

508 **Potassium chloride†**
(mineral salt)

509 **Calcium chloride†**
(mineral salt)

510 **Ammonium chloride†**
(flour treatment agent, mineral salt)

511 **Magnesium chloride†**
(mineral salt)

512 **Stannous chloride**
(colour retention agent)

514 **Sodium sulphate**
(mineral salt)

515 **Potassium sulphate**
(mineral salt)

516 **Calcium sulphate**
(flour treatment agent, mineral salt)

518 **Magnesium sulphate**
(mineral salt)

519 **Cupric sulphate**
(mineral salt)

526 **Calcium hydroxide**
(mineral salt)

529 **Calcium oxide**
(mineral salt)

535 **Sodium ferrocyanide**
(anti-caking agent)

536 **Potassium ferrocyanide**
(anti-caking agent)

541 **Sodium aluminium phosphate, acidic**
(acidity regulator, emulsifier)

542 **Bone phosphate**
(anti-caking agent)

551 **Silicon dioxide**
(anti-caking agent)

552 **Calcium silicate**
(anti-caking agent)

553 **Talc**
(anti-caking agent)

554 **Sodium aluminosilicate**
(anti-caking agent)

556 **Calcium aluminium silicate**
(anti-caking agent)

558 **Bentonite**
(anti-caking agent)

559 **Kaolin**
(anti-caking agent)

570 **Stearic acid**
(anti-caking agent)

575 **Glucono δ-lactone**
(acidic regulator, raising agent)

577 **Potassium gluconate**
(stabiliser)

578 **Calcium gluconate**
(acidity regulator, firming agent)

579 **Ferrous gluconate**
(colour retention agent)

620 **L-Glutamic acid**
(flavour enhancer)

621 **Monosodium L-glutamate (MSG)**
(flavour enhancer)

622 **Monopotassium L-glutamate**
(flavour enhancer)

623 **Calcium di-L-glutamate**
(flavour enhancer)

624 **Monoammonium L-glutamate**
(flavour enhancer)

625 **Magnesium di-L-glutamate**
(flavour enhancer)

627 **Disodium guanylate**
(flavour enhancer)

631 **Disodium inosinate**
(flavour enhancer)

636 **Maltol**
(flavour enhancer)

637 **Ethyl maltol**
(flavour enhancer)

900 **Dimethylpoly- siloxane**
(emulsifier, antifoaming agent, anti-caking agent)

901 **Beeswax, white and yellow**
(glazing agent, release agent)

903 **Carnauba wax**
(glazing agent)

904 **Shellac, bleached**
(glazing agent)

905a **Mineral oil, white**
(glazing agent)

905b **Petrolatum**
(glazing agent)

920 **L-Cysteine monohydrochloride**
(flour treatment agent)

925 **Chlorine**
(bleaching agent)

926 **Chlorine dioxide**
(bleaching agent)

928 **Benzoyl peroxide**
(bleaching agent)

941 **Nitrogen**
(propellant)

942 **Nitrous oxide**
(propellant)

950 **Acesulphame potassium**
(artificial sweetening substance)

951 **Aspartame**
(artificial sweetening substance)

952 **Cyclamates**
(artificial sweetening substance)

953 **Isomalt**
(humectant)

954 **Saccharine**
(artificial sweetening substance)

957 **Thaumatin**
(flavour enhancer, artificial sweetening substance)

965 **Hydrogenated glucose syrup**
(humectant)

967 **Xylitol**
(humectant)

1100 **Amylases**
(enzyme—flour treatment agent)

1101 **Proteases (papain, bromelain, ficin)**
(enzymes—flour treatment agent, stabiliser, tenderiser, flavour enhancer)

1102 **Glucose oxidase**
(enzyme—antioxidant)

1104 **Lipases**
(enzyme—flavour enhancer)

1105 **Lisozyme**
(enzyme—preservative)

1200 **Polydextrose**
(humectant)

1201 **Polyvinylpyrrolidone**
(stabiliser, clarifying

	agent, dispersing agent)	1410	**Monostarch phosphate** *(thickener and vegetable gum)*	1422	**Acetylated distarch adipate** *(thickener and vegetable gum)*
1202	**Polyvinylpoly- pyrrolidone** *(colour stabiliser, colloidal stabiliser)*	1412	**Distarch phosphate** *(thickener and vegetable gum)*	1440	**Hydroxypropyl starch** *(thickener and vegetable gum)*
1400	**Dextrin roasted starch** *(thickener and vegetable gum)*	1413	**Phosphated distarch phosphate** *(thickener and vegetable gum)*	1442	**Hydroxypropyl distarch phosphate** *(thickener and vegetable gum)*
1401	**Acid treated starch** *(thickener and vegetable gum)*	1414	**Acetylated distarch phosphate** *(thickener and vegetable gum)*	1450	**Starch sodium octenyl succinate** *(thickener and vegetable gum)*
1402	**Alkaline treated starch** *(thickener and vegetable gum)*	1420	**Starch acetate esterified with acetic anhydride** *(thickener and vegetable gum)*	1505	**Triethyl citrate** *(foam stabiliser)*
1403	**Bleached starch** *(thickener and vegetable gum)*			1518	**Triacetin** *(humectant)*
1404	**Oxidised starch** *(thickener and vegetable gum)*	1421	**Starch acetate esterified with vinyl acetate** *(thickener and vegetable gum)*	1520	**Propylene glycol** *(humectant, wetting agent, dispersing agent)*
1405	**Enzyme-treated starches** *(thickener and vegetable gum)*				

* To be deleted in March 1997
† May be contained in salt substitutes

adzuki beans. Tiny, reddish-brown, with a cream-coloured seam, adzuki beans are the seeds of a bushy bean plant grown extensively for food in China and Japan. They have a sweetish taste, and the mashed beans are sometimes used in cakes and desserts. They are also used in soups and stews. For information on preparation, storage, etc., see BEANS, DRIED. **To cook adzuki beans**, boil them gently until they are tender (1½–2 hours) or pressure cook them for 20–30 minutes.

agar-agar. A gelatinous substance obtained from various kinds of red seaweed. Agar-agar is used for thickening certain foods (approved additive no. 406) and, in Asia, for making soups and as a setting agent for desserts, etc. It is sold in long, dry, translucent ribbons or in thin leaves and strips. Agar-agar mixtures will set at room temperature.

aïoli. A cold sauce made from crushed garlic, olive oil, egg yolks and season- ing—in effect, a garlic-flavoured MAYONNAISE. It is served with boiled fish or meats and cold cooked or raw vegetables. In Provence, *aïoli* is the name of the dish itself, whatever the main ingredient, when it is served with this sauce (*ai* means 'garlic' and *oli* 'oil' in Provençal).

al dente. An Italian term meaning literally 'to the tooth', used to describe food, especially pasta but sometimes vegetables, which is cooked so that it is still firm to the bite, not soft or mushy. (See also PASTA.)

alfalfa sprouts. The leguminous plant *Medicago sativa*, known as lucerne in Australia and used as animal fodder, is also eaten at sprout stage as a health food, when it is known by its American name alfalfa. These fine sprouts with green stalks and tips are used in sandwiches and salads, as an edible bed of greenery on which to serve cold meats, and as a garnish. They can also be tossed with cooked vegetables and stir-fried in Asian dishes. Buy sprouts that look springy and smell fresh; avoid tired-looking or slimy ones and those that have brown tips to the roots. They can be stored for up to four days in a well-ventilated container in the refrigerator. (See also BEAN SPROUTS.)

allemande sauce. Also known as *sauce blonde* and *sauce Parisienne*, allemande is a VELOUTÉ reduced to half, enriched with egg yolks and a knob of butter and seasoned with a little nutmeg and mushroom liquor. It is served with white meat and fish. Allemande is not, as the name would suggest, a German sauce, but was so named because the colour of it reminded its creator, Antonin Carême, of 'Gretchen's' fair hair.

allspice is the dried berry of an evergreen tree from the West Indies which has a fragrance resembling a blend of cinnamon, nutmeg, and cloves. Allspice is not a mixture of these spices, as is sometimes thought by those who have only seen it in its powdered form. It is available both whole and ground. The berries are used in pickles, preserves, and chutney. In the ground form it is used as a flavouring for cakes, soups, meat dishes, milk and plum puddings, and vegetables. Allspice is sometimes called Jamaica pepper or Jamaican pimento (its genus is *Pimienta*) which causes confusion with *pimiento*, another name for CAPSICUM. (See also PIMENTO, PIMIENTO.)

almond. The seed from the fruit of a tree native to the eastern Mediterranean region and related to the peach and plum. There are sweet and bitter varieties; bitter almonds are not eaten as food but yield a fragrant oil that is used in confectionery making and for flavouring. Almonds can be bought in many forms: in the shell, as whole kernels with the skin on or off (blanched), toasted, salted, smoked, slivered, flaked, ground, and as a paste (see MARZIPAN), to name a few. They are eaten whole, fresh or dried, before meals with drinks or after meals with port; they are used as a garnish on cakes, cooked with chicken, devilled, mixed into salads, and set in toffee. (See also PRALINE, PRALIN.) Ground almonds are used in cakes and biscuits in place of flour. Like all nuts, almonds have a high oil content, but in the case of almonds it is 90 per cent unsaturated (68 per cent mono, 22 per cent poly).

To blanch almonds. Drop the almonds slowly into boiling water and boil them for about a minute, or simply pour boiling water over them and stand for 2–3 minutes. Drain, then slip the skins off between thumb and forefinger. Peeling almonds without treating them first with boiling water is harder, but they retain more flavour.

If you want to sliver almonds, slice them with a very sharp, small knife while they are still warm and wet after blanching, but it is much easier to buy them already slivered.

For toasting and other general information, see NUTS.

amandine, amardine. Amandine means prepared with almonds (*amande* is the French word for almond). Amardine is a sheet of dried or compressed apricots. A creamy pudding made from amardine is traditionally eaten in Egypt during Ramadan.

amaretti. Bitter MACAROONS made with bitter almond essence and often served with ice-cream desserts.

ambrosia. A mild cheese with a tangy flavour and smooth, buttery texture, originally from Sweden. In the southern United States it is the name of a dessert composed of segmented oranges and coconut, sometimes with the addition of other fruit. According to Greek mythology, ambrosia was the food of the gods; hence, it is anything particularly delicious or fragrant.

anchovies. The anchovy is a small member of the herring family which used to be abundant in southern European waters but is now almost fished out there. Much of the anchovies imported into Australia have been canned in Italy from fish caught and salted in Africa and South America. An anchovy processing plant has been established in Fremantle, WA, using the Australian anchovy, *Engraulis australis*, which produces good quality salted anchovies and anchovies in olive oil.

Anchovies have been savoured since Roman times and are much used in Italian cookery. They are a popular ingredient in pizza toppings. Canned or bottled anchovy fillets come either flat or rolled around a caper and packed in oil. They are also pounded or ground into a paste; however, the commercial product sold in Australia is usually made from some other fish flavoured with anchovy. You can make your own paste by mashing some fillets and mixing the mash with soft butter. **Anchovy toast** is toast spread with anchovy paste.

Some people soak anchovies in milk for 20 minutes or so to give them a milder flavour.

angelica. Ancient folklore holds that an angel revealed the medicinal qualities of angelica as a prophylactic against plague; hence its botanical name, *Angelica archangelica*. It is a perennial herb that grows freely in Europe. Oil distilled from the seeds and roots is used for making liqueurs. The leaves can be used to flavour stewed fruit. Candied angelica is made from the stalks and leaf stems of the plant. Chopped or sliced thinly, it is used in cakes and for decorating sweets and confectionery because of its beautiful green colour. It will keep almost indefinitely in a jar. Make sure that what you buy is real angelica; a jellied and candied green confection, and what appears to be candied celery, are sometimes sold in its place.

angels on horseback are oysters wrapped in bacon, skewered or fastened with thread, grilled and served on toast as an entrée. Stoned prunes wrapped in bacon and prepared in a similar way are known as devils on horseback, though they too are sometimes referred to as angels on horseback.

anise, aniseed. Anise is an annual plant, native to the Middle East, which is grown mainly for its small, oval, light brown seeds, although the leaves may be used in salads and as a garnish. Anise seed, or aniseed, tastes like licorice and is used to flavour liqueurs such as ouzo and Pernod. (French anisette is flavoured mainly with STAR ANISE, the fruit of a totally different plant.)

Anise has been known for thousands of years as an aid to digestion; the Romans ate cakes made with aniseed at the end of their enormous feasts. While aniseed is no longer a common cooking ingredient, it can be used in the preparation of bread, cakes, biscuits and pastries, and to flavour sauces, cheeses, milk puddings, and cooked vegetables and fish.

annatto. Also known as achiote and achuete, annatto is the red, triangular seed of a small tree native to tropical America. The seed is ground into an orange-red powder and used as a natural colouring agent (approved additive no. 160b) for food such as margarine, smoked fish and the red rind of cheeses. Annatto adds the characteristic colour and spicy flavour to many Mexican and Caribbean dishes. It is also used to some extent in Chinese and Vietnamese foods. When the seeds are used whole, they are heated gently in oil until they give off their colour and flavour; then the seeds are discarded and the oil used in the dish.

antipasto. An Italian word meaning 'before the meal' (or as the French have it, *hors d'oeuvre* 'outside the work')—in other words, an appetiser served at the beginning of an Italian meal. Antipasti usually consist of an assortment of cured meats, fish and shellfish, olives, tomatoes, capsicums, artichokes, mushrooms, cheese, and other ingredients, served with oil and vinegar.

apple charlotte. See CHARLOTTE.

apples. There are something like seven thousand varieties of apples grown around the world. New varieties are being bred all the time, and old ones drop from favour. The popular apple varieties available in Australia, in their order of ripening, are: Royal Gala (from early February), Jonathan, Red Delicious (from early March), Granny Smith, Golden Delicious, Fuji, Pink Lady (April), Bonza (May), Lady Williams (June). As a result of controlled-atmosphere storage, apples are available the year round, but as fresh apples of one variety or another are available for most of the year, these are the ones to look out for.

Select firm, smooth, even-coloured fruit with a pleasant aroma. A high gloss means they have been waxed, which is said to be harmless but is unnecessary. Store apples in your refrigerator crisper unless they are so firm that some ripening seems called for; small apples keep better than large ones. Don't store apples with ethylene-sensitive vegetables (see ETHYLENE) as the ethylene gas given off by apples causes these vegetables to deteriorate quickly. Wash apples thoroughly before eating them out of the hand.

Apples can be baked, stewed, frittered, and made into pies, tarts, puddings and apple sauce. They blend well with pork and also with chicken and fish. They can be sliced and added to salads and cheese boards. To keep peeled or sliced apples from turning brown, cover them with water to which some lemon or lime juice has been added.

Apples are also available dried and frozen as well as canned in the form of pie pack, purée, and juice.

apricots. The juicy, soft, orange-yellow fruit of the tree *Prunus armenica*, a native of China extensively cultivated in Armenia long ago and now grown in most temperate countries. Apricots are available from November to February, with heaviest supplies in January. Fragile and perishable, they should be eaten soon after purchase. Select firm, plump, uniformly coloured fruit; avoid soft or shrivelled ones and those tinged with green. Store slightly immature fruit in a brown paper bag or a dry place out of the light until they yield to gentle pressure. Ripe fruit can be kept in an unsealed plastic bag in the refrigerator for two or three days.

Apricots are also available dried, canned, frozen, and glacé. Dried apricots can be eaten as they are or reconstituted by soaking them in water overnight and then using them, as you can fresh or tinned apricots, to make apricot jam, pie, ice-cream, or COMPOTE, and in other dishes. Canned apricots are available unsweetened 'in natural juice' (pear or grape juice), in nectar (apricot purée and grape juice), and in sugar-and-water syrup.

Argenteuil. The French variety of asparagus, which has very thick spears with a pale purple tip (named after the district, north-west of Paris, famous for asparagus). Hence, any dish with the designation *Argenteuil* is one made or garnished with asparagus in one form or another.

arrowroot. A nutritious starch obtained from the rhizomes of certain tropical American plants. The name originated from the American Indians' practice of using the root to absorb poison from arrow wounds. Arrowroot is used in puddings, biscuits, etc., and as a thickening agent for sauces when you want the finished product to be clear and transparent.

arroz. The Spanish word for RICE. Arroz con Pollo is a dish consisting of chicken (*pollo*) with saffron rice, tomatoes, and peas.

artichoke / globe artichoke. The globe artichoke is not to be confused with the JERUSALEM ARTICHOKE, which is a tuber, like a potato, only sweetish and watery. The globe artichoke, also known as the crown artichoke or French artichoke, is the unopened flower head of a plant of the thistle family. The bottom of the artichoke is the choicest part, but the white base of the fleshy leaves (actually bracts) is also eaten. Fresh artichokes are available from June to November, the best value period being September–October.

Choose those that feel heavy, firm, and crisp. If you are not going to cook them straight away, cut about a centimetre off the stalks, wrap them in damp paper towels, and store them in plastic bags in the refrigerator; they will keep for several days. Artichokes are usually boiled or steamed and served hot or warm with melted butter or HOLLANDAISE SAUCE, or cold with MAYONNAISE or VINAIGRETTE.

To prepare and cook whole artichokes. Break off the stem, trim the base flat, and strip off the small bottom leaves and any bruised or tough outside leaves. Slice off about one-third from the top of the cone of leaves. Trim the points off the rest of the leaves with scissors. Rub all the cut edges with lemon to prevent them from discolouring; alternatively, drop each trimmed artichoke into a bowl of cold water mixed with lemon juice. (Wash your hands and any surface touched by artichokes, as they have a strong flavour when raw which can be picked up by other foods.)

Cook artichokes in boiling salted water with a slice of lemon. Use a stainless steel saucepan; aluminium tends to turn artichokes grey. Cooking time depends on size and age of the artichokes (15–20 minutes for fresh young ones; up to 45 minutes for larger ones). They are ready when a leaf pulls off easily; test the bottoms for tenderness with a skewer or the point of a knife.

To eat an artichoke. Pull off a leaf at a time, dip the bottom end into

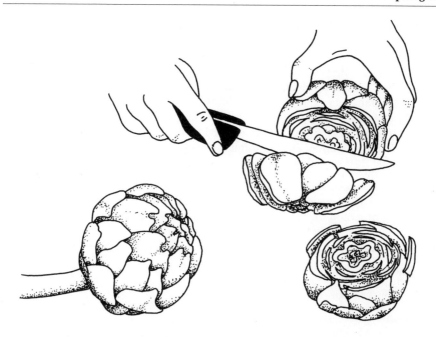

the sauce, and scrape off the flesh between your teeth. When you come to the central cone of leaves, pull off the cone in one piece. This will expose the hairy 'choke', which covers the delicious bottom, called the heart. Scrape off the choke with a teaspoon. The heart can be eaten with a knife and fork, dipping each piece into the sauce.

arugula. Another name for ROCKET.

asafoetida. Why anybody should have tried adding such an evil-smelling substance to food in the first place is a mystery. (It is known colloquially as Devil's dung and stinking gum.) Taking it as a medicine, yes; medicines were traditionally nasty, and asafoetida did ease flatulence. Perhaps someone originally added a pinch to food that gave you wind and found that the evil smell didn't transfer to the food. In India they use it in vegetarian dishes and to heighten the flavour of stews, curries, and sauces. Asafoetida is dried gum resin obtained from the roots of giant fennel. It comes as a red powder or waxy lumps. It is an acquired taste.

asparagus. The succulent young shoots of a plant with feathery leaves native to Eurasia. There are several varieties, which vary in thickness and colour of the spears. Available from September to December, asparagus is in heaviest supply during October–November. Choose well-coloured spears that are firm and brittle, with tightly closed tips and scales. Asparagus should be eaten as soon as possible after purchase; meanwhile, it can be kept in the refrigerator with the cut ends wrapped in a damp paper towel or standing in a little water and covered with a plastic bag.

To prepare and cook asparagus. Snap or cut off tough ends. If the stalks are stringy, pare off the skin near the base. Wash the spears in cold water, tie them loosely in a bundle, and stand them in a narrow, deep, covered

11

saucepan in boiling salted water over the base of the spears. In this way the delicate tips steam while the firm base cooks in the water. Asparagus may also be cooked horizontally, but the ends may be still tough when the tips are cooked. The Belgian white asparagus needs peeling and boiling in plenty of salted water. However, asparagus should never be overcooked. And never put asparagus in cold water and bring it to the boil. It can be eaten hot, cold or tepid.

Asparagus is said to stimulate the bladder—it certainly adds a pungent aroma to one's urine. (If you think it doesn't make your urine stink, it's just your inability to detect the odour, the scientists say.)

aspic. A savoury jelly originally made from meat STOCK but now often made from fish or vegetable stock and thickened with gelatine. It is used as a coating or mould for game or eggs and may be served separately as a garnish. The word originally referred to the dish itself—for example, chicken aspic— but the same dish would now more likely be called chicken in aspic.

au gratin. See GRATIN.

au lait. Served with milk.

aubergine. Another name for EGGPLANT.

avgolémono. A Greek soup made from chicken stock and rice, thickened and flavoured with a mixture of eggs and lemon juice.

avocados are the oval or pear-shaped fruit of a tree native to tropical America. The name *avocado* comes via Spanish from Nahuatl, the language of the Aztecs, who had their own idea of the fruit's shape; their word, *ahuacatl*, means 'testicle'. There are many varieties of avocado, which vary widely in size, shape, skin texture and colour. All have a green-yellow creamy flesh with a delicate flavour and buttery texture. The main varieties grown commercially in Australia are Fuerte, Sharwil, and Hass, but there are others such as Wurtz, Reed, and Shepard. There are also cocktail avocados. Because of their different harvesting seasons, one or another is available most of the year.

Fuerte is pear-shaped, with smooth, dark green, glossy skin; it is available in heaviest supply from March to July. Sharwil is oval and has a rough green skin; in heaviest supply from May to July. Hass is rounder in shape and smaller, with a rough skin that turns purple-black on ripening; in heaviest supply from July to November. The green-skinned Shepard is first to come on the market, from mid-February to the end of March.

Avocados should be eaten only when they are well ripe. Because they ripen satisfactorily off the tree—in fact they will not ripen on the tree as long as the skin remains unbroken—they can be bought firm (requiring four to five days ripening at room temperature) as well as mature (ready to eat). If you want to eat an avocado right away, choose one that yields to gentle pressure at the stem end; avoid very soft fruit with black / brown bruises or blemishes. Fully ripe avocados should be refrigerated until they are eaten, but don't refrigerate avocados until they *are* ripe. The Queensland Fruit and Vegetable Growers organisation suggest that ripening can be hastened by putting them in a brown paper bag with a ripe banana. They can be kept in the refrigerator for four to five days.

To prepare an avocado. Cut it in half lengthwise, twist it gently to separate the halves, and remove the seed with the point of a knife. It can be served 'in the shell' with lemon juice or VINAIGRETTE, the flesh being scooped out with a spoon. Skinned and sliced or cubed, it can be used in salads. Avocado is the main ingredient of GUACAMOLE. It is also recommended as a food for infants starting on semi-solids.

Avocado flesh is inclined to darken once it is exposed to air. You can prevent this by brushing or squeezing lemon juice over it. There is a theory that if the seed of the avocado is placed in any mixture in which avocado is included, it will stop the avocado from discolouring, but lemon juice is probably more effective.

Avocados have a high fat content, but it is unsaturated.

B

baba / rum baba / baba au rhum. A small rich sponge cake or dessert made from sweet, leavened dough, sometimes mixed with raisins or currants, and soaked while still hot in rum-flavoured syrup. A SAVARIN is made in a similar way. The baba is said to have been the inspiration of the eighteenth-century Polish king Stanislas I, who had the idea of sprinkling the cake with rum and flaming it. He named it Ali Baba after the character in his favourite book, the *Arabian Nights.*

baba ghanoush / baba ghannouj. A Middle Eastern creamy paste made from eggplant and TAHINA (ground sesame seeds), with lemon, garlic, and herbs, served as an appetiser with Arab bread or as a party dip.

babaco. As its botanical name (*Carica pentagona*) implies, the babaco is five-sided. An Ecuadorian member of the pawpaw family, and more elongated than the familiar species, it is now grown commercially in Australia and is available during the autumn.

The yellow flesh of the babaco has a taste reminiscent of strawberries and pineapple as well as pawpaw. Make sure it is fully ripe before you eat it; the thin, waxy skin should be yellow, not green. It is usually cut into cubes—the skin is edible—and eaten on its own, in fruit salad, with cheese or puréed in drinks. It can also be barbecued.

The babaco is an excellent source of vitamin C and is very low in kilojoules.

bacon. For something that can be defined simply as cured meat from the back and sides of a pig, bacon is prominent in the history of food. Consider the implications of the saying 'save one's bacon' and 'bring home the bacon'. Not only does bacon have a place in English idiom, but it holds pride of place in the traditional English breakfast. It has long been a favourite preserved meat.

Bacon is cured by salting, either with dry salt or by soaking in brine, and drying or smoking. Flavouring agents such as sugar, honey, or pineapple are sometimes added, in which case they are referred to as sugar cured, honey cured, and so on.

There are various kinds of bacon depending on the cut or which part of the carcase it comes from. Andre Simon in his *Encyclopaedia of Gastronomy* lists ten different cuts recognised in England: fore hock, collar, prime streak, thin streak, flank, back thick end, back and loin, corner of gammon, middle of gammon, and gammon hock. In New York, in a cornucopian delicatessen such as Balducci's, you would find a similar number but with different names. In Australian supermarkets, butcher shops, and delicatessens, the choice is narrower. **Middle cut bacon**, as the name implies, is from the middle rib area, and the rashers have a large eye of lean meat and an edging of fat. **Shoulder bacon** has little or no fat, and the thick, squarish cuts are often used in place of ham. **Streaky bacon** comes from the tail end and has alternate streaks of lean meat and fat.

Canadian bacon is not bacon imported from Canada but boned loin of pork, in one piece, which has been sugar cured and smoked—indeed, it is sometimes sold not as bacon but as smoked pork loin.

Green bacon is bacon that has been cured but not smoked and thus has a milder flavour than smoked bacon. To remove some of the salty and smoky flavour of smoked bacon, so as to make it resemble green bacon, place it in a pan of cold water, bring it to the boil and let it boil for a minute, then drain.

badiane. Another name for STAR ANISE.

bagel. A ring-shaped roll with a tough, chewy texture, made from yeast dough that is simmered briefly in hot water before baking. Bagels with lox (slices of smoked salmon) topped with cream cheese is a popular Sunday breakfast of New York Jews.

baguette. A long, slender, crusty French bread loaf, the kind you see poking out of shopping bags in films set in Paris.

bain-marie is a French term which comes from the Medieval Latin *balneum Mariae* 'bath of Maria', referring to the sister of Moses, an alleged alchemist; hence Ben Jonson's reference to 'St Mary's Bath' in his play *The Alchemist*. The bain-marie in the kitchen of today is a cooking device consisting of a large pan of hot water in which a smaller vessel is placed to heat or cook its contents gently. Cooking this way is slow, and it is used to make custards, sauces, meat loaves, and other things that require gentle cooking.

Those deep, rectangular dishes set in ranks above a trough of hot water, in which food is kept warm in fast-food shops, are also known as bains-marie.

bake, roast. Both words mean to cook by dry heat in the oven, although *bake* applies especially to bread, cakes, biscuits, and pastry, and *roast* to meat. However, many people use *bake* to describe all cooking in the oven (a 'baked dinner', for example), reserving *roast* for the cooking of meat on a spit over an open fire or in hot ashes. *Roast* also means to brown by exposure to heat, as with coffee or nuts. (See also ROASTING and OVENS.)

bake blind. To bake 'blind' is to bake a pastry case for a pie, flan, or tart before the filling is added. This ensures a crisp crust and avoids a soggy bottom. Baking blind is also necessary when the pastry case is to be filled with an ingredient that needs no cooking. After the pastry has been pressed into the tart mould, it is pricked with a fork, then the surface is covered with a piece of greaseproof paper weighed down with a layer of dried beans (you can also buy aluminium weights made specially for this). When the pastry has begun to brown and is set in the mould, the beans and paper are removed and the pastry case is returned to the oven for another 5 minutes to dry out the base and finish cooking. The beans can be used over and over again.

baked Alaska. A baked ice-cream dessert which consists of a piece of sponge cake topped with very firm ice-cream and completely covered with thick meringue. It is baked quickly in a hot oven and served immediately.

baked beans. Perhaps the best-known of Mr Heinz's 57 varieties (Do bingo callers still call 'Heens beans' as an alternative for number 57?), tinned baked beans of any brand are usually cooked navy beans (a variety of HARICOT BEANS) in tomato sauce. They make a handy, if prosaic, snack on toast and a stand-by sandwich filler. Home-made baked beans are made by soaking, boiling, and then slowly baking haricot beans in a casserole with ingredients such as onions, tomatoes, bacon (salt pork and molasses if you're from Boston), and seasonings. (See also BEANS, DRIED.)

baking powder. A powdered mixture consisting of SODIUM BICARBONATE and an acidic substance such as CREAM OF TARTAR with a filling of starch or flour. It is used to make cakes rise—the acid cream of tartar reacts with the alkali sodium bicarbonate in the moisture of a cake mixture to produce bubbles of carbon dioxide. A double-acting baking powder is used in some American recipes; double-acting and regular baking powders cannot be used interchangeably.

baking soda. See SODIUM BICARBONATE.

baklava. A Greek or Turkish sweetmeat made with layers of FILO pastry filled with nuts and spices, steeped in honey or a syrup flavoured with orange-blossom water, and usually cut into diamond shapes.

ballotine. See GALANTINE.

balm. See LEMON BALM.

Balmain bug, Moreton Bay bug. Although these flat-bodied crustaceans are classified under different genera, they are similar in appearance and are both known as shovel-nosed lobsters. They are equally good eating. The Balmain bug was named after the harbourside suburb of Sydney, some say because it was first found in Sydney Harbour, others because the trawlermen who pioneered the fishing industry in New South Wales were based at Balmain. It is actually found around the eastern and southern coast of Australia, while the Moreton Bay bug is found around the northern coast. Their ranges overlap in northern New South Wales. The Moreton Bay bug is slightly thinner in the body than the Balmain bug, and its eyes are set towards the outside of the head, whereas the Balmain's are set in the middle.

Bugs are sold cooked or uncooked, frozen or chilled. They are also sold live. Some people tell you to avoid any with a garlicky smell, which they say indicates they are no longer fresh enough to eat. However, the *Australian Seafood Catering Manual* states, 'This smell is unrelated to flesh quality.' Drown live bugs in fresh water or freeze them, then put them in cold water, bring them to the boil, and simmer them for 3–5 minutes. Serve them split down the middle. They can also be grilled or barbecued after first being split.

bamboo shoots. One of the basic ingredients of Chinese and other Asian cooking, bamboo shoots are the inner ivory-coloured part of the conical shoots that grow at the base of the bamboo plant. They are gathered usually at the end of the rainy season. Winter bamboo shoots are more tender and have a more delicate taste. Bamboo shoots are available in tins, cut in wedges or chunks, parboiled and packed in water, ready to use. Left-over bamboo shoots can be stored in fresh water in a covered container in the refrigerator for about ten days, but the water must be changed daily.

bananas. The banana palm is not a palm or a tree but a giant herb that grows from a rhizome and can reach a height of 8 metres in a year. The trunk is actually composed of compressed layers of leaf sheaths. Its fruit, one of the oldest known, is frequently referred to in myth and legend. 'Adam's fig' was an early name for the banana, and banana leaves were said to be the leaves Adam and Eve used to cover themselves in the Garden of Eden. Consequently, the first botanists of the Renaissance named the plant *Musa paradisiaca*. Ancient Chinese paintings show Buddha meditating under a banana plant.

The main variety grown commercially in Australia is the Cavendish, a dwarf plant really (growing to only 2 metres!) but which produces fruit 15–20 centimetres long. Also available are the smaller-fruited Lady Fingers and sugar bananas and the PLAINTAIN, a cooking banana which should not be eaten raw. Bananas are available all year round, with heaviest supplies from November to March.

Bananas are one of the fruits that are better picked green and allowed to ripen at a controlled temperature. When ripe, their skin is a bright yellow with brown flecks. Choose medium size fruit with no bruises or blemishes. It is better to buy a bunch, or hand, rather than individual fruit, as a banana pulled off the bunch may have its skin peeled slightly and the flesh exposed. Fruit that has green tips will ripen at room temperature. Contrary to some opinion, bananas may be stored in the refrigerator once they are ripe, to stop them from over-ripening. Wrap them in newspaper first. The skin will turn dark and unsightly, but the flesh will remain unchanged for up to a week.

Bananas may be baked, barbecued, and cooked as fritters but are mostly eaten raw out of the hand. They are an excellent source of potassium.

barbecuing. The word *barbecue* comes from the American Spanish word *barbacoa*, a corruption of the Haitian Creole *barboka* (but not as corrupt as the Australian signwriters' *barbeque* or *bar-b-q*). Originally a barbecue was a wooden framework used for smoking or drying meat. The word gradually came to mean an open-air gathering where animals were roasted whole. Now it means either a meal cooked over an open fire outdoors or the metal frame or portable stove or fireplace used to cook such a meal.

While meat of some kind is the usual food barbecued, some fruits and vegetables may also be cooked this way. Lean meat is often marinated before cooking to stop it becoming dry and tough (see MACERATE, MARINATE, MARINADE). The marinade or barbecue sauce can also be used to BASTE the meat while it is cooking. If you like salt on your meat, wait until the last minute to sprinkle it on, as salt draws out meat juices. Best cuts of beef to barbecue are sirloin, rib eye, fillet, blade, and T-bone.

Sausages are easier to barbecue if they are partially cooked. Put them in a saucepan of water, bring it to the boil, then take the pot off the heat and let the sausages stand in the water for 10 minutes before draining them.

The important thing about barbecuing is to allow the fire to reduce to a bed of flowing coals before you start cooking. Roaring flames are likely to turn your fine piece of steak into another piece of charcoal. Some rosemary or other herb or some green gumleaves thrown on the coals will gently flavour the meat. Seal the meat over high heat, about 2–3 minutes on each side, and then move it to a cooler spot until it is cooked to your liking— about 2–3 minutes more on each side for medium (slightly springy to the touch), 4–6 minutes more on each side for well done (firm to touch). Frozen steaks and chops can be barbecued without thawing, but naturally they take longer to cook. Never test meat to see if it is cooked by cutting it; this lets out the juices and makes the meat dry and tough.

barding. To bard is to cover or wrap meat, poultry, or game with a fat such as bacon rashers or pork fat before roasting. (You can flatten and spread pork fat by pounding it between two sheets of greaseproof paper.) Barding, like basting, prevents the food from drying out during cooking. (See also LARDING, LARDONS.)

barley. Although barley is used mainly in the brewing of beer and the distillation of whisky (hence John Barleycorn, the personification of malt liquor), this ancient cereal grain still has a place in the kitchen. It has a nutty flavour and is used in soups, casseroles, and vegetarian dishes as well as in the preparation of barley water. **Pearl barley**—dehulled and polished grains—is the form in which it is mostly used. It takes a long time to cook until tender—1½–2 hours.

Barley sugar is an amber-coloured sweet made from boiled sugar, traditionally shaped in the form of a twisted stick. It was originally made using an extract of barley.

Barley water, a refreshing drink highly regarded in the Victorian era, is made by simmering pearl barley in water for 2 hours and mixing the strained and cooled liquid with some lemon juice.

barramundi is an Aboriginal word meaning 'river fish with big scales', and the name was used by the Aborigines of northern Australia for three different fish. The one discovered by Ludwig Leichhardt on his first expedition in 1845 is a living fossil from fifty million years ago with so many needle-like bones that it is almost inedible. The second is the Queensland lungfish. The third, *Lates calcarifer*, is the one that has come to be regarded as Australia's most popular finfish. A deep-bodied, dark bluish-grey fish, it is found in rivers and estuaries around the northern coast of Australia from the Mary River in Queensland to Exmouth Gulf in Western Australia. It is also farmed at various places in Queensland as well as in Darwin and Adelaide. In the wild it grows to a quite enormous size, but the commercially farmed barramundis are immature and average 32 centimetres in length. (At this stage barramundis are asexual; they mature as males at three years, then turn into females two years later.)

The barramundi has a mild flavour and moist, fairly firm flesh with large flakes. A versatile fish, it can be fried, grilled, barbecued, or steamed. The Aborigines used to wrap it in the leaves of the wild ginger plant and bake it in hot ashes, which is said to be the best way of cooking it.

basil. 'If I had to choose just one plant from the whole herb garden,' Elizabeth David writes in *Italian Food*, 'I should be content with basil.' Originally from India, the wonderfully aromatic basil is much used in Italian cooking and is the basic ingredient of the Genoese pasta sauce PESTO. It is known especially for its affinity with tomatoes, both cooked and raw. It also goes well with eggs, mushrooms, and pasta, and in green salads.

Of the many varieties of basil, the two in most common use are sweet basil and the smaller-growing and milder bush basil. An annual herb, basil is available fresh from October to May, with heaviest supplies in the summer months. Although dried basil can be bought, it is a poor substitute for fresh, which is well worth growing each year in the garden or in a flower pot. In Italy, tradition has it that if a girl leaves a pot of basil on her window sill, it is an invitation to her lover to visit her.

Fresh basil will keep in the refrigerator for up to a week; remove the leaves from the stem, wash them, and put them in a plastic bag or container lined with a paper towel. To keep up your supply through the winter months, put the leaves in a jar and cover them with olive oil; store the tightly covered jar in the refrigerator, and take out the leaves as you need them. Alternatively, you can freeze basil leaves.

baste. To baste means to moisten food, usually meat or poultry, with pan drippings or sauce while cooking. The liquid may be spooned or brushed over, or you can use a *bulb baster*, a metal or glass tube with a rubber bulb on one end which acts like an eye-dropper, drawing up the pan juices to be gently squirted over the cooking meat.

batter is a mixture of flour, egg, and milk or water used mainly for making pancakes and for coating food before frying. In the United States the word *batter* is also used for cake mixtures, *dough* being reserved for bread and pastry mixtures. Batter to Americans is thinner than dough and may be stirred and poured; dough is kneaded.

When battering food for frying, make sure the food is dry before dipping it in the batter, or steam will form during cooking, separating the coating from the food. Too low a temperature of the frying fat will also cause the batter to drop off.

bavarois. A dessert made from custard, gelatine, and whipped cream with various flavourings. Also known as Bavarian cream, it is supposed to have been concocted in Bavaria in the seventeenth century.

bay leaf. Bay leaves are such a foundation ingredient of French cooking that it is characteristic of restaurants in provincial France to have a tub containing a standard bay tree, with its crown trimmed into a neat ball, by the doorway. Leaves from the bay tree, which were fashioned by ancient Greeks into laurel wreaths to decorate military and athletic victors, are fashioned by modern cooks into a BOUQUET GARNI or used to decorate a TERRINE and to flavour soups, stews and casseroles, poached fish, boiled corned beef or pickled pork, marinades, and even milk puddings and custards. They are usually removed from a dish before serving.

Bay leaves may be used fresh from the tree—better still, two or three days after picking—or dried. To dry your own, hang a twig of leaves in a cool, dry, airy place for a week or two, then remove the leaves and store them in an airtight jar. Avoid using dried leaves that are more than a year old as they will have lost much of their flavour.

bean sprouts are usually produced from green mung beans, sometimes SOYA BEANS, which have been allowed to sprout and grow for a few days. The crunchy-textured sprouts are used raw in salads and sandwich fillings or as an edible bed of greenery for cooked fish, chicken, or vegetables. They are also steamed or stir-fried for Asian dishes.

To grow your own sprouts. Place some dried beans in a large glass jar, fill it with water, then drain the water off through a piece of muslin or similar cloth secured with a rubber band over the opening of the jar. Leave the jar on its side in a warm place out of direct sunlight. Repeat the rinsing process every day, two or three times a day if practicable. Sprouts should appear in two days; allow them to grow for four to six days before eating. They can be stored for up to four days in a well-ventilated container in the refrigerator.

beans, dried. Dried beans are the seeds of various leguminous, or pod-bearing, plants. There are many kinds, the best known of which are included in this book under their individual names. Dried beans are used in soups, salads, stews, and other main-course dishes. Common characteristics and methods of preparation are given here to avoid repetition.

To prepare and cook dried beans. Before cooking them, discard any that are discoloured or float to the surface when covered with water and stirred. Wash them thoroughly, then drain. They will need to be soaked, by either the slow or the quick method. With the slow method, you soak them in cold water in a cool place for several hours or overnight. With the quick method, you put the beans in a saucepan with water to cover, bring them to the boil and continue to boil, uncovered, for 2 minutes, then remove them from the heat and allow to stand for 1–2 hours. Cook the beans in gently boiling water for 1-2½ hours depending on the kind of bean, or in a pressure cooker. As salt slows cooking and toughens the beans, it should be added towards the end of cooking time.

As a rule, dried beans are a good source of protein, starch and dietary fibre, B vitamins, and minerals. Unfortunately, they also contain certain substances people find hard to digest, and the intestines respond by producing large amounts of gas, causing flatulence. As they say in German, 'Jedes Böhnchen gibt sein Tönchen'—every little bean gives its little sound. To avoid suffering from the 'rooti-ti-toots', as Julia Child refers to this embarrassing condition in *The Way to Cook*, she suggests that since about 80 per cent of the substances that cause the trouble are soluble in water, you should throw away the soaking liquid and cook the beans in a fresh lot of water. You may be throwing away some of the nutrients as well, but for those who like beans but not the consequent rooti-ti-toots, this is an acceptable loss.

Store dried beans in an airtight container; keep them dry. They should not be stored for longer than a year, as they harden with age.

beans, green. Green beans, also known as French beans, snap beans, string beans (though most are stringless these days), or simply beans, are grown for their immature pods—which are not necessarily green; some are yellow or purple. The green bean plant, *Phaseolus vulgaris*, is thought to have originated in Central America. It was brought to Europe in the sixteenth century and became known in France as *haricot vert* (our haricot beans are the seeds of the mature pod of the green bean).

The two main kinds available in Australia are French beans and runner beans, but within these there are round-podded and flat-podded varieties, yellow wax or butter beans, and purple-podded ones that turn green when cooked. Green beans are available all year round, with heaviest supplies during the summer.

Snake beans, the long, thin, round-bodied beans known to the Chinese as **doh gok**, are an ancient Chinese vegetable of a different genus. They are available from November to March, with heaviest supplies in November–December. They are usually sold tied in bunches. Snake beans are cooked in the same way as green beans and are used in stir-fries, curries, and soups.

Beans should be eaten soon after purchase, but they can be kept for up to five days in the crisper or a plastic bag in the refrigerator.

To prepare and cook green beans. Cut off the tops and tails and remove strings, if necessary, by drawing an almost-detached top or tail downwards to see if the string comes away. Cook beans whole, or if they are large and not so young, slice them into slanting strips, then steam or cook them in rapidly boiling salted water until they are tender but still firm to the bite. Beans should never be overcooked. Drain them thoroughly. If you intend to serve them cold, plunge them into cold water to stop the cooking process and retain the bright green colour.

béarnaise sauce. A rich sauce similar to HOLLANDAISE, made from egg yolks, butter, and wine, vinegar, or lemon juice, but flavoured with tarragon, shallots, and chervil. Serve it hot with fillets of beef (FILET MIGNON, TOURNEDOS, or fillet steak) and other grilled meats. Any left-over sauce may be kept and served cold on chicken sandwiches or cold roast beef.

beat, whip, whisk. These three words mean the same thing: to mix or stir vigorously in order to thicken, aerate, or produce expansion. Though the words have the same meaning, they are generally associated with different ingredients; eggs are usually beaten, egg whites whisked, cream whipped, and so on; but the object is usually to produce a frothy mixture, whatever term is used. Implements used range from a fork, spoon, SPATULA, and wire WHISK to an electric beater or mixer of some kind. The extent and vigorousness of your beating, whipping, or whisking and the implement you use will depend on the recipe's instructions.

béchamel sauce. One of the basic French sauces, béchamel has been known to generations of Australians simply as white sauce. It is made by stirring milk into a mixture of melted butter and flour. 'To make a *Béchamel* in the old-fashioned and best manner,' says Andre Simon in his *Encyclopaedia of Gastronomy*, 'one should use butter and flour in equal quantities and the best and creamiest of milk.'

To prepare béchamel sauce. The milk is first boiled and allowed to stand for a while; the flour is mixed into the melted butter and cooked gently to form a ROUX, then the milk is added a little at a time and mixed, using a wooden spoon, until the sauce is the required consistency—thin and flowing if it is to be served as an accompaniment or used in cream soups, or a thicker mixture to coat or cover food.

This basic white sauce, combined with other ingredients, forms many well-known sauces. When béchamel is to be served straight, chopped onion, a bay leaf, and peppercorns are often added to the milk when it is heated, then allowed to infuse. The milk is strained before adding to the roux.

beef is the flesh of a full-grown ox (usually a bullock but also a bull, heifer, or cow) that has been raised and fattened for meat production (VEAL is the flesh of a calf).

A beef carcase is divided into several sections from which numerous cuts are made. Starting from the forequarter end of the carcase and working back along the top to the hind leg or butt, the sections are, first, the shoulder, from which come chuck and blade steak. Beyond the shoulder is the rib section, which provides rib roasts, rib steak, spare ribs and the rib eye, and below which is the brisket. The rear half of the carcase is where the best and most expensive cuts come from: the sirloin, which contains the fillet or tenderloin, and the rump. The butt yields topside, silverside, round, and shin.

Butchers' techniques and the names they give to the various cuts of meat vary from country to country. The regular cuts of beef available in Australian butchers' shops and supermarkets are given in alphabetical order below. For the various kinds of beef steak, see STEAK; for information on choosing and storing beef, see MEAT.

Blade. Meat from the shoulder section adjacent to the shoulder blade. It is available in one piece, with or without the bone, for roasting or pot roasting, or in steaks for frying, grilling, barbecuing, or braising. **Bolar blade** is the cut used for roasting; **oyster blade** the cut for pan-frying, grilling, and barbecuing.

Brisket. The breast or undersection of the forequarter and ribs of the animal, available either with the bone in or boned and rolled. It has a lot

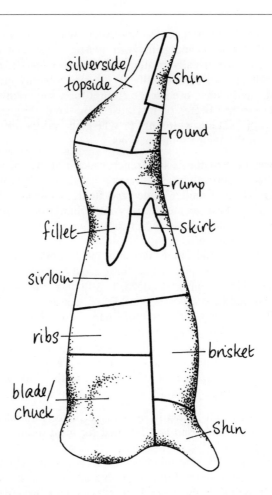

silverside/
topside

shin

round

rump

fillet

skirt

sirloin

ribs

brisket

blade/
chuck

shin

of fat and is usually pot-roasted or cooked in a casserole. It is also sold corned for boiling.

Chuck. The cut of beef from the shoulder between the neck and the shoulder blade. It is juicy and has plenty of flavour but is rather tough, so it is used in pot roasts, casseroles, curries, stews, meat pies (for which it is excellent), and also minced.

Fillet. The most tender but not necessarily the most flavoursome cut of beef, the fillet is a tapering strip of flesh, with almost no fat, on the underside of the rump and sirloin. It is sometimes sold as an entire piece, to be roasted or wrapped in pastry and baked (see BEEF WELLINGTON). More often, it is cut into steaks.

Rib. The rib section provides cuts that are cooked in all ways. Ribs with the bones in, or boned and rolled, provide the traditional roast beef. **Rib steak** has the bone in and can be pan-fried, grilled, and barbecued. **Rib eye**, also known as **Scotch fillet**, has the bones removed. In a piece it is oven-roasted; the steaks can be grilled, barbecued, pan-fried, and stir-fried.

Spare ribs are cut of the bottom of the ribs. Though they have a high proportion of bone to meat, the meat is sweet. Marinate and grill or barbecue spare ribs, or cook them in a casserole.

Round. A boneless cut from the top of the leg, the front of the butt. In the piece it can be roasted; steaks can be pot-roasted, braised, and (preferably when marinated) grilled, pan-fried, and barbecued; strips can be stir-fried.

Rump. A boneless cut from over the hip bone. It is a tender, juicy cut that may be roasted in the piece or pan-fried, grilled, and barbecued as steaks, and stir-fried in strips.

Shin beef comes from both fore and hind legs. It is lean, flavoursome stewing meat which takes a long time to cook. With the shank in, it is used for making soups and stocks.

Silverside. A boneless cut from the butt. Silverside is usually sold in a piece for oven-roasting or pot-roasting, and also salted and spiced to make the traditional corned beef.

Sirloin. Meat from the high or broad end of the loin between the rump and the ribs, part of which contains some of the fillet. In a piece with the bone in or boneless, it makes a fine roast. A double sirloin left on the bone and looking like a huge saddle is known as a **baron of beef**; it makes a truly noble roast, enough for a whole party to share. Sirloin steaks on the bone or boneless can be pan-fried, grilled, or barbecued.

Topside. A boneless cut from the inside of the butt. In a piece, topside can be oven-roasted or pot-roasted. As steak, it may be grilled, pan-fried, or barbecued. Topside is the cut used to make the better-quality mince.

Beef Bourguignon. See BOEUF BOURGUIGNON.

Beef Stroganoff. Like many famous dishes, Beef Stroganoff has been hybridised to such an extent that the original species is on the endangered list and rarely observed. The classic Russian version, so they say, is made with fillet of beef, cut into strips, sautéed in butter or oil, then combined with sautéed onions and mushrooms in a sour cream and mustard sauce.

Beef Wellington. Roasted whole fillet of beef, coated in PÂTÉ DE FOIE GRAS and sometimes mushrooms, enclosed in pastry, and baked. The name comes from its appearance, which was thought to be like the leg sheath of a wellington boot. Also called Boeuf en Croûte, it is usually served with a Madeira sauce.

beetroot was originally cultivated for its leaves, which were eaten by people living on the shores of the Mediterranean in pre-Christian times. While the leaves are still eaten—they taste like young spinach—the spherical red root is by far the most used part, as a hot vegetable, cold, cooked or grated raw in salads, in the famous Russian soup BORSCH, pickled or canned.

Beetroots are available all year round, with the peak period from June to December. Choose firm, smooth, clean specimens with at least 5 centimetres of stalk and the whiskery roots still attached. Beetroots can be kept in the refrigerator for up to five days, the leaves for one or two days.

To prepare and cook beetroots. Wash them in cold water and trim the stalks if necessary, leaving no less than 5 centimetres still attached. Cook them whole with skin on and whiskers untrimmed so that they don't 'bleed'—that is, the red colour doesn't leach away into the cooking liquid and leave a pale substitute for rich red beetroot. They are usually boiled; average size beetroots take about 40 minutes to cook. The skins will slip off easily after cooking, and the beetroots can then be used as the recipe requires. Beetroots can also be baked in the oven or cooked in a microwave oven.

beignet. A kind of FRITTER. **Beignets soufflés** are deep-fried balls of CHOUX PASTRY which are dredged in icing sugar after being cooked and drained.

Bel Paese cheese. A smooth, mild-flavoured, cream-coloured, firm cheese made by only one Italian company, which was founded in the 1920s. It is a table cheese that can also be used for cooking. (See also CHEESE.)

bergamot is a perennial herb native to North America where it was much prized by the Oswego Indians. After the Boston Tea Party, European settlers used it as a substitute for tea and referred to it as Oswego tea. Young leaves of the herb can be added to salads, meat loaves and other cooked dishes, but it is mostly used in dried form as a herbal tea.

    Bergamot oil is not extracted from this plant but from the bergamot orange (*Citrus bergamia*). It is bergamot oil that gives the distinctive flavour to Earl Grey tea.

berries. Botanically a berry is a fruit with seeds enclosed in a pulpy pericarp. So a banana and a tomato are berries in the botanical sense, while a strawberry is not. Those fruits that we non-botanists think of as berries are listed in alphabetical order under their common names. Berries deteriorate quickly but may be stored for a short time in the refrigerator; turn them out of the punnet onto a plate lined with paper towels.

    To dry freshly washed berries. Drain them as well as you can, then place them, not too close to one another, on a tray lined with paper towels. Shake them gently so that they roll about and allow the paper towels to absorb the moisture clinging to them.

besan. Flour made from finely ground CHICKPEAS, used extensively in India.

beurre blanc (white butter sauce). A warm sauce made from butter flavoured with shallots, wine or COURT BOUILLON (if it is to be served with fish), and salt and pepper. Beurre blanc is served with chicken, asparagus, cauliflower, terrines, and mousselines as well as with fish and shellfish.

beurre manié. A mixture of butter and flour, in equal quantities, kneaded together, which is used to thicken sauces, soups, stews, etc. It is added, in little balls, a few minutes before serving, and whisked into the hot liquid until the flour is cooked and the liquid has reached the required consistency.

beurre noir. Although its name translates to 'black butter', this sharp sauce is actually butter heated until it is nut brown. Just before serving, a little vinegar and sometimes capers are added. Beurre noir is served hot with grilled fish and eggs and is the classic sauce (made with capers) for brains.

big eye. Another name for BLUE EYE.

biltong. See JERKY.

bind. To hold a mixture of ingredients together with another ingredient such as egg, cream, mayonnaise or other sauce.

bird's-nest soup. A highly prized Chinese delicacy, this substantial soup is made from chicken stock, water chestnuts, mushrooms, pork, and, as *The Macquarie Dictionary* puts it, 'the gelatinous nests of any of several species of Indo-Australian swift of the Collocalia family'—well cleansed, I hope. As Tom Stobart explains in *The Cook's Encyclopaedia*, 'The birds nest in colonies in stupendous caverns . . . and, like swallows, stick their nests to the rocky walls and ceilings. They make them, however, not of mud but of a gelatinous spit which they secrete for the purpose.'

biryani / biriani. An Indian dish of saffron rice and highly seasoned meat, chicken or fish, nuts, etc., cooked in layers in a covered dish.

biscuits. *The Australian Concise Oxford Dictionary* defines *biscuit* as 'a small unleavened cake, usually flat and crisp and often sweet', an accurate description but one that does not fully indicate what Margaret Fulton refers to in her *Encyclopedia of Food and Cookery* as the 'infinite variety of crunchy, crisp, chewy or brittle baked goods, from the plain wafer biscuit to sweet confections nibbled with coffee'. In the United States a biscuit is what we call a scone. The American term *cookie*, applied to sweet biscuits, seems to be sneaking into Australian usage. I have even seen 'Anzac cookies' advertised for sale—a heresy if ever there was one.

Various biscuits are listed in this book under their common or generic names.

A few things to remember when making biscuits:

- Always preheat the oven.
- Have at least two baking trays so that you don't have to crowd the biscuits on the tray or place them too near the edges. Those near the walls of the oven get more reflected heat and will brown more quickly than those in the middle.
- Place the tray in the centre of the oven, and turn it during baking to compensate for uneven cooking.
- Some biscuits should be removed from the baking tray immediately they are taken out of the oven and cooled on a wire rack so that they don't stick to the tray and will cool quickly and remain crisp. Others need slower cooling and should be left for a while before removing from the tray. Follow the recipe.
- Store the cooled biscuits in airtight containers. Fragile biscuits may need to be separated by layers of greaseproof paper.

bisque. A bisque can be a smooth, creamy soup of any kind, but the term is applied mainly to one that has shellfish as its main ingredient. The shellfish, which may be anything from oysters to lobsters, is cooked in a COURT BOUILLON, puréed, and returned to the liquid. The soup is usually thickened with egg yolks or cream.

bitter melon. Shaped like a cucumber with a pointed end and ridged, wrinkled skin, the bitter melon is used in Chinese cooking as well as the cuisines of several South-East Asian countries. It is cooked unripe, when it is yellow-green in colour.

To prepare and cook bitter melon. The Chinese cut it in half lengthwise, scoop out the seeds, and blanch the melon halves for 2–3 minutes, then sprinkle them with sugar. The melon is then stuffed with minced pork and steamed with black bean sauce, or cut up to be used in stir-fries. The Indians use bitter melon to make a sharp pickle.

blachan / blacan is a pungent paste made from dried and fermented shrimps pounded with salt. It is used extensively as a flavouring in Asian dishes, especially Malaysian, Singaporean, and Thai food. Blachan is sold dried in flat slabs or cakes as well as in paste form packed in jars. Once opened, the jar must be kept in the refrigerator. The dried slabs will keep almost indefinitely in a tightly closed container stored in a cool, dry place. Blachan should be stir-fried or roasted in foil before use. This changes the naturally acrid flavour to a rich, aromatic seasoning.

black beans. See SOYA BEANS.

black sapote. A relative of the persimmon, and shaped like one but with a green skin, the black sapote has a pasty, pulpy, chocolate-coloured flesh; hence, its other name, the chocolate pudding fruit. It has a sweet taste and no smell. Originally from Mexico, it is commercially grown in Australia, and the fruit is available from June to December, with the peak period in June–July.

When ripe, the fruit is very soft and the skin turns dark green. Keep it in the refrigerator after it ripens, and eat it within two days. Halved, it can be eaten with a spoon, or you can purée the flesh to add it to custards, ice-creams, or sorbets.

blackberries. Originally introduced into Tasmania as far back as 1843, and planted in New South Wales twenty years later as a food for introduced birds, the prickly and highly invasive blackberry bush is now a certified noxious weed in a number of rural areas of Australia. However, as many a scratched and clothes-stained child has discovered in the Christmas holidays, the sweet wild fruit is delicious. Although some wild blackberries are marketed, a cultivated variety is grown in Tamworth and the Southern Highlands of New South Wales and at Hoddles Creek in Victoria; they are available from late November to February.

Blackberries deteriorate rapidly, so they should be used as soon as possible after picking. Choose large, firm berries with bright colour and no sign of crushed, leaking fruit or mildew. Keep them loose in a bowl in the refrigerator until required, then wash them and remove the stalks. Eat them fresh or stewed with cream or yoghurt, bake them in a pie or tart, or make jam out of them.

blackcurrant. See CURRANTS.

black-eyed beans. Also called black-eyed peas or cowpeas, these small, kidney-shaped seeds of the plant *Vigna sinensis* have a creamy-white skin with a distinctive black eye. They have been eaten since ancient times in Africa and are a favourite food in the southern United States, where the bean is eaten fresh as well as dried. Black-eyed beans are used in soups, stews, and salads. For information on preparation, storage, etc., see BEANS, DRIED.

To cook black-eyed beans. Boil them gently until they are tender (about 1 hour) or pressure cook them for 10–15 minutes.

blanch, parboil. To blanch means literally to whiten, and indeed when you blanch almonds you remove the brown skin and reveal the white flesh underneath. To do this, the nuts are usually plunged briefly into boiling water, after which the skin slips off when you squeeze the nut. So in a culinary sense *blanch* means much the same as *parboil*: food is boiled for a few minutes for one reason or another—to loosen the skin, to partly cook the food before finishing it off in another way, or to remove strong odours or flavours as with cabbage or bacon. When blanching green vegetables that are not needed immediately, they should be 'refreshed'—plunged into cold water straight afterwards—to stop further cooking and retain the fresh green colour.

Plants such as WITLOOF and ASPARAGUS are blanched—that is, kept white—by growing them in the dark or heaping soil around them while they are growing.

blancmange. 'White food' is how it translates from Old French. In medieval England a blancmange was a dish of chopped chicken or fish stewed with rice, dried fruits, almonds, and spices. Chaucer described it in *The Canterbury Tales* as a mixture of minced capon with flour, cream, and sugar. At some time or other the meat was omitted, and over the centuries the blancmange became a kind of creamy jelly stiffened with such things as egg yolks, isinglass, hartshorn, and arrowroot. In present-day Australia it is a sweet, opaque, jelly-like dessert made with milk thickened with cornflour and flavoured. It is often served with a blob of jam on top or with stewed fruit.

blanquette. This is another term that comes from the French word for 'white'. A blanquette is a French stew made from veal (*blanquette de veau*) or lamb (*blanquette d'agneau*) with blanched white onions, button mushrooms, eggs, and cream, which, when served, is creamy-white. It is similar to a FRICASSEE, but the meat for a blanquette is blanched instead of fried before cooking. White pepper is even used for seasoning, so that the whiteness is not blemished.

blend. While 'blend' may mean in some cases to process food in an electric blender, its traditional meaning is to combine ingredients with a spoon, usually a wooden spoon, using a wide, circular movement with a fairly light touch, until they are completely incorporated. This contrasts with beating, which is a more vigorous action. The context of the recipe will generally make it clear which meaning of *blend* is intended.

blini. Small Russian pancakes made with a yeast batter using BUCKWHEAT flour. They are traditionally served in Russia at Shrovetide (Pancake Day and the two days before it), with caviar and sour cream.

blintz. A small pancake rolled round a filling of cottage cheese and baked in the oven or fried. Blintzes are among the traditional dairy dishes eaten by

Jews at the festival of Shavuot (Pentecost). According to Leo Rosten in *The Joys of Yiddish*, 'blintzes, as eaten by Jews, are ordinarily smothered under thick sour cream. Jet-set Jews, aspiring to *crêpes suzettes*, have taken to smothering blintzes with honey or jam instead of sour cream. There is no accounting for tastes.'

blue eye / blue-eye cod. Also known as deep-sea trevalla / trevally, the blue eye is a big, thick-bodied, blue-grey fish found in deep water off the southern coast of Australia. It is available all year round and is commonly sold in fillets or cutlets. Its pale pink flesh is firm, moist, and mild-flavoured with only a few easily removable bones. It lends itself to all ways of cooking, particularly frying. (See also FISH.)

blueberries. Small, round berries, dark blue with a natural grey-blue bloom on the skin, and mostly seedless these days. They come from a variety of shrubs of the genus *Vaccinium*, native to North America and eastern Asia, which have been hybridised in North America for cultivation. (The huckleberry of the United States is a wild blueberry.)

Because of the number of varieties grown, blueberries are available from October to March. Choose plump, fresh-looking berries; avoid shrivelled ones. Keep them in the refrigerator, dry, and use them quickly. Otherwise freeze them; they freeze well. They can be eaten fresh or stewed, on their own or with cream or ice-cream, or in fruit salads.

bluefish. Another name for TAILOR.

bocconcini. See MOZZARELLA.

Boeuf Bourguignon. A French beef stew, popular throughout France (not just in Burgundy), made with red wine, bacon, onions, and mushrooms.

boiling. When water—and thus cooking liquid in general—reaches 100°C, it is said to boil: bubbles constantly rise to the surface and burst. However, there are degrees of boiling, and recipes may specify slow, medium, or rapid boiling. A **rolling boil** is the fastest of all, used for cooking pasta and also to speed up evaporation. To **simmer** is to cook gently just at or below boiling point. There is a slower stage yet, which the French call *frémir* (to shiver) when there is only the barest movement on the surface of the liquid.

Milk boils at 91°C (see also SCALDING). Oil boils at a much higher temperature than water, between 260°C and 399°C.

bok choy / bok choi / pak choi (Chinese chard, Chinese white cabbage). With loose, mid-green leaves and long, fleshy, white stems, bok choy looks more like spinach than the true cabbage (*Brassica chinensis*) it is. It has a mild cabbage taste and crisp texture. In China it has been cultivated for about three thousand years; in Australia it has been grown since the gold rushes of last century, although it has not been sold widely in this country until recent years. There are different varieties, some with wide, curved stalks forming a bulbous base, some with green stalks, some smaller than others (see also CHOI SUM).

Available all year round, bok choy is in heaviest supply from May to August. You can store it, after rinsing, in a plastic bag in the refrigerator for up to five days. Leaves and stems are both eaten—cooked in water and

served as a vegetable, sliced to use in stir-fries or in soups, steamed and served with oyster sauce. Cook it only a short time to retain the crisp texture.

bolognaise sauce. See RAGOÛT, RAGÙ.

bombe. A frozen dessert traditionally made in a spherical mould like an old-fashioned bomb, hence the name, but now often made in other shapes. It has an outer layer of plain ice-cream and a filling of a softer substance—flavoured cream, custard, mousse—to which fruit is sometimes added.

Bombe Alaska is a BAKED ALASKA in a bombe shape.

bonbon. French baby-talk for 'good' (perhaps 'good goodies'), *bonbon* means, in general terms, a piece of confectionery. Specifically it means a confection with a centre of fondant, fruit, or nuts and a coating of chocolate or fondant.

bone, fillet. These two words have meanings that are comparable but not exactly the same. To bone means to remove the bones from a piece of meat or fish. To fillet means to remove strips of fish from the bones.

bonne femme. Literally 'good woman', *bonne femme* (or *à la bonne femme*) means prepared 'country style'; in other words, food prepared in a simple, unadorned fashion. Potage Bonne Femme, made from sliced leeks and diced potatoes, is one of the basic and most versatile French soups. Puréed, it becomes Potage Parmentier, which is the basis for VICHYSSOISE.

borlotti beans. Like black and red kidney beans, cannellini beans, haricot beans, and pinto beans, borlotti beans are the dried seeds of a variety of the green bean plant, *Phaseolus vulgaris*. Borlottis, also called cranberry beans and Roman beans, are large, plump, and coloured beige to brown speckled with burgundy markings. They can be used in place of pinto beans or red kidney beans in recipes. Popular in Italian cooking, they are added to stews, soups, and salads. For information on preparation, storage, etc., see BEANS, DRIED.

To cook borlotti beans, boil them gently until tender (1½–2 hours) or pressure cook them for 15–20 minutes.

borsch / bortsch / borscht / borsht / borsh. There are even more versions of this Russian soup than there are ways of spelling the name, which comes from the Russian word for 'cow parsnip', the original base of the soup. Nowadays, the basic ingredient is beetroot. The soup may be made simply with beetroot and other vegetables or, as in the Ukraine, with beef and smoked or green bacon, garnished with pastries. The borsch served at the court of Csar Nicholas II had a whole duck in it. The soup may be thick or thin, served hot or cold. Each version has the characteristic wine-red colour derived from the beetroot, and it is usually served with sour cream.

botargo. Prepared mullet ROE.

bouchée. A 'little mouthful'—in other words, a little pastry case made with puff pastry, BAKED BLIND, usually with a savoury filling. A small version of the VOL-AU-VENT.

bouillabaisse. A stew or a thick soup? Take your pick. The important thing about this famous Provençal dish is that it should contain a large variety of fish and shellfish, together with oil and tomatoes, seasoned with garlic, saffron and other herbs and served with a separate ROUILLE to be added at the discretion of the individual diner. As it is made in Marseilles, the true home of the bouillabaisse, it requires at least seven or eight guests to do justice to the quantity that results from having such a variety of seafood in it. According to the gastronome M. F. K. Fisher, it is a main dish 'seldom served at night, being rich and eminently unsuited to peaceful slumbers'. The broth and the fish may be served separately.

bouillon. Another name for stock. See STOCK, BROTH, BOUILLON.

bouquet garni. A bundle of herbs, tied with string, used for flavouring soups, sauces, stews, etc. The herbs are essentially parsley, thyme, and a bay leaf, but celery and other herbs, even a piece of orange peel, may be added. If dried herbs are used, they are placed in a muslin bag and tied with string. The bouquet garni is removed at the end of cooking. To facilitate this, the loose end of the string is tied to the handle of the saucepan.

boysenberry. A hybrid berry developed in the United States by crossing various species of *Rubus*, the genus of BLACKBERRIES. Boysenberries look like blackberries but taste something like raspberries. They are available in late summer and autumn. Choose and use them the way you would blackberries.

brains. Sheep, lamb, pig, calf, and ox brains are all eaten, but lamb's and calf's are the ones usually available. Brains should be pink, moist, and plump when you buy them. Allow one set of lamb's brains for each person; one set of calf's brains for two people. Use them as soon as possible after purchase, as they deteriorate quickly. Brains contain a fair amount of fat.

    To prepare and cook brains. Soak them in cold, lightly salted water for two hours, changing the water three or four times. This softens the membranes that cover them. Drain the brains and carefully remove the membrane with your fingers or the point of a knife, then soak them again to dissolve any blood. Next, simmer the brains in ACIDULATED WATER for 15 minutes. They will then be ready to cook—gently fried or poached. Serve them with BEURRE NOIR.

braise, casserole, stew. These three cooking methods are similar, each requiring slow cooking in liquid in a covered container. The differences depend on whether the food is browned first and whether the final cooking is done on top of the stove or in the oven. When **braising**, the food (meat and / or vegetables) is browned in fat (oil, butter, etc.) and then cooked slowly with very little liquid on top of the stove. The food should fit snugly in the pot. For a **casserole**, the food is browned and the container, usually of earthenware or glass, is put in the oven to finish cooking. A **stew** is cooked on top of the stove without browning; meat, vegetables, and stock are put in a pan on low heat, covered and simmered. However, the terms are often used indiscriminately. (See also DAUBE and POT-ROASTING.)

bran is the outer layers of cereal grains such as wheat, oats, and rice. Most of the bran is removed in the milling of grain for flour. Although bran contains high amounts of nutrients, the fibre and phytic acid in wheat bran hinder, to some extent, the absorption of these nutrients, and calcium, by the human body. However, bran is effective as a laxative.

brawn. Also called head cheese, brawn is a jellied meat preparation traditionally made from pig's head but often from other boned and chopped cooked meats, pressed and set in gelatine. Brawn is served cold in slices with salad or dressed with vinaigrette, thin rings of sweet onion, and chopped parsley.

Brazil nut. The Brazil nut is not grown commercially but gathered from huge trees that grow wild along the banks of the Amazon River from the Atlantic Coast of Brazil across into the mountains of Peru. The curved, three-sided, dull brown nuts are packed like orange segments into hard, round, woody pods as big as coconuts, which drop from the trees with sometimes devastating effect on the Indian gatherers below.

The nuts are hard to crack—freezing them makes it easier—and the dark brown skin covering the creamy-coloured kernels can be removed by blanching (see ALMOND). Eat them raw or roasted, use them in cakes and tarts or ground in place of flour.

Brazil nuts are a good source of vitamins E and B1. Like all nuts, they have a high fat content; with Brazils it is 74 per cent unsaturated (36 per cent mono, 38 per cent poly). They are also high in kilojoules. (See also NUTS.)

Brazilian tree grape. See JABOTICABA

bread. The person who coined the phrase 'the greatest thing since sliced bread' was joking, of course. Sliced and packaged bread cannot bear comparison with a crusty whole loaf baked in the traditional way. If you look hard enough you can usually find a satisfactory loaf. If not, you can try making your own.

Bread is made from FLOUR, YEAST, water, and SALT. The gluten in the flour—strong flour, or baker's flour, which has a high gluten content—allows the mixture to be kneaded into an elastic dough that traps the bubbles of carbon dioxide formed by the yeast (see KNEADING). After kneading, the dough is set aside in a warm place to rise until it has doubled in bulk. The risen dough is punched down to break up the gas pockets, kneaded a second time, shaped into a loaf or loaves, and allowed to rise once again. It is then baked until the loaf sounds hollow when the bottom is tapped with the knuckles.

There are, of course, breads made without yeast—the flat breads of the Middle East, for example—and there are many kinds of leavened breads. Bread of some kind is an important daily element in the diet of most people of the world. It is a nutritious food which provides an excellent balance of energy and nutrients—protein, vitamins, minerals, complex carbohydrates, and dietary fibre—and it is low in fat. One nutritional disadvantage is the high sodium content.

While bread is best eaten fresh—crusty bread preferably on the day of baking—it can be kept for up to four months in the freezer. Allow it to thaw out at room temperature for about two hours, or put the frozen bread in the oven at 175°C for 20 minutes, bottom up for the first 10 minutes. Some people brush the top of the loaf with milk, but this is not necessary. The reheated bread tastes as though it has been freshly baked.

bread sauce. A very English sauce which is served with roast turkey, pheasant, or chicken. It is made from milk and breadcrumbs, with onion, cloves and seasonings. 'There are three secrets to it,' says Andre Simon: 'cook in a double boiler; beat with a fine whisk, and add a pat of fresh butter when removing from stove.'

bread stick. Some cookery writers use the term 'bread stick' when they are referring to a long, slender, crusty French loaf such as a BAGUETTE. This is confusing to those who are used to thinking of bread sticks as the Italian GRISSINI, which are little thin sticks like rusks.

breadcrumbs are used in various ways—to protect a piece of veal or a lamb cutlet from searing heat, as a gratin or casserole topping, to thicken sauces, to form the basis for poultry stuffing, and other important uses. There are two kinds of breadcrumbs: fresh (or soft) and dry. If a recipe calls simply for breadcrumbs, use fresh rather than dry.

To make your own breadcrumbs. Fresh breadcrumbs can be made by rubbing pieces of day-old bread through a sieve or by using an electric blender if you want especially fine crumbs. To make fine dry breadcrumbs, dry out slices of bread in the oven, then crush them with a rolling pin or grate them on a grater. Alternatively, you can get the blender to do the job.

To keep fresh breadcrumbs fresh. Put them in a plastic bag, gently squeeze out the air, fasten the top securely, and put the bag in the refrigerator. The breadcrumbs will stay fresh for quite a long time.

breadfruit. A staple food of the Pacific Islands, breadfruit is usually available only where there is an Islander community near by. The large, oval-shaped fruit has a knobbly green skin and a cream-coloured fibrous flesh which, when cooked, is said to taste like freshly baked bread; some say it tastes like yam or potato. It can be boiled or fried, served mashed, or eaten as a dessert with sugar and milk. The seeds can be roasted. It is an excellent source of vitamin C and iron.

bream. There are four species of bream sold commercially: yellowfin bream (also called silver beam, black bream, surf bream, and sea bream); black bream (also called golden bream, southern bream, and Gippsland bream);

pikey bream (also called black bream); and tarwhine. They are similar deep-bodied fish, of good size for the plate, with colours ranging from silvery-yellow to silvery-black. Their availability varies according to the species and where they are caught: yellowfin are available mainly in the autumn and winter, black bream in the summer. They are sold whole and in fillets, but what the retailer sells as bream fillets may well be frozen, imported fillets of a different species of fish or fillets cut from MORWONG. If you catch your own bream, bleed and gut it immediately, and remove the black lining of the abdominal cavity completely.

Bream have a sweet, distinctive flavour (tarwhine can be a little 'weedy'). The white flesh is moist and soft to medium in texture. Bream are best grilled or baked whole, but the fillets may be cooked in most ways. (See also FISH.)

Brie. A soft cheese, traditionally shaped like a large flat disc, with a white powdery crust (which is eaten) and a creamy-yellow inside that becomes softer as the cheese ripens. When ripe, it should bulge from a cut wedge but not be runny. Originally made in France, Brie was crowned 'king of cheeses' in a competition organised by Talleyrand during a break from setting Europe's borders at the Congress of Vienna in 1815. French Brie is available in Australia; it is at its best from December to March. Excellent Brie-type cheeses are made in Australia. Brie should be eaten at room temperature, so take it out of the refrigerator for a while before you serve it. A young cheese may need to be left overnight at room temperature to soften, while one near its use-by date will require only an hour. (See also CHEESE.)

brioche. A soft, light-textured, sweet roll or bun made from a yeast dough rich in butter and eggs. With the CROISSANT, the brioche is sacred to breakfast in France, where, as M. F. K. Fisher puts it, they are 'floated down on rivers of hot chocolate or coffee'. Eat them warm with butter and jam.

Brioche dough is also used to enclose roasts, sausages, and other meats (baked *en brioche*).

broad beans. One of the most ancient food plants of the Western World, the broad bean is cultivated mainly for its large, flat, oval seeds, although the pod also may be cooked and eaten like green beans when it is very young. The seeds are eaten either fresh or dried.

Fresh broad beans are available in spring and summer. Choose young, tender green pods. They may be stored in a plastic bag in the refrigerator for up to a week. With mature beans, shell the pods and boil, steam, or microwave the seeds until they are tender. Large seeds may need the outer skin removed; it can be tough and hard to digest.

Dried broad beans range in colour from green to beige and brown (green and beige indicate new season's crop). For information on preparation, storage, etc., see BEANS, DRIED.

To cook dried broad beans, boil them gently until they are tender (2–2½ hours) or pressure cook them for 25 minutes. They can be eaten with a little butter and pepper and salt, or with chopped ham. They are also used for making the Lebanese FELAFEL.

broccoflower is not a cross between BROCCOLI and CAULIFLOWER but a naturally occurring form of the cauliflower with a lime green head instead of a white one. It has a delicate flavour and retains its green colour when cooked.

broccoli. The image of broccoli has improved since E. B. White wrote his famous caption for the 1928 *New Yorker* cartoon in which a mother at table says, 'It's broccoli, dear', and her daughter replies, 'I say it's spinach, and I say the hell with it.' The daughter was wrong anyway; broccoli is one of the hundreds of varieties of the wild CABBAGE (*Brassica oleracea*) but, like its culinary cousin cauliflower, is grown mainly for its edible flower stalk and head.

Broccoli is available all year round but is in best supply from March to October. A sprouting variety known as asparagus broccoli, which produces an abundance of small flower branches and is usually sold in bunches, is available only in early spring. Because broccoli is eaten before the green, tightly clustered buds have opened, choose compact flower heads with no sign of yellow or open buds; leaves and stalks should be tender yet firm. Store it dry in a vented plastic bag in the refrigerator for up to five days; use preferably within one or two days.

To prepare and cook broccoli. As the stems take longer to cook than the buds, cut off the florets where they meet the central stalk and peel the stems. A cross cut through the thickest stems allows the broccoli to cook evenly. If you plan to cook the central stalk as well as the florets, cut off the tough butt end and peel the stalk down to the tender flesh. Cook in boiling salted water. Broccoli may also be steamed and stir-fried. The peeled, thinly sliced stalk may be eaten raw. Cooked broccoli florets are delicious eaten cold with a VINAIGRETTE dressing.

brochette. A small spit or skewer. *En brochette* means cooked on a skewer. *Shish* and *shash* from the Turkish also mean skewer, hence shish KEBAB and SHASHLIK.

broth. A thin soup of meat or fish stock (see STOCK, BROTH, BOUILLON). Just to confuse matters, Scotch broth is a thick soup made from beef or mutton, pearl barley, vegetables, and seasonings.

brown sauce, or *sauce espagnole*, is one of the basic sauces from which many others are made. It is prepared by whisking brown STOCK into brown ROUX and, when this is well blended, adding some chopped tomatoes or tomato purée, some cooked diced vegetables (see MIREPOIS), and a BOUQUET GARNI, and simmering it gently for 2 hours or more, skimming as necessary. The finished sauce should be lightly thickened, rich dark brown and deeply flavoured. A spoonful or so of brown sauce can be added to the pan juices when DEGLAZING.

brownies. The traditional Australian brownie is a bush cake—DAMPER sweetened with brown sugar and currants. American brownies are cake-like biscuits—fudgy chocolate squares made of flour, butter, sugar, eggs, cocoa or chocolate, and walnuts.

brunoise. A mixture of finely diced vegetables such as carrots, onions, leeks, turnips and celery made by cutting JULIENNE vegetables into evenly sized cubes. They may be cooked slowly and made the basis of a soup or stuffing, or used as an aromatic element of another dish.

bruschetta. The Italian version of garlic bread, made with slices of crusty bread grilled or toasted, rubbed with garlic, sprinkled with pepper and salt, and drizzled with olive oil, preferably extra virgin olive oil.

Brussels sprouts. Although one of the cabbage (*Brassica*) family, Brussels sprouts grow like buds sprouting from a stalk rather than as one big heart or head. They are said to have been first cultivated in Flanders, near Brussels.

Brussels sprouts are available in Australia from March to November, with the heaviest supplies in winter. Choose firm, round, brightly coloured sprouts preferably no bigger than a golf ball (the smaller, the tastier) and all the same size (for even cooking). You can store them in the refrigerator crisper or in a plastic bag lined with paper towelling in the refrigerator for up to a week, but they are better eaten as soon as possible after purchase.

To prepare and cook Brussels sprouts. Pull off any loose or discoloured leaves, and trim the stem end—not too short, or the outer leaves will fall off during cooking. If the stems are thick, cut a cross in the base so that they will cook faster. Brussels sprouts should not be overcooked or they will get an unpleasant smell. Steam them or cook them in boiling salted water until they are just tender.

Bubble and Squeak. Originally Bubble and Squeak was cold boiled potatoes and cabbage or other greens fried up together. First they bubbled in the boiling water and then they squeaked in the frying pan—at least that's what *Brewer's Dictionary of Phrase and Fable* says. Corned beef was often substituted for potatoes. Nowadays, Bubble and Squeak is any left-over meat and vegetables fried together.

buckwheat is not a cereal (grass) but an annual plant native to Central Asia which produces triangular seeds that are ground into a flour. It is a staple food in China, Russia, and Eastern Europe. The flour is used to make Japanese soba noodles, BLINI, and, mixed with other flours, special breads and cakes.

bunya nut. Australia's giant native pine nut. The bunya pine, *Araucaria bidwilli*, was a common tree in the rainforests of south-east Queensland and for centuries provided the Aborigines from near and far with fare for their regular bunya feasts. The tree's large pine cones contain numerous whitish to light brown, egg-shaped nuts with a starchy kernel. They are harvested in January–March and are available all year round.

To cook bunya nuts, boil them in the shell for 20–30 minutes or roast them like chestnuts. Eat them hot.

burghul / bulgur. Wheat that has been hulled and boiled or steamed until it is partly cooked, then dried and cracked. Burghul is an important food in the Middle East and is also used in Greek and Turkish cooking. It is a main ingredient in the Lebanese salad TABBOULEH.

35

burrito. A large warmed TORTILLA filled with potatoes, beans, meat, etc., and rolled into a cigar shape.

butter is made by churning cream until most of the water has separated from it; what's left is butter. By law it must contain at least 80 per cent fat and no more than 16 per cent water. The remaining small amount consists of salt and milk solids. Salt was originally added as a preservative, but nowadays it is there because people have got to like the taste. However, **unsalted butter** has a sweeter taste and is recommended for cooking. It is also a better frying fat than salted butter because it has few of the solids that burn at low temperatures. **Clarified butter**, from which all the solids have been removed, is better still for frying.

    To clarify butter. Cut the butter into pieces and heat it slowly in a saucepan until it melts. Take it off the stove, skim off any foam and allow it to stand until the milk solids have settled to the bottom, leaving a clear yellow liquid on top. Pour or strain this clarified yellow liquid into a bowl. It will keep for a long time in the refrigerator. (See also GHEE.)

    Cultured butter is made from cream to which a pure culture of lactic bacteria has been added. It can be either salted or unsalted.

    Drawn butter is melted butter used mainly as a fish sauce. To make it properly, some say, you should melt the butter in a warm spot on the stove, not over direct heat or you will cook it. According to Escoffier, it should be only just melted and not allowed to clarify or it will lose flavour. He also adds a little table salt and a few drops of lemon juice. Other cooks add chopped herbs.

    To measure a given volume of butter. If you want, say, half a cup of butter, put half a cup of water in a measuring cup, add butter in small pieces, one at a time, until the level of the water is at the one-cup mark, and Eureka! (as Archimedes said when he made the same sort of observation in the bathtub), you have the amount you need.

    Keep butter in the refrigerator well wrapped and away from strong-smelling foods, as it is easily tainted. Properly wrapped or in a sealed container, it can be frozen.

buttermilk. Originally the slightly acidic low-fat liquid left after making butter out of cream, buttermilk is now made commercially from skim milk fortified with milk solids, to which a benign culture of acid-producing bacteria has been added. It has a pleasant light tang and a thick creamy consistency. Mixed with fruit purée, it makes a low-kilojoule milkshake (buttermilk has a fat content of no more than 0.8 per cent). With French mustard and seasoning, it can be used as a salad dressing or sauce. It may also be used as a milk substitute in baking scones and cakes.

C

cabbage (*Brassica oleracea*) is an ancient vegetable which is thought to have originated in the eastern Mediterranean and Asia Minor. It has long been the national vegetable of northern Europe, where it is eaten raw as COLE-SLAW, pickled as SAUERKRAUT, and cooked in many ways. There are about four hundred varieties of *Brassica oleracea* cultivated round the world; included among them are broccoli, Brussels sprouts, cauliflower, kale, and kohlrabi.

Cabbages available in Australia may be green, red, or white (actually pale green); round, flattish ('drumhead'), or pointed; and wrinkled-leafed and greenish-yellow, as the Savoy. There is also the CHINESE CABBAGE which looks like cos lettuce and has thick white ribs and long, narrow leaves (see also BOK CHOY). Cabbages are obtainable all year round, with heaviest supplies in winter. Choose those that are solid and heavy, with firm heads and no limp leaves. They can be kept in the refrigerator for up to a week.

To prepare and cook cabbage. Green cabbage can be sliced thinly or quartered and then boiled or steamed until just tender; it is important not to overcook it. The smell of cabbage that has been boiled too long is reminiscent of rotten eggs and rotten boarding houses. A whole walnut added to the water will reduce the odour. Shredded cabbage can be eaten raw as a salad or stir-fried. Cabbage leaves can be blanched and used instead of vine leaves to make DOLMADES.

Red cabbage must be cooked with something acidic—vinegar, red wine, apples—to retain its attractive red colour; otherwise it takes on a nasty greyish-purple look. Red cabbage goes well with roast duck or pork.

cacciatore. An Italian stew made with fowl or game (*cacciatore* means 'hunter' in Italian). The most common version is Chicken Cacciatore, in which chicken pieces are browned in olive oil and garlic, then simmered in wine with tomatoes, seasonings, etc.

Cacciatore is also a kind of SALAMI sausage.

cacik. See also TZATZIKI / CACIK.

Caesar salad. There is some difference of opinion about this salad. It was apparently created in the 1920s, but whether by an Italian restaurateur named Alexander Cardini in honour of his brother Caesar or by Caesar himself, and whether in Tijuana, Mexico, or at the racetrack in San Diego (or by someone else, somewhere else) is uncertain. The recipe itself also has its variants. However, the essential ingredients are cos lettuce and garlic-flavoured croûtons, with grated Parmesan cheese and a dressing of olive oil, lemon juice, coddled egg, and Worcestershire sauce or Tabasco. Some recipes include anchovies, but Julia Child in *The Way To Cook* says that

Caesar Cardini's daughter told her the original recipe contained no anchovies.

caimo. See ABIU.

cakes. There are whole books written about cakes. Here are simply a few hints and tips about cake-making gleaned from the professionals (and one experienced amateur). Individual cakes are listed elsewhere in the book in alphabetical order.

Choosing cake tins. As a rule, choose heavy-gauge cake tins so that the heat is distributed evenly; thin or flimsy tins tend to develop hot spots to which cake mixtures may stick. Sponge cakes, however, cook quickly and need lighter, thinner tins so that the heat penetrates fast.

Always use the size and shape of tin specified in the recipe, as the capacity of the tin must be appropriate for the quantity of cake mixture or the cake may be spoilt. As a rule, the cake mixture should fill the tin by no more than two-thirds.

A dark-coloured tin will absorb and retain more heat than a light-coloured one, so the oven temperature may need to be lowered when baking a cake in a dark-coloured tin, to avoid burning.

A springform, or spring-clip, tin, which expands when the clip is unfastened and frees its loose base, allows fragile cakes to be removed easily and without damage.

Preparing cake tins. The recipe for any kind of cake will tell you to 'grease' or 'butter' the cake tin so that the cake doesn't stick to it. To do this, smear the baking surface—bottom and sides—evenly with soft butter or other fat. Some people use the butter wrapping for this procedure, a thrifty touch. The recipe may call for a thin layer of oil or melted butter to be brushed on. If the bottom is to be lined, cut a sheet of greaseproof paper or baking paper to fit it exactly, press it in place and grease the paper. If the tin is to be floured as well, add a couple of tablespoons of plain flour and shake it about, tipping the tin in all directions so that the flour makes a light film all over it, then knock the tin upside down over the sink to remove any excess flour. For cake mixtures that have a strong tendency to stick, you may need to **double grease**—that is, grease the tin as described, put it in the refrigerator until the film of butter hardens, then grease it a second time.

Some points to remember when baking cakes:

- Preheat the oven to the required temperature.
- If the cake mixture curdles while you are adding the eggs to the creamed butter and sugar, mix in a tablespoon of flour and then add the remaining eggs.
- Pour the cake mixture into the cake tin as soon as you have made it, and bake it immediately in the preheated oven.
- Don't open the oven door too soon. Wait until at least three-quarters of the baking time has elapsed, then do it gently. If the cake has not yet set, a sudden draught of cold air will make it collapse.

How you can tell if a cake is cooked. When a cake is cooked, it will begin to shrink away from the sides of the cake tin, the top of the cake will feel springy to the touch (if your finger leaves an impression, put the cake back in the oven) and a straw, skewer, or commercial cake tester poked into the centre of the cake will come out clean and dry.

After a cake is cooked, it should be allowed to cool on a wire rack for ten minutes or so before turning out, although some cooks say it should be turned out immediately unless the recipe specifically tells you to let it cool in the tin. Never stand a hot cake tin on a solid surface, or the bottom of the cake will become soggy.

To remove the cake from the tin. Gently run a knife blade between the cake and the tin all around to loosen the cake. Set the rack on top of the cake, lift the cake and rack together and turn them over, then give the tin a bit of a shake to dislodge the cake. If the paper is stuck to the bottom of the cake, lift one edge and gently peel it off.

calamari. Another name for squid (see SQUID, CUTTLEFISH, OCTOPUS).

Camembert. A soft, creamy-coloured, ripened cheese shaped like a small flat wheel, with a golden rind and a white, powdery surface. Near the village of Camembert, in Normandy, there is a statue in honour of Marie Harel, credited with being the creator of the modern camembert cheese through her development of the controlled mould flora used in its manufacture. The unpasteurised cow's milk used in the French cheese also gives it a distinctive flavour. However, good-quality camembert-style cheeses are made in Australia.

The flavour and texture of camembert change as it ripens. When young, the cheese has a mild flavour and a firmer texture than the fully ripe cheese, which is stronger tasting and almost runny. Serve camembert at room temperature, which means it should be taken out of the refrigerator a couple of hours before you eat it. (See also CHEESE.)

camomile / chamomile. A herb that is used to make a tea or TISANE out of its dried daisy-like flowers. The tea is rather bitter but is supposed to soothe the nerves and settle the stomach.

canapé. A small, thin rectangle of bread or toast with something savoury on top. The canapé's 'canopy' may be cheese, pâté, caviar, anchovies, or fish paste, etc. Served as an appetiser.

candied / crystallised / glacé fruit. *Candied* is a general term applied to fruit that is impregnated or encrusted with sugar. Candying is done by cooking the fruit (cherries, pineapple rings, angelica, orange slices, etc.) or citrus peel in a heavy SUGAR SYRUP. *Crystallised* fruit is candied fruit that has a coating of granulated sugar; *glacé* fruit has a smooth, glossy sugar-syrup coating. (See also CRYSTALLISED / FROSTED FLOWERS.)

caneton. The French word for duckling.

canistel. An egg-shaped fruit with a smooth, orange-yellow skin, yellow pulpy flesh, and several large, shiny seeds. Native to South and Central America, it is now grown commercially in tropical Australia and New Caledonia. Canistels are available most of the year, sometimes called egg fruit, marmalade fruit, or honey sapote. Ripen them at room temperature out of direct sunlight, until soft, then keep them in the refrigerator. Peel and eat them fresh out of the hand or with a spoon. The seeded flesh may be puréed and eaten with ice-cream. Canistels are an excellent source of vitamins C and A.

cannellini beans. Like black and red kidney beans, borlotti beans, haricot beans, and pinto beans, cannellinis are the dried, kidney-shaped seeds of a variety of the green bean plant, *Phaseolus vulgaris*. They are white, larger than haricot beans, and have squared-off ends. They are the most frequently used white bean in Italian cookery. Information on preparation, storage, etc., is given under BEANS, DRIED.

To cook cannellinis, boil them gently until they are tender (1–1½ hours) or pressure cook them for 15–20 minutes.

cannelloni. According to the best sources (Elizabeth David's *Italian Cooking* and Marcella Hazan's *Classic Italian Cookbook*, for example) cannelloni are made with rectangles of thin home-made egg pasta, briefly boiled, then spread with a meat and cheese stuffing, rolled up, placed side by side in an ovenproof dish with butter and grated Parmesan or a tomato sauce, and baked in the oven. For those who are not into making their own pasta, packaged cannelloni pasta comes in tubes about 10 centimetres long and 2–3 centimetres in diameter, which are boiled, stuffed and baked in the same way. (See also PASTA.)

canola oil is obtained from rape seed. It is used in some margarines and is a good cooking oil. When cold pressed, it becomes darker, thicker, and tastier, suitable for salads. Canola oil contains polyunsaturated fatty acids of the omega-3 series, which are believed to lower LDL cholesterol, although scientific studies have been inconclusive.

cantaloupe / cantaloup. See ROCKMELON.

cape gooseberry. A native of South and Central America rather than the Cape of Good Hope (where it is cultivated extensively) and not a gooseberry but a member of the tomato family, the cape gooseberry is a round, greenish-gold fruit the size of a cherry tomato, enclosed in a grey-green papery husk. It has a sharp, refreshing flavour which some people find reminiscent of passionfruit, tomato, and cherry.

Cape gooseberries are available from December to April, if you can find them. When ripe, the berry has a tight skin and the husk, if still on, becomes brittle. Keep them in the refrigerator once they are ripe. Eat them fresh in the hand or in a bowl with cream, or poach or purée them. They are an excellent source of vitamins C and A.

A green and purple variety of the cape gooseberry is known to Mexican food fanciers as the TOMATILLO or Mexican green tomato.

capers are not pickled nasturtium seeds, as some people think, but the unopened flower buds of a prickly shrub that grows around the Mediterranean. The olive green buds are pickled in salted white wine vinegar, which allows the capric acid in the bud to produce the condiment's strong aromatic flavour. They come in two sizes: the larger is called *capote*, the smaller *nonpareil*. Widely used in Mediterranean cooking, capers add a distinctive flavour to TARTARE and other sauces and make a tasty addition to salads.

capon. According to Andre Simon's *Concise Encyclopaedia of Gastronomy*, 'in the poultry trade the name applies to a castrated cockerel which has been superfed, usually in solitary confinement, and killed not less than six months and not more than nine months old'. The flesh is tender and marbled with fat, and capons have a high proportion of white breast meat to darker meat.

capretto. The Italian word for kid (see GOAT MEAT).

capsicums. Known also as peppers, sweet peppers, and bell peppers, capsicums are the fruit of the tropical American shrub *Capsicum annuum*. All capsicums are green at first; when ripe they turn red, yellow, orange, or purple-black according to the variety. They are available all year round, but are in best supply in summer and early autumn. Choose those with glossy, unwrinkled skin and no soft spots. You can keep them in the refrigerator crisper for up to a week. Either green or ripe, capsicums can be used raw in salads or can be fried in strips or stuffed whole and baked. They are also added to casseroles and other cooked dishes. Capsicums are an excellent source of vitamin C.

To prepare capsicums. Wash them and remove the stalk, seeds, and ribs. They may be left whole for stuffing, halved, or cut into strips or dice. Cutting on the rough side prevents the knife from slipping.

To skin raw capsicums. Hold them with a long fork over an open flame or halve them and place them skin-up under the griller until they are charred and blistered. Put them in a brown paper bag to steam for a few minutes, then rinse them under cold water and scrape off the charred skin with a paring knife. Red capsicums skin more easily than green.

carambola. Also known as five-corner fruit or star fruit, because the five prominent ribs on the fruit produce a star shape in cross-section, the carambola is thought to have originated in Malaysia. The fruit is about 10 centimetres long with waxy yellowish skin and crisp, juicy flesh. It is available most of the year. Allow it to ripen at room temperature out of direct sunlight, and when ripe, store it in the refrigerator where it will keep for up to three weeks. It can be eaten while still green.

To eat a carambola, wash it, cut off each end and trim the edges of the ribs, and eat it out of the hand or cut into star-shaped slices. It can also be

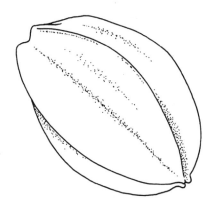
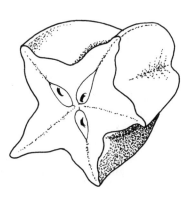

used in fruit salads, preserves, pickles and chutneys or as an edible decoration, and it can be puréed. It is a good palate cleanser between courses. And if you find you don't like the taste of a carambola, you can use the cut fruit for cleaning brass and copper.

Carambolas are an excellent source of vitamin C, vitamin A and iron.

caramel is burnt sugar which is used to colour or flavour foods (approved additive no. 150). It is also a kind of soft toffee made from sugar, butter, and milk.

To caramelise sugar. Heat three parts of sugar and one part of water in a saucepan over gentle heat until the sugar has completely dissolved, then boil over moderate heat without stirring (some cooks give the saucepan a swirl now and then; others say to tip it gently to and fro while boiling), until the syrup turns a rich golden brown. As soon as it is nicely coloured, take the saucepan off the heat and set it in a pan of cold water to stop the cooking process. Be careful you don't overcook caramel, or you might end up with toffee. You can caramelise sugar without any water, but you need to watch it carefully as it caramelises quickly, and stir it continuously.

caraway seeds. The use of caraway seeds predates recorded history. These tiny, crescent-shaped seeds, of a plant native to Europe and North Africa, have been found in the ruins of Bronze Age lake-dwellings in Switzerland. The Greeks and Romans used them as medicine as well as for flavouring food. They have been used in love potions and as a cure for hysteria.

Caraway seeds aid digestion and prevent flatulence, which is why they were traditionally served as COMFITS with baked apples in England. Germans, Austrians, and Hungarians use them extensively, adding them to sauerkraut, boiled cabbage, coleslaw, goulash and other stews, as well as to flavour the liqueur kummel (*Kümmel* is the German word for caraway seed). They are often added to rye bread and are the seed in English seed cake.

Store caraway seeds dry in an airtight jar away from direct sunlight.

The roots of caraway plants may be cooked and eaten like carrots.

carbohydrates are the body's principal source of energy. Bread, potatoes, rice, pasta, breakfast cereals, fruit and vegetables, sugars and sugary foods are all largely composed of carbohydrates. Once eaten they are converted by the digestive system into glucose, which is transported by the bloodstream to all parts of the body to supply the cells with energy. Glucose is the body's preferred fuel, and it comes mostly from carbohydrates, although it can be metabolised from fat and protein if the body is not receiving enough carbohydrate. When this happens for some time, the body wastes away. On the other hand, if we eat more carbohydrate than we can use up as energy, our body stores the excess as fat (see also KILOJOULES.)

Nutritionists make a distinction between simple and complex dietary carbohydrates. They advise us to eat more complex carbohydrates (starches) than simple carbohydrates (sugars). Refined sugar, honey, and anything that is mostly refined sugar may provide us with plenty of energy, but they provide us with little else, whereas fruit and vegetables, which contain both sugar and starch, provide us with vitamins, minerals, fibre, and some protein. Besides, refined sugar passes quickly into the bloodstream and puts a strain on the body's ability to regulate the amount of sugar in the blood. Starchy foods are more gradually broken down and assimilated by the body and don't overtax the body's regulatory system.

carbonade / carbonnade. Originally a French term for a grill over an open fire of coals, *carbonade* now refers to a traditional Belgian dish made with thin slices of beef and onions braised in beer (Carbonnades de Boeuf à la Flamande).

cardamom / cardamum / cardamon. A member of the ginger family, the cardamom plant has been cultivated in India since time immemorial. The flavour of cardamom, which is reminiscent of eucalyptus, is an essential part of all Indian curries. The plant bears fruit in the form of thin-skinned oval capsules (cardamom pods) about 1 centimetre long, each containing 15–20 irregularly shaped seeds.

While the seeds can be bought separately, it is better to buy the pods and remove the seeds as you need them. Some recipes call for the use of whole pods. Store the pods in an airtight jar. Crush the seeds between sheets of greaseproof paper with a rolling pin, or use a pestle and mortar.

Cardamom is used to flavour PILAF, PICKLES, and sweet dishes as well as curries. Scandinavians use it in cakes and pastries.

carob. It is the carob, or locust bean, not the locust insect, which John the Baptist is supposed to have survived on (with wild honey) during his spell in the wilderness of Judaea; hence, carob's other name, St John's bread. It is still a snack food in the Middle East.

The long, brown, dry carob pod is the fruit of a tree *Ceratonia siliqua*, native to the Mediterranean region. The pod contains hard seeds enclosed in a sweet pulp, and the whole pod is ground into a powder which can be used in place of cocoa powder in cooking. It is sweeter than cocoa, so less is needed. Health food stores sell a chocolate substitute made from carob powder with lecithin and other ingredients. It provides fewer kilojoules than chocolate and has no theobromine, which causes migraine in some chocolate eaters.

carpaccio. Very thin slices of raw meat or fish.

carrots of one sort or another have been around since prehistoric times. Today the sweet, orange-coloured, long and tapered or short and stubby carrot is one of the most popular root vegetables.

Carrots are available throughout the year but are in best supply during winter and spring. Choose firm, smooth, well-shaped roots without splits (although my mother-in-law used to say they were split with goodness). Tiny young 'Dutch' carrots are often sold in bunches with the tops on, but carrot tops are usually chopped off to prevent their sapping the roots of moisture and causing them to shrivel. If you buy carrots with tops on, cut them off before storing. Store carrots unwashed in the refrigerator crisper (not near apples; the ethylene gas given off by apples makes carrots bitter) or in a paper-lined plastic bag in the refrigerator. They will keep for up to a week.

To prepare and cook carrots. Wash and scrub the carrots with a vegetable brush, and cut off the tops and tails. Avoid peeling if possible (skin can be rubbed off young carrots after boiling), but if they need attention, scrape gently or peel finely, as the vitamin content is more concentrated near the skin. They can be cooked whole or sliced, eaten on their own or used in hearty winter soups and stews. Carrot soup and carrot cake are great pleasers.

Carrots are an excellent source of vitamin A, in the form of carotene, which turns into vitamin A in the digestive system. The deeper the orange colour of a carrot, the more carotene it contains.

cashew nuts are always sold already shelled, as the tree on which they grow, native to Brazil and the West Indies, is a member of the poison ivy family and the nut's shell contains a caustic oil that irritates the skin and eyes.

Cashew nuts are eaten as cocktail snacks and used in cakes, biscuits, desserts, and confectionery as well as in some Asian main dishes. They are also made into cashew nut butter. Like all nuts they have a high fat content, but with cashews it is 80 per cent unsaturated (62 per cent mono, 18 per cent poly). They are also high in kilojoules.

cassata. The traditional Italian cassata consists of a hard shell of cream or chocolate enclosing softer ice-cream. In Australia a cassata is likely to be a kind of ice-cream containing candied or dried fruit and nuts, not necessarily enclosed in a shell. (See also GELATO and ICE-CREAM.)

Cassata alla Siciliana is a rich cake layered with ricotta cheese and enclosed in chocolate frosting.

casserole. A covered dish, usually of earthenware or glass, sometimes of cast-iron, in which food is cooked slowly in the oven and often served from at the dinner table. The term also applies to the food, usually a mixture, cooked in a casserole (see BRAISE, CASSEROLE, STEW).

cassia. See CINNAMON.

cassoulet. A traditional French stew made with haricot beans and meat such as pork, sausage, goose or other poultry, usually with a crust of breadcrumbs, and simmered for a long time.

cauliflower. One of the many variant forms of *Brassica oleracea*, the cabbage, but cultivated for its large, compact head of unopened flowers rather than for its leaves. Cauliflowers are available most of the year but are at their best in winter. Choose firm, white heads with no brown spots or opened flowers. To store, remove the leaves and place unwashed in the crisper of the refrigerator. Use within five days.

To prepare and cook cauliflower. Cook whole or broken into florets. They can be steamed, boiled, stir-fried, or deep-fried, and can also be eaten raw in CRUDITÉS. Boiled or steamed cauliflower is usually served with a white sauce flavoured with cheese or *au gratin* (see GRATIN). Cold cooked florets in VINAIGRETTE are delicious. When cooking whole cauliflower, cut a deep cross in the base of the main stem so that it will become tender.

caviar. 'Caviar comes from virgin sturgeon' goes the old song, but what you buy as caviar may well come from salmon or lumpfish and only vaguely resemble the expensive Russian delicacy (which, incidentally, the Russians do not call caviar but *ikra*; *caviar* comes from the Turkish word for roe). True caviar is the ROE (eggs) of the beluga, osetrova, and sevruga, three fish of the family Acipenseridae which are known collectively as sturgeon.

The beluga is a very big fish, and the grain of its roe is correspondingly bigger than that of the smaller osetrova and sevruga. Their roe also varies in colour from light grey to almost black. Red caviar comes either from salmon, whose large-grain roe is naturally red, or from lumpfish, whose pink roe, about the size of a pinhead, is dyed red or black and sold as German or Danish caviar.

Caviar is preserved by salting and may also be pasteurised. Pasteurised caviar has a shelf life of more than a year; unpasteurised caviar should be used within three months of the day it is packed. Both should be stored in the refrigerator once opened, and used as soon as possible.

Caviar is supposed to be eaten with a spoon, but it is more often served chilled on plain bread or toast with a little lemon, sometimes with a garnish of chopped hard-boiled egg or finely chopped raw onion.

cayenne / cayenne pepper. A hot, pungent, orange-red condiment obtained from the ground pods and seeds of dried CHILLIES. It is named after Cayenne in French Guiana, where the chilli variety originally used in its making came from. The important thing to remember about cayenne is that it is very hot and should be used with discretion.

cedro. Glacé CITRON peel.

celeriac. A European variety of celery, celeriac is grown for its thick tuberous root rather than for its stalks, which are not eaten; for this reason, it is also known as celery root. The bulbous, rough-skinned, earth-stained root has a white flesh and a flavour like celery.

Celeriac is supposedly available from March to November, but it is essentially a winter vegetable and not widely available at the best of times. Choose small to medium-size roots, as large ones can be woody and have spongy or hollow centres. Trimmed of stalks and fine roots, they may be stored in the refrigerator crisper for weeks, though it is advisable to use them within one week.

Pare off the rough skin before cutting the flesh up into cubes or strips for salad or for cooking. As the flesh turns grey on exposure to air, the pieces should be dropped in ACIDULATED WATER to keep them white. Discard any soft centre flesh. Use celeriac in casseroles and soups or in the popular French way: cut into JULIENNE strips and mixed with RÉMOULADE sauce.

celery. Wild celery was known to the Egyptians in 2000 B.C. and is mentioned in Homer's *Odyssey*, but the plant as cultivated for eating derives from the sixteenth century, and today's crunchy, pale-green, 'stringless' variety is a fairly recent development. Available all year round, it is at its best in winter.

Fresh celery should be crisp and firm, without limp leaves or blemishes; a stick should snap easily. Store celery, unwashed and trimmed of its leaves and roots, in a plastic bag in the refrigerator. It will keep for up to a week. Limp celery can be revived by standing it in water.

The leaves and coarse outer sticks of celery can be added to the stockpot; the leaves can also be used in place of parsley as a garnish. Trim the base and remove any strings from celery sticks, which can be cooked in various ways—braised, parboiled and dressed À LA GRECQUE, cooked and served with a cream sauce, stir-fired, added to soups and stews—or eaten raw in salads.

celtuce. Chinese stem lettuce. A variety of the common lettuce, celtuce originated in China and is cultivated mainly for its stems. It is also called asparagus lettuce. Its flavour is said to be a blend of celery, lettuce, asparagus, and artichoke. The leaves are like cos lettuce and are also good to eat. Both stems and leaves may be eaten raw in salads or cooked—like celery and spinach or stir-fried. Peel the stems first.

cèpes. European wild mushrooms of the species *Boletus edulis* (see under MUSHROOMS).

ceviche. See SEVICHE / CEVICHE.

champagne melon. A small variety of WATERMELON with yellow flesh.

champignon. The French word for mushroom, usually applied to mushrooms that are small and unopened (see MUSHROOMS).

Chantilly / crème Chantilly. Sweetened whipped cream, sometimes flavoured with vanilla, chocolate, coffee, liqueur, or fruit purée, etc.

chapatti / chapati / chupatti / chupatty. A kind of flat, disc-shaped unleavened Indian bread made from wholemeal flour, cooked on a griddle, and served with curries and other savoury dishes. Chapattis should be eaten within a few hours of cooking, as they become stale quickly. They do not freeze well.

charlotte. One of the two different desserts traditionally made in a round, deep mould with sloping sides. Apple Charlotte has a casing of overlapping strips of buttered bread and a filling of apple purée. It is served hot. Charlotte Russe is surrounded by sponge fingers and has a filling of Bavarian Cream or similar custard or cream mousse mixture. It is served cold.

chateaubriand. A very thick beef steak cut from the butt end of the fillet, grilled and / or pan-fried, and usually served with BÉARNAISE SAUCE. One chateaubriand is enough for two people. The name was given to the steak by its creator, the chef of the Vicomte de Chateaubriand, whose wasteful method of cooking the steak was to grill it between two thinner steaks of the same size until they were burnt black. The charred outside layers were then discarded, leaving an evenly pink chateaubriand.

chaud-froid sauce. Prepared hot and eaten cold, chaud-froid is a rich white sauce thickened with gelatine which is used as a glossy coating to cold cooked meats, chicken, fish, etc. It is in effect an ASPIC, though not a clear one, and gives an elegant effect to cold food served buffet style.

Cheddar cheese. A firm cheese originally made in Somerset, England, Cheddar has been copied by cheese makers around the world. Australian Cheddar cheese is also known as 'tasty', 'matured', or 'vintage'. It varies in colour and flavour according to its place of production and its age, from palest yellow with a sweet, full flavour to a deep yellow and a sharp, rich, nutty taste. Used for sandwiches, savouries, toasting, etc., it also has its place on the dinner cheese board. (See also CHEESE.)

cheese. Cheese-making goes back to prehistoric times. It probably began with the natural curdling of warm milk or milk carried in animal skins. Cheese is the curd of milk separated from the whey, which may then be prepared and ripened or matured in various ways—pressed, salted, impregnated with bacteria, heat-treated, smoked, and so on. When a cheese is heat-treated, it is said to be 'uncooked' if the temperature does not exceed 40°C, 'scalded' if the temperature does not exceed 48°C, and 'cooked' if the temperature exceeds 48°C. Cheese can also be made from the whey; ricotta is one such cheese, although it is sometimes enriched with extra milk or cream.

In Australia, cheese must be made from pasteurised milk, which cheese makers and cheese fanciers agree places Australia at a disadvantage in the manufacture of specialty cheese. It is generally agreed that of the European specialty cheeses, those with the best taste and fullest flavour are made from raw, unpasteurised milk.

There are innumerable kinds of cheese; some of the most common are listed in this book under their individual names. They may be divided into four types: fresh, soft, firm, and hard.

Fresh cheese (COTTAGE CHEESE, CREAM CHEESE, etc.) was once known as green cheese—green in the sense of unripe—which makes the old saying about the moon being made of green cheese not quite so puzzling. It is the unripened curd set either by the natural acid in the milk or by the addition of a little RENNET, and drained of some of its moisture. The moisture content is still high, and storage life is short, so it should be kept in the coldest part of the refrigerator and eaten soon after purchase or after making it (it is easy to make). Fresh cheese is used for making cheesecakes as well as for savouries, spreads, and salads.

Soft cheese is ripened for a short while, more rennet is used to coagulate the curd, and it has less moisture than fresh cheese. Some soft cheeses, such as CAMEMBERT and BRIE, are ripened by a mould applied to the surface of the cheese which moves to the centre. They become runny as they mature. Others, such as **blue-vein cheeses**, are ripened internally by the introduction of a penicillin mould, or, like Blue Castello, by a combination of surface and internal moulds. FETTA CHEESE is pickled in brine, which makes it harder than other soft cheeses.

Firm cheeses make up the largest group. They include CHEDDAR, EDAM, GOUDA, GRUYÈRE and other Swiss-type cheeses, as well as the many locally produced cheeses that are known as 'tasty' or 'mature'. There are also some blue cheeses in this group. Firm cheeses are often pressed and heat-treated, encased in cheesecloth, wax, foil, or plastic and allowed to ripen and mature over a fairly long period.

Hard cheeses are subjected to pressure to make them dense, and they are left the longest time to ripen. They are also the driest and longest keeping. The hard, granular texture of cheeses such as PARMESAN and pecorino romano makes them ideal for grating.

With **processed cheese** the ripening is stopped at a given point by pasteurisation. The cheese itself is a blend of fresh and aged cheese, grated and mixed with emulsifying agents and preservatives to form a homogeneous plastic mass that remains constant in texture and flavour and keeps well. But it is not to be compared with a cheese that is allowed to ripen naturally to its peak.

To store cheese. Cheese should be stored in the refrigerator. To keep it from drying out, cover it with foil or plastic wrap, or wrap it in greaseproof paper and put it in a plastic bag. Rinded cheeses should have only the cut surfaces covered with plastic to allow the rind to breathe. If it is a particularly strong-smelling cheese, use an airtight container.

To freeze cheese. Freezing cheese is not generally recommended, although some cheeses freeze well enough—cottage cheese, for one, which may in fact have a better texture after freezing. Although some firm cheese—Cheddar, Edam, Gouda, Swiss—can be frozen, their texture becomes crumbly and furry on the tongue. They should be frozen in amounts of no more than 250 grams, in moisture-proof wrapping, immediately after purchase. Packaged cheese should be frozen in its unopened pack. Cottage cheese can be left in the freezer for up to a month, firm cheese up to six months.

To serve cheese. Serve cheese at room temperature. Allow a couple of hours out of the refrigerator before serving firm cheeses; somewhat less, depending on their ripeness, for soft cheeses. Different cultures have different ideas about when to serve cheese. In France and Italy the cheese is served before the fruit or dessert, perhaps accompanied by the remains of the red wine drunk with the main meal. In Britain the cheese is traditionally served after the dessert, with port. There are adherents to both styles in Australia.

Cheese is an excellent source of calcium and phosphorus and a moderate source of protein and vitamin A. As it is made from milk, it is high in saturated fat. It also contains between 1 and 5 per cent salt; hard, blue and brined cheeses contain the most.

cheesecake. 'Traditionally,' says Barbara Maher in *Cakes*, her definitive book on the subject, 'cheese cakes are baked from fresh cheeses, cream, eggs, butter, sugar and spices on a shortcrust pastry base—not made of crushed biscuit crumbs with a gelatined, plastic, uncooked, cream cheese topping.' Fresh cheeses of all kinds are used in the making of cheesecakes. The cheese is usually rubbed through a sieve or puréed in a blender before it is used in the cheesecake.

chef's salad. As the name implies, the ingredients of a chef's salad depend to some extent on the chef and what is available. According to Helen McCully in her book *Nobody Ever Tells You These Things*: 'Classically, a chef's salad is a combination of chicken, tongue or ham, and Swiss cheese, in equal proportions, all julienned, tossed in a vinaigrette sauce and served on greens. However, there are other variations.' Whatever the variation, it usually starts with a bed of crisp lettuce.

chelo. Steamed or boiled rice (Persian).

cherries are members of the *Prunus* genus and are closely related to plums, peaches, apricots, and nectarines, which are collectively known as drupes and commonly known as stone fruit. There are hundreds of varieties of cherry, loosely classified as sweet and sour. They range in colour from cream with a pink tinge to black, with cerise (the French word for cherry) in between. Cherries have a very short season. The New South Wales

Department of Agriculture says they are available from late October to mid February, but ripe and reasonably priced cherries seem to be available mainly in early summer. As they are highly perishable and do not travel well, they should be eaten soon after purchase. Choose glossy, brightly coloured fruit. They can be stored in a paper bag in the refrigerator for a few days. Wash them just before eating. They can be stewed, baked in pies and tarts, and preserved in brandy.

There is a special gadget to remove cherry pips. If you haven't one, a small pointed knife will do the trick. Roll the cherry between your fingers to loosen the pip, then insert the point of the knife in the stalk end and flick the pip out.

Maraschino cherries are a small Dalmatian variety known as damasca or marasca which are preserved in a syrup or candied. They are used for decorating desserts, pastries, cakes, and drinks.

chervil is a ferny-leafed herb that looks like parsley, tastes of aniseed, and is an essential ingredient in FINES HERBES. It is used in soups, sauces, and salads, especially potato salad, and goes well with eggs and fish. When used in cooked dishes, it should be added towards the end of cooking, as it loses its flavour if cooked for more than 10–15 minutes.

Chervil is available all year round. It can be stored for up to a week in a plastic bag lined with paper towelling.

chestnut. The nut of any of several species of tree of the *Castanea* genus. The species grown commercially in Australia is the Chinese chestnut, *C. molissima*. Chestnuts are available from March to June. They come in five sizes, and as a rule the bigger the better. Choose nuts that are glossy, heavy, and hard. Avoid any that rattle. As they don't keep well at room temperature, they should be stored in the refrigerator; you can keep them for a week or two. They can be eaten hot after roasting in the shell; the kernels can be boiled or braised and served as a vegetable, or chopped in turkey stuffing; made into a soup with dried beans; puréed and sweetened as a dessert; preserved and glazed as marrons glacés.

Unlike most other nuts, chestnuts have a low fat content.

To shell and peel chestnuts. Cut a slit or a cross in the shell at the pointed end, then put the nuts in a saucepan of cold water, bring them to the boil, and boil for a minute. The shell can then be peeled off and the bitter skin that covers the nut rubbed off. If the skin is stubborn, drop the nut back in the hot water for a while. Alternatively, bake them in an ovenproof dish for 8–10 minutes at 220°C. When cool enough to handle but still warm, the shells and skins can be removed.

To roast chestnuts. Cut or slit the pointed ends and bake the nuts in the oven for 20 minutes at 200°C or roast them over hot coals until the shell splits open.

chicken. About 140 million chickens are eaten in Australia each year, making Australians among the largest consumers of chicken in the world. Commercially raised crossbred chickens are fattened in cages above the ground on a regulated feeding mixture that produces a bland, standard-tasting bird ready for the table at six to eight weeks. Corn-fed chickens have a more yellowish appearance and, like free-range chickens, should have more flavour. The term *free-range* and *open-range* are loosely applied, however, and there are few truly free-range chickens sold commercially.

The youngest and smallest chickens, at six weeks old and about 500 grams, are sometimes called poussins or spatchcocks; at eight weeks and 900 grams they are known as spring chickens. A roasting chicken is one under six months old. A boiler can be eighteen months old or more. The numbering of chickens indicates directly the weight of the bird: size 5 weights 500 grams, 9 weighs 900 grams, 14 weighs 1.4 kilograms, 27 weighs 2.7 kilograms, and so on. A size 14 is three months old; a size 27, six months old. The bigger and older the chicken, the more flavour it should have. A large bird is better value too, as there is a higher proportion of flesh to bone than in a small bird.

To buy a chicken. As well as fresh and frozen whole chickens, you can buy chicken conveniently cut into portions: breasts, fillets, thighs, drumsticks, wings, etc. To assess the amount of chicken required, allow 375 grams for each person if the chicken is to be roasted (a size 15 for four people), and 500 grams each when grilling or frying; for a casserole, allow anything from 250 to 500 grams each, depending on the other ingredients. When buying frozen chickens, avoid any with pinkish ice in the pack—they will have been partially thawed and refrozen—or those with brown freezer burn marks.

To store chicken. Store fresh chickens in the coolest part of the refrigerator, and use within two or three days; giblets should be used within 24 hours. Frozen chickens can be kept in a separate freezer for six months or in the freezing section of a refrigerator for three months.

To thaw chicken. A frozen chicken must be thawed thoroughly before cooking; otherwise, harmful bacteria may not be killed by the heat of the cooking process. Leave it to thaw in the refrigerator for 24 hours. If you are in a hurry, put the chicken, still in its original wrapping, in a sink of cold water—not warm, or it will spoil the texture of the flesh. Do not refreeze a chicken after thawing.

To truss a chicken. Poultry is trussed to keep its shape while cooking and to make it look shapely when presented at table. Nowadays, trussing is

not recommended as it could prevent the poultry from cooking throughout and allow harmful bacteria to remain alive. However, if it is called for, you can truss a chicken as follows: Fold the wing tips under the bird and stretch the neck flap back and under the wing tips. Slip a piece of string underneath so that its centre is under the wing tips, draw the ends of the string around the sides, cross them over the cavity, then loop one around the left leg and the other around the right; draw them together and tie.

To joint a chicken. To cut a chicken into joints, first cut off the legs where the thigh joins the body. Slide a knife inside the chicken and cut each side of the backbone; remove the backbone. Turn the chicken over and cut along each side of the breastbone; remove the breastbone. Cut off the wing, with a small piece of breast, from each side. You then have six pieces: two legs, two breasts, and two wings.

The Chinese cut off the wings, legs, and thighs with a cleaver or large knife, then cut the body in half by cutting through the breastbone and along the backbone. The pieces of chicken are usually chopped across the bones into portions that can be managed with chopsticks.

To roast a chicken. To roast poultry in the French style, cook the bird on a rack in a roasting pan, with stock (or a mixture of stock and wine) in the bottom of the pan. Place the bird breast-side up at first and cook it for 10 minutes at a high temperature, then reduce the temperature to moderate, turn the bird on its side, and baste it with the liquid in the pan. Turn and baste every quarter-hour. The bird should be breast-side up for the last 15 minutes. Cooked in this way the flesh is kept moist while the skin becomes crisp and golden. A sauce is made with a reduction of the liquid after the bird is cooked (see REDUCE, REDUCTION).

To test if a roast chicken is cooked. Prick the thigh in the thickest part with a skewer. When the juice runs clear with no trace of pinkness, the chicken is done. It should take 1–1¼ hours to cook depending on the size of the chicken.

chicken livers. The secret of cooking chicken livers is to cook them quickly in clarified butter over high heat so that the juices are sealed in and the livers don't become tough. They should be a rich brown on the outside and pink inside. Before cooking them, remove the fibres with a sharp knife and make sure there are no yellow or green bile spots. If there are, cut them out; otherwise the liver will taste bitter. Mashed or puréed chicken livers are also used to make pâtés, terrines, pasta sauces, and a spread for CROSTINI.

chickpeas. Neither a pea nor food for chickens, the chickpea is the seed of a leguminous plant native to west Asia. There are two kinds available: the large white garbanzo and the smaller brown desi. They are eaten in many ways in many countries: roasted and eaten with drinks, cooked and dressed with oil as a salad, made into soups and stews, roasted with spices and chilli, milled into flour (BESAN), ground or mashed to become one of the main constituents of HUMMUS and FELAFEL, to mention a few. Chickpeas should be stored dry in an airtight container. Use them within a year.

To prepare and cook chickpeas. Before cooking, pick them over and discard any that are withered. For most uses, they need to be soaked first. If raw, softened peas are called for, soak them in water in a covered bowl in the refrigerator overnight; if cooked peas are required, boil them in water to cover for two minutes, then stand, covered, for 1–2 hours before further cooking. Some recipes require the skins removed; they can be rubbed off after soaking. Canned chickpeas, which are available, will relieve you of all this trouble.

Chickpeas are a good source of protein, dietary fibre, B vitamins and kilojoules.

chicory. A group of plants of the genus *Cichorium* are known by various names. The perennial plant *Cichorium intybus*, commonly known as chicory, used to be grown mainly for its roots, which were roasted and powdered and added to coffee. In the mid-nineteenth century some roots of this plant left lying in the dark were found to have grown a tightly furled mass of white leaves, which the Belgians cultivated and called WITLOOF (Flemish for 'white leaf') and others called Belgian endive. This has led to some confusion, as another species of chicory, *Cichorium endiva*, grown for its green curly leaves, was known as curly endive or, simply, ENDIVE (which, to add to the confusion, is called chicory in England). There is a broad-leaved Batavian endive known to many as escarole, and some Italian varieties of chicory that look like miniature red lettuces are called RADICCHIO.

chiffonade means 'ragged', and it usually refers to shredded or julienned lettuce and / or sorrel cooked in butter and used as a garnish for soups. It can also be the name of the soup itself. A chiffonade salad is made from shredded greens, beetroot, and hard-boiled eggs with a VINAIGRETTE dressing.

chill, cool. To chill means to refrigerate until cold (not frozen). To cool means to allow something hot to stand at room temperature until it no longer feels warm.

chilli con carne. The literal translation, 'chilli with meat', indicates that chilli is the predominant ingredient in this fiery Texan stew. The meat is traditionally diced or minced beef, and the dish is usually served with beans. The amount of CHILLI POWDER added depends on the pitilessness of the cook.

chilli paste (nam prik pao). A Thai paste made from dried chillies, dried prawns, roasted onion and garlic, sugar, and tamarind juice, which is used in many Thai recipes. If it is unavailable, a small amount of fresh or dried chilli can be substituted for it.

chilli powder. A blend of powdered chilli, capsicum, oregano, cumin, and garlic created in Texas to liven up dishes such as CHILLI CON CARNE. Local chilli powders may be made from various dried and powdered chillies and other spicy powders.

chillies / chilli peppers. The hot members of the capsicum family. Like all capsicums, chillies are of American origin. The pods come in all shapes, colours, and sizes. As a rule, the smaller the hotter, but colour is not an indicator of pungency. Chillies lose their flavour quickly, so they should be kept in the refrigerator.

To prepare chillies. Chillies need careful handling, as their volatile oils irritate sensitive skin and burn the eyes. Make sure you don't touch your face or eyes while you are handling chillies, and wash your hands thoroughly immediately you are finished. Rinse the chillies under cold running water, and pull off the stem. If the seeds, which are the hottest part, are to be removed, cut the chillies in half lengthwise and brush out the seeds with your fingers under the running water. If the ribs are coarse, cut them out with a paring knife.

Dried chillies should be torn into small pieces, covered with boiling water, and left to soak for 30 minutes before use.

Canned chillies should be rinsed in cold water to remove the brine in which they are preserved.

When you are cooking for guests and the recipe calls for chopped chillies, cut it into pieces big enough for the diners to see and avoid if they want to. Chilli should be used with discretion in any case.

To make fresh chillies less hot, soak them in cold salted water for an hour.

chine. The chine is the backbone, or the backbone and adjoining parts, of an animal carcase. When the butcher chines a joint of meat, he loosens the backbone from the ribs to make it easier to carve.

Chinese broccoli (gai laan). A stem vegetable similar to the European sprouting BROCCOLI with dark green leaves and small florets, Chinese broccoli has a crisp texture and slightly bitter taste. Stems and leaves are both eaten. It is available all year round and can be stored in a plastic bag in the refrigerator for up to a week.

Boil or steam Chinese broccoli for a short time to retain the crisp texture, and serve it with oyster sauce. It is also good stir-fried or added to soups and pork dishes.

Chinese broccoli is extremely nutritious. It is said to have the highest calcium content of any food and is an excellent source of vitamin C, as well as vitamin A, iron, potassium, and dietary fibre.

Chinese cabbage (wong nga baak). Also known as Peking cabbage and *pe tsai*, Chinese cabbage looks like a large cos lettuce with crinkled, pale green leaves and wide, thick ribs. It is available all the year round, with heaviest supplies from March to November. Provided it is wrapped in plastic to prevent the leaves from drying out, it can be stored in the refrigerator for up to a fortnight.

To prepare and cook Chinese cabbage. Shred or tear the leaves into bite-size pieces, and slice thick stems into narrow strips. Steam, braise, or stir-fry it, or add it to soups and noodle dishes.

Chinese flowering cabbage (choi sum) is similar to BOK CHOY, with tender, white, fleshy stems, bright green leaves, and also yellow flowers. All parts of the plant are eaten. It is available all year round and can be kept in a plastic bag in the refrigerator for up to five days. Cook it in a small amount of water or steam it for a short while. Stir-fry in large pieces or add to meat dishes.

Chinese gooseberry. See KIWI FRUIT.

Chinese mustard cabbage (gai choi). There are many varieties of mustard cabbage, an ancient Chinese vegetable. The common variety, dai gai choy, has pale green, curved, thick stems and wrinkled, fringed leaves. Mustard cabbages have a strong bitter flavour and are usually pickled in China. They may be cooked in braised dishes and soups and also stir-fried and served with oyster sauce.

Chinese parsley. See CORIANDER.

Chinese spinach (een choi) resembles English spinach rather than silver beet and can be used in place of those green vegetables. It is available from February to October, usually sold as an entire plant. After rinsing and shaking dry, it can be stored in a plastic bag in the refrigerator for up to a week. Before cooking, remove the roots and stem ends, then steam, boil or stir-fry briefly to retain its crisp texture. (See also WATER SPINACH.)

Chinese white cabbage. See BOK CHOY / BOC CHOI / PAK CHOI.

chipolata. A small, thin, fresh sausage (see SAUSAGE). According to Andre Simon's *Concise Encyclopaedia of Gastronomy*, chipolatas 'should be plentifully seasoned with chives, the name being derived from the Italian for chives'. *Larousse Gastronomique*, on the other hand, makes no mention of chives but says the name comes from the Italian *cipolla* (onion) 'and was originally applied to a stew made with onions and sausages'. Chipolatas are sometimes served as a garnish for meat or poultry dishes or as a snack on cocktail sticks.

chitterlings. The small intestine of pigs, usually fried.

chives. The chive is a member of the onion family, together with garlic, shallots, and leeks. The regular onion chives have slender green tubular leaves; garlic chives have flat leaves like blades of grass. The colour and delicate flavour of chives make them an ideal garnish. You can snip them with scissors straight over the food. They go well with eggs, especially omelettes, cottage or cream cheese, potatoes, carrots, salads, and soups.

chocolate. For three hundred years after cocoa beans were brought back to Europe from the New World, chocolate was consumed only as a drink, as the Mayans and Aztecs had done for centuries and the Mexicans still do. It was not until the nineteenth century that powdered cocoa and eating chocolate were developed. Cocoa beans—the seeds of the small, evergreen tree *Theobroma cacao*—are fermented, roasted, husked, and ground into an oily paste, also called cocoa liquor, which contains about 50 per cent of a fat known as cocoa butter. Varying amounts of cocoa butter are extracted from the paste, the residue being ground to make cocoa. Block chocolate is made from cocoa paste mixed with sugar and extra cocoa butter; milk powder is added for milk chocolate. **Couverture** chocolate has a high proportion of cocoa butter and is used for covering sweets and cakes. Compound chocolate is made with vegetable fats instead of cocoa butter.

    To melt chocolate. Break the required amount of chocolate into pieces and place them in a bowl over hot water—not boiling water, because the steam might condense and drop into the melting chocolate. Water and chocolate don't mix, and even a tiny amount can harden the chocolate and make it unusable. (If this happens, add some vegetable shortening or oil, which will make it liquid again.) Some people melt the chocolate in the oven so that there is no risk of moisture. You can also melt it in the microwave, but be sure to check it every 15–20 seconds as it can burn very quickly. Gently stir the chocolate until it has melted. Don't stir vigorously, or air bubbles will form. And don't heat the chocolate over 50°C (hot to touch). If it is too thick, add some shortening or oil to thin it out.

choi sum. See CHINESE FLOWERING CABBAGE.

choko. For those old enough to remember the ubiquitous choko vine covering the outside dunny and the Depression dessert of stewed 'pears' that were, in fact, choko quarters cooked in sugar syrup and tinted pink with cochineal, it still comes as a surprise to see chokos *sold* in vegetable markets. Once upon a time you had trouble giving them away.

Originally from Central America, where it is known as chayote, the choko has been eaten there since the time of the Aztecs. It is cultivated around the Mediterranean as well as in Australia. The Chinese also use it in their cooking; they call it *faat sau gwa*. Chokos are available most of the year, with heaviest supplies in summer and autumn. Choose small, light green ones without shoots. You can store them in a cool dark place or in the vegetable crisper of the refrigerator for up to ten days.

To prepare and cook chokos. Cut them into quarters and remove the seed if the choko is large; soft seeds can be eaten. Peel them, under water if you don't like the sappiness; otherwise rinse afterwards. Steam, boil or microwave them, and serve them with a sauce to give some flavour to their natural blandness. They can be used in soups and casseroles or stuffed and baked. And of course you can stew them as 'pears'.

cholesterol. The cholesterol in the food we eat does not have a major effect on the amount of cholesterol in our blood. The body makes its own cholesterol, which it does for important reasons. Unfortunately, it makes an over-abundance of cholesterol when we eat food containing a lot of saturated fatty acids or trans fatty acids (see FAT), and the spare cholesterol tends to clog the blood vessels leading to the heart and other parts of the body. However, there is good and bad cholesterol. Low-density lipoprotein (LDL) cholesterol is the harmful kind. High-density lipoprotein (HDL) cholesterol appears to protect against coronary risk.

As for advertising the fact that a certain fruit or vegetable contains no cholesterol, it is an empty claim. Cholesterol is uniquely an animal product. No fruit or vegetables contain cholesterol.

chop suey. An American Chinese dish, its name comes from a Cantonese phrase meaning 'mixed bits'. It consists of small pieces of meat or chicken cooked with bean sprouts and other vegetables and served with rice.

chops. A chop is a slice of lamb, mutton, veal, or pork containing some bone. For buying and storing chops, see MEAT.

chorizo. A spiced, coarsely textured cured sausage very popular throughout Spain. It is made usually with pork and pork fat and spiced with garlic and paprika, and it is eaten either thinly sliced in a selection of TAPAS or in a crusty bread roll, and cooked in stews and soups. In Portugal a similar sausage is called chouriço.

choucroute. The French name for SAUERKRAUT. Choucroute Garni is sauerkraut cooked with chopped onion, carrot, and apple, and garnished with ham, pork, or sausage.

chow mein. A traditional Australian Chinese restaurant dish composed of fresh noodles with shredded vegetables and small quantities of chicken, pork, or seafood served over them in a sauce (chicken chow mein, prawn chow mein, etc.). Dictionaries say the Chinese phrase means 'fried flour'.

chowder. Derived from the French word *chaudière*, meaning 'stew pot', *chowder* has been pretty much taken over by the Americans, who can't even agree among themselves how their celebrated clam chowder should be made. The American *Heritage Illustrated Dictionary* defines chowder as 'a thick soup or stew containing fish or shellfish, especially clams, and vegetables, often in a milk base'. This is all very well, but the New Englanders insist on milk alone as the base and include salt pork or bacon. They scorn the Manhattan version, which calls for water rather than milk—and tomatoes, no less. They almost passed a law to prohibit this.

chutney is a word of Indian origin, as is the pungent condiment itself. There are two kinds of chutney: cooked and fresh. Cooked chutneys are made from chopped fruit and vegetables with sugar (roughly half as much sugar by weight as the fruit and vegetables), spices, and vinegar. The mixture is cooked for 1–2 hours, sometimes longer, until it becomes thick, dark, and jam-like. Cooked chutneys are bottled and allowed to mature for weeks or months before eating. Fresh chutneys are made to eat immediately, so they need no sugar or vinegar to act as preservatives. The ingredients, which may include lemon or lime juice and sometimes yoghurt, are often combined in a food processor.

Chutney is a traditional accompaniment to curry and is also served with cold meats and cheese.

cilantro. Another name for CORIANDER leaves, although some suppliers use the term to denote a fashionable variety of coriander that originated in America.

cinnamon is the dried inner bark of the evergreen tree *Cinnamomum zeylanicum*, native to Sri Lanka, where most of the world's cinnamon is produced. The peeled bark curls into sticks, or 'quills'. Cinnamon is available either whole or powdered. As it is not easy to grind, it is handy to have in both quill and powdered form—but buy the powder in the smallest quantity available, because it does not keep its aroma for very long.

Cinnamon sticks are used in mulled wines, poached fruits, PILAF, etc. Powdered cinnamon is widely used to flavour cakes, buns, and milk puddings. Cinnamon toast—hot buttered toast sprinkled with sugar and cinnamon—is an old favourite in tea and coffee shops. Cinnamon is also used in many Middle Eastern and Indian dishes.

The dried bark of *Cinnamomum cassia*, though properly called cassia, is also known as cinnamon and is used as a substitute for cinnamon. It is also available in powdered form. It is more pungent, and the sticks are thicker than those of true cinnamon.

citron. An ancient member of the citrus family, the citron is grown for its peel, which is candied and used in fruit cakes. Citrons are like large lemons with thick rough skins and a flesh too bitter to eat.

citrus fruit. The popular citrus fruits are ORANGES, LEMONS, LIMES, mandarins · (see MANDARIN / MANDARINE, TANGERINE), and GRAPEFRUIT, but other members of the *Citrus* genus include the CITRON, KALAMANSI, POMELO or shaddock, TANGELO, and ugli fruit. The CUMQUAT used to be considered a citrus but has been reclassified by botanists. Citrus fruits ripen on the trees and stop developing once they are picked. They can therefore be kept for quite a long time. Store them in a cool place or in a plastic bag in the refrigerator (but eat them at room temperature). Don't store oranges with lemons, as they both tend to become mouldy.

The skin of citrus fruits sometimes turns partially green after picking. This is simply the chlorophyll in the skin reacting to the temperature; the flesh remains unaffected.

All citrus fruits are a source of vitamin C, some varieties providing more than others.

To grate and squeeze citrus fruit. If a piece of citrus fruit is to be both squeezed and grated, it is best to grate first, because a whole, firm fruit is easier to hold while grating than a pliable, slippery, squeezed half. If you are simply grating the fruit and want to keep it, wrap it in plastic wrap or place in a well-sealed plastic bag so that it doesn't dry out and go hard before you want to use it; keep it in the refrigerator.

To segment citrus fruit. Peel the fruit, round and round, removing all the pith with the skin. Hold the peeled fruit in one hand over a bowl to catch the juice, and, with a small sharp or serrated knife, cut down as close as possible to the membrane on each side to loosen the segment. Drop each segment into the bowl as you continue round the fruit.

clarifying. To clarify is to remove sediment or cloudiness from a liquid such as stock so that it becomes clear, or to remove the milk solids from butter so that it will not burn when used for sautéing. For the techniques of clarifying, see under STOCK, BROTH, BOUILLON and BUTTER.

cloves are the dried, unopened flower buds of an evergreen tree of the myrtle family native to the Molucca Islands and now grown in many hot countries. The word *clove* comes from the Latin *clavus*, meaning 'nail', which the clove resembles, especially when used to stud a crumbed baked ham or an orange pomander.

Cloves are available whole or ground. Ground cloves should be stored in an airtight container, as they lose their aroma and flavour fairly quickly.

Whole cloves are used to flavour stewed fruits, particularly apples, pickles and chutneys, mulled drinks, boiled corned meats, and soups and stews. As it is not very gratifying to bite on a whole clove (unless you have a toothache, which is traditionally relieved by the clove's numbing effect), they are often fixed in an onion and removed from soups and stews before serving. Ground cloves are used in cakes, buns, milk puddings, and various sauces and vegetable dishes.

cobbler. A deep-dish fruit pie with a thick top crust made of dough arranged in overlapping circles or cut in squares. The name presumably comes from the appearance of the topping, which resembles cobblestones. Serve it with ice-cream or whipped cream.

cock-a-leekie / cocky-leeky. A traditional Scottish soup made with a boiling fowl and leeks, sometimes with added rice. Applying traditional Scottish thrift, you can serve the broth first and the fowl as the main course.

cocoa. A powder made from the hardened residue of ground cocoa beans after a certain amount of the fat or cocoa paste has been extracted (see CHOCO-LATE). As well as being used to make the hot cocoa drink, cocoa powder is used to flavour biscuits, cakes, cake icing, and desserts. It can also be substituted for cooking chocolate—three tablespoons of cocoa and one tablespoon of vegetable shortening is equivalent to 30 grams of chocolate; add a teaspoon or two of sugar if it needs to be sweetened.

To make a hot drink. First mix the cocoa powder with a little cold milk or water to form a smooth paste so that it does not become lumpy. Then add hot milk and stir. Some cocoa fanciers boil it gently for a couple of minutes and then whisk it to a froth before serving. Others add cream, or coffee (when it is known as MOCHA).

coconut. With such a diversity of prepared coconut products on the supermarket shelves—tinned coconut milk and coconut cream, instant coconut milk powder, grated, flaked, and desiccated coconut flesh—it might seem hardly worth while buying a fresh coconut and preparing it yourself. However, the nuts are available all year round, and some recipes do call for fresh coconut. Besides, home-made products are usually more satisfying and tasty.

When buying a coconut, choose one that is heavy for its size and full of juice; the more juice, the fresher it is. Shake it and you will hear the liquid sloshing about. Avoid nuts without juice and those with wet or mouldy 'eyes'.

To open a coconut. Remove the fibrous outer husk if it hasn't already been removed. Pierce two of the eyes with a sharp pointed implement (skewer, screwdriver, bradawl, etc.) and drain off the juice, which makes a refreshing drink. The shell will be easier to crack if the nut is put in the oven at 200°C for a few minutes or in the freezer for an hour. Then hit it sharply with a hammer. The flesh should fall away from the broken pieces of shell; use a small knife to prise off the bits that cling.

To grate coconut. Pare off the brown skin and grate the white pieces on a hand grater or in a blender.

To make coconut milk and cream. Put 1½ cups of flaked, grated, or desiccated coconut in a saucepan with 1½ cups of hot water and simmer it for about 5 minutes. Strain the liquid through a sieve, pressing on the pulp with the back of a spoon to extract as much liquid as possible. This will produce a cup of rich coconut milk. Coconut cream is obtained by chilling the coconut milk for a few hours and skimming the creamy liquid off the top. Coconut milk and cream are used extensively throughout India, Thailand,

Malaysia, and Indonesia in traditional recipes—curries, meat, vegetable and seafood dishes, and in desserts.

Coconut is high in fat, which is 90 per cent saturated, and provides lots of kilojoules.

cocotte. A round or oval ovenproof dish for cooking individual mousses, soufflés, or egg dishes; a ramekin. Food cooked in one of these dishes is described as *en cocotte* and is usually served in the dish.

coeur à la crème. A mixture of cream and cream cheese is packed in a cheesecloth-lined heart-shaped basket or perforated mould and allowed to drain. Unmoulded, with the cheesecloth removed, it is served as a dessert with sweetened strawberries or other berries or with redcurrant jelly.

coffee. Coffee beans are the half-seeds of the fruit from a small tree belonging to the *Coffea* genus, especially *Coffea arabica*, native to Arabia but cultivated in many parts of the world, including Brazil and other Central American countries, Jamaica, Kenya, Mysore, Java, and Papua New Guinea. All produce their own particular style of coffee. The beans are fermented, dried, and roasted, the degree of roasting determining the flavour. At one extreme, a light roast produces a cinnamon-coloured bean and a flavour that is either delicate or thin according to whether you like it or not. At the other extreme is the Italian or espresso roast where the bean is almost burnt black and the flavour is very intense.

To buy, grind, and store coffee. Coffee is at its best when it is freshly roasted and freshly ground. Buy it in small quantities so that it is all used within a week or two, and keep it in an airtight container in the refrigerator or freezer. Unless you roast your own beans, the best you can do to obtain them freshly roasted is to buy from a specialist supplier or one with a high turnover. You can, however, grind your own coffee when you need it. If you buy coffee ready ground, make sure it is the grind suitable for your coffee-making machine or the way in which you brew coffee: pulverised for Turkish-style coffee; very fine for the filter-paper method; fine for espresso or drip-pot; medium for the percolator, vacuum pot, or plunger pot. Otherwise you may end up with coffee that is either insipid because of under-extraction or bitter because of over-extraction.

To brew coffee. There is much difference of opinion among coffee drinkers about which is the best way to make it, and the various proprietary coffee-makers have their own instructions about how to use them to the best advantage. However, you can make coffee in a simple pot or jug as you would make tea, by pouring boiling water over the grounds, leaving it to infuse for 4–5 minutes, and straining it into cups. Use a tablespoon of medium-grind grounds per 200-millilitre cup. Plunger and percolator coffee makers work in much the same way. Turkish-style coffee is traditionally made in a long-handled metal jug with a heaped teaspoon of pulverised coffee per tiny, 75-millilitre cup of water and plenty of sugar, brought to the boil and simmered to a froth. It is poured into cups and allowed to stand until the grounds settle to a sludge and the liquid can be sipped off the top.

colander. A perforated bowl-shaped utensil used for draining off liquid after cooking or rinsing food. Lined with two or three layers of muslin or a clean linen tea-towel, it can be used to strain fruit jellies and the like.

coleslaw. Dutch in name (it means 'cabbage salad') and American in origin (it rivals potato salad as America's favourite, according to Julia Child), coleslaw is essentially finely shredded raw cabbage mixed with a dressing. However, various additions are often made: grated carrot, diced celery, cucumber, onion, capsicum and apple, walnut pieces, caraway seeds, and so on. The cabbage can be of any kind, and the dressing is usually a mustardy mayonnaise. Coleslaw is the ideal accompaniment for barbecued meats.

comfit, confit. A comfit is a sugar-coated nut or seed. The name is an old English word not used very much these days. French confits are fruit and vegetables preserved in sugar, sometimes with brandy added; but they are also pieces of pork, goose, or duck preserved in their own fat. Both words come from the Latin *confectum* 'preparation', from which *confection* and *confectionery* are derived.

compote. A preparation of fresh or dried fruit, or a mixture of both, poached in a SUGAR SYRUP, often with spices or other flavourings. The shape of the fruit, whether whole, halved or sliced, is retained by the gentle cooking. The fruit is served in the syrup, usually cold but sometimes hot. (However, 'compote of peaches' listed on a dinner menu could mean peach halves straight out of the can.)

condiment comes from the Latin word for 'spice' or 'seasoning', and the term is used to denote something that gives a special or additional flavour to food, such as mustard, chutney, sauces, pickles and relishes, as well as various spices.

confectioner's sugar. The American name for ICING SUGAR.

conserve. A kind of JAM but made with whole or large pieces of fruit and often with a mixture of two or more fruits. Conserves may be served as a dessert.

consommé. Beef or chicken STOCK that has been clarified (see under STOCK, BROTH, BOUILLON) and simmered for a while to reduce the liquid and concentrate the flavour. (This is also known as a double consommé, the French *consommé simple* being strained stock, unclarified.) Consommés can be served hot or chilled. A little dry sherry or Madeira added just before serving enhances the flavour. Sometimes a chilled consommé will set into a jelly, which can be served as a first course to a summer meal.

cooling. See CHILL, COOL.

Copha. A proprietary SHORTENING agent made of coconut oil that has been purified and processed into a white, waxy solid. Copha is used especially in making uncooked, chilled confections such as chocolate crackles.

coppa can mean several things, but it usually refers to cured but uncooked pork, prepared in much the same way as ham and shaped into a hard, thick sausage. It is served raw in very thin slices.

coq au vin. A classic French dish consisting of chicken cooked in red wine with onions, mushrooms, bacon, garlic, and herbs.

Coquilles Saint Jacques. The French term *coquille-Saint-Jacques* simply means 'scallop', *coquille* being 'shell' and Saint Jacques being Saint James the apostle, whose emblem was the scallop shell. The dish Coquilles Saint Jacques has a number of variations but usually consists of scallops in a sauce made of cream, egg yolks, and wine, topped with grated cheese and baked in their shells. However, Elizabeth David in her *Book of Mediterranean Food* says that, in her belief, 'scallops should not be served in their shells; they tend to dry up when baked in the oven'. (See also SCALLOPS.)

coral trout. A medium-size fish caught near reefs all round the northern coast of Australia. The skin of the coral trout is pink to reddish-brown (sometimes other colours), covered with fine blue spots and sometimes vertical bars. Its moist, firm-textured flesh is very white and has few bones. Coral trout are available all year round but mainly from April to November. They are sold whole and in fillets. Whole fish may be steamed, poached, or grilled but should not be stuffed owing to the fine, delicate flakes of the flesh. Fillets may be fried or grilled. (See also FISH.)

coriander is an ancient herb and spice mentioned in the Bible and Sanskrit literature. An annual plant native to the Mediterranean region, it is grown both for its green leaves and for its dried seeds, which are different in flavour and should not be substituted for one another in recipes. Fresh, green coriander, which is known also as Chinese parsley and cilantro, is usually sold with the roots attached. Store it, with the roots still on, standing in a jug of water with a plastic bag over the top. It is used in many Thai and Indian dishes (Thai cuisine makes use of the entire plant—leaves, stems, and roots). The Chinese use it as a seasoning for soups and steamed foods and on baked fish.

The round, light brown seeds are available whole or ground. They are used in curries, to flavour meat, poultry, and fish dishes, in anything prepared À LA GRECQUE, and in many spicy meat dishes of North Africa and the Middle East.

corn is a general term meaning any edible grain, although in various English-speaking countries it refers especially to a particular grain: in England, wheat; in Scotland and Ireland, oats; and in the United States and Australia, maize.

Maize is native to the American continent and was cultivated by the Incas, Aztecs, and Mayans for thousands of years before it was taken to the Western World. There are countless varieties, soft and hard, coloured from cream to purple. Maize is an important crop economically, although only 12 per cent of the world's crop is used for culinary purposes. The remainder is used in the manufacture of starch, glue, alcohol, paper, nappies, and embalming fluid, among other things. Apart from SWEET CORN, the main culinary products of corn are corn meal, cornflour and corn oil.

Corn meal is a yellow-white granular flour available in coarse or medium grinds. In the southern United States, corn meal is used to make corn bread, muffins, stuffings, and other things. In Italy corn meal is known as POLENTA, and is a staple food in certain regions. In Central America, a finely ground corn meal known as *masa harina* is used to make the ubiquitous TORTILLA. *Masa harina* is treated with lime water or another alkali to release the niacin

61

and vitamins, which are otherwise not biologically available from maize. Store corn meal in a screw-top jar in a cool place; it can be kept for up to six months.

Cornflour is a fine white starchy powder (in the United States it is called cornstarch) which is used mainly as a thickening agent for sauces, gravies and pie fillings and in cakes. It is also much used in Asian cooking. Cornflour is prepared from the white heart of maize or from wheat. The package will specify whether it is '100 per cent pure corn', or 'wheaten cornflour'. One can be used in place of the other, but the quantity has to be adjusted, as maize cornflour produces a thicker mixture than wheaten cornflour.

Corn oil or **maize oil** is pressed from the maize kernel and is usually refined to improve flavour and keeping quality. It is used as a salad oil or cooking oil. Its high smoke point makes it good for frying. The fat in the oil is predominantly polyunsaturated, and it is an excellent source of vitamin E.

corn salad. Another name for lamb's LETTUCE.

corned beef. Corned means salted—the term derives from the corns or grains of salt that were rubbed over meat to preserve it. Corned beef nowadays is soaked in and / or injected with brine, with a little sodium nitrate added to keep the meat pink. The cut of beef may be a solid piece of silverside or a flatter piece of brisket that has been rolled and tied. Before cooking, corned beef may be soaked to remove some of the salt. It is usually boiled in water with an onion, peppercorns, bay leaf, cloves, celery, and carrots. It may be served hot or cold. Serve it hot with cabbage, carrots, or potatoes and white sauce. When it is to be served cold, let the meat stand in the cooking water until cool.

cornichon. The French word for GHERKIN. There is also a large, bluish-purple, thick-skinned grape known as a cornichon.

Cornish pasty. A very practical portable meal, the pasty is made from a round piece of pastry which is folded around a filling of some kind—usually a savoury combination of vegetables and perhaps meat, but sometimes sweet fruit—and baked without a mould to shape it. It was designed, they say, to fit neatly in the pocket and created to provide the miners of Cornwall with an all-in-one lunch. Some pasties had meat and vegetables at one end and a sweet filling at the other. 'The Devil and all goes into a pasty', as the Cornish people are wont to say.

cos. A kind of LETTUCE, also known as romaine.

cottage cheese is a soft, unripened, white cheese traditionally made from the strained curds of skim milk, the curds having coagulated by the action of the natural acids in the milk (see 'Fresh cheese', under CHEESE). However, commercially made cottage cheese may have cream added to give a softer texture, food acid to set the curd, and salt as a preservative. Cottage cheese is quite perishable and should be eaten as soon as possible after it is made or bought; keep bought cheese in a covered container in the refrigerator for no more than a week.

Cottage cheese is low in kilojoules and provides a low-fat alternative to CREAM CHEESE for people watching their weight.

cottage pie. See SHEPHERD'S PIE.

coulis. A strained purée of fruit or vegetables, usually made from red berries (strawberries, raspberries, redcurrants) or tomatoes. The modern coulis is a product of the NOUVELLE CUISINE period and is used to add a splash of colour and a dash of flavour to a plate. You can make a fruit coulis simply by puréeing 500 grams of berries and a cup of sugar in a food processor and rubbing the purée through a sieve to remove the seeds. It will keep for weeks in a covered jar in the refrigerator.

coupe (pronounced 'coop'). A shallow, stemmed glass or bowl-shaped dish in which a chilled dessert of fruit and ice-cream is served. The word may also refer to the dessert itself.

courgette. Another name for ZUCCHINI.

court bouillon. A liquid used for poaching whole fish, or large pieces of fish, and shellfish. The composition of the court bouillon depends on the type of fish. It is usually made from water with some wine, lemon juice, or vinegar to make it slightly acid, together with aromatic vegetables, herbs, and seasonings, simmered for a while to draw out the flavours, and then strained. It may also be based on milk. The object of the court bouillon is to enhance the flavour of the fish, not to mask it.

couscous is the national dish of Algeria, Tunisia, and Morocco. It is also the name of the tiny pellets of flour-coated semolina with which the dish is made. To cook couscous it helps to have a *couscousier*, the traditional cooking vessel consisting of a large pan in which a stew or broth of lamb or chicken and vegetables is cooked, with a sieve-like top in which the couscous is steamed. A double steamer or a metal sieve that fits neatly over a large pan will do as a substitute. The important point is that the couscous must not touch the liquid below but should cook in the steam.

To prepare and cook couscous. According to Claudia Roden in her *Book of Middle Eastern Food*, the couscous is first moistened with a little cold water, working it in with the fingers to prevent lumps from forming. After the stew has been cooking for some time, the couscous is turned into the sieve, given a raking with the fingers to air the grains and help them swell, and left to steam, uncovered, over the simmering liquid for 30 minutes. The couscous is then turned into a bowl, sprinkled with cold water (which makes the grains swell very much), stirred with a wooden spoon to break up any lumps, and put back in the sieve to steam for a further 30 minutes. However, instructions on packaged couscous available in Australia tell you simply to add 1 cup of boiling water to each ½ cup of couscous and let it stand until the water is absorbed.

Couscous is served with the stew over which it is cooked or, if it has been steamed over or soaked in boiling water, with any meat or vegetable dish usually served with rice or pasta. In Egypt it is served with honey, nuts, and dried fruit as a dessert.

couverture. Chocolate containing a high proportion of cocoa butter, which is used for covering sweets and cakes.

crab. The two main edible crabs available in Australia are the mud or mangrove crab and the blue swimmer. They are sold cooked or uncooked. A cooked crab should be heavy for its size, with legs intact and not limp. Although uncooked blue swimmers may be bought dead, uncooked mud crabs are sold alive because they deteriorate quickly once they have been killed.

To prepare and cook a crab. Some people tell you to plunge the crab into rapidly boiling salted water, sea water, or COURT BOUILLON, which kills it quickly, then boil it for about 8 minutes per 500 grams of crab. Others say that this makes the flesh tough and the legs fall off. They recommend killing the crab by drowning it in fresh water (add a handful of flour or dried milk powder to hasten the process), or by freezing (a more humane method). Once the crab is dead, place it in a pan of cold water, cover, bring to the boil, and simmer for the same amount of time—that is, about 8 minutes per 500 grams. Keith Floyd, in *Floyd on Fish*, says to pop the live crab into cold salted water and bring it to the boil. However, you may find the crab's attempts to get out of the pot before it expires distressing.

To extract the flesh from a crab. Pull off the claws and legs, crack them carefully with a nutcracker or mallet, and remove the flesh. Insert a rigid knife between the main shell and the part the legs were attached to, and lever out this body section. Discard the stomach sac and its appendages. Remove the brown and white meat with a teaspoon or, from the crevices, with a skewer.

crab-apples are not usually seen in fruit shops, no doubt because they are small, sour, and mostly core. But crab-apple trees are grown as decorative blossom-bearers in the garden, and the attractive yellow, red, or green fruit are used to make clear, golden-pink crab-apple JELLY, a delicious spread for breakfast toast or brioches. Crab-apples can also be cooked whole in SUGAR SYRUP until tender, and served cold with cream.

crayfish. The sea-dwelling crayfish in Australian waters are commonly known as lobsters or rock lobsters (see LOBSTERS). Among the fresh-water crayfish are the Murray crayfish, the marron, the redclaw, and the yabby, which got its species name, *Cherax destructor*, from its habit of undermining the banks of irrigation channels and bore-water drains by its industrious burrowing. Crayfish are found in lakes, creeks, billabongs, and farm dams, the Murray crayfish only in the Murray River system, the marron only in Western Australia, the redclaw in the Northern Territory and Cape York. There are also large crayfish found only in Tasmania. Crayfish are now farmed commercially. They are available cooked (frozen or chilled) or live. It is inadvisable to buy a dead, uncooked crayfish. Look for crayfish that have a clean, full tail and both claws intact.

To prepare and cook crayfish. Remove the intestinal tract by twisting off the middle tail fin, which will draw out the dark thread with it. Although crayfish may be grilled, baked, barbecued, or made into a BISQUE, they are usually boiled. Place live crayfish in cold water, bring to the boil, and simmer until pink-red.

cream (noun). The fatty part of milk which is used to make butter and cheese. Cream separates of its own accord, floats on top of the milk, and can be skimmed off. It is separated mechanically for commercial purposes. The butterfat content of the cream produced determines its description:

rich cream	48 per cent minimum
pure cream	35 per cent minimum
reduced cream	25 per cent minimum
light cream	18 per cent minimum
extra light cream	12 per cent minimum

There are some very rich creams that have much more than the 48 per cent minimum.

Cream is high in saturated fat and kilojoules. However, it is an excellent source of vitamin A.

The regular cream sold in Australia is 'pure cream', that is, cream which must have a minimum fat content of 35 per cent. It is best consumed as fresh as possible, but it will keep for up to ten days stored in the coldest part of the refrigerator. It is used for most purposes where cream is required—to pour over desserts, add to coffee, use in soups and sauces, and for whipping. When used in cooking, cream is added towards the end and should not be boiled or it may curdle.

Clotted cream is the traditional rich cream served with scones for Devonshire tea. Known also as scalded cream, it is made by gently warming cream until bubbles appear on the surface, then cooling it for twelve hours. The thick, clotted cream skimmed off the top is richer in butterfat and thicker than the cream it is made from.

Double cream is a term sometimes used for cream having a minimum 48 per cent butterfat content (i.e., rich cream).

Long-life cream or UHT (ultra high temperature) cream is cream that has been briefly heated to about 135°C to sterilise it, then packed in cartons lined with aluminium foil or polythene to exclude all light and air. It will keep for up to five months unrefrigerated, but after it is opened it must be kept in the refrigerator and used within a day or two. It is kept on the shelf in the supermarket rather than in the refrigerated section.

Sour cream is cream that has been treated with a special culture to produce a slightly sour flavour. Commercially produced sour cream is homogenised and pressure-treated, which results in a thickened consistency. You can make your own by adding a few drops of lemon juice or white wine vinegar to regular pure cream. Sour cream is used in soups and sauces and on jacket potatoes.

Thickened cream is pure cream to which a small amount of gelatine, rennin, or other thickening agent is added. It whips more easily than pure cream, with less risk of curdling or separating.

Tinned reduced cream is a long-life cream that has been sterilised and will therefore keep for many months without refrigeration, but, like long-life cream, must be kept in the refrigerator once it has been opened and used within a few days. The sterilising process coagulates some of the protein in the cream which thickens it a little, but it will not whip readily.

Whipping cream means different things in different places. A container marked 'whipping cream' may contain rich cream, pure cream, or thickened cream. Cream will whip more readily when it is two days or more old. Reduced cream and light cream will not whip however hard you try. When whipping cream, make sure the bowl and whisk are chilled as well as the cream. A little added sugar will help to avoid curdling and separating.

cream (verb). To work butter (or other fat) and sugar together until light and fluffy, at which stage the butter is about twice its original volume. Use a wooden spoon or an electric beater.

cream cheese is a soft, unripened cheese made from whole milk or a mixture of cream and milk (see 'Fresh cheese' under CHEESE). It can be made simply by introducing RENNET or an acid to the milk or cream so that it curdles, then hanging the curds in a cheesecloth to allow the whey to drain off. There are several well-known varieties of cream cheese, including NEUFACHÂTEL, Philadelphia cream cheese, and MASCARPONE, each with its own characteristics. In some, the curd is cooked. Cream cheese is high in saturated fat and kilojoules; it is a good source of vitamin A.

cream puff. You would expect a cream puff to be made with puff pastry, but it is in fact a confection of choux pastry with a cream filling, traditionally CRÈME PATISSIÈRE.

cream of tartar. Tartar is a reddish-brown acid compound deposited on the sides of casks during wine-making; chemically it is potassium bitartrate (approved additive no. 336). When purified and crystallised, it is called cream of tartar and is used as the acidic ingredient in BAKING POWDER.

Crécy. A designation meaning made of, or garnished with, carrots. Potage Crécy, for example, is carrot soup.

crème anglaise. A light CUSTARD made from egg yolks, sugar, and milk, sometimes thickened with cornflour and flavoured with vanilla, heated together into a creamy sauce. It is served hot or cold, on steamed puddings, stewed fruit, and compotes; it is used in trifles and as the 'sea' on which meringue icebergs are placed to make the attractive dessert Floating Islands. If crème anglaise happens to be spotty, it is the tiny black seeds of the vanilla bean infused in the milk that cause it.

crème brulée. A French name (meaning 'burnt cream') for an English dessert, said to be a specialty of Trinity College, Cambridge. It is a rich custard which, after being cooked and allowed to cool and set in a dish or individual ramekins, is sprinkled with a layer of caster sugar and placed under the grill to caramelise. The custard is made with high-fat cream and egg yolks flavoured with vanilla—Sydney chef Gay Bilson also includes cinnamon and lemon peel. Serve crème brulée chilled.

crème caramel. A baked custard with a coating of CARAMEL. It is made by pouring caramelised sugar into a bowl and swirling it about, adding the custard mixture, then baking in a BAIN-MARIE. When cooked and unmoulded, the custard emerges with its caramel coating.

crème Chantilly. See CHANTILLY.

crème fraîche. Although this French term translates as 'fresh cream', crème fraîche is in fact matured cream—that is, the lactic acids and natural culture in the cream are allowed to ferment gently so that it thickens and takes on a slightly sour, nutty flavour (see also 'Sour cream' under CREAM). The advantage of crème fraîche over sour cream in cooking is that it doesn't curdle when boiled or reduced.

Commercially made crème fraîche has a butterfat content of at least 35 per cent, often as much as 48 per cent, and is treated with an added culture. You can make your own by mixing 2 parts of rich fresh cream with 1 part of sour cream (or a little buttermilk) and leaving it covered at room temperature for 5–6 hours, then refrigerating it in a covered container.

crème frangipane. See FRANGIPANE.

crème patissière (pastry cream) is the standard filling for cream puffs, éclairs, profiteroles, cream horns, and fruit tarts. It can also be used as an alternative to cream for filling sponge cakes. It is made from a rich egg custard mixture flavoured with vanilla, thickened with flour, with an egg-white folded into it, gently cooked, and then cooled.

crème Saint Honoré. This is CRÈME PATISSIÈRE lightened with beaten egg-whites.

crêpes, pancakes. *Crêpe* is the French word for pancake. The difference between a crêpe and a pancake, according to dictionary definitions, is a matter of thickness; a crêpe is 'a thin pancake', or 'a very thin pancake'. However, the dictionaries also define pancake as a thin flat cake. Which makes a crêpe a thin, or very thin, thin cake. Perhaps the difference is social: a crêpe is something fine and fancy, a pancake ordinary and down-to-earth, otherwise the same thing. They are traditionally cooked and eaten on Shrove Tuesday, or Pancake Day. There are variations of the pancake around the world with other names—the Mexican TORTILLA, the Russian BLINI, the Jewish BLINTZ, the Chinese egg roll, the American griddle cake or flapjack.

Crêpes (or pancakes) are made from a batter of eggs, flour, milk, and salt. They may be sweet or savoury, flat or rolled, and can be used from entrée to dessert. They cook in a minute or less and can be made hours before serving. They freeze well, too. Stack them with a piece of greaseproof paper between each.

As the name implies, pancakes (or crêpes) are cooked in a pan, the ideal pan being made of cast iron with rounded or low, sloping sides so that a spatula can be slipped under the pancake to turn it over when it is cooked on one side. Suzanne Gibbs in her *Sweet Things* says a crêpe pan should be seasoned before the first use. Half-fill it with oil, gently heat it for at least 30 minutes, and leave it to stand overnight, then discard the oil and wipe the pan with a paper towel. Some say the pan should never be washed, simply wiped over with clean oil and a paper towel after each use.

Crêpes Suzette. There are as many variations of the recipe for Crêpes

Suzette as there are stories about how it got its name. Essentially, the crêpes are heated in butter, sugar, and orange juice and flamed with a liqueur such as Grand Marnier or Kirsch, usually at the table.

crépinette. What distinguishes a crépinette from a fresh sausage is its covering of pig's caul (*crépine de porc*). The caul is the fat-webbed membrane that covers a pig's intestines. It is cleansed and some of the fat is removed, and pieces of the caul are wrapped around minced meat (traditionally seasoned pork but also a mixture of pork and veal) in flattened sausage shapes. Crépinettes may be fried or grilled and served with mashed potatoes.

cress / garden cress. The tiny sprouts from the seeds of *Lepidium sativum*, a European plant mentioned by Xenophon in 400 B.C. The small, bright green leaves have a sharp, peppery flavour and are used in salads and sandwiches. Cress is often grown in combination with mustard seed and sold, growing in punnets, as mustard and cress or mustard cress. (See also WATERCRESS.)

crocodile. Crocodiles are farmed for their meat and skins in various locations around northern Australia. In one of those economic ironies, almost all of the crocodile meat produced in Australia goes to export markets, while that for local consumption is imported from Papua New Guinea. Crocodile meat, mainly taken from the tail, is pale-coloured, medium-textured, and mild in flavour, like a combination of pork and chicken, some say, but a little fishy. It needs a sauce to enhance the flavour. Although crocodile steaks can be grilled or pan-fried like beef, some cooks say crocodile is best cooked as you would veal or chicken, or even seafood.

croissant. A rich, buttery roll shaped like a crescent and customarily served in France for breakfast with butter, jam, and coffee. Croissants were originally made from bread dough rather than the yeast-leavened puff pastry used today, and they were created not by the French but by the Viennese or the Hungarians. 'Their crescent shape was supposed to celebrate the defeat of the Turks in the siege [of Vienna] of 1683,' writes Maguelonne Toussaint-Samat in her *History of Food*. 'It was said a baker going to bake a batch of bread had raised the alarm.' Other sources say it was a Hungarian baker in Buda in 1686.

croquembouche. A festive French confection consisting of dozens of cream-filled PROFITEROLES dipped in warm caramel and placed around the inside or the outside of a conical metal mould, like a dunce's cap, to set. When the caramel is cool, the croquembouche is unmoulded and decorated with spun toffee, marzipan and cream flowers, or other decorations (see opposite). *Croquembouche* means 'crunch in the mouth'.

croque-monsieur. A French sandwich filled with ham, cheese, and mustard and lightly fried on both sides. The name translates literally as 'munch-sir', meaning, perhaps, a gentleman's bite. It is not to be confused with *croque-mort*, which means 'pall-bearer' or 'undertaker' and comes from the old French custom of biting a corpse on the toes to see if the person is really dead.

croquette. A little ball, cake, or roll of minced or chopped meat, fish, or mashed

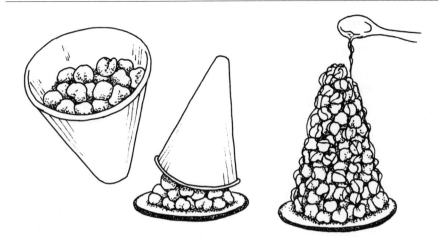

potato with herbs and seasonings, coated with egg and breadcrumbs, then deep-fried.

crostini is the Italian word for CROÛTONS or CROÛTES—that is, pieces of bread prepared in some way. They are usually cubed and fried and served with soup. However, Elizabeth David in *Italian Food* gives a variation: 'a round of bread spread with cheese, which is heated in the oven until the bread is crisp and the cheese melted'. Food writer Margaret Fulton makes tomato crostini with a topping of cooked tomatoes, basil, capsicum, and anchovies, finished off in the oven. Crostini are also sometimes spread with a paste of chicken livers.

croustade. A hollowed-out bread roll or small loaf which is deep-fried until golden and then filled with chopped meat, chicken, game, or a savoury mixture of some kind. The shell may be made of pastry or even mashed potato instead of bread.

croûtons, croûtes. Both of these are pieces of fried or toasted bread. *Croûton*, being a diminutive of *croûte*, naturally refers to the smaller of the two. Croûtons are cube-shaped, made from slices of bread with crusts removed, cut into dice. They are either fried or toasted and are served with soups or used as a garnish. The bigger croûte, which may be a whole round of French bread, is often fried and used as a foundation for meat or savoury mixtures to serve as an hors d'oeuvre. A pastry case (puff or shortcrust) BAKED BLIND and used in the same way is also known as a croûte. Croûtes may also be thin slices of bread, toasted or dried out in the oven, which are served with soup or added to soup at the time of serving.

　　En croûte means 'entirely encased in pastry'.

crown roast. See 'Loin' under LAMB.

crudités. Raw or blanched vegetables served as an hors d'oeuvre. The vegetables should be young and fresh, washed and in bite-size pieces: cherry tomatoes or larger tomatoes halved or quartered, trimmed spring onions, celery and carrots cut into strips, radishes 'trimmed of excess greenery but otherwise left as God made them, rather than disguised as water lilies' (as

Elizabeth David pleads in *French Provincial Cooking*), cauliflower florets, blanched asparagus and snow peas. The prepared raw vegetables are crisped in iced water and served with bowls of AÏOLI and VINAIGRETTE for dipping.

crumpets are made from a yeast batter with bicarbonate of soda added. The batter is cooked in metal rings on a hot griddle, producing straight-sided, round, flexible products that are smooth and brown on the bottom and otherwise pale and honeycombed with holes. 'All crumpets should be toasted on both sides,' says Dorothy Hartley in *Food in England*, 'the smooth side first, the holey side last, as this produces a suitable concavity for the butter.'

crystallised / frosted flowers. Violets, honeysuckle, sweet peas, wattle blossoms, rose petals, mint, and scented geranium leaves are some of the flowers that can be preserved by crystallising or frosting and used for edible decorations on cakes and desserts. The flowers must be not only edible but clean and free of garden sprays. They are crystallised by immersing them in SUGAR SYRUP boiled to the hard-crack stage, then drying them on a rack. Frosting is done by painting the flower parts with a stiffener such as egg-white or rose water and gum arabic, then dusting them with castor sugar. Crystallised and frosted flowers will keep for weeks in an airtight container away from humidity.

crystallised fruit. See CANDIED / CRYSTALLISED / GLACÉ FRUIT.

cube, dice. Both words mean to cut food—vegetables, meat, bread, etc.—into fairly precise cubes. When a recipe specifies cubes, the approximate size is usually given. Dice are very small cubes.

cucumbers. It is thought that the cucumber originated somewhere in Asia, but since it has been cultivated for possibly nine thousand years its original habitat is uncertain. It is now grown around the world.

There are several types of cucumber sold in Australia: the large, firm, common green cucumber; the Lebanese or Continental cucumber; the longer telegraph or hothouse cucumber, usually wrapped in plastic; the small pickling or dill cucumber; and the round, yellow apple cucumber.

Green cucumbers are available all year round, with heaviest supplies in summer; apple cucumbers are normally available only in summer. Choose firm, bright-coloured cucumbers with no soft spots. Store them in the refrigerator crisper and use them within a few days. Don't store them with apples, which will make them deteriorate quickly.

The cucumber's former bitterness has been bred out of it by modern horticulturists, so there is no need to peel off the skin unless it is tough (it is not poisonous, as some people used to think). The flesh may be fluted with the tines of a fork before slicing for a decorative effect.

Cucumbers are usually eaten raw, sliced or cubed, or combined with yoghurt and spices to make an accompaniment to Indian dishes. They may also be boiled, steamed, or stuffed and baked. The Queensland Fruit and Vegetable Growers say they are delicious sautéed with butter, salt, pepper, lemon juice, and herbs.

Cucumbers are 95 per cent water but contain a fair amount of vitamins A and C, with some fibre and minerals; they are very low in kilojoules.

cuisine minceur. Developed by the French chef Michel Guérard in the 1970s to cater for the health and weight conscious, cuisine minceur ('slimming cookery') makes use of light and simple foods, low-fat ingredients such as FROMAGE BLANC, and sugar substitutes.

Cumberland sauce. Although Cumberland sauce is regarded as a traditional English sauce, it was not mentioned by name in print until 1904, and only then in a book about English cookery by a Frenchman writing in French. Elizabeth David, in her book *Spices, Salt and Aromatics in the English Kitchen*, also quotes a recipe which is without a doubt Cumberland sauce given by Alexis Soyer fifty years before as a German sauce to go with boar's head. Whatever its origin, Cumberland sauce is made from julienned orange rind (or a mixture of orange and lemon), with redcurrant jelly, mustard, port wine, and sometimes vinegar, shallots, and ginger. It is served cold, traditionally with venison but with any cold meat.

cumin / cummin. The small annual herb *Cuminum cyminum* is indigenous to Egypt and is cultivated along the coast of North Africa and in India for its seeds—really the fruit. Cumin is an essential ingredient in CURRY powder and Mexican CHILLI POWDER, and it provides the characteristic flavour of many lamb, chicken, vegetable, and rice dishes of the Middle East and North Africa. It is also used in pickles and chutneys. Like caraway seed, which cumin seed resembles, it is said to aid digestion. Cumin is sold whole or in powdered form. Powdered cumin loses its aroma and flavour quickly. Store seeds and powder in airtight jars in a cool, dark place.

cumquat / kumquat. Formerly classified as a citrus fruit, the cumquat is now included by botanists in the *Fortunella* genus. It nevertheless resembles a miniature orange and, like citrus fruits, is an excellent source of vitamin C. It is a native of China and is often grown in Australia as an ornamental in a pot. Cumquats can be eaten raw, with the skin on, if they are quite ripe. They are often preserved in heavy syrup or in brandy. They are also used for making marmalade.

cup measurements. The standard metric cup holds a *volume* of 250 millilitres (ml), which is equivalent to just under 9 fluid ounces in imperial measurement. The *weight* of a cupful of dry ingredients, of course, varies with the ingredient. It is useful to have a graduated metric measuring cup for measuring liquids up to 1 cup, and also a set or nest of cups—¼, ⅓, ½, and 1 cup—for measuring dry ingredients. To measure fine dry ingredients such as flour or icing sugar, spoon the ingredient into the cup until it is heaped, then level off the excess with a straight-edged knife or spatula.

The standard British cup and the standard American cup both contain 8 fluid ounces. (However, as the fluid ounce in the US customary system of measurement has a slightly greater volume than the imperial fluid ounce, the American cup contains 237 ml compared with the British cup's 227 ml.) Recipes formulated in Australia before 1970 employ 8 fluid ounce cups.

curd has two meanings in culinary parlance: the coagulated part of milk and the edible whitish flower head of a cauliflower.

When milk is allowed to stand in a warm place, friendly bacteria produce lactic acid which causes the milk to coagulate or curdle. This effect can also be produced by the introduction of a coagulating agent such as RENNET. The curd, which is mainly the protein casein, is used to make cheese; the watery liquid that separates from the curd is called WHEY or serum.

curd cheese. Fresh, unripened cheese such as COTTAGE CHEESE, made from curds without rennet. (See also CHEESE.)

cure. To cure is preserve meat, fish, or fruit by salting, drying, or smoking. **Sugar-cured** is preserved with a preparation of sugar, salt, and nitrates— usually with reference to bacon or ham.

currants. Fresh currants are small, juicy, tart-tasting berries that grow on bushes of the *Ribes* genus, indigenous to much of the Northern Hemisphere. Dried currants are dried miniature grapes.

Fresh currants come in red, white, and black varieties. They are available for only a short period in midsummer. Choose firm, ripe fruit, and store them in the refrigerator. Red and white currants keep longer than black, and they are better for eating raw. Remove them from their stems by drawing the stems upward through the tines of a fork. Serve them fresh, sprinkled with sugar, or in a fruit salad. Currants are an excellent source of vitamin C and fibre. They also contain a lot of pectin, which makes them ideal for jelly-making. **Redcurrant jelly** can be eaten either as a garnish for cooked meat or, like jam, on croissants. A spoonful is added when cooking red cabbage, and it is one of the main ingredients of CUMBERLAND SAUCE.

Dried currants are produced from tiny purple, seedless grapes originally grown on the slopes around Corinth in ancient Greece. They are now grown and dried on the Murray Irrigation Area in Australia; the sweet fresh grapes (Corinth and Zante varieties) are sometimes available in fruit shops during February. Dried currants are used in cakes, biscuits, and pastries; they are also mixed with rice and pine nuts to use as stuffing for vine leaves in Middle Eastern cooking.

curry. The word *curry* probably comes from the Tamil *kari*, meaning 'sauce'. This sauce has many variations, depending on country, province, region, and personal taste of the cook. It is a mixture of spices, seeds, vegetables, fruits, coconut milk, etc., and is usually eaten with rice but may also be combined with other food. Curry has also come to mean the dish prepared with curry paste or curry powder—or, indeed, any hot, spicy dish originating in the East.

Curry powder is a blend of powdered spices and other ingredients used for making curry sauce or for seasoning food. Indians rarely if ever use curry powder; the closest they get to it is GARAM MASALA. Instead, they use different proportions of individual spices for different dishes. Curry powder was an invention for Europeans. It may include ground cardamom, coriander, cumin, turmeric, black or white pepper, cayenne pepper or chilli powder, paprika, cinnamon, mustard seed, fenugreek, garlic, ginger, cloves, nutmeg, mace, and allspice, though not all of them together in one mixture.

Curry leaf comes from a plant native to southern India. It is a common ingredient in Madras curry and gives a distinctive smell to Madras curry powder.

custard. There are two kinds of custard: custard sauce, also known as boiled custard (which is something of a misnomer, because the sauce should not be boiled or it will curdle); and baked custard, which is heated in the oven until it sets. Both are made from milk, eggs, and sugar, with some vanilla flavouring and, for the sauce, some cornflour to thicken it.

If custard sauce does curdle, you can uncurdle it in much the same way as you would uncurdle a mayonnaise. That is, take a teaspoon of milk and a tablespoon of the curdled custard and beat them together briskly with a wire whisk until creamy. Add the remaining custard gradually—no more than a tablespoon at a time—beating each addition until creamy. Sometimes you can uncurdle the sauce simply by pouring it all into a cold bowl and beating it vigorously with a wire whisk.

To prevent a baked custard from separating, heat the milk to boiling point and cool it before mixing it with the other ingredients (see also SCALDING and VANILLA). The custard should be baked gently in a BAIN-MARIE.

Custard sauce is available ready prepared in cartons from the refrigerated section of the supermarket.

Custard powder—a mixture of cornflour, artificial flavouring, and colouring agents—can be made into a kind of custard by mixing it with sweetened milk. It is also used sometimes for making cakes and biscuits.

custard apple. The fleshy, heart-shaped, lumpy-skinned fruit of a tropical American tree. Custard apples have a smooth white flesh with the texture of custard and a flavour that some describe as a cross between a banana and a pineapple and others as a blend of pineapple and strawberries. They are available in autumn and winter, with heaviest supplies from April to July. Custard apples are picked mature but not ripe, so if you want to eat them straight away, choose fruit that are dull brownish green and yield to gentle pressure; firm ones may take five or six days to ripen at room temperature. When ripe, keep them in the refrigerator, but no longer than a day or two.

Break or cut them open, and eat the flesh raw with a spoon. Discard the seeds. The flesh may also be used in fruit salads (sprinkle it with lemon juice to stop it discolouring) or to garnish curries. Puréed custard apples can be used in ice-creams, sorbets, and drinks.

cutlet comes from the French *côtelette*, which is a diminutive of *côte*, meaning 'rib'. So a côtelette, and thus a cutlet, is a little rib, or, as Andre Simon puts it in his *Concise Encyclopaedia of Gastronomy*, 'one of the smaller ribs of lamb, mutton or veal, cut off and cooked with its bone attached'. Some books seem to use *chop* and *cutlet* interchangeably, but a cutlet is a rib chop. When the ribs are left attached to one another, they are known as a rack. Cutlets are usually trimmed by the butcher so that the tail of the bone is laid bare, often ornamented with a paper frill. Lamb cutlets are usually flattened; veal cutlets are not. They are often coated with egg and breadcrumbs and fried.

cuttlefish. See SQUID, CUTTLEFISH, OCTOPUS.

D

daikon. A Japanese variety of the giant white radish, which grows to more than 40 centimetres and is almost cylindrical. It is one of the commonest Japanese vegetables, resembling a white turnip in flavour. It is eaten cooked or raw, grated, juiced, and cut into a great variety of shapes. A skilled Japanese chef with a big knife can peel a daikon lengthwise into a single thin, continuous sheet, which is then finely shredded.

dal. See DHAL / DAL.

damper. A form of unleavened bread widely used by early settlers and bushmen in Australia. The name apparently derives from the dampening effect on the appetite. Damper was originally made from plain flour mixed with water, kneaded into a round, flat cake, and baked in the ashes of a camp-fire. Salt, powdered milk, and baking powder were added when and if they were available. A camp oven later replaced the camp-fire coals. As damper did not keep well, it was usually made fresh for each meal. It was customarily cut into wedges.

   Damper is usually made today with self-raising flour, salt, milk or milk powder, butter, and water, mixed to a dough and baked in the oven. In one of Keith Floyd's television programs on Australian food, an old Aboriginal man made a fine-looking damper using beer instead of water, which no doubt acted as a leavening agent. Yeast-leavened dampers (if that is not a contradiction in terms) are sometimes available from bakers.

dandelion. The world-wide weed with its tooth-shaped leaves (*dent de lion* or 'lion's tooth' in French) and its fluffy 'twelve o'clock' seed heads has come into its own as a salad green. It can be bought in bunches in some shops. There are cultivated varieties with larger leaves than those of the common 'pee-the-bed' (it has a reputation as a diuretic). Wild dandelion can also be eaten if picked in early spring and if you're careful to avoid any that have been sprayed by council workers or dogs. Dandelion leaves are rather bitter tasting, but they add variety to the salad bowl and take a vinaigrette dressing well. They can also be cooked like spinach. The roots may be dried and used as a coffee substitute.

Danish blue cheese. A soft, crumbly cheese made from cow's milk, ripened internally (see CHEESE). When buying Danish blue, choose white cheese with even blue-green veining; avoid dull-looking dry cheese and any with brown or grey colouring. Store it in the refrigerator, well wrapped to avoid contaminating other food with its strong aroma. It will keep for two to three weeks. Take it out of the refrigerator and unwrap it an hour or so before serving. Serve it on the cheese board at meal's end. Use a separate knife to cut it.

dariole. A high-sided circular mould used for making moulded creams and MOUSSELINES, and for savoury mixtures set in aspic. The dish made in the mould is also called a dariole. Darioles for individual servings are of about 200 millilitres capacity.

dashi. A basic Japanese soup and cooking stock. Dashi is made from *katsuobushi* (flakes of dried bonito) and *kombu* (dried kelp; see SEAWEED). It is used as the stock for cooking many meat, poultry, and fish dishes, and it becomes a soup itself with the addition of various garnishes.

dates. The date palm, which originated in the fertile country between the Tigris and the Euphrates rivers in present-day Iraq, has been cultivated for its fruit for more than seven thousand years. Dates are now produced commercially in various parts of the world. Those sold in Australia are imported from such places as China, Pakistan, and the United States as well as Iraq and Iran. They are available all year round, fresh (that is, imported frozen and thawed for sale) and dried. Choose fresh dates that are plump and have a shiny smooth skin. They range in colour from pale gold to dark brown. Dried dates are shiny brown and not as plump as fresh ones. Poorer quality dried dates are stoned and pressed into blocks.

Fresh dates should be washed and drained before eating. They may be eaten out of the hand or stuffed with cream cheese or blue-vein cheese. Dried dates should also be washed if they are to be eaten as they are. They may be stuffed with nuts or marzipan as well as chopped for use in breads, puddings, and cakes. Store fresh dates in the refrigerator, covered. Dried dates can be kept for up to six months in a jar stored in a cool, dry place.

daube. 'To cook *en daube*,' says Elizabeth David in *French Provincial Cooking*, 'is much the same as to braise.' A daube is essentially a country housewife's dish, she says, so it is apt to be rougher than a braise. 'What goes in apart from the meat is largely a matter of what is available.' The meat is usually beef, cut into cubes, but instead of being browned as in a braise (see BRAISE, CASSEROLE, STEW) it is usually soaked for a few hours in a marinade of red wine, garlic, and herbs. It is also cooked in this marinade, together with whatever else is available, in a heavy pot with a tight-fitting lid such as the tall, earthenware *daubière*, for 4–5 hours in the oven.

deep-frying. To deep-fry is to cook food, usually coated with flour, batter, or egg and breadcrumbs, in sufficient fat or (preferably) oil to cover the food. A deep pan is used, sometimes with a removable wire basket for easy removal and draining of the cooked food.

Use clean oil that can be heated to a high temperature without burning (peanut oil or maize oil, for example). It should be very hot, 170–180°C, before adding the food, so that the food is sealed quickly and absorbs little fat. It should not be too hot, however, or the food will burn on the outside and be uncooked on the inside. To test the temperature of the oil without a thermometer, drop a small cube of bread in; the oil should begin to bubble and the bread should become crisp and golden in about a minute.

Make sure the food is dry before dipping it in batter, or excessive steam may form during cooking, separating the coating from the food. The coating also protects the food from the intense heat and prevents nutrients from leaching out.

Large pieces of food should not be deep-fried, as they take longer to cook and absorb too much oil. Fry small amounts at a time; adding too much at once reduces the temperature of the oil. Drain the food well before serving.

deep-sea trevalla. Another name for BLUE EYE.

defat. Remove the fat from a liquid (see DEGREASING).

deglazing. To deglaze is to dilute the juices in which food has been browned or cooked and detach the particles that have adhered to the bottom and sides of the pan. This is done by adding liquid—wine, stock, water, cream, or whatever is called for—scraping the bottom and sides of the pan to incorporate the juices and particles into the liquid, and simmering it until you have a sauce to go with the dish you have cooked. The French term is *déglacer*, and the technique is important in making sauces to accompany meat, poultry, fish, etc.

degorge / disgorge. A term that comes from the French *faire dégorger*, meaning to soak meat or other food in water to remove impurities or strong flavours or to soak out blood (as with BRAINS and SWEETBREADS). However, the term seems to be used mostly in reference to removing excess moisture and bitter juices from eggplant by sprinkling it with salt and leaving it for 20 minutes or more to 'disgorge' the juices (see EGGPLANT). The same treatment can be given to cucumber to make it more digestible and to pumpkin to enhance the flavour.

degreasing. To degrease (French *dégraisser*) is to remove the fat from a liquid such as stock or sauce. One way is to put the liquid into the refrigerator until the fat sets on the top and then lift it off with an egg slice or palette knife. Any small particles that remain can be wiped off with a cloth wrung out in hot water. To remove the fat from a liquid while it is still hot, skim off what you can with a spoon or suck it up with a bulb baster (see BASTE), then sop up the remainder with paper towels.

devil. Prepare food with hot spices or sharp seasonings: for example, devilled eggs, which are sliced hard-boiled eggs covered with a sauce made from butter, cream, Worcestershire sauce, cayenne pepper, chutney, and mustard to taste.

devils on horseback. Stoned prunes wrapped in bacon, skewered or fastened with thread, grilled, and served as an hors d'oeuvre.

devon. A bland, finely textured, large cooked sausage made from pork and / or beef trimmings. It used to be called fritz or pork fritz until wartime patriotism replaced a German nickname with an English county name. Devon contains a large amount of fat and salt.

dhal / dal. An Indian name for all members of the legume or pulse family. They include *arhar dhal* (pigeon peas), *chana dhal* (CHICKPEAS), *masur dhal* (LENTILS), *mung dhal* (mung beans), *lombia dhal* (BLACK-EYED BEANS), and *rajma dhal* (RED KIDNEY BEANS). In India they are available fresh as well as dried. The name dhal is also used for a dish cooked with any of the dried pulses, especially lentils.

dhania. An Indian name for CORIANDER.

dhufish. A variation of jewfish (see MULLOWAY and WESTRALIAN JEWFISH).

dice. See CUBE / DICE.

dietary fibre. Cereals, wholemeal bread and other grain products, vegetables, fruit, and nuts contain a certain amount of cellulose and related material which is digested to only a small extent. This undigested fibre adds bulk in the digestive tract, which stimulates the bowel to function properly and helps to prevent constipation. Certain types of fibre (in oatmeal, barley, pulses and fruits) are digestible, and these are believed to reduce the level of cholesterol in the blood and help control blood sugar levels.

dill. A tall annual herb which is grown for its seeds as well as its delicate, fern-like leaves. The seeds have an aniseed flavour, while the leaves are reminiscent of caraway. Although the plant originated in the Mediterranean region, it is used widely in the cookery of northern Europe, especially Scandinavia (see, for example, GRAVLAX). The chopped leaves go well with fish, potatoes, and eggs, in sauces, butters, and cheese dips, and in salads and soups. The seeds transform cucumbers into dill pickles.

   Dill has a reputation for relieving indigestion and flatulence. Dill water is a traditional remedy for colic in babies.

Fresh dill should be kept in water or wrapped in foil in the refrigerator to prevent it from wilting.

dim sim, dim sum. Although these terms come from the same Cantonese source, loosely meaning 'snack', dim sim came to refer to a small parcel of seasoned minced meat and vegetables wrapped in a thin sheet of noodle dough and steamed or deep-fried, whereas dim sum is a meal or course of savoury and sweet titbits, of which the dim sim is only one. Back in the days when Cantonese dishes adapted to Australian taste were just about all that was on offer from Chinese restaurants in Australia, dim sims were the regular choice for a starter or snack. Ella-Mei Wong, in her popular book of the 1960s, *Chinese Cookery*, gives a recipe for dim sims which contains minced pork, prawns, dried mushrooms, and water chestnuts, but the mixture may vary. She also says that the dim sum hour is generally between the first meal of the day and midday. (See also YUM CHA.)

dolmades / dolmas. Stuffed vine leaves. Little rolls of savoury rice and minced lamb or pine nuts are wrapped in blanched vine leaves and cooked in a small amount of stock or tomato juice with oil and lemon juice. Eaten cold, dolmades are a popular first course in Greece, Turkey, and all countries of the Middle East. They may be served with lemon juice squeezed over them or with yoghurt. Dolmades are also eaten hot, usually when made with a meat and rice stuffing.

Blanched cabbage leaves may be used in place of vine leaves to make cabbage rolls, stuffed and cooked in the same way.

doneness. A barbarous word but a convenient one for cookery writers to use when they want to tell you to test whether food has been cooked adequately. There are various 'tests for doneness', depending on the type of food being cooked; they are given under CAKES; CHICKEN; ROASTING; and STEAK.

döner kebab. A kind of Middle Eastern hamburger, with meat, salad, and sauce wrapped in a round of flat, unleavened bread. It is also known as a Lebanese roll. The term *döner kebab* is actually Turkish for thick slices of marinated lamb, alternating with pieces of fat to keep it moist, threaded and packed tightly onto an upright spit which revolves in front of a charcoal fire. As the meat cooks on the outside, thin slices are cut off with a long, sharp knife. In Australian fast-food outlets the meat may be chicken or beef as well as lamb, and the lamb may be minced and combined with emulsifier before being formed into a reconstituted mass on the spit. The heat is usually gas or electric rather than charcoal. Salads of lettuce, sliced tomato and onion, and TABBOULEH, with HUMMUS and TAHINI sauce are added to the meat in the warmed round of flat bread. (See also KEBAB / KEBOB / KABOB.)

dory. Four species of three different genera of fish are known as dory—john dory, mirror dory, king dory and silver dory. They are similar deep-bodied, silvery smooth fish and can be substituted for one another, although the john dory is the most highly regarded and expensive. Dories are caught around southern Australia and are available all year round but mainly in the winter. They are sold whole and in fillets. John dory is sold with the skin on, probably to display the distinguishing dark spot on its side—the imprint of

Saint Peter's thumb when he took a coin out of the fish's mouth (unfortunately for legend, there are no john dories in the Sea of Galilee).

The moist, medium-textured white flesh has a mild, delicate flavour (distinctly sweet in the case of john dory, which is regarded by many as the finest-tasting Australian fish) that should not be overpowered with highly flavoured accompaniments. Dories can be cooked in all ways (see FISH).

dough. A soft, thick mixture of flour or meal, liquid such as water or milk, and other ingredients (yeast in the case of bread dough) which is baked as bread, pastry, cakes, and the like. The word *dough* comes from the old English *dag* 'to knead' which suggests that it should be used only in reference to bread dough, as the Americans do; they refer to cake mixtures as batter.

doughnut. A doughnut doesn't have to be ring-shaped, but the American doughnut with a hole (which came into being, they say, either when an Indian shot an arrow through some bread dough and it fell into some hot bear fat, or a dissatisfied son cut the soggy centres out of his mother's dough and fried the rings—believe what you will) seems to have become the accepted version. Whatever the shape—ring, twist, or ball—doughnuts are made from yeast dough or a dough made with baking powder, deep-fried, and covered with icing sugar or spiced sugar after they are cooked and drained. Ball-shaped doughnuts sometimes have jam injected into the centre.

drawn butter. Melted butter, used mainly as a fish sauce (see under BUTTER).

dredge. To dredge is to coat food lightly but completely with a powdered ingredient such as flour or icing sugar. An effective way of dredging pieces of meat, chicken, or fish with flour is to place them in a paper bag with the seasoned flour, hold the bag closed at the top, and give it a good shaking. The food will be covered with flour, but your kitchen won't be. Icing sugar can be dredged over the top of a cake by holding a fine-mesh sieve containing icing sugar over the cake and gently tapping the side of the sieve.

dress. To dress poultry or game is to get it ready for cooking by plucking, cleaning, or trussing it. To dress a salad is to add VINAIGRETTE or some other salad dressing. Vegetables may be dressed with melted butter or sauce.

dried fruit. Fruit has been preserved by drying for thousands of years. Dried fruit was found in the tombs of Egyptian kings. The Romans included dried fruits in their banquets. Dates, figs, prunes, and grapes (currants, raisins, sultanas) are the traditional dried fruits, but apples, apricots, peaches, pears, and even bananas are also available in dried form. Drying concentrates the sugar and nutrient content, including dietary fibre, of the fresh fruit but also reduces vitamin C content. Store dried fruit in an airtight container in a cool, dry place; it will keep for six months to a year, depending on the variety.

dripping. The fat that drips from roasting meat, or is produced commercially by the rendering of meat, muscles, and bones of cattle or sheep. In the days before people became concerned about saturated fats, dripping was used extensively for frying and as a pastry shortening. It was even spread on bread or toast and eaten with relish by some and out of necessity by others who couldn't afford much else. The drippings exuded by meat while it is roasting, now usually referred to as pan juices, are still used effectively for basting the meat during the cooking process and for making gravy or sauce afterwards.

dry roast. To roast meat or poultry on a rack placed inside a roasting pan in the oven, with no added fat or liquid (see BAKE, ROAST and ROASTING).

duck is more likely to be ordered in a restaurant than cooked at home. It is very fatty, and the smaller proportion of flesh to bone compared with chicken means that you have less to go round when you carve it up. When buying a fresh duck, you should allow 500 grams per person. The experts tell you to test the webbing of the feet, which should be soft, and the underbeak, which should be pliable enough to bend back easily, before you buy. Ducks are available frozen as well as fresh; they should be thawed slowly and thoroughly before cooking.

To prepare a duck. As well as the thick layer of fat under the skin (to insulate the duck from the cold water it swims in), a duck has two oil glands near the base of the tail. You can press the glands to empty them, or cut off the tail and glands. Wash the duck under cold running water; pat it dry with paper towels. Remove any visible fat, inside and outside, and prick the skin all over to allow the subcutaneous fat to drain out while the duck is cooking.

Ducks are often cooked or served with orange or cherries, or with turnip or onions, to offset the richness of the meat. Young green peas are a traditional accompaniment.

dumplings. 'Dumpling' means different things in different places and contexts. Characteristic English dumplings, according to Andre Simon, are made from chopped beef fat, flour, and breadcrumbs moistened with egg and milk, formed into balls the size of a turkey's egg, tied in a cloth, and boiled for three-quarters of an hour. German dumplings come in all shapes, sizes, and contents, some flat or sausage-shaped, some the size of golf balls and others the size of cannon balls, made with breadcrumbs, with potatoes, with or without flour, with semolina, with meat, with or without yeast. Some are little 'sparrows' of batter dropped into the simmering water, which rise to the top when they are cooked. Chinese dumplings are like ravioli: finely minced delicate ingredients wrapped in squares of fine noodle dough, which are often served in a clear broth.

A dumpling may also be an apple or other fruit wrapped in dough and baked.

Dundee cake. The story goes that Dundee, the Scottish city renowned for its marmalade, had more left-over orange peel than it knew what to do with. So the marmalade manufacturer came up with an idea to make use of the peel—the Dundee cake. This rich, dark fruit cake is made with brown sugar, sultanas, and candied orange peel. What gives the Dundee cake its distinctive appearance is the concentric circles of blanched almonds decorating the top.

durian. The fruit of a tropical tree native to Malaya, the durian is much prized by the people of Malaysia and Indonesia. The spiny, green-yellow fruit is very large—it can weigh up to 10 kilograms. It also has a revolting odour, especially when overripe, which has caused the fruit to be banned from hotel rooms and aeroplanes. People who can withstand the smell say that its buttery-textured flesh tastes heavenly, like strawberries and cream flavoured with almonds. Author Anthony Burgess described the experience of eating a durian as being 'like eating sweet, pink raspberry blancmange in the lavatory'. Chilling the fruit is said to reduce its smell. The flesh is eaten with ice-cream, used in cakes, cooked with Indonesian rice and meat dishes. The seeds may be roasted and eaten. Canned durian is available.

duxelles. Finely diced mushrooms sautéed in butter with chopped onions, shallots, or spring onions. This concentrate of mushroom flavour is used as a foundation for various sauces and stuffings.

E

Eccles cakes. Flat, round cakes made of pastry filled with a mixture of currants, chopped mixed peel, spices, etc. Nowadays the pastry used is commercially produced puff or flaky pastry instead of home-made shortcrust. A teaspoon of the filling is placed on a circle of the rolled pastry, the edges of the pastry are gathered up and pressed together, and the cake is turned over and gently flattened into a circle. Small slits are made in the top to let the steam out while the cakes are baking.

éclairs. Small, finger-shaped cakes made of choux pastry filled with CRÈME PATISSIÈRE or FRANGIPANE and iced with chocolate or coffee icing. *Éclair* means 'lightning' in French, and it is said that the cakes derive their name from the lightning speed with which they are consumed.

Edam cheese. One of Holland's oldest and most famous cheeses, Edam is an uncooked, firm cheese made from partially skimmed milk and produced in a distinctive cannonball shape covered with red wax for export. It is mild and smooth-textured, with perhaps a few tiny holes, and has a minimum fat content of 21 per cent. Edam is a good all-round cheese with exceptional keeping quality. Locally made Edam-style cheese is also available. (See also CHEESE.)

eels. Fresh eels are not often to be found in fish shops. Most of the eels sold in Australia are smoked. Fresh ones are mainly exported, as is a large amount of the smoked eel production. Eels are caught commercially in rivers in Tasmania, eastern Queensland, northern New South Wales, and parts of Victoria. Before being sold, they should have been purged for three to five days. Eel skin is very tough and is usually removed from fresh eels before cooking. They are usually cut into lengths and poached, deep-fried, or made into a soup or casserole. Smoked eel can be eaten on bread and butter or as you would eat smoked trout or smoked salmon.

een choi. See CHINESE SPINACH.

egg noodles. See NOODLES.

egg wash. A mixture of egg yolks and cream, milk or water (1 or 2 tablespoons per yolk), which is brushed over pastry before baking to glaze it and give it a golden colour. It is also used to stick pastry seams together. Egg wash is sometimes used on freshly baked bread.

eggah. The Middle Eastern version of the OMELETTE. Unlike a French omelette, an eggah is thick, firm, and cake-like. The egg is more of a binding to hold together a filling of lamb or other meat, chicken, vegetables such as zucchini, eggplant, beans, and potatoes, nuts, etc. Eggahs are cooked either on top of the stove or in the oven. They may be served hot or cold and are often cut into slices or square pieces. They can be eaten as a starter, side dish, with salad, or as a main dish.

eggplant. The fruit of a perennial plant belonging to the potato family and probably native to southern or central Asia. Eggplants, also known as aubergines, come in a variety of shapes and sizes, with colours ranging from white through green and red to almost black, but the common varieties are egg-shaped or long and thin and deep purple. The spongy white flesh has many small brown seeds dispersed through it.

Eggplants are available all year round. Choose those that are heavy for their size, with smooth, glossy, firm unblemished skin and a fresh green stem. They can be stored in the refrigerator for up to a week.

To prepare and cook eggplant. Wash the eggplant and cut off the stem. You don't have to peel eggplants unless they are to be puréed. To extract an eggplant's bitter juices, slice it or cut it up, sprinkle it liberally with salt, and let it stand in a colander with a plate pressed on top for 20–60 minutes to allow the juices to drain away; then rinse off the salt under cold running water and pat the eggplant dry with paper towels (baby eggplants and the long, thin ones may not need this treatment). Preparing eggplants in this way also prevents them from soaking up oil when they are fried. As well as being fried, eggplants may be grilled or stuffed and baked. They are also used in Asian curries and are an essential ingredient in MOUSSAKA and RATATOUILLE.

Avoid using carbon steel knives or metallic dishes when preparing eggplant, as they may cause the flesh to discolour. Cut eggplant turns brown fairly soon after exposure to air; this can be avoided by immersing the cut eggplant in ACIDULATED WATER.

eggs must be the most nutritious, versatile, compact, convenient, inexpensive and useful food item in the kitchen. Boiled, fried, poached, and scrambled on their own, the main ingredient of omelettes, soufflés, and mayonnaise, an essential ingredient in most cakes and biscuits, used as a thickening agent, an aerating agent, a binder, a glaze—these are just a few ways in which eggs are used in cookery. Yet the consumption of eggs has declined in recent years. Perhaps this is partly because they contain significant amounts of cholesterol, and people mistakenly believe there is a direct connection between dietary cholesterol and blood cholesterol. However, research has found that certain fatty acids are the substances to be concerned about, not dietary cholesterol. Some egg producers market eggs containing additional omega-3 fatty acids, believed to reduce cholesterol and triglycerides and thus help to prevent heart disease, the eggs being laid by hens fed a special vegetarian diet. However, all eggs are now regarded as fine in moderation and an important part of a balanced diet.

Another mistaken belief is that brown eggs are more nutritious than white eggs. The colour of the shell has no bearing on the food value or flavour of the egg. The breed of the hen that laid it determines an egg's colour.

Eggs are sold in five grades according to the minimum weight of each egg in the carton: 45 grams, 50 grams, 55 grams, 60 grams, and 65 grams. The fresher the egg, the better it is. As an egg gets older, the white, which is thick and gelatinous in a new-laid egg, becomes thin and runny, and the yolk becomes less firm and more likely to break. Because the shell of an egg is porous, moisture seeps out as time goes by and is replaced by air, which gathers in a chamber between the shell and the membrane at the rounded end of the egg. The freshness of an egg can therefore be tested by covering it with water. A fresh egg, with little air in the cell at the rounded end, will remain lying on its side; one that has acquired some air with age will become buoyant at the rounded end and, if three weeks old, will float.

Eggs should not be washed unless they are to be used immediately. They have a natural protective film; if it is washed off, the egg will go bad quickly.

Eggs should be kept in the refrigerator, still in their carton (to protect them from damage and to slow down moisture loss) with the rounded end upwards to allow the air cell to breathe. Before using an egg it should be taken out of the refrigerator and brought to room temperature. A cold egg will crack in boiling water, cold whites will not whisk well, and a cold yolk will not emulsify satisfactorily.

To boil eggs. To ensure eggs don't crack in boiling water, prick a hole in the rounded end to allow the air to escape—there is a special gadget for this. Put room-temperature eggs in a saucepan and cover them with cold water. Bring it to the boil over high heat. As soon as the water boils, take the saucepan off the heat, cover it, and let it stand for 1–3 minutes depending on how firm you like your eggs.

For hard-boiled eggs, bring them to the boil and *simmer* them for 6 minutes, then plunge them into cold water to stop the cooking process. Don't cook them for too long or on too high a heat. If they are overcooked, the whites become rubbery and unsightly dark rings form around the yolks, and the longer they are cooked the harder they are to digest.

To separate an egg. Crack the egg sharply mid-centre on the edge of a bowl. With the egg held above the bowl, pull the halves apart, holding them upright. The yolk will stay in one half, and some of the white will drop into the bowl. Tip the yolk back and forth between the two half-shells until all the white has separated itself from the yolk and fallen into the bowl. Italian chef Lorenza de Medici, in one of the programs in her television series *The Medici Kitchen*, worked the yolk back and forth between her bare hands, allowing the white to slip through her fingers. There are gadgets shaped like spoons with holes or slots halfway up the bowl for those who are unable to master either of the above techniques; the yolk stays in the bottom of the gadget while the white runs out through the slots into a cup or basin below. If you happen to break the yolk and a little of it gets into the white, lift it out with the edge of the shell. Egg-white will not whisk up if there is the slightest bit of yolk in it.

To beat egg-whites. The bowl and the beater or whisk must be perfectly clean and dry, with no trace of oil or grease, and there must be not a particle of yolk in the whites or they won't whip up. A round-bottomed copper bowl is best to use, but enamel or glass is satisfactory; plastic is least acceptable. Julia Child in *The Way to Cook* recommends preparing the bowl by pouring a tablespoon of vinegar and a teaspoon of salt into it and then wiping it clean with paper towels. The traces of vinegar and salt help to stabilise the egg-whites. Others suggest rubbing a cut lemon round the bowl or adding a pinch of salt while beating. A little cream of tartar (¼ teaspoon to 4 whites) is usually added as a stabiliser. Because egg-whites do not whisk well when they are cold, have them at room temperature, or heat the bowl and beater. Use a hand-held electric heater or a balloon-shaped wire whisk. The whites are beaten to the point where they stand up in peaks, look wet and shiny, and cling to the beater. Do not overbeat so that they lose their sheen and become grainy. Egg-whites will triple in volume if beaten properly. Use them immediately, as the aerated mixture quickly disintegrates. (See also FOLDING IN.)

To beat egg yolks. Before beating egg yolks, rinse the bowl with cold water; the beaten yolks will slide out of the bowl easily. When adding sugar, do so a tablespoon at a time. Beat until the yolks and sugar are thick and pale yellow and when the mixture falls from the beater it forms a ribbon that slowly dissolves on the surface.

Eggs Benedict. When the American banker and yachtsman Commodore E.C. Benedict called for poached eggs on slices of ham on toast covered with HOLLANDAISE SAUCE, he was acting in the tradition of Lord Sandwich and ensuring his name would be remembered, at least in a simple item of food.

Emmental / Emmenthal / Emmenthaler. The quintessential Swiss cheese. Emmental is a firm, ivory-yellow cheese with a sweet, nutty flavour and large shiny holes which are produced by bubbles during fermentation. (It is sometimes confused with GRUYÈRE, which has smaller and fewer holes.) Emmental is made in large wheels with a smooth, dry, yellow rind. The cheese is good for cooking—in sauces, soufflés, quiches, and pies—as well as for sandwiches, cheese platters and salads. It may also be grated. Locally produced Emmental-style cheese is also available.

empanadas. Spanish pies. They may be huge flat pies, cut and sold in wedges, or home-made turnovers the size of a Cornish pasty. Fillings may be savoury or sweet or a mixture of both. The South American version is made with beef, chopped black olives, hard-boiled eggs, and raisins.

emperor. See RED EMPEROR and SWEETLIP EMPEROR.

emu. Both the Australian national animal symbols now appear on the dinner table as well as on the Commonwealth coat of arms. While kangaroo has been legally eaten since the 1980s, emu meat was made available for consumption more recently. Farm bred, mainly in Western Australia, emus are raised on grain and pasture and processed in licensed abattoirs. The meat is lean and tender with a delicate flavour, more like beef than poultry, and less than 3 per cent fat. It can be grilled, pan-fried, roasted, or casseroled. Because of the small amount of fat in it, emu meat should not be overcooked or it will become dry and tough. The producers suggest that the meat should be sealed at high temperature to prevent loss of juices and served when the meat is slightly rare (when the juices rise).

en croûte means 'in a crust', and it designates food, usually meat and pâté, which is cooked entirely encased in pastry; for example, BEEF WELLINGTON.

en papillote means 'in curl paper'—but, presumably, only metaphorically. Food cooked, and often served 'en papillote' is wrapped in paper or enclosed in a paper bag, preferably of baking paper. Avoid paper that may have been treated with chemicals which could be released with the heat of cooking. Aluminium foil is an effective substitute for baking paper. Cooking *en papillote* retains all the juices, flavours, and aroma of the food.

enchilada. A TORTILLA rolled around a filling of chopped meat, chicken, cheese, etc., covered with a tomato sauce spiced with chilli, and baked. A Mexican specialty.

endive. The various endives are species of CHICORY. Curly endive, with its finely divided frizzy leaves (it's known as *chicorée frisée* in French), and the broad-leaved Batavian endive (also known as escarole) are grown mainly for eating as salad greens, although they may also be cooked like spinach. They are rather tough and bitter as salad, requiring a highly flavoured dressing, but less so if they have been blanched. They are usually sold with the inner, blanched leaves folded back over the outside ones. Curly and broad-leaved endives are rich in vitamin A.
    Belgian endive is another name for WITLOOF.

entrecôte. Rib steak. A cut of beef which should be taken from 'between the ribs' which is what *entrecôte* means in French.

entrée is another one of those terms that mean different things to different people. For those who go in for old-fashioned multi-course dinners, the entrée is the course that comes between the fish and the roast (soup, fish, entrée, joint, etc). For the more restrained, it is as *The Macquarie Dictionary* defines it, 'a dish served at dinner before the main course'—provided, of course, you're not in America where the entrée *is* the main course.

escabeche. A Spanish and Portuguese method of pickling fish. The fish is first fried in olive oil, then allowed to stand for 24 hours or more in a marinade of cooked onions, carrots, garlic, bay leaves, herbs and spices, and vinegar. It is served cold, usually from the dish in which it was marinated. Poultry and game prepared in this way are also known as escabeche.

escalope. An escalope is a thin slice of meat without any bone. It is usually veal cut across the grain from the fillet end of the leg, but it may also be a thin slice of pork or beef. Veal escalopes, or SCALOPPINE in Italian, are prepared in many ways (see, for example, SALTIMBOCCA), but are commonly flattened, coated with egg and breadcrumbs, and fried in hot oil (when they are also known as Wiener schnitzels). The butcher will usually flatten escalopes for you, but you can do it yourself by placing the meat between two pieces of plastic film and pounding with a rolling pin.

escarole. Another name for broad-leaved or Batavian ENDIVE.

eschalot. See SHALLOTS.

espagnole, sauce. Another name for BROWN SAUCE.

essences are extracts of plants or other foodstuffs obtained by distillation or other means and bottled usually in an alcoholic solution. They are used in small amounts as flavourings. In culinary French, *essence* means the pan juices of whatever has been cooked, after they have been reduced to concentrate their flavours.

ethylene is a gas given off naturally by certain fruits. Some vegetables are sensitive to this gas and may deteriorate quickly or be adversely affected in some way if stored together with fruits that produce it. Carrots, for example, may become bitter if stored with apples. The *ethylene-producing* fruits are apples, apricots, avocados, bananas, figs, mangoes, rockmelons, nectarines, pawpaws, passionfruit, peaches, and pears. The *ethylene-sensitive* vegetables are artichokes, asparagus, beans, broccoli, Brussels sprouts, cabbage, cauliflower, celery, cucumber, endive, lettuce, leaf greens, okra, parsley, potatoes, rhubarb, silver beet, squash, sweet corn, sweet potatoes, and zucchini.

F

fabada. Fabada Asturiana is a famous Spanish stew of dried white beans, smoked blood sausage, salted pork fat, and CHORIZO, with chilli, garlic, and seasoning.

farce. Theatrical farce and culinary farce have a common derivation: the French word for STUFFING. The comic theatrical stuffing came about when buffoonery was inserted into early religious dramas. Culinary stuffing—known as forcemeat rather than farce these days—is a mixture of minced or chopped seasoned ingredients used to stuff poultry, game, meat, fish, eggs, etc., and as a garnish.

farina. Flour or fine meal usually made from cereal grains but also from nuts and starchy roots. It is cooked as breakfast cereal and used in puddings and other cooking.

fat. A great deal of the food we eat contains fat of some kind in some degree. There are 'visible' fats—butter, cream, oils, the fat on meat—and 'invisible' fats such as in milk, cheese, egg yolks, nuts and seeds, and those in processed and takeaway foods. Animal foods generally contain more fat than plant foods, although the avocado contains more than 20 per cent and some nuts more than 60 per cent in the form of oil.

Chemically, fat is a combination of glycerol (glycerine) and fatty acids, composed of carbon, hydrogen, and oxygen atoms. Depending on the way the atoms of carbon and hydrogen are attached to each other, the fat is referred to as saturated, mono-unsaturated, or polyunsaturated. Saturated fats are the bad ones. They raise blood CHOLESTEROL and should be avoided where possible, the National Heart Foundation warns us. Mono-unsaturated and polyunsaturated fatty acids are believed to reduce the level of cholesterol and triglycerides (a form of fat where three fatty acids are attached to a molecule of glycerol) in the blood. There are essential fatty acids (polyunsaturated) which the body can't do without, but there are also trans fatty acids, which recent research has found to be as harmful as saturated fats. So the recommendation is to limit the intake of fats, especially saturated fats, which are thought to contribute to heart disease, obesity, and certain types of cancer, and replace them where possible with polyunsaturated and mono-unsaturated fats (see under OIL).

That having been said, it should be remembered that fats are the richest source of energy in food, providing some 3700 kilojoules per 100 grams. They also add flavour to food. Some cooks say that fat should be taken off meat and poultry only after it has been cooked, as the fat does not penetrate the flesh but forms an insulating layer that enhances tenderness and keeps the food moist and flavoursome. (For removal of fat, see DEGREASING. See also DRIPPING; LARD; MARGARINE; SHORTENING; and SUET.)

feijoa. *Feijoa sellowiana* is more likely to be mentioned in a gardening book than a cookery book. This bushy, evergreen shrub from South America, with its fuchsia-like red and white flowers followed by egg-shaped green fruit, has been grown as an ornamental shrub in Australia for many years. Its popularity with the fruit fly, however, makes it a bit of a nuisance in the suburban garden.

The fruit itself has a smooth, dull green skin and a yellow-green, granular flesh. Depending on your taste buds, it has a flavour of pineapple, strawberries, or guava (it is known as the Brazilian guava and the pineapple guava). It is available only during its brief season in February–March. Choose fruit that yields to gentle pressure for immediate eating, or ripen fruit at room temperature away from direct sunlight, then refrigerate. The flesh can be eaten with a spoon from the halved fruit, or the fruit can be peeled and sliced or cubed and added to fruit salads. It may also be puréed and made into jam.

Feijoas are an excellent source of vitamin C and low in kilojoules.

felafel / falafel. What is certain about this Middle Eastern dish is that the ingredients are formed into little balls and fried. The ingredients themselves are a matter of opinion. Claudia Roden in her *Middle Eastern Food* gives the Egyptian version of felafel, or *ta'amia*, which she says is one of Egypt's national dishes. It contains dried broad beans (*ful nabed*), onions, garlic, parsley, cumin, and coriander, mashed to a paste, formed into walnut-size lumps, and deep-fried. However, the Israelis have practically adopted felafel as their own national dish, only they have substituted chickpeas for the broad beans. Recipes for felafel from various sources include crushed wheat (burghul), capsicums, cayenne, chilli sauce, eggs, tahini, celery—it seems whatever is at hand can go in. But then, variations on the rissole abound.

fennel. The fennel plant is indigenous to southern Europe and Asia Minor, but from the way it grows wild along railway lines and roadside banks and ditches in Australia you could be excused for thinking it was an Australian native—or a perennial weed. The cultivated variety, Florence fennel, known in Italy as *finocchio*, is grown as an annual, and almost all of the plant is eaten in some way. Its fine, feathery leaves, resembling dill and, like dill, tasting of aniseed, are used as a herb to flavour and garnish many dishes, especially fish, and in dressings and sauces. The stalks may be dried and used as an underlayer to cook on. The bulbous base is eaten raw like celery or cooked in various ways: boiled or steamed and served with a white sauce, braised, sautéed, stir-fried, or added to soups. The yellowish-brown aromatic seeds are used to flavour pickles, soups, beans, and cakes.

Florence fennel is available from June to November. It should be crisp, clean, and fresh looking. Keep it in the vegetable crisper of the refrigerator.

fenugreek. The light brown, furrowed seed of an annual herb belonging to the pea family native to south-eastern Europe and western Asia. Ground fenugreek, which has an aroma of burnt sugar, is an essential ingredient of most curry powders and may be added to chutneys, stews, and soups.

fetta / feta. A soft, white cheese ripened in brine, originally made from ewe's milk or goat's milk by Greek shepherds on the mountains near Athens. Fetta is now made in countries around the world, including Australia, usually from cow's milk, though Bulgaria still makes it from ewe's milk. The cheese is sharp and salty, with a crumbly texture that makes it suitable for crumbling into Greek salads with black Kalamata olives. It is also eaten as an appetiser and cooked in cheese and spinach pies.

fettuccine is the Roman name for home-made noodles. Like TAGLIATELLE, only a little narrower and thicker, fettuccine are long, flat ribbons of egg PASTA about 5 millimetres wide. According to Marcella Hazan in *The Classic Italian Cookbook*, they are 'ideally suited to carry sauces in which heavy cream is an essential ingredient'. She says the famous Roman restaurateur Alfredo prepared fettuccine with a sauce of heavy cream and butter, giving each serving a final toss with a gold spoon and fork before dispatching it to the dining room. Other recipe books suggest using butter alone as the sauce. Whatever is used, the cooked pasta is tossed in it with a generous addition of grated Parmesan cheese, a tiny grating of nutmeg, and a few grinds of pepper.

fibre. See DIETARY FIBRE.

figs. It's no wonder fig leaves are associated with Adam and Eve; *Ficus carica* is one of the oldest known plants, probably originating in Syria or there-abouts in western Asia. Figs play an important part in ancient mythology and early recorded history.

The bulbous or pear-shaped fruit is actually a collection of many tiny, single-seeded fruits inside a fleshy receptacle which is a specially adapted stem. It takes a wasp to pollinate some kinds of fig. Fresh figs vary in colour and shape according to the variety. In Australia the main varieties grown are Brown Turkey, White Adriatic, and Black Genoa. They are available from December to April, with best supplies in January–February. St John's figs, originally from Malta but grown in Darwin, have a purple-black skin and an intensely sweet flavour. They are available in winter and spring when other figs are out of season.

When you buy figs, choose plump, sweet-smelling fruit that yield to gentle pressure. Avoid any with skin breaks or mould. Eat them as soon as possible after purchase, as they are highly perishable; meanwhile, keep them in the refrigerator (but serve them at room temperature, because chilling dulls their delicate flavour). They can be eaten out of the hand, stuffed with a cream cheese mixture, served with prosciutto in place of the usual melon, poached in SUGAR SYRUP and served with cream, and made into jam.

Dried figs are higher in carbohydrates and kilojoules than fresh figs. They can be eaten out of the hand, stewed, and cooked in cakes and puddings. Locally produced glacé figs are also available.

filbert. Another name for HAZELNUT.

filet mignon. A small, tender slice of beef cut off the end of the FILLET. As the end is quite narrow, the slice may be cut thick and beaten gently with the back of a cleaver to flatten it out into a wider piece. Filet mignon is usually lightly grilled or fried.

fillet. The fillet, or tenderloin, of an animal carcase is a tapering piece of boneless flesh that runs parallel to the backbone on the underside of the rump and sirloin. It is a particularly tender cut of meat and contains very little fat.

A fillet is also a slice or strip of fish cut off the bones. For the verb to fillet, see BONE, FILLET.

filio / fillo / phyllo pastry. A fine, tissue-thin pastry popular throughout the Middle East. Although the dough is simple enough to make—high-gluten flour, salt, water, and a little oil— kneading and stretching it into sheets as thin as onion skin requires such skill (professionals spin it in the air) that no one can be blamed for buying it ready made and frozen or chilled. Filo is used for making a variety of savoury pies and pastries. The Greek spinach and cheese pie is a popular favourite. Several sheets of filo, each one brushed with melted butter before it is laid on the other, form the base and the top. The same spinach and cheese mixture (or cheese on its own) is used in small pastries made with a strip of buttered filo folded in a tricky zigzag that produces little triangles of several layers of pastry.

When using frozen filo, let it thaw slowly in the packet, then take out the sheets and stack them on a dry cloth and cover them with a thick sheet of plastic to stop them drying out, which they do quickly on exposure to air. When they do, they become brittle and tend to crumble when folded. So you must use them quickly. An effective way to butter the sheets for a pie is to place the required number in a stack, butter the top one, then pick up two corners of the top sheet and turn it over on the stack. Continue buttering and turning, each time picking up an extra sheet until they are all buttered.

fines herbes. A mixture of parsley, tarragon, chives, and chervil, finely chopped. Fines herbes add a subtle flavour when tossed in with a green salad or added to an otherwise plain omelette. They can be mixed with butter and lemon juice to garnish fish or grilled steak, blended into TARTARE and BÉARNAISE sauces, and used in many other ways.

finnan haddie. The porters at London's Billingsgate fish market were never renowned for their use of Received Pronunciation, and the Scots too have their own way with words. Consequently, smoked haddock from the Scottish fishing port of Findhorn became finnan haddie. (Just as well, or Mary Martin would have had trouble with the rhyme in 'My Heart Belongs to Daddie'.) Finnan haddie as a dish is traditionally cooked in milk and butter or a cream sauce, however, as smoked haddock, it may be grilled or poached like other smoked fish.

fish. Many kinds of fish are caught in the sea around Australia and in its rivers and lakes, although overfishing has drastically reduced catches of a number of species. The popular varieties available are listed under their individual names. Common features and some general information on fish are given here to save repetition.

Fish is a good source of protein; it is rich in vitamins A and D and contains iodine and various minerals; its oils (long-chain highly polyunsaturated omega-3 fatty acids) help to reduce blood cholesterol. It is easily digested, and can be cooked in all ways and even eaten raw.

To buy fish. As anyone who has eaten a freshly caught fish will know, the fresher the fish, the tastier it is. A fresh whole fish should have bright, clear, prominent eyes, firm flesh (your finger shouldn't leave an impression when you press it), clean, red gills, scales with a high sheen or shiny skin, and a pleasant smell. Fillets should have a translucent, lifelike quality (not dull).

How much do you need? When buying whole fish, allow 500 grams (including the weight of bones and head) per person. With fillets, 500 grams will give three average servings or two large ones.

To store fish. Fish should be eaten as soon as possible after you catch it or buy it. Meanwhile, keep it in the coldest part of the refrigerator, cleaned and scaled, in an airtight container for no more than a day or two. Frozen fish should be thawed slowly in the refrigerator. If you are in a hurry, put it in a plastic bag, seal it, and thaw under cold running water.

To scale fish. Lay the fish on a board and hold it by the tail. Using a blunt knife or a fish scaler (you can make one by nailing two crown-seal bottle tops on a piece of wood), scrape off the scales from the tail end, working against the grain towards the head. To prevent scales flying all over the kitchen, scale the fish in a sink of water.

To clean a fish. Trim off the fins with kitchen scissors. Slit the fish's belly with a sharp knife and pull out the entrails. Then wash the fish inside and out under running water.

To skin a flat fish. Lay the fish on a board, dark-side up, and cut a slit

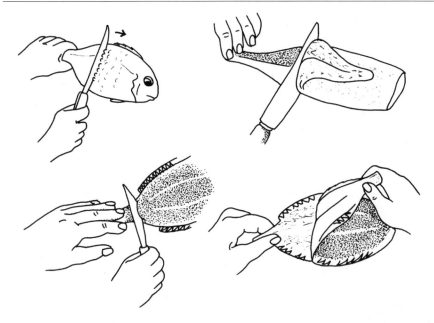

in the skin at the tail end. Ease the skin up with the knife or your fingernails until there is enough to get a grip on (dipping your fingers in water and then salt will help you get a firm grip), then draw the skin towards the head. When you come to the mouth, turn the fish over and pull the skin back towards the tail.

To fillet and skin a round fish. Cut through the skin along the backbone. Starting just below the gills, slice down the length of the fish, following the slit, and sever the fillet from the bones. Do the same thing on the other side. To skin a fillet, lay it skin-side down on a board and cut about 1 centimetre of the flesh away at the tail end so that you have some exposed skin to hold down with your fingers. Then insert the knife almost flat on the skin and cut away from you in short strokes until you have separated the fillet from the skin.

To fry fish. Coat the fish in flour and pan-fry in clarified butter or oil over fairly high heat until the fish flakes when it is probed gently with a fork in the thickest part. To reduce the smell of frying fish, take care not to let the cooking fat reach smoking point. Deep-frying is best suited to whole small fish or thin fillets. Coat the fish in batter, flour, or egg and breadcrumbs, and fry quickly in oil heated to 190°C.

To poach fish. Simmer the fish in stock or COURT BOUILLON—it should not boil, merely shiver—until the fish flakes easily. Delicate fish should be wrapped in cheesecloth to prevent it from falling to pieces.

To grill fish. Preheat the griller. Heat the grill pan (don't use a rack unless covered with foil), and coat the fish with a little oil or clarified butter. Fillets or fish steaks need not be turned when cooking; the heat of the tray cooks them from underneath. Whole fish are grilled on both sides. Slash larger fish on the thicker part so that they cook evenly.

To bake fish. Most fish would dry out in the oven if simply exposed to the dry heat. To prevent this from happening, wrap the fish in foil or vegetable leaves (lettuce, spinach, vine leaves); bake it in a liquid (wine, FUMET, water) and baste while it is cooking; or cover it with vegetables. Leave the head and tail on when baking a whole fish.

fish sauce. See NAM PLA.

five-corner fruit. See CARAMBOLA.

five-spice powder. A traditional Chinese mixture of five spices—star anise, cloves, cinnamon, Sichuan pepper, and fennel seeds—and dried mandarin peel, which is used to flavour stews, sauces, and other Chinese dishes. As it has a strong taste and aroma, it should be used sparingly. It is sometimes mixed with salt and sprinkled over fried dishes. Store it at room temperature in a tightly covered container.

flageolets. See HARICOT BEANS.

flake (noun). The fish-shop euphemism for SHARK and STINGRAY. The flesh of various sharks and rays are sold in shops, sometimes as 'boneless fillets'.

flake (verb). When a fish is cooked, its flesh will separate into individual flakes if gently probed with a fork. To flake a whole fish, remove the flesh carefully from the bones and skin, and then pull it apart with two forks to bite-size pieces or flakes.

flambé. Flamed. Certain dishes—CRÊPES SUZETTE and Christmas puddings, for example—are flamed before serving. Heated brandy, rum, or other spirit is poured over the food and ignited. For a bright, dramatic touch it is done at the table in front of guests. The purpose of flaming is to burn off the alcohol but keep the flavour, so the spirit should be good and the flavour appropriate to the food.

flamiche. A famous vegetable pie of France, the flamiche has a filling of sliced leeks that have been cooked gently in butter and then mixed with egg yolks (or whole eggs and cream). It is best made with BRIOCHE dough. Served hot or warm.

flan. See PIE, TART, FLAN.

flapjack. Another name for pancake (and, at one time, for BALMAIN BUG).

flathead. There are a number of flathead species found in Australian waters, the most common being the dusky, tiger, deepwater, and sand flathead. They are bottom-dwelling fish with a flattened head and body and eyes on the top of the head. Flathead are caught all year round but are more abundant from October to May. They are sold whole or in fillets. (Gurnard fillets are sometimes sold as flathead fillets by unscrupulous retailers.) The flesh of the flathead is white-cream with fine to medium flake and a soft to firm texture depending on the species. It can be cooked in most ways but is commonly battered or coated with flour and fried; served with chips and TARTARE SAUCE or MAYONNAISE. (See also FISH.)

fleurons. Scraps of puff pastry rolled out thinly, baked or fried, and served hot as a garnish for soup or as entrées.

florentine. A florentine is a thin, crisp biscuit containing nuts (usually almonds), dried fruit, peel, etc., and topped with chocolate. The designation Florentine means served with spinach.

floret / floweret. Each of the clusters of unopened flowers, or flowering stems, that form the head of a cauliflower or broccoli.

flounder. See SOLES AND FLOUNDERS.

flour. Humans have been grinding flour from grains of various kinds since prehistoric times. Today flour in cookery generally means wheat flour (but see also BESAN: cornflour under CORN; POTATO FLOUR; RICE FLOUR; RYE FLOUR). Hard and soft varieties of wheat produce flour of different qualities—hard-wheat flour, with its high gluten content, for bread and pasta making, soft-wheat flour for cakes, biscuits, and general use. The milling and bleaching processes also result in different types of flour which are used for different purposes.

Plain flour is a general-purpose flour produced from a blend of hard and soft wheats that have been milled, refined, and bleached, removing about 25–30 per cent of the grain, including the germ and bran. Plain flour is what is used whenever 'flour' is called for in the recipe.

Strong plain flour, or baker's flour, is produced from a blend of hard and soft wheats but has a higher protein content than plain flour and is better for bread making and other yeast cooking. It is available from some health food stores and from flour mills.

Wholemeal flour contains at least 90 per cent of the grain, which means it has more B vitamins, minerals, and fibre than white flour. It does not keep as well as white flour. It is used to make bread and in other yeast cookery and may be substituted, at least in part, for white flour in recipes. However, their textures are different, and the cooked products may be different in texture and moisture content, so some adjustments may have to be made to produce a satisfactory result.

Self-raising flour originated in the United States and was introduced into Australia in the 1930s. It is plain flour with baking powder added. Self-raising flour is used for making cakes and scones. As the baking powder loses its strength over the course of time, the flour should be used before its use-by date. You can make your own self-raising flour by adding 1¼ teaspoons of baking powder per cup of flour and sifting it twice.

Unbleached flour is plain flour that has not been through the final bleaching process. Its baking quality is not as good as that of bleached flour.

To measure flour. Using a dry measuring cup, spoon in the flour (sifted or unsifted) until it is heaped, then level it off with the edge of a knife or spatula. Do not press the flour down in the cup.

To sift flour. There are sifters of various design, some with revolving metal arcs worked by turning a little handle, others with oscillating spokes operated by squeezing the handgrip. But they all have a sieve at the bottom, and the object is to separate and aerate the fine particles of flour and disperse any added baking powder, etc. Using an ordinary fine sieve and tapping it on the side works just as well. If a cake recipe in which precise measurements are important calls for a cup of sifted flour, it expects you to sift the flour before measuring it, as sifted flour measures less by weight than unsifted flour; otherwise you may put too much flour in the cake and end up with a heavy, dry end product.

fluff. To fluff is to separate and loosen cooked cereal grains by lightly lifting and tossing them with a fork. (See also RICE.)

flummery. People don't seem to make flummeries these days. Instead they make creams, custards, jellies, and mousses, which are what flummeries could be variously described as. According to Sarah Paston-Williams in *The National Trust Book of Traditional Puddings*, the flummery began in medieval England with cereals such as oats and sago being cooked long and slowly with milk and flavourings. 'In Tudor and Stuart times it became a much richer dish of cream flavoured with spices, orange flower water, rose-water, almonds or wine, set with calves' feet or isinglass.' Gelatine later came to be used as the setting agent, and beaten egg-whites were added to make flummeries mousse-like. They are traditionally set in elaborately shaped jelly moulds.

focaccia. This flat, crusty Italian bread harks back to the origins of bread: a flattened piece of dough cooked on a stone in the coals of the hearth. The name *focaccia* comes from the Latin *panis focacius*, 'hearth bread'. Now usually made from leavened dough with olive oil and baked in the oven, focaccia is sometimes topped with coarse salt or onions and may contain pieces of bacon or sausage or herbs.

foie gras. An abbreviation of PÂTÉ DE FOIE GRAS.

folding in. To fold in is to mix a light, delicate mixture such as beaten egg-whites into a heavier one such as a soufflé base or a main cake mixture. The idea is to combine the two without losing the air whisked into the whites. It is one of the most important techniques in cookery.

First stir a quarter of the egg-whites into the heavier mixture to lighten and loosen it. Then tip the remaining whites onto the top. Plunge a rubber spatula or a large metal spoon down edgeways from the centre of the whites

to the bottom of the bowl and run it along the bottom and the side toward you, lifting the mixture and turning it over the top. Repeat this plunging and turning operation, while rotating the bowl, until all the egg-whites have been incorporated. Don't overdo it or you will lose the air and defeat the purpose.

fondant is a thick, creamy sugar paste made from icing sugar, liquid glucose, and egg-white. It is soft and pliable and can be rolled out to cover cakes or moulded into decorative objects that dry hard and can be painted with food dyes. It is also used as a filling for sweets. The name comes from the French *fondre*, 'to melt', and fondant does indeed melt in the mouth.

fondue. Another term from the French *fondre*, 'to melt', this time applied to melted cheese. Fondue is a famous Swiss dish composed of grated Gruyère and / or Emmental cheese, dry white wine, Kirsch, garlic, and seasonings. The ingredients are cooked in a casserole and then placed on the table over a burner, together with a basket of bite-size cubes of bread. Each person round the table spears a piece of bread on a fork—preferably a special long-handed fondue fork—dips it in the bubbling mixture, swirls it round, and eats it immediately.

fonduta. See FONTINA.

Fontina. The true Fontina cheese is produced only in the Aosta valley in Piedmont, Italy. Similar cheeses produced elsewhere are sometimes called fontal or fontinella. Fontina Val d'Aosta was originally made from ewe's milk but is now made mainly from cow's milk. A rich, buttery, nutty-flavoured cheese with a smooth texture and a few small holes, it is considered among the world's best. While essentially a table cheese, it can be used in cooking and is the basis for the Piedmontese specialty fonduta, made by melting the cheese with egg yolks, milk, and butter and topping the creamy mixture with sliced white truffles.

foo gwa. The Chinese name for BITTER MELON.

fool. There's no fool like an old fool, which in this case is the gooseberry fool, a cold dessert developed in eighteenth-century England and extremely popular in the Victorian era. *Fool* is an English term usually indicating puréed fruit with a thick cream or custard folded into it. How the name came about is uncertain, although *Brewer's Dictionary of Phrase and Fable* says it comes from the French *fouler*, 'to crush'. The fruit in a fool is indeed crushed—or bruised or pushed through a sieve or puréed—usually after being stewed. Fools are usually served in glasses or cups, accompanied with shortbread or similar biscuits.

forcemeat. STUFFING. (See also FARCE.)

fouet. The French name for the looped-wire whisk (see WHISKS).

four spices. See QUATRE-ÉPICES.

frangipane. The Marquis Muzio Frangipani, a sixteenth-century Roman nobleman, gained renown by inventing a perfume for scenting gloves. (The gloves were known in France as *gants de frangipane*.) The perfume, based on bitter almonds, inspired the creation of an almond-flavoured pastry filling made with milk, eggs, sugar, and vanilla mixed with either crushed macaroons or ground almonds. This rich custardy filling came to be known as frangipane, as did the pastry filled with it. Kirsch, orange zest, or orange flower water are often included as additional flavourings.

frankfurts / frankfurters. Just as well it was Berlin rather than Frankfurt that President Kennedy visited in June 1963; he would have sounded even sillier declaring 'Ich bin ein Frankfurter.' (In declaring 'Ich bin ein Berliner', Kennedy was telling the people of Berlin that he was a doughnut, or a sausage. He should have said, 'Ich bin Berliner.')

The 'continental' frankfurt is a sausage made from finely minced pork and veal seasoned with spices, smoked and cooked in hot water. Ordinary frankfurts may also contain beef, chicken, meat, and other meat scraps. They also contain plenty of fat and salt. A frankfurt can be eaten without further cooking, but it is usually heated in simmering water for 5 minutes or so before being served, traditionally with sauerkraut and mustard or with potato salad, or in a bread roll with mustard or tomato sauce—the ubiquitous hot dog. Frankfurts may also be grilled or fried and are sometimes added to soups.

French beans. See BEANS, GREEN; and HARICOT BEANS.

French dressing. Another name for sauce vinaigrette (see VINAIGRETTE).

French-roasting. See under CHICKEN.

French toast. How the French came to be credited with this way of using up stale bread is anybody's guess. Unlike French leave (absence without permission), French gout (syphilis), and other indelicate backhanders by the British against their neighbours across the Channel, French toast is something commendable. Slices of firm-textured bread, crusts trimmed, are soaked in a mixture of lightly beaten eggs and milk and then fried in butter on both sides. A little freshly ground nutmeg is sometimes sprinkled on top. It is more interesting than the British version of French toast as given in the *Concise Oxford Dictionary*: 'bread buttered on one side and toasted on the other'.

frenched. A CUTLET is said to be frenched when the rib bone is stripped of fat and meat from the tail to the eye of the fillet.

fricassee. A fricassee is similar to a BLANQUETTE, the difference being, as the great Escoffier quaintly puts it, the meat for a fricassee is 'stiffened in butter without colouration', in other words fried without browning (the French verb *fricasser* means 'to fry'). The meat in question is usually chicken or veal, cut into pieces, though people do fricassee tripe and onions, brains, rabbits, and best neck chops. Whether the meat is first stiffened or not, it is stewed in stock or water with whatever additions are called for, and the liquid is thickened and whitened with flour and milk or, as in a blanquette, with egg yolks and cream. The fricassee is served with the white sauce.

frijoles refritos. Refried beans, a popular dish in Mexico and other parts of Latin America. The beans—pinto beans, red kidney beans, or similar—are first cooked in water until tender and then mashed and fried with onions and garlic that have been sautéed in oil. Recipes vary, and ingredients such as chilli or capsicum, tomatoes, cumin, coriander, and other herbs, even grated cheese, are sometimes added. Frijoles refritos are served in tostadas (see TORTILLAS) or with plain cooked rice and tortillas, or stuffed into green capsicums and baked.

frittata. A frittata is an Italian version of the OMELETTE, but it differs from the French omelette in three important ways: it is cooked slowly over low heat rather than quickly over high heat; it is firm and set, not creamy and moist like an omelette; and it is flat and round, not folded over into an omelette's roll shape.

A frittata is cooked on both sides. If you have the courage and the necessary skill, you can flip it over in the air as you would a pancake. The less adventurous turn it onto a plate and slide it back into the pan with the cooked-side up. The faint-hearted put the pan under a hot griller for a little while to cook the top once the underside is done. The result is just as good.

All kinds of fillings can be incorporated in frittatas: cheese, ham, vegetables such as artichokes, asparagus, beans, tomatoes, and onions, and herbs; frittatas are very adaptable. They are eaten hot or (even better) cold, cut into wedges.

fritters. A fritter can be as simple as a spoonful of batter fried in deep fat. Mix some kernels of sweet corn in the batter and it becomes a corn fritter. It can be a piece of fruit, vegetable, meat, fish, or shellfish dipped in batter and either deep-fried or sautéed in a frying pan (see also TEMPURA). A soufflé fritter is made using sweet or savoury choux pastry.

fritto misto is Italian for 'mixed fry'. The dish is variable and may consist of up to half a dozen ingredients, including thin slices of veal, precooked and sliced brains, artichoke wedges, slices of Florence fennel, zucchini, or eggplant, cauliflower florets, mushrooms, etc. The pieces may be dipped in batter and deep-fried in oil or coated with egg and breadcrumbs and pan-fried. With *il grande fritto misto* the entire meal is fried, from a first course of, say, fried cheese to a dessert of fried sweet cream and apple fritters.

Fritto misto di mare, mixed fried fish, is one of the most common fish dishes in Italian coastal restaurants and what is popularly regarded as fritto misto in Italian restaurants in Australia. A variety of fish and shellfish are dusted with flour and fried in hot oil.

fromage blanc. A light fresh cheese (see under CHEESE) that originated in France and achieved popularity with the advent of CUISINE MINCEUR. It is made from skim milk soured with an added culture. A substitute can be made with skim-milk yoghurt and cottage cheese, with a little salt or lemon juice, whipped at high speed in a food processor. Fromage blanc is used to make low-fat sauces and as a topping for desserts.

frosting. See ICING and CRYSTALLISED / FROSTED FLOWERS.

fruit, dried. See CANDIED / CRYSTALLISED / GLACÉ FRUIT and DRIED FRUIT.

fry, pan-fry, sauté. To fry means to cook in hot fat. The fat may be oil, butter (or a mixture of oil and butter, which raises the burning point of butter), margarine, lard, or dripping, and the cooking implement may be a frying pan or saucepan. *Fry* is the general, serviceable term used by people who have no use for the terms *pan-fry* and *sauté* (See also DEEP-FRYING and STIR-FRYING).

Pan-fry and sauté mean much the same thing—to cook in a small amount of fat. Pan-frying—sometimes called dry-frying, because only a light coating of oil or butter is spread on the base of the pan (or nothing at all when the pan has a non-stick surface)—usually refers to meat, which is cooked first on high heat to seal in the juices and then on medium heat until the meat is cooked to the desired stage: rare, medium or well done (see STEAK). With sautéing, the food may be potatoes, onions, or other vegetables as well as meat, generally in small pieces, and it is cooked quickly and lightly, sometimes just to brown the food before finishing it off in some other way. The pan is usually shaken (*sauter* means 'to leap' in French) to ensure that the food is browned all over.

When pan-frying, don't turn the meat too often, and don't fry with a lid on, as the lid traps the steam in and the meat stews. Frozen meat doesn't need defrosting; just allow longer cooking time.

With both pan-frying and sautéing, don't use too much fat, and make sure it is hot enough before the food goes into the pan. The food should not be damp; moisture prevents it from browning and searing properly. Don't crowd the pan or the food will steam.

fudge is a soft, rich confection made out of milk, butter, or cream (or a combination of all three) with sugar and a flavouring, popularly chocolate. The ingredients are boiled together to soft-ball stage (see SUGAR SYRUP), then beaten, and the mixture is poured into a shallow, flat container to set. When cool, it is cut into squares.

ful medames. Egyptian brown beans. The dried bean *Vicia faba* var. *minor* is a smaller, more rounded variety of the broad bean, native to the Mediterranean region. It is a staple food of Egypt, where it has been eaten since the time of the Pharaohs. Ful medames is the name of a simple dish of cooked beans, seasoned with oil, lemon and garlic, sprinkled with chopped parsley, and accompanied by hard-boiled eggs. The beans are also served as a filling in Arab bread. Like other dried beans, ful medames must be pre-soaked and simmered for hours until tender (see also BEANS, DRIED).

fumet. A concentrated stock usually made by simmering fish and fish bones in wine with herbs and seasonings. This strong, well-reduced stock is used as the basis of fish VELOUTÉ SAUCE and fish-poaching liquid. A fumet can also be made from chicken, game, mushrooms, truffles, etc., to give flavour to sauces and other stocks.

fungi usually means mushrooms, and indeed most of the edible fungi sold in Australia are cultivated mushrooms or field mushrooms. However, with an increasing migrant population, especially from Asia, Australia has been importing, and to some extent growing, exotic mushrooms and other fungi. Among such fungi (see also MUSHROOMS) available in Australia are:

Bamboo fungus. A rare, and thus expensive, lacy fungus that grows on bamboo plants in the Sichuan region of China. It is only available dry and is used in Chinese vegetarian and banquet dishes.

Cloud ear fungus. Also called black fungus, tree ears, and wood ear fungus. It has a crunchy texture when fresh. The curled and crinkly dried fungus expands to five times its size and becomes flexible and tender when soaked. It is widely used in Chinese cookery in soups, braises, and stir-fries.

White fungus, also known as silver fungus and snow fungus, is used for its texture (crunchy) and appearance rather than for its flavour, which is slight. The dried form increases dramatically in size on being soaked. It is served as part of a vegetable dish or in SUGAR SYRUP as a dessert.

G

gai laan. See CHINESE BROCCOLI.

galangal is a member of the ginger family native to China. It is also known as *Siamese ginger* or *ground laos* and, in Thai, as *kah*. Galangal has a peppery flavour with a hint of ginger and cardamom and is used extensively in Thai and Laotian cooking. The rhizomes are pinkish-cream in colour with pink nodules and sprouts. They are available fresh, dried, and in powder form. A teaspoon of the powder equals a little less than 1 centimetre of fresh galangal. Dried galangal needs to be soaked for 10 minutes or more before being sliced.

galantine. The word *galantine* seems to have come from the same source as *gelatine* and *jelly*; the dish is served cold in its own jelly or coated in aspic. The main ingredient can be poultry or meat, even fish, which is boned, stuffed with a forcemeat that includes the meat trimmed off the bones, cooked in a rich stock, then taken out of the stock and pressed into a symmetrical shape. The stock is turned into an aspic.

A **ballotine** is a similar dish, originally made only with meat (a boned shoulder of lamb, for example), whereas the galantine was made only with poultry. A ballotine may be served hot as well as cold in aspic.

galette. The French name for a thin, round cake or pastry. Galettes are also made with potatoes cut in very thin slices and cooked in a pan on both sides until crusty. Sometimes there are layers of flavourings—herbs, mushrooms, grated cheese, a MIREPOIS, etc.—between the potato slices.

gammon is a term used mainly in England. In one sense it means the lower part of a side of bacon, including the leg. It also applies to the leg, or ham, cut from the cured side of bacon. (With a regular ham, the leg is cut from the carcase first and then cured.) Gammon as sold in an Australian butcher's shop, however, is likely to be a leg of pork that has been boned, rolled, and salted but not smoked or pre-cooked. Gammon is usually boiled and served with root vegetables, or boiled (to remove some of the salt) and then fried or grilled.

garam masala is probably the nearest an Indian household gets to CURRY POWDER. The name means 'hot mixture', and it is a blend of spices mixed and ground together to use as a basic seasoning for food. The mixture varies according to the dish and the cook's preference; it might contain coriander seeds, cumin seeds, cardamom seeds, peppercorns, cinnamon sticks, cloves, and nutmeg, or it could consist simply of coriander, chillies, and pepper. Garam masala is usually added to a dish towards the end of cooking. It can also be used as a condiment to be sprinkled on, say, pumpkin soup or vegetable kebabs.

garfish. A small, slender, silvery fish with a lower jaw that is elongated into a little sword or beak. Garfish have white, sweet-tasting flesh containing little oil but have many soft, fine, rib bones which, when the backbone is removed, may be eaten. Garfish keep well in the refrigerator, but be sure to gut and scale them first. The best way to cook them is by deep-frying them whole. Larger ones can be filleted and either coated with batter and fried or lightly dusted with seasoned flour and grilled on a very hot plate. (See also FISH.)

garlic. You either love or hate garlic, and it seems it was ever thus. The Roman emperor Nero obviously loved it; he is said to have invented AÏOLI, the garlic-flavoured sauce. On the other hand the priestesses of Cybele in Rome refused to allow anyone who had been eating garlic to enter their temple. Unfortunately for those who hate garlic, its pungent flavour, which lingers on the breath, is hard to ignore.

Garlic has been around for a long time: it is mentioned in the Old Testament, and bulbs of garlic were found in the tomb of Tutankhamen. A member of the onion family, it probably originated in central Asia but is now grown round the world. It has long been recognised as an antiseptic. Many people eat garlic to ward off colds, aid digestion, cleanse the skin, and for other medicinal purposes. The edible bulb, known as a head, is a cluster of cloves encased in a paper-thin skin ranging in colour from white to pinkish-purple. The cloves themselves have a skin, which is usually (but not always) peeled.

Garlic is indispensable in innumerable dishes. It goes well with meat, especially lamb, and many vegetables; it is essential in aïoli and any dish designated *Provençale*; a sliced clove wiped around a salad bowl gives a subtle flavour to salad, or a clove can be added to the salad dressing. A famous chicken dish has as many as 40 cloves cooked whole with it in a casserole; the flavour is surprisingly mild, and the gently braised olive-oil-soaked garlic cloves can be eaten separately or on crusty bread.

To peel and crush garlic. To separate the cloves from a head of garlic, some people slice off the top of the head and then bang down on it with their fist, which does the job. If you find peeling the cloves a problem, an easy way is to drop them into boiling water for a few seconds, drain and run cold water over them, then slip off the skins with your fingers. To smash or bruise a clove, place it on a board, lay the blade of a broad knife on it, and hit it with your fist. This splits the skin, making it easy to remove. You can then chop the garlic or mash it with salt as you prefer. Garlic presses are available, but they release every bit of volatile oil and produce a more pungent flavour than chopping or crushing with a knife does.

garlic chives. See CHIVES.

garni. Garnished.

garnish. To garnish food is to decorate or embellish it for the table. The garnish may be eaten; often it is an essential part of the dish or, like chopped chives, impossible to avoid eating. Or it may be simply there to add a decorative touch—a sprig of parsley, for example—or to be used if you wish, such as a lemon wedge. Garnishes include CROÛTONS, FLEURONS, various sauces, sour cream, diced tomatoes or potatoes or hard-boiled eggs, garlic cloves or mushroom caps, and so on.

gateau is the French word for cake, but a gateau as we know it is not just any old cake; it is a celebration cake, an elaborate confection made for a special occasion. It may have a sponge or pastry base, and it is usually layered and / or topped with cream, fruit, jam, or nuts. A gateau is often served as a dessert.

gazpacho. A cold soup, of Spanish origin, made from raw vegetables. (Sydney chef Gay Bilson has referred to gazpacho as 'a kind of very wet salad rather than a very salady soup'.) There are many ways of preparing it, and the ingredients are fairly flexible. The Andalusian version is usually made with a base of breadcrumbs, crushed garlic, olive oil, and wine vinegar into which goes puréed tomatoes and finely chopped cucumber, green capsicum, Spanish onion, with perhaps some crushed almonds or cumin seeds. It is then chilled for a couple of hours. Ice cubes are often added when it is served. Sometimes the chopped vegetables, and hard-boiled egg, are served separately for the diners to garnish the soup as they please.

gefilte fish. A dish from the Jewish cuisine, the name meaning 'filled fish'. It seems that the ingredients—chopped or minced fish mixed with egg, breadcrumbs, and seasonings—were originally stuffed back into the skin of the fish. Nowadays they are usually formed into balls and cooked in broth, although variations on the recipe are almost endless. Gefilte fish may be served hot with the strained broth (warm or cool), or cold with the broth jellied and horseradish accompaniment.

gelatine is a protein setting agent which is extracted from the ligaments, bones, and skin of animals. It is available as a powder and in leaf or sheet form, 5–6 leaves being equivalent to 1 tablespoon (10 grams) of powder. As a rule, a tablespoon of powdered gelatine will set half a litre (2 metric cups) of liquid or stiffen the same amount of cream.

Gelatine must be softened and dissolved before being added to the main mixture. Sprinkle a tablespoon of powdered gelatine on top of a half-cup of the hot liquid to be set, or hot water, and stir it briskly with a fork. When leaf gelatine is being used, soak the leaves in cold water for 5 minutes first to soften them, then squeeze the excess water out of the softened sheets and either add them to the hot liquid or gently heat them in a pan until they are dissolved.

Leaf gelatine, which contains some water and sulphur dioxide, produces a softer result than powdered gelatine.

gelato is Italian for ICE-CREAM. The Neopolitans are said to have invented ice-cream. The original *gelati* were water ices, eaten as a digestive as well as a refreshment. You can still buy a fruit- or water-based gelato, which is more like a SORBET or a GRANITA than an ice-cream made with a milk or cream base. Some of the ice-cream kind have an icy, lumpy consistency that has given gelato a bad name. A good gelato should be smooth, stable, not too aerated, and fairly solid. The original milk-based gelato was perhaps the one given in a recipe book published in Naples in 1694, with pine nuts, candied fruit, and cinnamon as the ingredients. It is still a favourite in Naples three hundred years later. Custard cream and hazelnut are the Italian ice-cream maker's two basics, but the ingredients and flavourings that can go into a gelato are many and varied.

gem scones. Gem irons are not regarded as essential equipment in the modern kitchen, but if you have inherited some of these cast-iron baking trays with recessed, half-sphere moulds you might be familiar with the light, sweet, round scones they produce. A mixture of creamed butter and sugar, with egg and milk added and flour and salt folded in, is placed in pre-heated gem irons and baked for a few minutes in a hot oven.

gemfish. Formerly known as hake, this long, silver fish with tiny scales which inhabits the deep waters off eastern Australia was one of Australia's most important commercial fish in the 1970s and 1980s. The annual catch reached 5000 tonnes, an unsustainable level of exploitation. Quotas were introduced, but it was too late; there weren't enough gemfish left for the trawlermen to meet their quotas. The familiar gemfish fillets (the fish was too ugly to present whole) are now not so common in fish shops. (See also FISH.)

ghee. Indian-style clarified butter (see under BUTTER) made from either cow's milk or buffalo's milk. The difference between ghee and ordinary clarified butter is that, with ghee, the butter is melted and then simmered for about 45 minutes before the clear liquid is strained off. By this time all the water in the butter has evaporated and the milk solids are golden brown. This cooking not only removes the water content but also gives the ghee a distinctive nutty flavour.

Commercially produced ghee is available in tins. It will keep for many months in the refrigerator and will even keep for some weeks unrefrigerated. Because it can be heated to higher temperatures than unclarified butter, ghee is good to use in frying.

gherkin. A gherkin is a small, rough-skinned variety of cucumber which is picked immature and pickled in spicy wine vinegar or brine, often with dill flower-heads or some other herb or spice. When the pickling liquid is sweetened, the cucumbers are known as sweet gherkins. Gherkins are used as a garnish for cold meats and pâté; chopped, they are an essential ingredient in TARTARE SAUCE.

giblets are the edible entrails of a fowl—the heart, liver, gizzard, and neck. They used to be tucked into the carcase of the bird when you bought it, but nowadays the only part you may get is the neck; the rest you have to buy separately. CHICKEN LIVERS, of course, are prepared in many ways (see separate entry). The other giblets are used for making stocks, soups, and gravy. Trim the fat, blood vessels and membrane off the heart, and cut off the outer skin and inner sac of the gizzard before cooking them.

gigot. A leg of lamb or mutton.

gingelly oil. An Indian name for the oil pressed from unroasted sesame seeds (see SESAME OIL).

ginger. A perennial plant native to tropical Asia, ginger is grown in China, India, Africa, the West Indies, and Australia for its thick, tuberous root (more properly rhizome), the source of the spice. The ginger factory at Buderim in Queensland is the world's largest, exporting ginger to seventeen countries around the world. Ginger is available fresh, also called green ginger; preserved in syrup, or glacé; crystallised; and dried and ground into powder.

Fresh ginger is used extensively in Chinese cooking. For stir-fries it is usually chopped; for dishes that require longer cooking, the piece of root is bruised with the flat of a cleaver. As a rule, powdered ginger should not be substituted for fresh in Chinese cooking, though preserved ginger may be at a pinch. Fresh ginger is also an important ingredient in Indian curries. Store fresh ginger root, wrapped in foil or plastic, in the refrigerator. To keep it for a long time, peel it and place it in a jar of dry sherry in the refrigerator.

Fresh ginger will not grate satisfactorily using a standard metal grater; what you need is a special bamboo grater, obtainable at Asian stores.

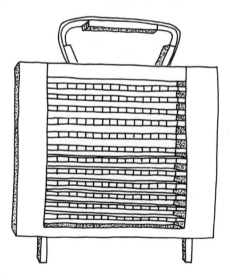

Preserved ginger is probably bought often for the attractive jars it is packed in, but it is used in cakes and puddings and eaten with its syrup as a dessert sauce, on ice-cream, or chopped and mixed with yoghurt.

Crystallised ginger is eaten as a sweetmeat, especially at Christmas.

Powdered ginger is used in making ginger snaps, brandy snaps, gingerbread and other cakes and puddings, as well as in the ginger beer 'plant' which is the basis for making ginger beer.

gingerbread is a dark-coloured cake made with treacle or golden syrup and flavoured with ginger and other spices. It is usually iced with lemon icing. In nineteenth-century England, gingerbread men and other gilded toy shapes fashioned out of gingerbread were sold at country fairs. As a result, the word *gingerbread* came to refer to something gaudy or tawdry (*tawdry* was itself a corruption of *Saint Audrey*, a town where cheap and showy goods were sold at the annual fair). Nevertheless, gingerbread, together with gingerbread men and gingerbread houses, retains its popularity.

glacé. Generally speaking, glacé means having a glossy surface. Glacé fruit is preserved using sugar (see CANDIED / CRYSTALLISED / GLACÉ FRUIT). Glacé icing is made from icing sugar, water, and vanilla essence.

glaze. To glaze is to give a glossy finish to food. This is done in various ways: pastry is glazed by brushing it with EGG WASH before cooking; a cooked tart is glazed with syrup or jelly; some cakes are glazed with apricot jam; carrots steamed with butter and sugar acquire a glaze; cold fish or meat in aspic are glazed. Basting meat or poultry while it is roasting glazes it.

Glaze also refers to the browned, dehydrated juices from meat and vegetables that form on the bottom of the roasting pan during cooking. This glaze is used to make a sauce (see DEGLAZING).

Meat stock reduced to about a quarter of its original volume is known as a meat glaze or *glacé de viande*. It becomes a jelly when cold and is used to strengthen the flavour of gravy or sauce and as a glaze for cold meats.

glucose is a form of sugar (see also CARBOHYDRATES). Liquid glucose, also known as glucose syrup and corn syrup, is a combination of sugars obtained from starch (for example, maize). It is used as a sweetener in drinks and desserts and for making FONDANT and other confectionery.

gluten. In wheat and some other grains there is a mixture of proteins which form an elastic substance called gluten when flour is mixed with water. This gluten is important in bread-making, because it forms a skin for the millions of tiny bubbles of gas produced by the fermenting yeast and thus keeps the dough aerated and the bread light. High-gluten flour is consequently preferred for bread-making, and gluten may be added to flour to increase its strength and its protein content. Gluten is an important source of protein for vegetarians.

Some people, however, have a congenital intolerance to gluten and must avoid it in their diet. This can be difficult, as it is present in rye, oats, and barley as well as wheat and it is used in the commercial manufacture of breakfast foods, soups, salad dressings, sausages, and other products. However, it is not present in rice, and food prepared with rice flour instead of wheaten flour is acceptable. Cautious parents start their infants on rice cereal to avoid the risk of ill effects in case they are among the unfortunate minority suffering from coeliac disease.

Powdered gluten is available from supermarkets and health food shops. Store it in an airtight container in the refrigerator.

gnocchi. It seems everything about these little Italian dumplings—ingredients, shape, and method of cooking—is variable. *Gnocchi verdi*, for example, are made with puréed spinach mixed with ricotta, grated Parmesan, eggs, flour, and seasonings, formed into croquettes the size of a cork, dropped into simmering salted water to cook (they rise to the surface when they're ready), then drained and placed in a baking dish with some butter and grated Parmesan and cooked for a few minutes more in the oven. They may also be simmered in stock instead of water and served as soup.

Potato gnocchi, as might be expected, have puréed potato substituted for spinach and cheese and are shaped with the aid of a fork into ridged crescents. They are cooked in the same way.

Gnocchi alla romana are made with a semolina mixture, rolled out and cut into discs, which are placed, overlapping, in an ovenproof dish, dotted with butter and sprinkled with Parmesan, and baked in the oven.

A point to remember when forming the little gnocchi shapes: keep your fingers floured to avoid the mixture sticking to them.

goat cheese. Cheese has been made from goat's milk for centuries in countries around the Mediterranean. The goat's milk cheeses imported from France are known generally as *chèvre*. They are mainly soft cheeses and should be kept no longer than a fortnight. Goat cheeses are also produced in Australia, mostly in Western Australia but also in Victoria and Tasmania. Both fresh and mature cheeses are available. By law, cheese made in Australia must be made with pasteurised milk, which does not give as fine a flavour as unpasteurised milk, traditionally used by European cheese makers. Goat cheese has a distinctive nutty, sweet flavour. To appreciate it, take the cheese out of the refrigerator at least an hour before serving to allow it to reach room temperature and its full flavour.

goat meat is the most widely eaten red meat in the world. But not in Australia, where kid, or *capretto*, as young goat meat is also called, is hard to find, and then mostly in butcher's shops that cater for ethnic groups. Much of the goat meat sold here is from feral animals and their offspring or from goats bred for wool production. This meat, particularly if it is mature, can be gamy and should be treated like venison. Kid raised for meat, however, is fine-tasting—a cross between pork and chicken, some say—rich in flavour, easy to digest, and having only a moderate amount of fat. A leg of kid can be cooked as you would cook a leg of lamb, rubbed with olive oil and flavoured with rosemary. The cutlets can be braised, the loin pan-fried.

A program of breeding goats for meat production has been set up in South Australia. Though aimed largely at the export market, it could mean that goat meat will become more freely available locally.

golden syrup is one of the by-products of the refining of SUGAR from sugarcane. A syrup remains after the crystallised sugar is extracted from the concentrated cane juice. This can be further refined to produce golden syrup and treacle. In bygone days 'cockatoo farmers' found golden syrup a cheap substitute for jam, and consequently it became known as cocky's joy. It is used in making brandy snaps, treacle tart, gingerbread and some cakes and also as a sauce for dumplings and puddings. It goes well on a chunk of damper hot from the camp oven, too.

goose. 'Christmas is coming, the geese are getting fat' goes the old beggar's rhyme. It's mainly at Christmas that goose is eaten, and even then the few people who do eat it would have to order one from a supplier. It would probably be three to nine months old and weigh 3–5 kilograms. About 500 grams per diner would be needed.

Goose is not tender like chicken; the all-dark meat has a kind of chewy texture. Geese also run to fat. Before roasting a goose, remove all visible fat and prick the skin all over to allow the subcutaneous fat to run out during cooking. Put the bird on a rack in the roasting pan. It is traditionally stuffed with onion and sage; the French use chestnuts and / or apples. With an older bird it helps to steam or poach it before roasting.

Goose fat, sold in tins, can be used in place of cooking fat or salad oil.

gooseberries. There are many kinds of gooseberry, some round, some oval, some smooth, some hairy, coloured green or white or yellow or red-black when ripe. No matter what their ripe colour is, they are green when immature, and that is the way they are often picked and used. Although the unripe fruit is too sour to eat out of the hand, it makes delicious tarts, pies, and puddings. The berries are topped and tailed and washed before cooking. They can also be cooked in a SUGAR SYRUP and puréed. Fully ripened, gooseberries are a sweet dessert fruit.

Gooseberries are grown commercially in Victoria. The main variety grown is Roaring Lion, a smooth-skinned fruit that is ruby red when fully ripe. It is harvested in November.

Where the name *gooseberry* came from is uncertain. The famous English horticulturist John Loudon suggested it was a corruption of gorseberry, since the prickly gooseberry bush resembled the gorse. How 'playing gooseberry' came to mean being the unwanted third party when sweethearts are together is anybody's guess.

Gorgonzola cheese. The town of Gorgonzola, north-east of Milan in northern Italy, was a stopping place for cows tired from their journey to or from the Alpine grazing slopes. The 'tired' milk from these cows was used to make a cheese that has become one of the great veined cheeses of the world. It is now made throughout the Lombardy plains. The milk is uncooked and curdled with calf's RENNET, and the cheese is internally ripened.

The veining of Gorgonzola cheese is blue-green, and the cheese at its peak is smooth, soft, and creamy with a flavour distinctively its own. Make sure the cheese you buy is not dry and crumbly or heavily moulded. Though its aroma is potent, it should not be overpowering or excessively musty. Wrap the cheese well before storing it in the refrigerator. It will keep for up to a fortnight.

Like other veined cheeses, Gorgonzola is a fine dessert cheese. The Milanese stuff pears with it. It goes well also with figs, dates, and grapes. Use it in salads with cos lettuce and walnuts, for example. It can also be used in cooking. (See also CHEESE.)

Gouda cheese. The equally famous Dutch cheeses, Gouda and Edam, are often compared and sometimes confused. Both are mild, firm cheeses with a buttery taste. Each has a few tiny holes. Whereas Edam is produced in a grapefruit-sized ball with a red wax coating (for export), Gouda comes in a wheel shape with a yellow waxed rind. Gouda is creamier than Edam, with a minimum butterfat content of 26 per cent to Edam's 21 per cent. As Gouda ages, its colour becomes a deeper yellow and the flavour matures. An old Gouda—that is, seven or more years old—is identified with a black skin instead of a yellow one.

Like Edam, Gouda is a general-purpose cheese good for slicing, cooking, and adding to the cheese board. It can be grated into sauces, melted over vegetables, even made into a kind of fondue. Australian-made Gouda-style cheeses are also available.

goulash. Hungary's most famous export, the hot, spicy stew Hungarians call *gulyás*, has lost much of its identity as well as the spelling of its name in the course of its assimilation around the world. Goulash has come to be just about any kind of meat stew provided it is cooked with plenty of paprika.

The original goulash was a simple meat-and-onion stew of the Magyar herdsmen. It was carried about in dehydrated form by the shepherds, and when they were hungry they popped some in a pot, added water, and heated it into a reconstituted stew or a soup depending on the amount of water. The authentic Hungarian goulash of today is made with cubed beef, preferably from the rib or shoulder, cooked with finely chopped onions and diced potatoes in beef or chicken stock with caraway seeds, salt, and paprika. These are the essential ingredients. Usually added are tomatoes, green capsicums, and garlic, all finely chopped. No flour is used to thicken the stew, and no wine is added. A Transylvanian version is made with cubed pork and sauerkraut and is finished off with sour cream.

granadilla. Another name for PASSIONFRUIT.

granita. The Italians invented two mouth-cooling and delightfully refreshing finales to a meal: the GELATO and the granita. The granita is a water ice made of fine-grained frozen crystals of fruit juice or coffee. As the texture of a granita is grainy (more or less a translation of the Italian word), it does not need to be made in an ice-cream churn. The fruit juice (usually orange juice, lemon and water, or strawberry purée) or sweetened black coffee is poured into a shallow dish such as a Swiss roll or lamington tin, or freezer trays without the ice-cube grids, placed in the freezer, and stirred every few minutes right up to the last. The liquid should not be allowed to set solid; the ice crystals must be broken up each time they form. The finished granita should have a fine, snowy texture. Serve it in a martini glass, goblet, or glass bowl. Top a coffee granita with some whipped cream if that's your fancy.

grapefruit. The origin of the grapefruit is something of a mystery. It is derived from the POMELO, an ancient citrus fruit that grows wild in Indo-China and Indonesia. In the seventeenth century a Captain Shaddock of the East India Company is said to have taken a pomelo (which he called a shaddock) from the East Indies to the Bahamas, where it reproduced itself in abundance.

Whether the grapefruit was a sport of the pomelo or a cross between it and a sweet orange is unclear, but it appeared in the Bahamas and was later cultivated in Florida. It was recognised as a separate species, *Citrus paradisi*, in the nineteenth century. Grapefruit are now grown commercially in citrus-growing areas around the world.

There are several varieties of grapefruit, including some that have pink or red flesh, which are sweeter than the yellow-fleshed variety. Grapefruit are available all year round, with heaviest supplies in winter and spring. Choose firm, bright-coloured fruit that are heavy for their size. Those left longer on the tree to mature and sweeten, known as goldfruit, may have skin blemishes or discolouration. Keep grapefruit in a cool place or in the refrigerator.

Grapefruit are traditionally eaten halved with a spoon at breakfast time. Segmented, they are added to salads and fruit salad. The juice is used in mousses and sorbets. Grapefruit are also used in marmalade. For information on segmenting, etc., see CITRUS FRUIT.

Grapefruit has lots of vitamin C and is low in kilojoules.

Some people with a hiatus hernia, and others with arthritis, find that grapefruit aggravates their condition.

grapes. The noble vocation of the grape is to be turned into wine, and most of the grapes grown in Australia are used for that purpose. But grapes are nice to eat, too, and there are many dessert varieties produced for the table. (Some are also used for drying into CURRANTS, RAISINS, and sultanas.) Grown as far north as Charters Towers in Queensland as well as in all the other states, grapes are consequently available most of the year, beginning in November and going through to September.

Grapes are roughly divided into white or black varieties—though the colours range from pale green through yellow and red to purple and blue-black—and whether they are seeded or seedless. Some of the popular table grapes in their order of maturing are: Cardinal (reddish purple, large, round seeded); Menindee (white, seedless); Flame Seedless (bright red, medium to large, round); Thompson Seedless, otherwise known as Sultana (yellow-green, medium size, oval, seedless); Black Muscat, or Muscat Hamburg (medium size, oval, blue-black, seeded); White Muscat (greenish-yellow, large, round, seeded); Waltham Cross (golden-green, large, long oval, seeded); Italia (golden, large, oval, seeded, with a mild Muscat flavour when ripe); Ribier (black, very large, round, seeded); Purple Cornichon (purple with bloom, large, lady-finger shaped, thick-skinned, seeded); Ruby Seedless (red, small to medium, oval); Nyora (dark purple, large, long oval, seeded); Emperor (red, medium to large, oval, thick-skinned, seeded); and Ohanez (golden white, medium to large, cylindroidal, seeded). The tiny, white seedless currant grapes are also available in mid-season.

Choose bunches of grapes that are plump, firm and well-coloured, with a fresh, green stem. Taste one before you buy, as grapes don't ripen any more once they've been picked. Handle them carefully, and store them in a plastic bag in the refrigerator, but eat them soon after purchase. Rinse them under cold water before eating. They go well with cheese after a meal and can be added to fruit salads, made into jam, cooked as a filling in tarts, used as a garnish for poultry, and frozen or chilled and frosted.

Grapes contain a fair amount of sugar, which is good for wine making but something to consider when weight watching.

gratin generally refers to a dish sprinkled with breadcrumbs or grated cheese, or both, and then baked or grilled until the cheese melts and the topping browns. There are many gratins, including the old stand-by macaroni cheese and even French onion soup. They can be made with either cooked or raw foods and are often mixed or masked (see MASK) with a white sauce, although this is not essential. Food prepared in this manner is said to be served *au gratin* or *gratiné* (from the French *gratter*, to scratch or scrape). Certain oval dishes are known as gratin dishes.

gravlax is a traditional Scandinavian dish of raw salmon prepared with coarse salt, sugar, dill, and peppercorns and buried in the snow for two or three days. Nowadays the salmon fillets, sandwiched with the seasonings and pressed together with weights, are left in the refrigerator to cure. The cured salmon is cut into slices on the diagonal and served with mustard sauce as part of a smorgasbord.

gravy. 'Madam,' said the Reverend Sydney Smith to Lady Holland, 'I have been looking for a person who disliked gravy all my life; let us swear eternal friendship.' They were probably thinking of the brown, lumpy mixture of uncooked flour and fat too often served up as gravy. The secret of gravy making is not to use too much flour, just enough to give the gravy a little body. Better still, use no flour at all; then you have sauce. Sauce is considered to be more elegant than gravy. (See DEGLAZING and SAUCES.)

To make a smooth brown gravy. Pour or skim off most of the fat in the roasting pan after the meat is cooked, leaving mainly the juices. Season with salt and pepper, and sprinkle a little flour evenly over the surface. Stir constantly over medium heat until the flour begins to brown, then add some hot stock or water in which the vegetables have cooked (or some plain hot water if you haven't anything else). Add it a little at a time, stirring continuously to dissolve any lumps, until the gravy is smooth and has thickened slightly. Taste it for seasoning, and strain it into a warmed gravy boat.

greasing. To grease is to coat with butter or oil or other fat, depending on the recipe. For greasing cake tins, see 'Preparing cake tins' under CAKES.

griddle. A heavy iron or cast aluminium flat plate, round or square with a handle, used over a heat source to cook such things as griddle cakes, English muffins, chappatis, and other flat, unleavened breads or pancakes.

grilling. To grill is to cook under or over direct heat. It may be done on a grill pan under the grilling element of the stove, or on a ribbed grill (a kind of heavy frying pan with raised ridges across the cooking surface) on top of the stove. Grilling is a fast and low-fat method of cooking steak, chops, sausages, kebabs, fish, chicken, etc.

Defrost frozen meat before grilling it, and trim off any fat. Don't salt the meat first, as salt draws out the juices and makes the meat tough. Fat left on steak shrinks and makes the meat curl. To stop it from curling while cooking, nick the edges.

Always preheat the grill on high to provide a searing temperature. Meat should be quickly seared to seal in the juices. Once the meat is browned on both sides, the heat can be reduced to medium or the grill pan lowered. Cooking time varies according to the type of meat and its thickness (see also STEAK). Don't cut the meat to see if it's done; the juices will escape. Turn the meat no more than three times during cooking, only once for rare.

When grilling fish steaks or thick fillets, lay them on the bottom of the grill pan without the rack, or line the rack with aluminium foil. The fish will cook on the underside with the heat from below; it shouldn't be necessary to turn the fillets. Small whole fish can be cooked in the same way. Larger whole fish are grilled on both sides. Score the flesh at thick parts for even cooking.

grissini. Long, slender, rusk-like Italian bread sticks.

groper. The blue groper of southern Australian waters is a medium to large fish with prominent, thick lips. There is a red or brown form of the fish as well as the blue. The flesh of smaller fish has a good texture and flavour, but larger fish are coarser and less palatable. Groper is available in steaks, cutlets and fillets, and occasionally a smaller fish is sold whole. (See also FISH.)

Gruyè is often confused with EMMENTAL, the classic Swiss cheese with holes big enough for cartoon mice to lounge about in. Gruyère has smaller and fewer holes and a sharper taste than Emmental. The rind of Gruyère is brown and wrinkled, unlike the smooth, amber colour of Emmental. A firm, yellow cheese with a nutty, fruity flavour, Gruyère is both Swiss and French in origin. It is used for sandwiches, in salads, and as an after-dinner cheese with fruit and nuts. It is also a good cooking and melting cheese and is traditionally used in FONDUE. Gruyère-style cheeses are made in various countries, including Australia.

guacamole is a dip or spread made from very ripe avocado mashed with chopped onion, tomato, and chilli together with lemon juice, salt and pepper, and sometimes other ingredients. It is traditionally served as a dip with TORTILLAS or NACHOS chips, as a sauce with TACOS, and as a dressing for tomatoes and green salad.

guard of honour. See 'Loin', under LAMB.

guava. Originally from tropical South America, guavas are grown commercially in northern Australia and are available intermittently throughout the year. The small, round or fig-shaped fruit has a thin, smooth yellow-green skin, pink flesh with small edible seeds and a sweet aroma. Allow guavas to ripen at room temperature—they turn yellow and soften as they ripen—then store them in the refrigerator. They can be peeled and eaten fresh out of the hand or in a bowl with cream, added to fruit salads or fruit platters, and made into guava jelly, which is used as a spread on toast or as a garnish for meat or game. Guavas contain more vitamin C than any other commonly available fruit and are high in fibre.

White guavas, popular in South-East Asia, have white flesh and remain green-skinned and hard when ripe. They can be eaten like an apple, unpeeled.

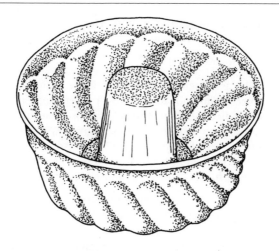

gugelhupf / gugelhopf / kougelhopf / gouglof, etc. A tall, sugar-dusted cake with fluted sides and a hole in the middle. The gugelhupf is extremely popular in Austria, Germany, and Alsace, where there are as many varieties of the recipe as there are variations of the spelling of the name. What has come to be regarded as the traditional version is made with a sweet yeast dough filled with sultanas. Blanched almonds are often set in the top of the cake. It is cooked in a mould with slanting, furrowed sides and a central funnel through which the oven's heat penetrates the cake's centre.

gumbo. Another name for OKRA. Gumbo is also the name given by the Creoles and Cajuns of Louisiana to a soup or stew usually thickened with okra. There are many variations, but it is commonly made with chicken or seafood flavoured with onions, garlic, capsicums, tomatoes, herbs, and various spicy seasonings including *filé* (powdered dried sassafras leaves), which is itself a thickening agent and may be used in place of okra.

haggis. Robert Burns called it 'great chieftain o' the puddin' race', and his memory is honoured each year with the piping-in of the haggis at Burns Night celebrations around the world.

This national dish of Scotland is made from the liver, lungs and heart of a sheep, which are cooked and then chopped and mixed with suet, onions, oatmeal, herbs, and seasonings. The cleansed stomach bag of the sheep is half-filled with this mixture and sewn up. Then the bag is put in a pot of boiling water and cooked for three hours. Haggis is traditionally served hot with mashed potatoes and turnips.

hake. Another name for GEMFISH.

haloumy. A Middle Eastern cheese originally made with ewe's milk, the curd being cut into pieces and cooked in its own whey (see CHEESE). The pieces of cooked curd are flattened out, sprinkled with dried mint or cumin seeds, folded in three, and then matured in brine. Cow's milk is also used to make the cheese, which is often home-made in Cyprus, Lebanon, and Syria. Haloumy is a fairly firm cheese which is often grilled and fried in olive oil. It is also eaten with bread or biscuits and added to green salads.

halva comes from an Arabic word meaning sweet and is applied to various Middle Eastern sweets and puddings made from SEMOLINA, RICE FLOUR, or FARINA with oil and sugar, flavoured with nuts, fruit, chocolate, spices, or flower petals. The halva you are likely to find in Australia is made from crushed sesame seeds and sugar, glucose or honey, and halva root, an extract from the root of a Mediterranean tree, which gives halva its characteristic light, crunchy texture. It can be eaten with after-dinner coffee and also as a spread.

ham. A ham is the hind leg of a pig, although the word *ham* usually refers to a leg that has been cured in some way, a fresh ham being referred to as a leg of pork. (Pigs are raised for one purpose or the other: 'porkers' to be sold as pork, 'baconers' for curing into bacon and ham.) A ham can be cured in many individual ways. However, the popular leg ham 'on the bone' is first injected with a sweet-flavoured brine, allowed to marinate for several hours, and then smoked. After smoking, the ham is partially or fully cooked by boiling or steaming. A fully cooked ham is ready to eat, although it may still be cooked in some way; a ham that is partially cooked should be baked or boiled until the internal temperature reaches 76°C before it is served, either hot or cold.

Some hams are given a second smoking, which produces a richer flavour and a firmer texture for cutting. Others are not smoked at all, just salt-cured. These are sometimes known as GAMMON, and are usually boneless. Smoked hams are also available boneless and compacted into a flat or round shape. Some forms of ham, such as PROSCIUTTO and COPPA, are meant to be eaten raw.

To prepare and store ham. For a commercially produced ham on the bone or boneless ham, the Australian Pork Corporation recommends the following: Remove the bag or wrapping, and wipe the ham with a clean cloth. Loosen the rind around the edge, then pull it off in one piece. Trim off the layer of surface fat (you can render this down into lard or use it to wrap pieces of lean meat for roasting). Put the ham on a tray or platter, preferably with a rack so that air can circulate underneath it, and cover it with a clean tea-towel or a light cloth bag (a clean cotton pillowcase is handy for this) that has been dipped in a solution of 2 cups of water and 1 teaspoon of vinegar and squeezed out. Replace this vinegar cloth or bag every three days with a fresh one. Store the ham in the coolest part of the refrigerator; it will keep for up to three weeks. Some people use a fold of fat as well as a cloth to keep the ham fresh.

To carve a ham. First cut a slice off the underside parallel to the bone to allow the ham to sit flat. Holding the shank with one hand, make a cut straight down to the bone near the shank end; make a second cut a little higher up, slanting it to meet the first cut at the bone. Remove the wedge formed and discard it (it is mostly fat). With a long, thin, sharp knife, start carving thin slices parallel to the angled cut. Some people lift each slice off as they carve it; others make a number of cuts down to the bone and then cut along the bone to remove the slices. When you reach the middle or broadest part of the ham, start carving alternately from one side and the other—in other words, half slices, because a whole slice would be too big to fit on a plate. When the top is carved, turn the ham over and carve it parallel to the bone.

hamburger. An American creation, the hamburger has nothing to do with ham and little if anything to do with the German city of Hamburg. According to H. L. Mencken in *The American Language,* the minced beef that now goes into a hamburger was known in the nineteenth century as hamburg steak 'and was served like any other steak, not in the form of a sandwich . . . By 1889 it had become *hamburger steak,* and soon afterward it degenerated from the estate of a steak to that of a sandwich and became a simple *hamburger.*' Apparently the early American hamburgers were made with slices of bread or toast rather than a bun, and inside was only the patty of cooked minced beef, with perhaps a slice of raw onion. The early Australian hamburger had shredded lettuce, a slice each of tomato and beetroot, tomato sauce, and fried onions with the minced beef. A fried egg was an optional extra, and the lot was held between the toasted halves of a bun more substantial than the cake-like buns nowadays supplied with the assembly-line product from the hamburger specialty chains. The additional fillings have varied over the years—pickles, cheese, pineapple, bacon, and so on as well as those already mentioned.

hard sauce. Brandy butter or rum butter is a more descriptive term than hard sauce for this simple garnish, which is made by creaming butter with castor sugar or brown sugar flavoured with brandy or rum (or lemon juice for total abstainers). Hard sauce is kept refrigerated until it is to be used, mostly for a Christmas pudding or other rich pudding, when pieces of it are cut off, shaped, and served.

hare. 'First catch your hare,' some ignorant reviewer misquoted the eighteenth-century cookery writer Hannah Glasse, and so the saying has gone ever since. (What she wrote was 'Take your hare when it is cased', meaning skinned.) First order your hare from a specialist supplier would be more in keeping nowadays. A young hare preferably, one that has not yet developed the distinctive harelip, which is hardly noticeable until about a year old. Hares are usually either roasted (marinated first if old) or jugged. In the original method of jugging, the jointed hare was placed in a jug with herbs, spices, and port and the jug put in boiling water to cook. Now the pieces are braised with vegetables and herbs in a red-wine sauce, with some of the hare's blood added at the last moment if you are a purist.

haricot beans. Like black and red kidney beans, borlotti beans, cannellini beans, and pinto beans, haricot beans are the dried, kidney-shaped seeds of a variety of the green bean plant, *Phaseolus vulgaris.* They are white, smaller than cannellinis, and are also called **navy beans** (and used for canned baked beans), **soissons,** and, in a semi-dried state, **flageolets.** Information on preparation, storage, etc., is given under BEANS, DRIED.

To cook haricot beans, boil them gently until they are tender (1–1½ hours) or pressure cook them for 15–20 minutes. They are traditionally used in making CASSOULET and Boston BAKED BEANS.

harissa / hrisa. This fiery paste is used to flavour almost everything except sweet dishes in North Africa. The combination of spices that go into harissa vary from country to country, but the main one is dried red chilli. Harissa is available from specialist food shops and will keep for up to two months in the refrigerator. Covering the top with a little olive oil every time you spoon some out will stop the remainder from drying out. You can make your own harissa by mixing together 2 tablespoons each of chilli powder, ground cumin, tomato paste, and olive oil with 1 teaspoon of salt. Serve it with COUSCOUS.

hash. One of the drawbacks of eating processed and take-away foods is that you don't have leftovers to make hash. Leftover corned beef or roast lamb can be turned quickly into a satisfying extra meal by chopping it into small cubes (*hash* comes from the French *hacher*, 'to chop') and frying it with chopped potatoes and onions and perhaps other vegetables. The Swedes add a delicious finishing touch: they mix a raw egg yolk into each serving of the hot hash when it is about to be served.

hazelnut. Native to Europe and North America, where the cultivated nut is known as a filbert, the hazelnut can be eaten raw or roasted and is used in cakes, puddings, breads, ice-cream, desserts, and in soup with Jerusalem artichokes. Hazelnuts may be ground into a meal and used in place of flour and fat in making pastry and cakes. They are an excellent source of vitamin E. Like other nuts, they have a high oil content, but it is 92 per cent unsaturated (82 per cent mono, 10 per cent poly). Just the same, they supply lots of kilojoules. (See also NUTS.)

Though the skin is usually eaten and adds to the flavour of the nut, it can be removed by lightly toasting the nuts under the griller or in the oven until the skins are loose, then rubbing them between your hands until the skins fall off.

head cheese. Another name for BRAWN.

hearts. For the most part, hearts are used as pet food. However, lamb, calf, and ox hearts can be cooked, usually braised or casseroled. First remove outside fat, trim off lobes and flaps, and soak the hearts in ACIDULATED WATER or a MARINADE. Hearts are also stuffed and roasted.

herbs. Individual herbs are dealt with separately in their alphabetical order. Information on herbs in general is given here to avoid repetition.

When to add herbs. For foods that take a long time to cook, add selected herbs or a BOUQUET GARNI during the last hour of cooking. With quickly cooked foods, add the herbs with the other ingredients. Basil, however, should only be added towards the end of cooking, and chives are almost always scattered over hot dishes or mixed into salads just before serving. Mint is added to peas and new potatoes at the beginning of cooking, and a few extra sprigs can be added for the last few minutes to give a fresh mint flavour.

Dry or fresh? Fresh herbs are best to use in most recipes, but dried herbs can be substituted if fresh are unavailable. As dried herbs are more concentrated than fresh, you need to use half the quantity or less. Some cooks tell you to soak dried herbs in a little milk before adding them.

To dry herbs. Spread fresh herbs on some kitchen paper or aluminium foil on a baking tray and leave them in the oven on its lowest setting for 12 hours or until the leaves are brittle, then take them out and allow them to cool. If you are fortunate to live in a place with unpolluted air, you can hang the herbs for a week or two in a cool, dry, airy position. In either case, remove the leaves from the stalks when they are dry and put them in airtight containers to store.

To store herbs. Fresh herbs will keep for a fortnight in the refrigerator. Wash and dry them first, then wrap them loosely in kitchen paper and put them in an airtight container. They can also be frozen: wash and blanch the freshest leaves, dry them in a clean tea-towel, and seal them in plastic or foil packages of recipe size. Dried herbs should be kept in screw-top jars or other airtight containers away from light. They do not last indefinitely, so sniff them from time to time, and if they are losing their punch, throw them out and buy some more.

herrings used to be so abundant in the North Sea that it was inconceivable that their stocks could be diminished by fishing fleets. That was before modern technology. For periods of years herring fishing has been almost halted to allow exhausted stocks to revive. Although there are species of herring found in Australian waters, they have not been exploited commercially to a great extent. Herrings are available pickled or soused, as ROLL-MOPS, and as KIPPERS.

hibachi. A Japanese-style barbecue. Hibachis are small, black, cast-iron troughs—round, square, or rectangular—with wooden-handled grilling irons on top. They stand low on the ground and can be used on a garden wall or steps or on a tabletop. Draught vents in the sides of the trough allow the heat to be adjusted. (See also BARBECUING.)

hoisin sauce. A sweet, spicy, reddish-brown sauce made from fermented soy beans, garlic, sugar, and spices. It is used in Chinese cooking to marinate meat and poultry for roasting, to flavour stir-fries, as a dip or sauce for grilled and roasted foods, and as the sauce with PEKING DUCK.

hollandaise sauce. One of the great basic sauces, hollandaise is a rich mixture of butter and egg yolks seasoned with lemon juice and salt and pepper. Elizabeth David feels that this is apt to be insipid and suggests beginning with some greatly reduced white wine or vinegar and water (so does Escoffier). The egg yolks are whisked into this reduction, and then the butter is gradually added. This is done in a double saucepan over gentle heat. Like

MAYONNAISE, hollandaise is an emulsion, and care must be taken to prevent it from curdling. The sauce is served warm, traditionally with asparagus but also with other vegetables, fish, and chicken.

honey is probably the original sweetener; it has certainly been used since the dawn of time. Honey varies in colour and consistency depending on the blossoms from which the bees extract the nectar to convert to honey. Most honey is sold in a clear liquid form that has been strained and heat-treated before packaging. Candied and creamed honey are also available.

Store honey at room temperature. Liquid honey may granulate after standing for some time. If this happens, take the lid off the jar and stand the jar in hot water until the crystals dissolve and the honey liquefies again.

honeydew melons are oval in shape and have a smooth, creamy-yellow skin and sweet, delicate green flesh. They are available all year round, with heaviest supplies in late summer. Choose melons with a good creamy colour and a fragrant aroma, as melons do not ripen further after picking. Store at room temperature for up to a fortnight. Eat them as you would rockmelons.

hors d'oeuvres. Like the Italian ANTIPASTO, the French term *hors d'oeuvre* ('outside the work') refers to food served at the beginning of a meal, or with drinks before a meal, to whet the appetite. CAVIAR, CANAPÉS, CRUDITÉS, PÂTÉS and dips, ANCHOVIES, savoury pastry, and the like are served as hors d'oeuvres.

horseradish is a perennial herb cultivated for its thick, whitish, pungent roots, which are grated or shredded and mixed with vinegar and other ingredients to make a hot condiment or sauce. Horseradish is served with roast beef, pork, poultry, cold meats, and shellfish. Prepared horseradish is always available in jars.

hotpot. A Lancashire hotpot is like an Irish stew. Neck of mutton and / or mutton chops are cooked with some onions in a casserole dish with slices of potato on the bottom and the top. More elaborate versions of hotpot include mushrooms, kidneys, and oysters, with perhaps three layers of sliced potato.

huevos rancheros. Ranch-style eggs, a famous Mexican dish of fried eggs served on tortillas surrounded with a hot sauce of tomatoes, capsicums or chillies, garlic, and onions. The eggs are often cooked in depressions made in the simmering sauce and garnished with sliced avocado.

hummus bi tahina. *Hummus* is the Arabic word for chickpeas; *tahina* is a paste made from crushed sesame seeds. In combination they make a savoury dip / spread that is probably the best-known Middle Eastern hors d'oeuvre. The chickpeas are soaked, cooked, and puréed. This purée is mixed with crushed garlic, lemon juice, and the tahina paste, and the creamy mixture is poured into a bowl with a dribble of olive oil and paprika and a scattering of chopped parsley to decorate the top. Hummus bi tahina is served with Lebanese bread or as an accompaniment to cold meats.

I

ice-cream. Whether it was the Tuscans, the Neapolitans, or the Sicilians who invented ice-cream in the sixteenth or seventeenth century (or the Chinese thousands of years before), it has turned out to be an extremely popular invention, especially with Australians, who consume about 18 litres of ice-cream per head a year, second only to the Americans, who get through 22 litres. Commercially produced ice-creams are often made from synthetic ingredients, but the premium commercial ice-creams contain the basic natural ingredients—cream, milk, egg yolks, and sugar. An important constituent is air; without it, ice-cream would be like an iceblock.

Home-made ice-cream is not hard to make, especially with the modern equipment available. Old-style manual ice-cream makers required a bucket of crushed ice and salt (to lower the temperature of the ice) and 20 minutes of hand cranking to swirl the mixture round a stationary paddle. Electric machines, called sorbetières, are small enough to fit into the refrigerator freezing compartment, and the flat flex fits through the rubber seal on the freezer door to the power point. Paddles on the motor stir the mixture. Once the ice-cream is frozen, the paddles lift out and the power switches off. You can even make ice-cream in the ice trays in your freezer if you have a custardy mixture that is well beaten and cooked to thicken.

icing. The simplest decoration for a cake is icing sugar dredged through a fine-mesh sieve.

To prepare glacé icing, add water to sieved icing sugar and mix until the desired consistency is obtained. Usually a little flavouring is added— vanilla essence, lemon juice, rum or a liqueur, coffee, or cocoa. Glacé icing is suitable for light cakes and biscuits, but it must be used quickly and lasts for only a few days before it cracks.

Royal icing, or glacé royale, makes a harder and longer-lasting covering. It is a mixture of egg-white, icing sugar, and lemon juice, with some food colouring if needed.

Boiled icing is made by boiling sugar, water, and a pinch of cream of tartar to soft-ball stage (see SUGAR SYRUP), then whisking in some beaten egg-white. Boiled icing has a rough finish when spread on a cake.

Fondant icing, or sugar paste, can be rolled out to cover cakes. It is firm but pliable and is also used for moulding decorations. Colours can be kneaded into it.

MARZIPAN, or almond paste, is used to cover fruit cakes before the icing is added, to prevent the icing from being discoloured by the cake.

Some of the butter creams and other cake fillings may also be spread or piped on the top of the cakes. Another simple topping is flavoured and sweetened whipped cream.

Before a cake is covered with a firm icing or with chocolate or marzipan,

117

it should be spread with a strained apricot-jam glaze. This forms a bond joining the two different textures and prevents the icing from cracking and breaking away from the cake in pieces.

icing sugar, also known as confectioner's sugar, is a finely ground, powdered white sugar which is used for making cake icing. It is also used in cooking when sugar is required to dissolve quickly. Pure icing sugar turns lumpy when stored for a long time, so manufacturers produce an icing sugar mixture which has a small amount of cornflour or other substance in it to prevent it from caking. But it also prevents royal icing (see ICING) from holding its shape, so only pure icing sugar should be used for making royal icing. Storing icing sugar in the refrigerator will help prevent it from going hard or lumpy.

Indian fig. The Indian fig, or cactus berry, is the fruit of the prickly pear. Not, we are assured, the dreaded prickly pear that caused devastation in Australia after it was introduced in the early colonial days to provide food for the cochineal insect, which was used to produce red dye for the soldiers' coats. Indian figs are available from December to March. The fruit is yellow-orange to red-purple in colour and covered with fine bristles that are hard to remove. It must be handled with care. Rubber gloves and tongs are recommended. Cut off the top first, then slice downwards to remove the skin. The flesh may be white, pink, yellow, orange, or red. It is sweet tasting, and the seeds, if any, are edible.

infuse, steep. Both words mean to soak something in a hot liquid to extract its essence or flavour. The most common infusion is tea, though we're just as likely to say brew as infuse or steep when we make tea.

Irish stew is made with neck or loin or mutton (or lamb) trimmed of fat and cut into cubes and cooked in a covered casserole between layers of sliced potatoes and sliced onions. Water, pepper, and salt are the only other ingredients. Irish stew is traditionally accompanied with pickled red cabbage.

J

jaboticaba. Also known as the Brazilian tree grape, the jaboticaba is native to Brazil, grows on a tree that can reach a height of ten metres, and resembles a large black grape or a small dark purple plum. It has a tough, thick skin and a sweet, juicy, pinkish-translucent flesh with one to four seeds. The taste is something like a grape, and the fruit is used in Brazil for making wine. Jaboticabas are grown commercially in Australia and are available mainly in summer, though trees can bear fruit throughout the year. Store jaboticabas in a covered container in the refrigerator, where they will keep for up to a fortnight. Eat them out of the hand or in a fruit salad.

jalapeño. Many years ago, people used to take a purgative known as jalap (pronounced 'jollop'). It was obtained from the root of a Mexican plant and named after the city of Jalapa in eastern Mexico. Someone or something native to Jalapa is referred to as jalapeño (pronounced roughly 'halapenyo'), and the culinary jalapeño best known these days is a small, grass-green smooth-skinned chilli. Though considered relatively hot to the general palate, jalapeños are quite low on the various scales used by growers and canners of chillis to rate their pungency or heat. They are sometimes available fresh, otherwise preserved in jars and cans.

jam. 'Money for jam' would lead you to think jam required little effort to make. Although jam-making is not hard once you get the hang of it, there are a few things to remember and some effort needed to produce a well-set finished product with a fine colour.

Jam is made essentially from fruit and sugar, with added water if there's not enough juice in the fruit. PECTIN is essential for the jam to set properly. Some fruits are high in pectin—cooking apples, plums, citrus fruits, and grapes, for example. Other fruits, such as apricots, peaches, cherries, blackberries, raspberries and strawberries, melons, and figs, are low in pectin, so more has to be added. Commercial pectin can be used, but lemon juice (and peel and pips) will do as well.

Sugar preserves the fruit and enables it to set. Too little sugar will prevent the jam from setting; too much will darken the jam. As a rule, in jam making the fruit is given a long and slow cooking, with a stir from time to time, before the sugar is added. Once the sugar has dissolved, the jam is cooked hard and fast, with little or no stirring, until the setting point is reached.

There are three ways to determine the setting point:

1. Drop a little jam on a cold saucer. As the jam cools, it should wrinkle rather than roll if you push it with your finger, and the jam should stick to the saucer when you turn it upside down.
2. Dip a wooden spoon in the jam. Lift it out, and turn it sideways; if the jam is at the setting point, it should fall off the spoon in heavy flakes.
3. Use a sugar / jam thermometer. The temperature should be 105°C.

As soon as the setting point is reached, take the saucepan off the heat and let it stand for 10–15 minutes to allow the fruit to distribute evenly. Skim off any scum. Before you bottle the jam, sterilise the jars by heating them in a low oven for half an hour. Fill the jars to the top, as jam shrinks as it cools. Get rid of any air bubbles, which could harbour bacteria. Cover the jars with screw tops, cellophane, or a layer of melted paraffin wax.

jambalaya. A Louisiana Creole and Cajun dish of rice cooked with such things as smoked pork sausage or ham, capsicums, shrimps, tomatoes, onion, garlic, and seasonings, garnished with parsley. A chicken jambalaya can be made by substituting chicken thighs for the shrimps.

Jarlsberg is the Norwegian version of Emmental—a firm, rich yellow cheese with large holes—but it has a more delicate taste than Emmental and a rubbery texture. (See also CHEESE.)

jelly. 'It must be jelly, 'cause jam don't shake like that,' the old jazz song explains. The other difference between jam and jelly is that jelly is made with the strained juice of cooked fruit rather than fruit pulp (see JAM). The juice is strained through a JELLY BAG and then boiled with sugar. The pectin in the fruit sets the liquid into a clear, soft, elastic preparation for using as a spread.

Another kind of jelly, also made with fruit juice (or wine) but set with gelatine, is firmed in a mould and eaten as a dessert. This jelly can also be made with commercially prepared jelly crystals. Boiling water is poured over the flavoured crystals to dissolve them; the liquid is allowed to cool and then put in the refrigerator to set.

To make it in a hurry, dissolve the crystals in a cup of hot water and add a cup of cold water or, for quicker results, ice cubes.

To unmould a jelly, stand the mould in a bowl of hot water for a few moments and then turn it out onto a plate. Rinsing the mould in cold water and coating it with salad oil before adding the jelly liquid will make the jelly drop out easily and give it a sheen. If you rinse the plate in cold water before turning the jelly out, the jelly will slide to where you want it by tilting the plate.

Jelly can also be obtained by boiling bones and tissues rich in gelatinous matter, such as calf's foot or pig's trotters and cheek, skimming off the scum and allowing the rest to cool and set. This jelly is used for garnishing various dishes and for glazing hams, tongues, and other meats.

A well-made CONSOMMÉ will often set into a natural light jelly which can be served as the first course of a summer meal.

jelly bag. To make fruit jellies or wines, the juice of the fruit, cooked or raw, has to be extracted without pressure in order to get clear, pure juice. The best way to do this is to put the fruit pulp in a cloth jelly bag, hang it up, and let the juice drip through slowly into a container below. This may take all night, but on no account must the bag be squeezed to hasten the flow, or the juice will become cloudy.

Jelly bags are made of very closely woven fabric; the finer the mesh, the clearer the juice. The bags have loops at the top to hook over a special frame or, for improvisers, onto the legs of an upturned stool. A jelly bag should be scalded before using. Not only does this sterilise the bag, but the water soaks into the very absorbent cloth and prevents the loss of too much juice.

If you haven't a jelly bag, a reasonable substitute can be made by lining a colander with three layers of muslin or a clean linen tea-towel. Place the colander over a large bowl. You could also tie the muslin or tea-towel to the legs of the stool.

jerky, also called jerked beef, is meat that has been cut into long strips and dried in the sun and wind or cured by smoking. It is very tough, dry, and unattractive; its great advantage is that it will keep for years. Jerky can be grated or sliced and eaten raw. The name is a corruption of *charqui*, the Chilean word for the same thing. It is also known by its South African name, biltong. An Australian version of jerky is made from emu meat. It has a strong, smoky flavour.

Jerusalem artichoke. This gnarled and knobbly tuber has nothing to do with Jerusalem (it originated in America) or with the globe artichoke. The Jerusalem part is a corruption of the Italian *girasole,* meaning 'sunflower'— the tuber's flower turns towards the sun. It's called an artichoke, it seems, because of its similarity in flavour to the globe artichoke. (In early spring, when their seasons overlap, they can be satisfyingly sautéed together in olive oil.)

Jerusalem artichokes are in season from autumn to spring but at their best in early winter. Select large, firm tubers with the fewest knobs, so that they are less of a nuisance to peel. Store them in the refrigerator crisper or in a cool, dry place. They are usually boiled, sliced, and served in a white sauce with parsley. But they can also be sliced and sautéed, or mashed with potatoes. They make a thick winter soup with onions and milk. Some people eat them finely sliced and raw, like radishes.

As their flesh discolours when exposed to air, peeled or sliced Jerusalem artichokes should be dropped in ACIDULATED WATER if they are not cooked immediately. A little lemon juice added to the water when they are boiled also prevents them from discolouring.

Jerusalem artichokes are apt to cause flatulence, especially when eaten raw. Long cooking lessens the problem. They contain a lot of iron and few kilojoules.

jewfish. See MULLOWAY and WESTRALIAN JEWFISH.

john dory. See DORY.

johnny cake. A small, thin damper, not much bigger than a scone, made of flour and water and cooked on both sides in the ashes of a fire or in a camp oven.

joint. A joint is any of the portions into which an animal carcase is divided by a butcher for cooking. Generally it refers to a shoulder or leg used for roasting.

To joint poultry is to divide a bird into serving pieces either before or after cooking. (See 'Jointing' under CHICKEN.)

julienne. Whoever Julienne was (or perhaps it was Jules or Julien), she (or he) liked to cut food, especially vegetables, into very thin strips. The length of julienne strips is a moot point. Some authorities are quite precise: about 5–7.5 centimetres, or the length of a matchstick. Others simply say short. Others still, just to be contrary, specify long, thin strips, while the non-committal simply go for thin strips. The thickness can be as precise as 3 millimetres square or as loose as 'it depends on the dish and use'.

Potatoes, carrots, capsicums, and beans are common vegetables that are 'julienned'. The strips are often used as a garnish.

A CONSOMMÉ garnished with strips of julienne vegetables is known as a julienne.

juniper berries are the main flavouring ingredient of gin, especially Hollands gin. (The word *gin* comes from *genever,* an old Dutch word for juniper.)

These hard, bluish-black, aromatic berries grow on a prickly evergreen tree and take two years to mature. Dried whole berries are obtainable from herb and spice suppliers. They are used in game dishes, in stews, with red cabbage and sauerkraut, in marinades, and in stuffings for chicken and other poultry. The berries are usually crushed with a rolling pin or the back of a spoon before use.

junket is milk that has been transformed into CURD by the addition of RENNET in the form of junket tablets. The milk is often sweetened with sugar and flavoured with vanilla or other flavouring. Junket tablets are available already flavoured. Junket is served as a dessert, sometimes with a topping of whipped cream, fresh strawberries or other fruit, candied orange peel, meringue, grated nutmeg, etc.

To prepare junket, dissolve a junket tablet, or tablets, in a little cold water, and gently heat the milk to lukewarm (milk straight out of the cow used to be considered ideal). Stir in the dissolved junket tablets, then quickly pour the warm liquid into individual serving dishes. Leave them to stand undisturbed in a warm place for about 15 minutes, when the junket should be set, then put them in the refrigerator until ready to serve.

Long-life milk and some milk powders may not set into junket. Homogenised milk usually needs double the amount of junket tablets—that is, 2 tablets for half a litre of milk, rather than the 1 tablet for ordinary milk.

junket tablets are essentially RENNET compressed into tablet form. Plain (unflavoured) tablets are used not only for making junket but also for curdling milk to make cottage cheese and cream cheese. A dissolved junket tablet added to a glass of cold milk makes the milk much easier to digest.

K

Kaffir lime leaves. The Kaffir lime is a member of the citrus family with leaves that are rich in aromatic oils. Fresh leaves, and also the zest of the fruit, are used in Asian cooking, especially by the Thais, but they are not always available in Australia. Dried leaves, however, are obtainable in Asian food shops. When dried leaves are used in casseroles or dishes with a fair amount of liquid and a cooking time of more than a few minutes, they can be added as they are. Otherwise they need to be soaked in warm water for 5–10 minutes to reconstitute them. You can then slice the leaves, which some recipes require. Kaffir lime leaves are used in soups, sambals, curries, and fish dishes.

kalamansi is a small citrus fruit, something like a cumquat, with yellow-orange flesh and an acid but flavoursome juice. It is native to the Philippines, where it is used extensively in cooking. The juice is the basis of some of the popular cocktails served in Asian bars. Kalamansi juice is available, canned or bottled, from Asian food stores in Australia.

kale / cole / borecole. One of the many varieties of cabbage *(Brassica oleracea)*, kale does not form a solid head or heart like an ordinary cabbage but produces its coarse leaves on a central, upright stem. Curly kale has crimped leaves and is better tasting than the smooth-leaved kind. Kale is rich in vitamins and minerals, especially vitamins A and C and calcium. Cook as for cabbage.

kangaroo. High in protein, low in fat and cholesterol, kangaroo meat is healthy to eat as well as versatile to cook. It is available in various cuts, including saddle, leg, rack, rump, topside, round, and silverside, and in steaks, fillets, diced meat, or mince. It can be roasted, grilled, pan-fried, stir-fried, barbe-cued, cooked in a casserole, and of course made into kangaroo-tail soup. It also goes well smoked and served like prosciutto. Seared kangaroo with batterd baby beetroots has been suggested as a contender for Australia's national dish. Kangaroo is less dense than beef and has the flavour of young venison.

There are a few things to remember when cooking kangaroo meat. Have the meat at room temperature before cooking. Always brush it with olive oil, and perhaps some cracked pepper, before frying, baking, or barbecuing; marinating is not recommended. The meat should be cooked quickly at a high temperature and should not be overcooked; rare to medium is best. Allow the meat to rest before serving it: larger cuts like rump and topside for 5–10 minutes, leg and saddle for at least 15 minutes.

Bear in mind that kangaroo meat oxidises quickly. Once the cryovac (vacuum) pack is opened the meat will soon turn dark, so you should buy the amount you need for one meal and cook the meat as soon as you take it out of the pack.

kebab / kebob / kabob. Kebab is the Turkish word for lamb or mutton. A shish kebab, possibly the best-known of all Turkish dishes, consists of chunks of lamb grilled on a skewer (shish comes from the Turkish word for skewer or sword). In Australia, kebab and shish kebab are more or less synonymous, and the meat on the skewer may be beef, veal, pork, chicken, or fish as well as lamb, the chunks alternating with pieces of onion, tomato, capsicum, mushroom, and other vegetables and fruit. The meat is usually marinated before cooking.

kedgeree. This is a dish the English picked up from the Indians during the days of the raj and adapted to their own taste. The Western version is made with cooked, boned, and flaked fish (smoked or white or a mixture of both), mixed into cooked unpolished rice together with hard-boiled egg, cream or butter, and seasonings.

khoresh. The name for any of a multitude of sauces (almost stews) served on rice and eaten every day in Iran. These sauces are made with cubed meat or poultry and vegetables, fruit, nuts, herbs, and spices—almost anything in season and available at the market—sautéed in butter, then, after a little water is added, allowed to cook gently for a long time.

kid. See GOAT MEAT.

kidney beans. Like borlotti beans, cannellini beans, haricot beans, and pinto beans, kidney beans are the dried seeds of a variety of the green bean plant, *Phaseolus vulgaris.* There are two kinds, black and red, both native to the Americas, where they are a staple food item, but the black kidney bean is not generally available in Australia. Red kidney beans are probably best known as an essential ingredient in CHILLI CON CARNE and FRIJOLES REFRI-TOS. They may be used in place of borlotti beans and pinto beans. For information on preparation, storage, etc., see BEANS, DRIED.

To cook red kidney beans, boil them gently for 1–1½ hours with 10 minutes of rapid boiling at the end of cooking time, or pressure cook for 20–30 minutes.

kidneys. The kidneys of sheep, cattle, and pigs, though classed as offal, are good to eat and a rich source of protein and iron. Kidneys are encased in a layer of fat (suet) which is usually removed by the butcher. Before cooking, the covering membrane should be slit and removed and the hard core cut out. Lamb's kidneys need only be split in half; calf's and ox kidneys, which have many lobes, are usually cut in slices or small pieces.

Soak kidneys in cold water for a few minutes before cooking. The highly flavoured ox kidneys need longer soaking, with some vinegar in the water. They are usually braised or cooked in a steak and kidney pie. Lamb's and calf's kidneys may be fried, grilled, or roasted. A mustard sauce is a popular accompaniment. Pig's kidneys are larger than lamb's and have a stronger flavour, but they too may be grilled or fried.

kilojoules are what we used to call calories, the energy value of food. The energy contained in the food we eat is used up by our bodies in exercise and through our own particular metabolism; what we don't use up is stored by the body as fat, for use in lean times. When you don't experience lean times and don't use up the energy in some way, you put on more fat. If that worries you, eat food that has fewer kilojoules or exercise more.

kingfish. See YELLOWTAIL KINGFISH and MULLOWAY.

kippers. A kippered fish is one that has been split open and cured by salting and drying or smoking. What is normally referred to as a kipper is a kippered herring. Imported whole kippers are available in Australia, as are kipper fillets canned in brine. Kippers may be eaten cold with salad or grilled with a lump of butter on top. To keep them moist when grilling, put a tablespoon or two of water in the pan under them.

The canned fillets also may be grilled, or they may be heated in the can by putting it in boiling water and simmering for a few minutes. You have to careful opening the can after heating it; put it in cold water for a few seconds and cover it with a cloth while you break the seal.

kiwano. Also known as the African horned melon, the kiwano looks like a squat yellow cucumber with spikes. It is indeed a member of the cucumber family but is regarded more as a kind of fruit, not eaten out of the hand but sliced or cubed in fruit salad. It is also added to green salad and may be served with smoked salmon or trout, or as a purée or sauce.

kiwi fruit. Originally known as Chinese gooseberry (it is a native of China), this brown, fuzzy, egg-shaped fruit was given such a successful promotional campaign by New Zealand growers and exporters that it has become known as kiwi fruit throughout much of the world. It is also grown in Australia and is available all year round, with heaviest supplies from May to October. Select plump, firm fruit that yield to gentle pressure. Hard fruit can be ripened at room temperature, then stored in the refrigerator for a week or two.

Once the fruit's furry overcoat is removed, the bright green flesh with the small black, edible seeds can be sliced or diced and added to fruit salads or fruit and cheese platters, used as a garnish for desserts, and puréed to use as a cake filling. You can also cut the unpeeled fruit in half and eat the flesh with a spoon.

Kiwi fruit are rich in vitamin C—one will supply your daily needs—and low in kilojoules. They also contain an enzyme that acts as a meat tenderiser; rub the flesh over meat just before cooking.

kneading. The purpose of kneading is to work dough into a uniform mass and join the gluten particles in the dough into an elastic skin or web to hold in place the tiny bubbles of carbon dioxide gas freed by the yeast, which keep the dough aerated. To do all this by hand takes time and effort. Begin by flouring your hands so that they don't stick to the dough. Flatten the dough on a lightly floured board, then lift the end farthest from you and fold the dough over itself. Press down on it with the heels of your hands, pushing the dough away from you. Give the dough a quarter turn, fold it back on itself again, press and push. Keep doing this until the dough is smooth and elastic. It will take 5–10 minutes, with fifty or more folds and presses. Keep you hands and the board lightly floured.

knives. To work efficiently, a cook needs at least four knives:

1. A chef's knife (also called cook's knife and French knife). These knives have a strong, broad, pointed blade with an edge that is straight from the heel to about half way along the blade and then curves gently to the point. They come in various sizes; one between 18 and 23 centimetres would be suitable. Chef's knives are used for chopping, mincing, slicing, dicing, cutting up a chicken, smashing garlic with the flat of the blade—in other words the workhorse knife.
2. A 26-centimetre slicing knife for carving and slicing hot or cold cooked meat and poultry.
3. A 20-centimetre filleting knife, not only for filleting fish but for cutting thin slices of raw meat for escalopes and for intricate slicing and cutting.
4. A 7-centimetre paring knife for peeling fruit and potatoes, trimming vegetables, etc.

You will, of course, also need a serrated-edged bread knife. A vegetable peeler, or swivel-bladed paring knife, is also useful.

Keep your knives sharp. Sharpening steels, made from a harder steel than that used for knife blades and grooved so that they act like a file, are

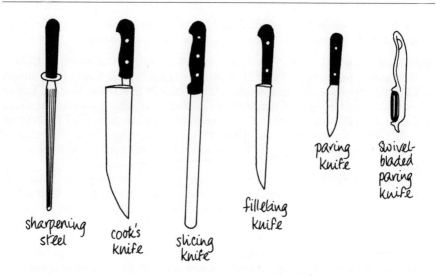

sharpening steel   cook's knife   slicing knife   filleting knife   paring knife   swivel-bladed paring knife

traditionally used for regular sharpening. However, they require a knack to use them properly. Patent sharpeners that require only the knife blade to be drawn through a slot make knife sharpening possible for those who can't master the art of using a steel. A good honing with an oilstone three or four times a year will keep a knife really sharp. Always wipe a knife after using it. Clean knives stay sharper; acid material dulls the edge.

kohlrabi means cabbage turnip, and this mutant variety of the cabbage has a turnip-like purple or green root (actually a swollen stem which grows just above the ground). Although the young leaves can be cooked like spinach, the root is the better part. It resembles a turnip in flavour and is best when young and small; it becomes coarse and fibrous as it gets older and bigger. Small ones can be cooked whole; trim and peel them either before or after cooking. Larger ones should be peeled, sliced or diced, and steamed or boiled in salted water until tender. Use them as you would turnips.

Kohlrabi are available in winter and can be stored in the refrigerator crisper for up to a week. They are an excellent source of vitamin C.

kombu. Dried kelp (see SEAWEED).

kosher means fit to eat, lawful, or ritually permitted, according to Jewish dietary laws. Among these dietary laws are rules forbidding the eating of meat and milk at the same time—separate cooking utensils must be used for milk and meat. Only those four-footed animals that chew their cud and have a cloven hoof are kosher, and the animals must be slaughtered according to strict procedure. Only fish having both scales and fins are kosher, which makes shellfish taboo.

kumara. A New Zealand variety of sweet potato, which has a red skin (see SWEET POTATOES).

L

labna / labneh. A Middle Eastern CREAM CHEESE made with yoghurt. The yoghurt is salted and placed in a cheesecloth to let the whey drain away. The creamy white curd cheese is then shaped into little balls and covered with olive oil and paprika.

ladies' fingers / ladyfingers. Several items of food which by willing suspension of disbelief could be thought to resemble a lady's finger are known by this name: certain biscuits and cakes, especially sponge fingers; thin rolls of FILO pastry with a spicy filling; various small bananas; an elongated dessert grape; OKRA; and even the strips of toast that children dip in their boiled eggs.

laksa. A spicy, aromatic soup popular in Malaysia and other parts of South-East Asia. There are different versions, some with coconut, tamarind and lemon grass, chicken, prawns and other seafood. Laksa is a meal in itself and is eaten at any time of day, including breakfast.

lamb. Meat sold as lamb should be from a sheep less than a year old, one that has not yet grown any permanent teeth. Meat from a sheep with a pair of permanent incisors, usually aged between fifteen and thirty months, is called hogget; from an older animal the meat is classed as mutton. Hogget and mutton are generally sold only in butcher's shops catering for certain ethnic communities.

Lamb should have light reddish-pink flesh and firm, white fat. Store it in the coldest part of the refrigerator, or in the meat compartment, loosely

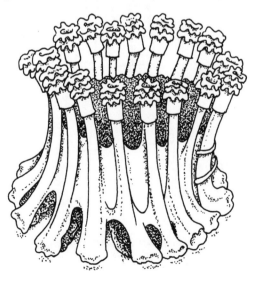

covered with foil. Never leave it in a plastic wrap. As a rule, the larger the cut, the longer it will keep: roasts for three to five days, chops two to four days; diced lamb should be cooked within two days of purchase (see also MEAT).

Cuts of lamb, beginning at the leg and working down one side to the neck (as the carcase is hung by the butcher) are:

Leg. Usually roasted on the bone, the leg may also be boned (tunnel-boned or butterflied) and stuffed or rolled for roasting. The leg can also be corned for boiling.

Chump. This is the part between the leg and the loin. It can be roasted as one piece or cut into chump chops for grilling, frying, or barbecuing.

Loin. The loin comprises the mid-loin, or short loin, and the rib loin. Again, the mid-loin can be bought in one piece, with bone in or boned, for roasting, or cut into short loin chops for grilling, frying, or barbecuing. The rib loin contains eight ribs which may be separated into cutlets or sold in a piece for roasting as a rack of lamb. Two racks can be cooked as a crown

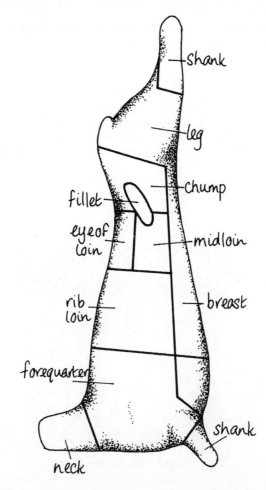

roast (in a circle, bones curving outwards) or as a guard of honour (parallel with bones interlinked).

Forequarter. The whole forequarter consists of the neck, shoulder, shank, and part of the breast or flank. This can be roasted whole or boned. Forequarter chops may be grilled, fried, or barbecued (they are known as barbecue chops), and also braised or stewed. The **shoulder** is usually roasted, either on the bone or boned and rolled, sometimes stuffed. The shoulder is sweeter tasting than the leg. The **shank** (the foreleg below the shoulder) has a high proportion of bone to meat and a lot of connective tissue. Shanks may be cooked whole or sawn in pieces; either way they are best braised or used for soup. The **neck** is divided into the best neck and the scrag. Best neck chops are braised, stewed, casseroled, or used for soup. The scrag is traditionally used in Irish stew.

Breast. The bony parts may be barbecued, and the boneless breast is usually roasted or braised, and also corned.

Trim lamb is lamb that has been cut off the bone and trimmed of much of its fat. As well, it is made available in cuts similar to beef cuts: round and topside roasts, steaks, and schnitzels; eye of loin roasts and butterfly steaks; the fillet, for grilling, frying, and barbecuing. Strips from Trim lamb cuts are suitable for stir-frying, traditional lamb cuts being unsuitable because of the wasteful and time-consuming preparation involved.

lamb's fry. See LIVER.

lamington. Lord Lamington, governor of Queensland from 1895 to 1901, left his name on some noteworthy geographical and cultural features: a plateau and national park in Queensland, a mountain in Papua New Guinea, and a cube of sponge cake coated with chocolate and rolled in desiccated coconut. As early as 1909 the Holy Trinity Church Ladies Working Guild had published in their *Guild Cookery Book* a recipe for a lamington. Since then the lamington drive—an organised effort by church, school, and other community groups to raise money from the sale of lamingtons—has become an Australian institution.

Lancashire hotpot. See HOTPOT.

lard is rendered and clarified pig fat, much used in the past for deep-frying and as a shortening in pie pastry, but largely superseded by vegetable oils and shortenings.

larding, lardons. To lard is to insert thin strips of pig fat or fatty bacon into the flesh of lean meat or poultry before cooking to impart flavour and prevent the meat from drying out as it cooks. These strips of fat are called lardons (or lardoons). They are inserted with a larding needle, which has a sharp point and a long, hollow body with sometimes a hinged jaw at the end for holding the lardon.

lasagne are broad, flat ribbons of PASTA, 8–10 centimetres wide, sometimes with curled edges, sometimes coloured green with spinach. A narrower variety is called **lasagnette.** Lasagne are usually boiled first (although there is an instant variety that does not require pre-boiling) and then baked in an ovenproof dish in layers alternating with meat sauce, BÉCHAMEL SAUCE, and grated Parmesan cheese, finishing with a layer of béchamel and Parmesan on top. Green and uncoloured lasagne are sometimes layered alternately. It is important not to overcook lasagne, or the pasta will turn mushy.

lassi. An Indian drink made from yoghurt. Lassis can be sweet, with sugar and rose water and perhaps some cream; salty, with salt and pepper; or spiced, with cumin and coriander. The yoghurt and other ingredients are mixed in a blender with ice cubes to produce a smooth, frothy, cool drink. A longer drink can be made with half yoghurt and half cold water or soda water.

leatherjacket. Once regarded as an inferior fish, perhaps because of its rough skin in place of scales and its unprepossessing appearance, the leatherjacket is now acknowledged as an excellent eating fish, white and tender, with easily managed bones. Leatherjackets are usually sold skinned, headed, and gutted, which makes them more attractive to the public. As they are rather dry, they are best pan-fried. (See also FISH.)

leavening agents. A leavening agent, or simply a leaven, is anything that is incorporated into a dough or other mixture to cause it to ferment and form a gas which aerates the mixture and makes it rise. Yeast in its various forms is the common leavening agent, especially for bread dough, but baking powder, sodium bicarbonate, egg-whites and yolks or whole eggs, even beer, are other leavening agents.

leeks. Legend has it that when the Welsh fought the Saxons back in the seventh century, King Cadwalader's soldiers wore a leek in their caps to distinguish them from their Saxon foes, and as the Welsh were the victors, the leek was adopted as the national emblem of Wales. Perhaps there is more to it than that. The Romans thought that licking a leek cured a sore throat, and the emperor Nero was said to eat large quantities of leeks to improve his voice. Who knows, the leek may well be the secret of the Welsh people's ability to sing.

Leeks are members of the onion family; they look like fat, overgrown spring onions (too big for a Welsh soldier to wear in his cap). They are available all the year round, with heaviest supplies in winter. Choose small to medium size leeks with crisp white bottoms and fresh green tops. Store them unwashed in the refrigerator in the vegetable crisper or a plastic bag.

To prepare and cook leeks. Before cooking leeks, cut off the roots, remove coarse leaves and filmy skin, and trim the green tops, as only a little of the green is edible (but the tops can go in the stockpot). Fan the leaves open and wash them well under running water to rinse out any dirt (the bottoms are blanched by heaping up the soil to cover them as they grow). You may need to push a knife blade through the white part and slit up through the green leaves to separate them.

More delicate in flavour than onions, leeks are ideal for making stocks and soups, as the Scots can vouch for with COCK-A-LEEKIE and the French with potage bonne femme (see BONNE FEMME). As well as being used for making soup, leeks can be steamed or boiled and served with a cream sauce, baked, braised, and used as a savoury filling for pies (see FLAMICHE) and QUICHES.

legume. In French, any vegetable is a *légume,* but in English legumes are vegetables such as peas and beans, where the pods and seeds are eaten rather than the leaves or the roots of the plant. Specifically, a legume is a seed-bearing pod that splits into two halves with the seeds attached to the lower edge of one of the halves. When dried, the seeds of legumes are collectively known as PULSES.

lemon balm. The generic name for lemon balm, *Melissa,* is the Greek word for bee. Ancient Greek and Roman bee-keepers grew lemon balm for their bees and rubbed the herb on the hives to stop the bees hiving off elsewhere. The fresh green lemon-scented leaves, which resemble mint, are not widely used in cooking, but they may be added to fruit drinks and wine cups or tossed in a salad. Fresh or dried, they make a pleasant herbal tea (see TISANE), and a few dried leaves in a pot of regular tea is a refreshing additive. (See also HERBS.)

lemon cheese / lemon butter is a mixture of lemon juice and rind, butter, eggs or egg yolks, and sugar cooked until it thickens. It is used mostly for filling tarts and pies but can also be spread on bread or toast.

lemon grass is a popular herb in Thai cooking, often combined with chilli to give a spicy, lemony flavour to seafood, chicken dishes, and curries. A tropical plant that forms clumps of sharp-edged, strap-like green blades, it grows abundantly in South-East Asia. It is easy to grow in the garden, being propagated by root division, but it can be bought fresh at Asian specialty food shops. Dried and powdered lemon grass are also available. Fresh is preferable to dried for cooking. Generally, the pale lower part of the fresh leaves is chopped finely for use in recipes calling for lemon grass. When larger pieces are specified, the tougher, greener part can be bruised with a pestle before being added to the dish.

lemonade. Home-made lemonade is a simple, refreshing summer drink. An easy way of making it is to boil some sugar and water together to form a syrup, add some fresh lemon juice when it is chilled, and keep this lemon syrup in the refrigerator until it is needed, when the addition of chilled water and ice makes lemonade; soda water or mineral water makes it sparkling.

lemons are the most useful of all citrus fruits. Lemon juice and rind add flavour to soups, main dishes, marinades, sauces, puddings, sorbets, cakes, icings, and drinks; wedges of lemon are an almost essential garnish for fish; the high pectin content of the juice, pith, and pips of a lemon helps set jams and jellies; and a little lemon juice will prevent apples, pears, bananas, avocados, sweet potatoes, and Jerusalem artichokes from discolouring.

A lemon tree should be one of the first choices for a kitchen garden. With a variety such as Eureka, ripe fruit are carried for much of the year, and there is nothing more satisfying than being able to pick a fresh lemon when you need it for use straight away. Another advantage of having your own lemon tree is that the fruit you pick is not waxed. Waxed lemons are awkward to grate.

Lemons are available all year round, with heaviest supplies in winter. Choose fruit that are firm and heavy for their size, with clean, fine-textured skin. (Lemons that are still slightly green are best for jam-making.) Store them in a cool place. Lemon juice can be frozen for later use.

For information on grating, squeezing, and segmenting, see CITRUS FRUIT. Like other CITRUS FRUITS, lemons are rich in vitamin C.

lentils. The red pottage for which the biblical Esau sold his birthright was made of lentils, which gives an indication of the longevity of their use. These round, flat, dried seeds are still a popular item of food in the Middle East and Europe, where they are used for making soups and casseroles, served hot as a vegetable or cold as a salad, and also puréed.

There are red, yellow, green, and brown lentils. Before cooking, they should be picked over to eliminate stones and other foreign bodies, then washed. To soak, or not to soak: that is the question. Red and yellow lentils don't need soaking; in fact they disintegrate completely after about half an hour's cooking and thus are good for soups and purées. Brown and green lentils are better soaked, as this reduces cooking time. They take between 30 minutes and 1½ hours to become tender and will remain whole if not overcooked. Use brown lentils for salad.

Lentils are an excellent source of protein, dietary fibre, and B vitamins. They can also be used for sprouting (see BEAN SPROUTS).

lettuce. By far the most popular of all salad greens, lettuce comes in various types. There are the common crisp-head or cabbage-head, such as Iceberg; butterhead, with its soft, buttery leaves loosely folded round a head; the small mignonette, either with burgundy-tinged outer leaves or completely green; cos, called romaine in other parts of the world, with elongated deep green leaves and a tightly folded, elongated head; oakleaf, coral, and other leaf lettuces with loose leaves branching from a stalk and no head.

Lamb's lettuce, also known as corn salad or *salade de mâche;* is not a real lettuce but an edible member of the valerian family; its large, round or oval, grey-green leaves are tender and very mildly flavoured.

Lettuces are available all year round. Ironically, the crispest and tastiest

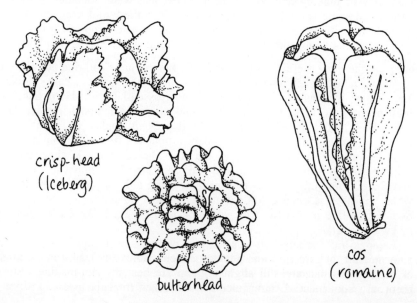

crisp-head
(Iceberg)

butterhead

cos
(romaine)

are those harvested in winter, when warming soups are more in mind than cool salads. Whenever you buy them, choose lettuces with bright, crisp and tender leaves free of blemishes. Crisp-head lettuces should be cored, held under a strong stream of cold water, and left to drain with the core down. Other lettuces should be washed under running water and dried with a tea-towel. Store lettuces in a plastic bag or covered container in the refrigerator and use them as soon as possible. Hydroponically grown lettuces store better with the roots cut off.

As well as being used in salads, lettuces can be braised (especially with peas—braised in butter with a little water), cooked with bacon, and made into a delicious soup with green peas. Crisp lettuce cups can be used to hold savoury concoctions such as stir-fried pork to be eaten out of the hand; or they can be blanched and used as a wrapping around a stuffing in the manner of cabbage rolls.

liaison. Though an illicit sexual relationship has no doubt occurred more than once in the kitchen, a cook's liaison is usually something less exciting—a thickening agent used to bring sauces and soups to the right consistency. The liaison may be as simple as a mixture of flour and water which is added to a soup, or it may be egg yolk in a tricky mixture with oil for MAYONNAISE, or eggs and cream mixed together and whisked into a sauce at boiling point, carried out without having the ingredients separate.

lima beans. Also known as butter beans, lima beans are flat and kidney shaped. The larger ones are white; the smaller ones, or baby limas, either green or white. Limas are native to central South America, where they are a staple food, and are named after the capital city of Peru. They have a floury texture, which makes them suitable for soups and purées, but they are also popular in salads and go well with lamb.

For information on preparation, storage, etc., see BEANS, DRIED.

To cook lima beans, boil them gently until tender (1–1/2 hours) or pressure cook them for 20–25 minutes.

lime leaves. See KAFFIR LIME LEAVES.

limes. As anyone who has referred to British sailors as limeys should know, lime juice was issued to them to prevent scurvy, as limes are an excellent source of vitamin C. So too are lemons and other CITRUS FRUITS. Limes can in fact be substituted for lemons in cooking and flavouring. Indeed, some cooks prefer lime juice and zest to lemon in certain recipes, although this may be just a fashionable trend.

Limes are available all year round, when you can find them. In the past there were two types to be had: the Mexican or West Indian (also known as the Key lime), small, round, and yellowish-green; and the larger Persian or Tahitian, which is oval in shape and lime green. Both are acidic and fragrant. Since 1992 the Australian Giant has been on the market. Developed in Australia, it is much larger and has 50 per cent more juice by volume. Limes are more perishable than other citrus fruits.

ling. A member of the cod family found in deep water off the southern coast of Australia. Because of the ling's unprepossessing appearance—like a large pink eel with irregular brown spots—it is usually sold as skinless fillets.

(Chilled or frozen fillets are also imported from New Zealand, and those of a related species known as kingclip are imported from South America and South Africa.) Ling is available all year round, but mainly in winter. The white flesh is moist and firm, with dense, large flakes. It has a fine, mild flavour. The large, thick, boned-out fillets are suitable for cooking in all ways, especially grilling because it is moist. (See also FISH.)

linguine. Long, narrow, flat pasta that tapers slightly at the edges. Very slithery.

Linzertorte. A round, single-layered cake made with almond pastry filled with raspberry jam and covered with latticed strips of pastry sprinkled with icing sugar. Really a jam tart, the Linzertorte is one of the most popular cakes for festive occasions in Austria and Germany.

Liptauer cheese. Originally a fresh cheese made in Hungary from ewe's milk, Liptauer is now usually a combination of any cottage cheese or cream cheese, often home-made, and butter, paprika, caraway seeds, mustard, chopped onions, capers, and seasonings mixed together to form a spread or dip.

liquorice / licorice. A black extract from the root of a leguminous plant native to Europe and Asia, used in confectionery. Liquorice is also an ingredient of Guinness stout. As a sweet, it is safe for diabetics.

liver. Of the various items of offal we eat, liver is probably the most nutritious and widely consumed. It is rich in iron, vitamin A, and B vitamins (though also rich in cholesterol) and traditionally prescribed for those suffering from anaemia. Liver's popularity is attested to by the permanent inclusion of lamb's fry and bacon on the breakfast menu of many an eatery.

Sheep's (lamb's fry) and calf's are the two livers most commonly eaten. Ox liver and pig's liver are coarse or granular in texture and have a strong flavour (which can be reduced by soaking the sliced liver in milk for 1–2 hours). They are usually braised, stewed, or, in the case of pig's liver, roasted. Calf's and sheep's livers are sliced thinly and fried quickly. Over-cooking makes liver tough and leathery.

Before cooking, the membrane around the liver must be removed. Make an incision with the point of a knife, and pull the membrane off gently. Then cut off any fat and gristle attached to the liver.

Goose liver is used to make PÂTÉ DE FOIE GRAS. (See also CHICKEN LIVERS.)

liverwurst is a soft sausage of preserved meat that includes a large proportion of cooked liver. Many regions of Europe, especially Germany, produce distinctive liver sausages, some made with pork liver, others with calf or ox liver, others still with goose liver. Some are fine in texture, other coarse. Some contain onions and seasonings, others are smoked. All are rich in fats, mainly mono-unsaturated. Liverwurst is used mainly as a spread and is more of a PÂTÉ than a sausage.

lobsters. Australian rock lobsters, or marine crayfish, have become an expensive rarity in Australia. Much of the commercial lobster catch (practically the whole of the West Australian, South Australian, Tasmanian, and Victorian catch, according to Sydney seafood marketer and restaurateur Peter Doyle) is exported. Fisheries departments have imposed restrictions on catches to prevent over-fishing and secure future stocks. Meanwhile, lobsters are imported from Chile, Cuba and Mexico.

There are three main species of rock lobster in Australian waters: the eastern, the southern, and the western. They vary in colour from dark green through pink to maroon but all turn bright red when cooked. When buying an uncooked lobster, make sure it is alive and, if not kicking, at least active and still in possession of its limbs; lobsters deteriorate quickly once they are dead. Keep a live lobster in a damp hessian bag until you cook it. It is best not to buy an uncooked chilled lobster, as you don't know how long it has been dead. A cooked whole lobster should have all its legs and be evenly coloured. If you straighten its tail, it should flip back into a tight curl.

To prepare and cook a lobster. Before cooking a live lobster, drown it in fresh water, or kill it by freezing, then put it in a pot of cold water and bring it to the boil. Allow 8 minutes of cooking time for each 500 grams of the lobster's weight. Green lobster tails can also be grilled.

(For sand lobsters or shovel-nosed lobsters, see BALMAIN BUG, MORETON BAY BUG.)

loganberry. When the American judge and horticulturist J. H. Logan crossed a variety of blackberry with a raspberry in 1881, he produced a purplish-coloured fruit that resembles both its parents and may be treated as one or the other as regards eating, cooking, etc.

longan. The fruit of a large evergreen tree native to China, but which grows in many parts of tropical Asia, the longan is similar to the LYCHEE but smaller. It has a dull greenish-brown skin and translucent, white, juicy flesh with a single brown, inedible seed. Longans are grown commercially in Australia and are available in the autumn. Canned and dried longans can also be obtained. Eat and use longans as you do lychees.

loquat. Loquat trees used to be common in Sydney backyards, and their fruit was plunder for marauding urchins. Like the equally common chokos, loquats were never seen in fruit shops. Then the fear of fruit fly caused the growing of loquat trees in the suburban garden to be discouraged for some years. Now the loquat is regarded as an exotic fruit and takes its place in fruit shops together with nashi pears, rambutans, star fruit, and the like.

The loquat is, of course, exotic. It is a Chinese native, though it is known as a Japanese medlar or Japanese plum. The yellow-orange, fig-shaped fruit with large brown seeds has a tart-sweet flavour and crisp texture. Commercially grown loquats are available in October-November. They are harvested ripe and should be stored in the refrigerator. Eat them out of the hand, peeled, or add them to fruit salads. They can be stewed and puréed, and they make good jelly.

lovage is a southern European herb resembling celery or angelica in appearance. It has a strong, peppery flavour. Lovage is not used very much in cooking, but it can be added to soups and sauces and used, sparingly, in the same way as parsley.

lychee / litchi / lichee. The lychee is a delicately flavoured fruit that has been cultivated, and honoured in verse, by the Chinese for thousands of years. Grown commercially in Australia, lychees are available fresh for a short season during summer. They are about the size of a small plum and have a rough, leathery, red skin when ripe. Avoid buying green fruit, as it doesn't ripen after being picked. The skin peels off to reveal a translucent white flesh enclosing a large brown seed. The flesh is sweet, with a slight acidity, tasting something like a grape. Although lychees are best eaten soon after purchase, they will keep for up to a fortnight in a plastic bag in the refrigerator. They are eaten fresh in fruit salad, with ice-cream, or on a fruit and cheese platter. The Chinese find them a perfect cleansing finish to a meal. Lychees can also be poached. They are used in many Chinese dishes, particularly sweet and sour pork, chicken, and fish.

Lychees are also available canned and dried.

M

macadamia nut. Although the macadamia is a native Australian tree and the nuts were an important food item for the Aborigines of the Queensland coastal rainforests, it took the Hawaiians to grow and market the nut commercially. Since the 1960s, however, macadamia plantations in Australia have increased by a multiple of sixty, and the price and availability of these sweet, buttery nuts have improved markedly.

The Queensland nut, bopple nut, or macadamia supplies about 3000 kilojoules per 100 grams, so it is inadvisable to overindulge in macadamias if you are watching your weight. Like other nuts, they have a high fat content, but about 84 per cent of it is unsaturated (82 per cent mono, 2 per cent poly). The extremely hard, brown, spherical shells need a special nutcracker or a hammer to crack them. Once out of their shells, the creamy-white kernels should be kept in a screw-top jar in the refrigerator to stop them going rancid. When buying shelled nuts, choose kernels vacuum-packed in foil or plastic.

Macadamias are usually eaten whole as a snack but can be chopped and ground and added to stuffings, cooked in biscuits and cakes, sprinkled over ice-cream, and used in both sweet and savoury dishes.

macaroni. The origins of the word *macaroni* are obscure, but it seems to have been used for the earliest forms of Italian PASTA of any kind. Today macaroni usually refers to tubular pasta—of medium thickness, often produced in short pieces or curves (elbow macaroni) suitable for baking as well as boiling. Other hollow pasta in various shapes and sizes are known by specific names—for example, penne, cannelloni, and rigati.

Macaroni cheese is a dish of macaroni baked in a white cheese sauce (see MORNAY SAUCE), with perhaps some chopped ham, topped with breadcrumbs.

macaroons. The origin of the macaroon can be traced back to seventeenth-century Italy (the name is derived from macaroni). Macaroons are round biscuits or small cakes made of sugar, egg-white, and ground almonds, sometimes flavoured with spices or perfumes. There are many variations from different parts of the world. Some use coconut, hazelnuts, or walnuts instead of almonds. Some are flavoured with chocolate, coffee, orange, or lemon. The Italians make a version with bitter almond essence which they call amaretti. Whether you beat all the ingredients together or cook the nuts with the sugar and egg-white first in a double boiler is a matter of choice.

mace is the lacy red membrane that surrounds a NUTMEG. It is removed from the shell and allowed to dry out, then distributed separately either whole as 'blades' of mace or ground into a reddish-brown powder. Mace is a more pungent spice than nutmeg, but they can be substituted for each other if you bear in mind that mace is stronger and less is needed. Mace is used in pickles and chutneys, in potted meats, pâtés, and terrines, on fish and in sauces for fish, and to add spice to vegetables such as creamed spinach, steamed carrots, and mashed potatoes. Blade mace is used generally in recipes where there is some liquid—a stew, for example—and in fruit jelly, where ground mace would cloud it.

macédoine. The mixture of peoples in Macedonia was such that any mixture, medley, or hotchpotch came to be known as a macedonia or macédoine. The culinary macédoine is a mixture of fruit or vegetables cut into dice. A macédoine of fruit is essentially a fruit salad; the diced fresh fruit is usually macerated in orange and lemon juice, with sugar and Kirsch or maraschino, then chilled. It is served as a dessert, sometimes with fresh cream. A vegetable macédoine is composed of vegetables that have been cooked separately and diced. It is served hot or cold and dressed with VINAIGRETTE or MAYONNAISE or in ASPIC.

macerate, marinate, marinade. To macerate or marinate food is to soak it in a special liquid before serving or cooking. The liquid is known as a marinade. The object is to impart flavour to the food and sometimes to soften it or preserve it. *Macerate* is generally used with regard to fruit, and the word essentially means to soften or break up, although this is not always the case. Fruit is usually macerated in brandy or some other spirit and sugar.

Marinate usually applies to meat or fish, and the liquid in which it is soaked often tenderises the meat as well as flavouring it.

Marinades for meat and fish vary according to the recipe and the method of cooking. Usually they have a basis of wine, vinegar, or citrus juice and oil, seasoned with herbs and spices. The acid content has a tenderising effect, and the oil prevents the food from drying out. For Chinese food the marinade might include honey, soy sauce, rice wine, sesame oil, and ginger. For Thai food, the marinade would probably include NAM PLA, chilli sauce, and coconut cream.

The longer food is left in a marinade, the more effective the process will be. After marinating, meat or fish should be allowed to drain before cooking.

mackerel. There are several species of mackerel in Australian waters. They are streamlined, irridescent fish, ranging widely in size. Available all year round, with seasonal peaks in each state, they are usually sold in fillets, steaks, or trunks (the gutted main body section without the head, gills, or fins). Their pearly-pink to white flesh may be oily or rather dry and has a strong fishy flavour. Mackerel can be fried, baked, grilled, poached, or barbecued. It should not be overcooked, and when fried it should be first lightly salted. Its oiliness can be counteracted by marinating in a lemon-based marinade and using vinegar in the cooking. Mackerel is good smoked. (See also FISH.)

Madeira cake. A rich, plain cake, lemon in colour and flavour. The name comes from the nineteenth-century practice of serving it with a glass of Madeira.

madeleine. Whoever made the first madeleine—and that is lost in the mists of time, although Talleyrand's chief pastrycook is said to have named it—this dainty little cake was made for ever famous by Marcel Proust in *Swann's Way,* where he dips one in his tea and sets his memory off *á la recherche du temps perdu.* The cake's ingredients are nothing unusual: flour, butter, sugar, and eggs, with some lemon juice and rind or some vanilla. It is the mould that makes a madeleine special—a grooved, paw-like shape rather than the scallop it is usually said to resemble. Turned out so that the ridges are on top, and dusted with icing sugar, madeleines make attractive and tasty teacakes which, despite Proust, are better left undunked.

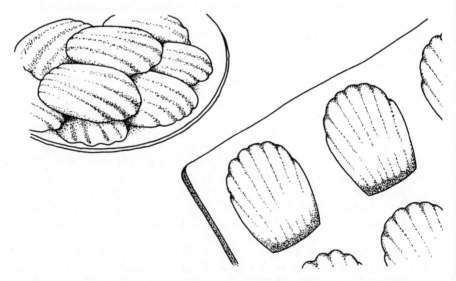

madrilène is short for *consommé madrilène,* a consommé in the Madrid style. You begin with a rich chicken stock, strengthen it with beef, colour and flavour it with tomatoes, clarify and strain it, then chill it until it sets into a light jelly. Serve it chilled, garnished with chopped red capsicums or lemon wedges. It may also be served hot.

maids of honour. According to legend, King Henry VIII discovered the delight of these sweetened cheese tartlets at the same time as he discovered the charms of Anne Boleyn, who was then his sister's maid of honour, and he dedicated them to her. There are many recipes for maids of honour, but all have a cheese and lemon filling. They are usually made with shortcrust pastry (originally puff pastry) and filled with a mixture of CURD CHEESE, butter, eggs, and sugar, flavoured with ground almonds, lemon juice and zest, and brandy. Fit for a king.

maître d'hôtel. Apart from meaning chief steward of a great household in France and the head waiter of a restaurant in the United States, MAÎTRE D'HÔTEL means served with a sauce made by creaming butter with finely chopped parsley, lemon juice or vinegar, and seasonings. This parsley butter is often formed into a roll, wrapped in aluminium foil, and chilled. Pats are cut off when needed to be served on grilled steak, grilled or fried fish, and other dishes.

maize. See CORN and SWEET CORN.

mandarin / mandarine, tangerine. One of the citrus family, the mandarin crosses easily and consequently has a few near relatives in the various parts of the world where it is cultivated, as well as an alias or two. It originated in the East, and because it was imported from China became known as a mandarin orange. This was shortened to mandarin or, in French, mandarine. Those grown near Tangiers in Morocco became known as tangerines.

Mandarins are available from April to October, with heaviest supplies in winter. Imperials, with a skin that is not as loose as others, are first to appear. Other varieties, such as the large Ellendales and the sweet Murcotts, make their appearance in May. Choose brightly coloured fruit with no soft spots, though puffiness is normal. Heaviness for their size means a lot of juice. Store them in a cool place or in the refrigerator for a longer time. They don't keep as long as oranges. Best eaten out of the hand, they can also be used for making marmalade. They are an excellent source of vitamin C.

mangetout. Another name for snow peas (see under PEAS).

mangoes are thought to have originated in India—they have been cultivated there for four thousand years—but are grown in tropical areas around the world, including Queensland and the Northern Territory. There are many varieties, with a range of sizes, shapes, and colours. Those generally available are medium sized, round to oval with a point, and ripen to a yellow-orange colour, some with a red blush. They are in season from November to February. Choose fruit that are well coloured, with no soft spots or bruises. However, sap from the stem which sometimes squirts onto the fruit may cause dark marks on the skin. These do not affect the flavour of the fruit. Ripe mangoes have a perfumed aroma and will yield to gentle pressure. Those slightly underripe, but not completely green, will ripen at room temperature, after which they should be kept in a plastic bag in the refrigerator.

Eating a mango can be messy, especially if you simply peel the skin off and eat the voluptuous, juicy flesh out of the hand. A less messy way is to cut off the sides of the unpeeled mango as close as possible to the seed, then score the flesh in a criss-cross pattern down to the skin without cutting through it. When the skin is pushed inwards as if to turn it inside out, the cut cubes of flesh pop up for easy eating.

Mangoes can also be peeled and the flesh cut off in chunks or slices to be served in a salad or as a dessert sprinkled with lemon juice or rum, or with cream or ice-cream. They are also used in curries and chutneys, especially when green. Some of the green varieties, such as those known as *nam doc mai* and *keow savoey* in Thailand, where they are used raw in salads and sometimes as a vegetable, are now grown in the Atherton Tableland in Queensland.

Mangoes are rich in vitamins C and A.

mangosteen. A tropical fruit from South-East Asia now grown commercially in tropical Australia. The mangosteen is round with a smooth, purple skin, white, segmented flesh, and one or two brown seeds. The flavour, reminiscent of pineapple, is deliciously sweet with an acid aftertaste. Mangosteens are picked ripe and should be eaten soon after purchase; meanwhile, store them in the refrigerator. Peeled and segmented, they can be eaten out of the hand like an orange, or they can be added to a fruit salad or served with ice-cream.

marengo. After Napoleon defeated the Austrians in the Battle of Marengo on 14 June 1800, he dined, so they say, on a dish specially created by his cook for the occasion. Chicken is the main ingredient, although the dish can also be made with veal. Pieces of chicken are browned in oil and cooked in a sauce of tomatoes, mushrooms, garlic, parsley, and white wine—ingredients Napoleon's cook could purloin from the surrounding Piedmont countryside. Chicken Marengo is often served with fried CROÛTONS and a fried egg for each person, and prawns cooked in their shells.

margarine. In 1869 Napoleon III launched a competition to discover a cheap product that could replace butter for the French navy and the 'less prosperous classes of society'. The product invented by Hippolyte Mège-Mouriés— essentially an emulsion of fat and water, which was named after a Greek word meaning 'pearl-like'—did not meet with universal approval. However, subsequent development, particularly during the two world wars, led to a much improved margarine.

Table margarines, especially polyunsaturated table margarine, are generally made from vegetable oils, whereas cooking margarines may have animal fats included in the margarine mixture, which is a minimum of 80 per cent oil / fat and a maximum of 16 per cent water, the remainder being made up of emulsifiers, colouring and flavouring agents, antioxidants, skim milk or whey, and salt. They also have added vitamins A and D.

In June 1994, however, the National Heart Foundation released a report which stated that all but one margarine contained trans fatty acids, which are recognised as having a similar effect as saturated fats in raising blood cholesterol. So it would seem that margarine's reputation as a healthier alternative to butter is not so good. And margarine doesn't have the flavour of butter.

marinade, marinate. See MACERATE, MARINATE, MARINADE.

marinara. A dish prepared *marinara* or *alla marinara* is one prepared in the manner of sailors—southern Italian sailors, that is. It is based on a sauce made with tomatoes, garlic, olive oil, and herbs—basil, oregano, or parsley. The sailors in question being mainly fishermen, there may well be some seafood included. The sauce is usually served on pasta, but also with rice or simply with crusty bread.

marjoram is a perennial herb native to the Mediterranean. It has small, soft, grey-green leaves and a delicate perfume and flavour. There are three main types, sweet marjoram, pot marjoram, and wild marjoram, better known as OREGANO. Sweet marjoram is the one most used, often in combination with thyme, to which it has a great affinity. Marjoram goes well with veal, poultry, pork, and beef, with vegetables such as beans, peas, mushrooms, and potatoes, in salads, omelettes, sauces, meat loaves, and pizzas, with cream cheese on sandwiches. It is one of the herbs that go to make up a BOUQUET GARNI.

marmalade is jam made with citrus fruits. It can be made with one fruit or a combination of two or more. The method of making marmalade is much the same as that for jam (see JAM for directions), although marmalade takes longer to cook because of the tougher skins of citrus fruits. Marmalade sets more readily than jam because of the amount of pectin in citrus fruit.

The fruit should be fresh and slightly underripe. It should be scrubbed to remove any wax and then sliced thinly or cut up and prepared according to the recipe.

To make jelly marmalade, fine shreds of peel without pith are needed; for bitter, chunky marmalade, the fruit is cut up roughly and the pith left on. Much of the pectin in citrus fruit is in the pith and pips, so these are placed in a muslin bag and cooked with the fruit. The bag is removed just before the sugar is added, after being squeezed to extract all the pectin.

The amount of sugar required depends on the fruit, but it is usually twice the weight of the fruit or more. If the fruit is not tender before the sugar is added, the peel will remain tough and the colour will be poor. Overcooking will make the marmalade too dark.

marmite. The French marmite is a round, tall, straight-sided or slightly bulbous stewpot or stockpot, usually made of earthenware, which is used for cooking dishes such as CASSOULET and POT-AU-FEU and a rich beef CONSOMMÉ known as petite marmite.

Marmite is also the proprietary name of a yeast extract spread.

marron is the French word for CHESTNUT. The fresh-water crayfish known as marron is dealt with under CRAYFISH.

marrow. Bone marrow is the soft, fatty substance in the cavities of large bones. It is a delicacy which goes to flavour soups and sauces and such dishes as OSSO BUCO. It can be scooped out of bones that have been cut into sections and cooked, to be used on CANAPÉS or on toast.

Vegetable marrows are members of the squash family (see SQUASHES). They are grown to giant size as show pieces, but the smaller they are the better they are to eat, although the taste is fairly bland on its own and the texture can be mushy if they are boiled too much. They are best cooked with a PROVENÇALE sauce or stuffed with a savoury stuffing and baked.

marshmallows are light, spongy confections, usually cube shaped, sometimes coloured pink, and either dusted with icing sugar or rolled in toasted coconut or coated with chocolate. The marshmallow is made with SUGAR SYRUP and gelatine boiled for 20 minutes, then flavoured, coloured, and whipped until thick. The whipped mixture is poured into cake tins or trays to set, then cut into cubes.

maryland. The combined thigh and drumstick of a chicken. Chicken Maryland is a dish of maryland portions coated in egg and breadcrumbs and deep-fried in oil. Traditional accompaniments to this American dish are corn fritters, banana fritters, and grilled tomatoes.

marzipan is a confectionery paste made from ground almonds. It is used to cover fruit cakes beneath royal icing to provide a smooth surface and to prevent the icing from becoming discoloured. Being very pliable, marzipan can be used for moulding into animals and other decorations for a cake. Ready-made marzipan is available from supermarkets and health food shops. A simple, uncooked marzipan can be made by mixing together ground almonds, castor sugar, icing sugar, eggs, and a little flavouring such as brandy or rum, lemon juice, rose water, and almond essence.

Store marzipan between sheets of greaseproof paper in a covered container in a cool place. In the refrigerator it will keep indefinitely.

masa harina. Finely ground corn meal (see under CORN).

masala is a mixture of spices and other seasonings ground together to provide a base for an Indian sauce. A wet masala is produced when liquid is added during the grinding process. (See also GARAM MASALA.)

mascarpone. A luscious CREAM CHEESE made from very rich cream, mascarpone has the consistency of soft butter and a sweet, slightly acidic flavour. It is usually served with strawberries or stone fruit. Sometimes it is whipped up with brandy or a liqueur, or the liquor can simply be poured into a depression made in the top of some mascarpone spooned onto a plate alongside the fruit.

mask. To mask is to cover or coat food with a sauce or aspic. For example, the eggs in EGGS BENEDICT are masked with HOLLANDAISE SAUCE. Vegetables, fish, or poultry are sometimes masked with BÉCHAMEL SAUCE to prevent them from drying out while they are being browned under a grill for a GRATIN.

matzo / matzoh. According to Leo Rosten in *The Joys of Yiddish,* the pronunciation of *matzo* rhymes with 'lotsa'. Who knows what you'd get if you asked for a 'motsa'. What you'd be expecting to get is a flat, crisp, oblong of unleavened bread. Made from flour and water only, like water biscuits, matzos commemorate the flight from Egypt by the Israelites, who had no time to wait for bread to rise. While these crispbreads are naturally appropriate to eat during Passover, when yeast and leavened products are off the menu, they are ideal for eating with cheese or spreads at any time. Matzos are covered with rows of perforations to facilitate even breaking.

Matzos are also ground into meal which is used in Jewish cooking—for example, to coat food in place of breadcrumbs and to make into matzo balls (*knaidlach*), dumplings usually served in chicken soup.

mayonnaise. Home-made mayonnaise is so much better than the commercial product that it is worth the trouble to make this most useful of sauces. And you'll know what's in it: egg yolks, oil, lemon juice, and seasonings. With a food processor it is much quicker and easier to make than by hand.

What you have to remember is that mayonnaise is an emulsion—that is, the uncooked egg yolks have to hold the oil in a suspension that does not separate. The trick is to beat the yolks fairly thoroughly, with half the lemon juice, before you start adding the oil, which is added drop by drop at first. When the mixture thickens, the oil can be added in a thin, steady stream until it is all incorporated.

The proportions of the ingredients are 2 egg yolks to 1 cup of oil, with 2 teaspoons of lemon juice and salt and pepper to taste. The kind of oil depends on what the mayonnaise is to accompany. The taste of straight olive oil may be too overpowering for delicately flavoured food, so peanut oil or salad oil of some kind, or a blend of that with olive oil, may be more appropriate. Wine vinegar may be used instead of lemon juice. And some cooks add a teaspoon of French mustard. Have all the ingredients at room temperature. The mixing bowl should be warm.

If the mayonnaise shows signs of curdling during the beating, add a teaspoon or two of boiling water. If it really curdles or refuses to thicken, take a clean warmed bowl and beat an egg yolk with ½ teaspoon of vinegar, then gradually whisk in very small amounts of the curdled mayonnaise until you have a thickened mixture; then you can add the curdled mayonnaise more quickly. Another way is to beat 1 teaspoon of prepared mustard with 1 tablespoon of the curdled mayonnaise (stir it up first so that you spoon out both egg and oil), then whisk in successive trickles of stirred-up mayonnaise, increasing the amounts when it thickens.

meat originally meant food of any kind ('One man's meat is another man's poison'), just as in Italian the word for *bread* stands for food, and in some Asian languages the words for *rice* and *food* are one and the same. The English, being traditionally large eaters of meat rather than bread or rice, came to use the word to mean specifically animal food. Beef, lamb, veal, pork, and other meats are dealt with separately elsewhere in this book, as are some methods of cooking meat. Here are a few points about meat in general, as recommended by the Australian Meat and Live-Stock Corporation:

Purchasing tips
Allow 125 g of lean, boneless meat or 200 g of bone-in cuts per person.
Meat should be bright pink to red in colour with a fresh (not dry) appearance.
Check that supermarket meat is packed on day of purchase. Don't buy packs where there is meat juice, as this means the meat has lost some juice and will be dry when cooked.

Storage tips

When storing in the special meat compartment of the refrigerator, unwrap meat or remove from supermarket pack, and arrange in stacks no more than 2–3 layers high. Make sure there is some air space between each piece of meat. Cover top of meat loosely with foil or waxed paper to stop surface drying. Do not cover with plastic, as this causes the meat to sweat, which shortens storage time.

When storing in the general refrigerator area, place a rack in a dish deep enough to catch any meat drips. Unwrap the meat and store it as for the meat compartment in the coldest part of the refrigerator. In a 'refrigerator only' unit, this is at the bottom. In a combination refrigerator and freezer, the coldest air is at the top, because of the closeness to the freezer.

If meat is to be used on the day of purchase, it can be left in its original wrapping.

Meat kept in the refrigerator for 2–3 days will be more tender than meat cooked on the day of purchase. This is because natural enzymes soften the meat fibres.

Follow this guide for refrigerator storage of meat before cooking:

- Mince and sausages — 2 days
- Beef and lamb cubes or strips — 2–3 days
- Steaks, schnitzels, chops and cutlets — 2–3 days
- Mini roasts — 2–3 days
- Roasting joints, boned — 2–3 days
- Roasting joints with bone in — 3–4 days
- Corned beef — 1 week
- Vacuum-packed meat, unopened — 4 weeks

The more cutting the meat has had, the less time it will last.

Vacuum packaging extends the storage life of chilled meat by removing all air and vacuum sealing the pack. In the pack, the meat is purple-red in colour due to lack of air. Once opened, the meat returns to its usual bright colour (bloom). You might notice a slightly 'off' odour when opening the bag. This is only 'confinement odour' and will disappear in a short time.

Once opened, vacuum-packed meat's storage time is 1–2 days less than fresh meat.

Freezer storage

Mince, strips and diced meat can be frozen for up to 2 months. Other cuts can be frozen for up to 6 months. Longer storage doesn't cause contamination, but it will cause dehydration and give the meat a 'fridgy' taste.

Interleave steaks and chops with freezer wrap so that they separate easily.

Freeze mince in flat packages for quick defrosting.

Place meat in a sealed freezer bag to stop 'freezer burn' (dehydration). Label with name of cut and date frozen.

Vacuum-packed meat can be frozen in its bag without re-packing.

Defrost meat in the refrigerator, never at room temperature or in water. Allow 2 days for a roast, 1 day for smaller cuts. To defrost quickly, use defrost setting of a microwave oven. Follow manufacturer's instructions.

Cooking

Dry-heat methods—that is, pan-fry, stir-fry, grill, barbecue, and oven roast—are best suited to tender cuts of meat. Timing is a key factor when cooking them, as overcooking will give a tough, dry result. Cooking times depend on the size and thickness of the cut, as the bigger the cut, the more time is needed.

Moist-heat methods—pot-roast, casserole, braise, stew—are ideal for less tender cuts of meat. Timing does not depend on the size of the cut as much as the connective tissue (gristle and sinew) which needs long, slow cooking to soften it. This is why casseroling diced meat often takes as long as pot-roasting whole cuts.

Never use tender cuts for moist-heat cooking. First of all it's a waste of money. Second, the long cooking time will make the meat fibre shrink and toughen.

meat loaf. A meat loaf is made from minced or chopped beef, lamb, veal, or pork—or a mixture of meats—seasoned with herbs and spices and possibly mixed with breadcrumbs and other ingredients, then moulded into a loaf shape and baked. It may be served hot or cold.

medallion. A medallion, or *médaillon,* is a thickish piece of lean, boneless meat (or poultry or fish, for that matter) cut in a round or oval shape for cooking. A medallion of beef might be cut from the middle of the FILLET; this is also known as a TOURNEDOS. A medallion of veal or pork, if cut thinner and flattened, would be an ESCALOPE. Medallions are often sautéed but may be cooked in any way.

Melba sauce is a purée of sieved fresh raspberries, sweetened with castor sugar, which is used in PEACH MELBA and may be poured over ice-cream, yoghurt, cream cheese, orange segments, poached pears, or anything requiring a raspberry sauce.

Melba toast. Very thin crisp toast. One way to make it is to toast a slice of white bread until it is brown on both sides, then cut off the crusts and slice the piece horizontally through the middle so that you have two pieces, each browned on one side. Put these in the oven for a few minutes to crisp.

Another method is to remove all the crusts from a square, unsliced loaf of white bread, cut it in half across to make it more manageable, then cut each half diagonally to make four triangular prisms of bread. With the flat side down, these pieces can be cut into wafer-thin slices. Bake them in a moderate oven for 15–20 minutes.

meringues. When Napoleon visited the Swiss town of Meiringen, so the story goes, a local pastrycook named Gasparini created something special for the occasion, using nuts, sugar, and egg yolks. Having the egg-whites left over, and not wanting to waste them, he whipped them stiff with some castor sugar, formed the mixture into small cakes which he baked until they were crisp and light, and served them with cream. Napoleon was more impressed by these makeshift confections than the specialty, and named them after the town.

To make meringues. Don't make meringues in rainy or humid weather, or they will droop; for the same reason, avoid moisture in the air from other cooking. Have the egg-whites at room temperature, use clean utensils, and avoid getting any grease or egg yolk in the whites (see 'To beat egg-whites' under EGGS). Beat the egg-whites slowly at first, then add a little cream of tartar and beat quickly until peaks hold their shape. Add the sugar gradually and continue beating until the mixture is thick and glossy.

Dessertspoonfuls of the mixture are baked on a tray lined with greased greaseproof paper. The meringues may be served separately or sandwiched together with whipped cream or some other filling in between. The meringue mixture may also be used to top pies (lemon meringue pie, for example), to make the famous dessert cakes VACHERIN and PAVLOVA, to form into icebergs for the dessert Floating Islands, and to mould into fingers and other shapes.

Meringues should be kept in an airtight container. If they absorb moisture and begin to weep, they can be dried out in a very slow oven for 15 minutes or so.

mesclun is not the opposite of feminine but a French word that comes from the Niçois *mesclumo,* meaning 'mixture'—in the culinary sense a mixture of fresh baby salad greens. A mesclun might consist of various LETTUCE leaves—crisp Iceberg and cos, soft butterheads and mignonette, red and green oakleaf, peppery lamb's lettuce—with ROCKET, curly and broad-leaved ENDIVE, RADICCHIO, snow pea shoots, nasturtium leaves, edible flowers, and so on.

meunière. The miller's wife must have done some fishing in the mill stream, for the designation *meunière* or *à la meunière* ('in the manner of a miller's wife') usually applies to fish—Sole Meunière, for example. She certainly would have had no shortage of flour on hand in which to dredge the fish, which is part of the process. The fish is then sautéed in butter. The distinctive feature of meunière is the sauce with which it is served: lightly browned butter with lemon juice and parsley.

mezze. Middle Eastern appetisers or hors d'oeuvres eaten throughout Greece, Turkey, the Arab states, and the Balkans. The innumerable items that comprise mezze include dips such as TARAMASALATA, TZATZIKI, TABBOULEH, and HUMMUS BI TAHINA, raw tomatoes and cucumbers, stuffed vine leaves, black and green olives, cubes of FETTA cheese, nuts, fish sticks, mussels, fried chicken livers or cubes of calf's liver, meat and fish balls, sliced sausage, as well as many others.

milk. By milk we usually mean cow's milk, though milk from goats, ewes, mares, and camels is used in various parts of the world. Milk is highly nutritious. Since it was intended by nature to be the sole diet of the young, it contains most of the nutrients required for health and growth: protein; all the known vitamins, though light in vitamin C; minerals, especially calcium; as well as fat, sugar, and water. But since milk was intended by nature only for the young, the ability to digest it diminishes as we pass from babyhood, and many adults can digest comfortably only a limited amount of milk.

Cow's milk in many forms can be found in the refrigerated section and on the shelves of the Australian supermarket: whole, skimmed, reduced, evaporated, powdered, long-life, modified, flavoured, and variations on these themes (see also BUTTERMILK). Goat's milk is fairly freely available, in both liquid and powdered form. It is more easily digested than cow's milk and does not need to be pasteurised.

The cow's milk we buy is always pasteurised—that is, the temperature of the milk is raised to 72°C briefly and then quickly cooled. This kills any disease-carrying organisms. It also kills some beneficial organisms, such as the acidophilus bacterium, which aids the digestion of milk. And it makes the milk unsuitable for producing certain cheeses of an equivalent quality to their counterparts in Europe, where pasteurised milk for cheese is not compulsory.

What benefit there is in having **homogenised milk** is hard to fathom. It doesn't taste as good as ordinary whole milk; it is not as good for making sauces; and it gives tea with milk a different taste. With ordinary whole milk there was always a handy tablespoon of cream on the top if you needed it in a recipe. In homogenised milk the globules of fat are evenly suspended throughout instead of being allowed to rise to the top. Some scientists believe the tiny particles of fat in homogenised milk are absorbed directly into the bloodstream, a characteristic that doesn't seem to be in its favour.

Skim milk is milk that has had the cream removed (not nowadays by skimming but by machines using centrifugal force), leaving a fat content of less than 0.15 per cent. All the protein and calcium are left in; only the fat is taken out.

Low-fat, reduced fat, or **modified milk**, under various brand names, is milk that has had some of the fat removed (sometimes replaced with mono-unsaturated vegetable fat). These milks may be fortified with skim milk powder or concentrated skim milk. They are produced for people concerned about reducing their cholesterol intake and increasing their calcium intake for health reasons.

Long-life milk, also known as UHT (ultra high temperature) milk, is pasteurised milk that has been further heated to 135°C for 2–3 seconds and then cooled and packed in special cartons. Unopened, the milk will keep without refrigeration for up to five months. Once opened, it should be refrigerated and used fairly quickly.

Evaporated milk is whole milk that has had the water content reduced by evaporation to about 40 per cent of its original content. It is thus thicker than ordinary milk. It is pasteurised and homogenised and is packed in cans. Unopened, it will keep indefinitely. Once opened, it should be refrigerated and used fairly quickly. It may be reconstituted by adding 3 parts of water to 2 parts of milk.

Condensed milk is evaporated milk that has had a little more of the water content removed and has been sweetened and thickened by the addition of about 40 per cent sugar. It can be stored indefinitely and when opened need not be refrigerated.

Powdered milk, which has had the moisture removed by mechanical processing, is available as full cream or skim. It is used in cooking both in powdered form and reconstituted with water according to the instructions on the package.

millefeuille. A thousand leaves, as the French name implies, may seem something of an exaggeration. But when you consider that in making puff pastry six folds produce 729 layers, and two or three pieces of puff pastry go into the making of a millefeuille, it could be a considerable underestimation. The oblong pieces of puff pastry are baked and then sandwiched with a filling of CRÉME CHANTILLY. Sometimes strawberry or raspberry jam or purée is included in the filling, and the top is dusted with castor sugar.

mincemeat is what goes into mince pies and is not to be confused with minced meat, which is meat cut up very fine. The composition of mincemeat is variable, but it may contain all or a large selection of the following: raisins, sultanas, currants, apples, candied peel, beef suet (traditionally) or butter, blanched almonds, sugar, spices, lemon juice and rind, and brandy or rum. The larger solid items are chopped or minced to blend with the smallest, and all are mixed together and allowed to stand for a week, the mixture being stirred from time to time. Stored in sterilised jars, it will keep for months if necessary to wait until Christmas to make mince pies.

Originally mince pies did contain finely chopped meat, but for a long time suet has been the only meat ingredient of mincemeat.

minestrone. There are innumerable versions of this hearty Italian vegetable soup. Almost any fresh vegetables in season may be included, as well as dried beans, canned tomatoes, herbs, garlic, and oil. In the south of Italy the soup is usually thickened with pasta; in the north, with rice. Genoese minestrone is distinctive for the PESTO added at the last moment, either floated on top or swirled in. All versions are served with grated Parmesan cheese.

As a robust soup, minestrone can serve as a meal in itself. If you follow it with a meat course, you won't need vegetables with the meat. Minestrone may also be served cold.

mint. A patch of mint in the garden seems almost a law of nature. With its invasive roots and its tendency to hybridise, this hardy perennial herb of Mediterranean origin is pretty much a law unto itself. Mint is one of the most commonly used culinary herbs (see also HERBS). Traditionally placed in the pot with boiled or steamed peas and potatoes and made into a sauce to accompany roast lamb, mint is also used in pea soup and as a garnish for drinks and fruit salad. It blends well with orange. In India it is used in some curries and in fresh chutneys that accompany curries. In the Middle East it is an essential ingredient in the Lebanese salad TABBOULEH.

There are many varieties of mint, including apple mint, peppermint, eau de cologne mint, and pennyroyal, each with its own distinctive aroma and flavour. The common variety used in the kitchen is spearmint, which has a clean-tasting, tangy freshness.

To prepare mint sauce. Chop some mint leaves finely and put them in a bowl with 1–2 teaspoons of sugar. Pour over 2–3 tablespoons of boiling water and stir until the sugar has dissolved. Stir in 3 or more tablespoons of malt vinegar and allow to stand for at least an hour. Serve at room temperature with roast lamb.

To prepare mint tea. Put some fresh or dried mint leaves in a teapot and pour boiling water over them as you would if making ordinary tea. Leave the tea to infuse for 4–5 minutes, then serve it with sugar or lemon according to your fancy.

mirepois. A preparation of diced vegetables (and sometimes diced ham) fried in butter. It is used to flavour stocks, sauces, and stews, as a garnish, and as a base on which to braise meat or poultry. The vegetables in mirepois are essentially carrots (the red part only, according to Escoffier), onions, and celery, with perhaps a bay leaf and some thyme. The preparation was named, for some reason, after the Duc de Mirepois, an eighteenth-century French general. Perhaps he was renowned for chopping the enemy to pieces.

mirin. A straw-coloured, viscous, sweet rice wine used in Japanese cookery.

Mirin gives a distinctive sweet flavour and gloss to sauces, and it is mixed with soy sauce and other ingredients to form a marinade for TERIYAKI as well as a sauce for other dishes. As mirin is used only in cooking, it is available from Asian food shops rather than liquor stores. It will keep indefinitely after being opened. Sherry may be substituted for mirin.

mirror dory. See DORY.

miso. A paste made from fermented soya beans, used in countless ways in Japanese cuisine and eaten by most Japanese almost every day. There are many kinds of miso, which vary in colour from white to dark red according to the other fermented grains in the paste and the time it is left to mature (sometimes for ten years). Miso has a distinctive, pleasant nutty flavour and aroma. It is used in Japanese dishes of various kinds—soups, grilled and fried dishes, marinades, dressings, and so on. The favourite breakfast dish, misoshiru, is a soup made from DASHI, the basic Japanese stock, and miso.

mizuna. A Japanese green vegetable of the *Brassica* genus, with long, finely lobed leaves. Eaten mainly as a salad green, mizuna may also be cooked in braises and stir-fries.

mocha. Apart from being the name of a type of coffee which originally came from the town of Mocha in Yemen, mocha is also a combination of coffee and chocolate, or a drink of hot cocoa to which coffee has been added, perhaps topped with whipped cream.

molasses. The fluid that drains off the clarified, boiled, and crystallised juice of crushed sugar cane during the refining of SUGAR. Molasses itself undergoes refinement to extract the sugar remaining in it, becoming darker and more concentrated until it becomes 'blackstrap' molasses. Treacle and molasses are more or less interchangeable in recipes.

monosodium glutamate (MSG). A white crystalline powder used in Chinese and other cooking as a flavour enhancer. MSG occurs naturally in many foods. Some people are allergic to it, experiencing burning sensations, facial tightness and numbness, pressure in the chest, and other reactions, however, research suggests that adverse reactions occur less often than is generally believed. MSG has the food additive code number 621, which allows those who are allergic to it to avoid it in packaged foods, although not in Chinese restaurants.

mornay sauce. A cheese-flavoured white sauce. It is made by mixing grated cheese (a combination of PARMESAN and an EMMENTAL-type cheese) into BÉCHAMEL SAUCE, together with some French mustard or cayenne pepper. The sauce may be served with pasta, eggs, fish, or vegetables. It is used to coat food that is reheated in the oven or under the grill. Sprinkle with grated cheese and / or breadcrumbs to serve the food *au gratin*.

Moreton Bay bug. See BALMAIN BUG, MORETON BAY BUG.

mortadella. A large slicing sausage originally from Bologna in northern Italy. It is made from finely chopped pork, or a mixture of pork and beef, studded with cubes of pork fat, spiced and smoked. The name comes from the mortar in which the pork was traditionally crushed with a pestle—*mortaio della* *carne di maiale* ('mortar for the meat of a pig')—a mouthful that was shortened to *mortadella.*

morwong. The morwong is a silvery, bream-shaped fish (it is also sold as deep-sea bream) with a distinctive elongated ray of its pectoral fin. It is found off the southern coast of Australia from New South Wales to Western Australia. In Tasmania is is known as the black perch or silver perch, in Victoria as the jackass fish— the morwong and the jackass fish are in fact similar, related species. Another related species is called the queen snapper in Western Australia. The morwong and its relations have moist, medium to firm white flesh with a distinctive flavour. They are good eating and may be cooked in all ways. (See also FISH.)

moussaka. A favourite dish throughout the Middle East and the Balkans, but known especially in its Greek version, moussaka consists of alternate layers of eggplant, minced lamb or beef, onions, and a tomato sauce, topped with a thick white sauce and baked. The eggplant is sliced and salted to extract the juices (see under EGGPLANT), then fried lightly in oil. The minced meat may be fried with the onions and tomatoes or separately to make individual layers. Whichever way, the layers are arranged so that the eggplant is on the bottom and the top. The sauce, seasoned BÉCHAMEL with added egg yolks, covers the top with a brown crust when baked.

mousse. A mousse can be either a sweet, cold dessert or a hot or cold entrée. Chocolate mousse is probably the best known of the dessert mousses. It is made by mixing chocolate, egg yolks, and cream, folding in beaten egg-whites, then chilling the mixture. But dessert mousses can be made in various ways, with or without cream, with puréed fruit or fruit juices, with gelatine to make a more jelly-like than frothy preparation. Savoury mousses can be made with fish, chicken livers, ham, tongue, etc.

mousseline. A light, airy-textured mixture of puréed fish (or meat or poultry) combined with egg-whites and cream. The mixture can be cooked by itself, made into little dumplings called QUENELLES and poached, and used as an ingredient of a decorative moulded dish.

Mousseline is also HOLLANDAISE SAUCE or MAYONNAISE with whipped cream added.

mozzarella cheese. True mozzarella, the main cooking cheese in the south of Italy, is made from buffalo's milk. However, as there are far more cows than buffaloes in Italy, even there it is made mostly from cow's milk, which gives the cheese a milder flavour than the buffalo-milk kind. The mozzarella-type cheeses produced in Australia are made from cow's milk. A smooth, white, elastic cheese, mozzarella comes in round, oval, and pear shapes. The whey from mozzarella is traditionally used for making RICOTTA.

Small fresh mozzarella cheeses, sometimes called bocconcini, are sold in bags containing whey to keep them moist. The slightly acid, walnutty-flavoured cheese is often sliced, sprinkled with olive oil and pepper, and served with tomatoes and basil. The mature cheese is used mainly for cooking, especially in pizzas.

muesli. It was some time in the 1960s that muesli came into fashion, though it was created at the beginning of the century by a Swiss nutritionist named Birchner-Brenner. The name, a Swiss German dialect word meaning mixture, was adopted everywhere with the breakfast food itself. There's no question that muesli is good for you. A mixture of oats, wheat germ, chopped dried fruit and nuts, raw sugar, and a piece of fresh fruit, served with milk, is a complete, nutritious meal that should set you up for the day. There are countless variations on the basic recipe—added bran, the oats toasted, other cereals included, honey instead of sugar, yoghurt rather than milk, and so on. Create your own version to suit your taste.

muffins. English or American? The English muffin is (or was, when muffin men roamed the streets) a thick, flat, round, soft cake made from risen yeast dough cooked on a GRIDDLE over gentle heat until biscuit-coloured on both sides. The muffin is usually split open, revealing a slightly honeycombed inside, then toasted and spread liberally with butter. In Australia, if the Country Women's Association's *Coronation Cookery Book* is any guide, the American muffin has been traditionally favoured over the English. American muffins are made with a sweet dough and baking powder, cooked in muffin pans or patty tins in the oven. Fruit such as blueberries, orange, apple, and dates, or nuts, chocolate chips, carrot, bran, etc., may be included. The muffins are served hot.

mulberry. Though mulberries are not sold extensively in fruit shops, the large, bountiful trees are fairly common in suburban gardens and the shiny purple-staining fruit is available in summer. Mulberries deteriorate rapidly and should be eaten soon after picking. Meanwhile, keep them in the refrigerator. They freeze well. Like raspberries, blackberries, loganberries, and boysenberries, they may be eaten fresh, turned into Summer Pudding (see under PUDDINGS) and sorbet, cooked in pies and tarts, and made into jam.

mullet. Sea mullet, yellow-eye mullet, and related species are small to medium size, slender, silvery-grey fish with a blunt nose. Fish of this kind are known as grey mullets in Britain and America to distinguish them from red mullets (highly prized in France, where they are known as *rougets*), which belong to another family of fish, different in appearance and taste. Mullets (grey) are found around the eastern and southern coast of Australia from north Queensland to Western Australia. They are available all year round, but mainly in autumn and early winter, and are sold whole and in fillets. Their pink-to-grey flesh is moist, fairly soft, and quite oily, so they are best grilled, baked, or barbecued but may also be fried. Filleting and skinning lessens the amount of oil. Mullets are strong-flavoured and get an earthy taste at certain times of the year; soaking the fish in milk for 30–60 minutes helps

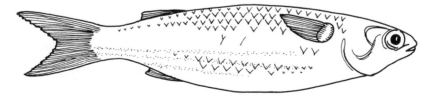

to remove this. Mullet ROE is highly prized, especially when smoked; fresh mullet roe is used to make TARAMASALATA.

mulligatawny. The word *mulligatawny* comes from a Tamil word meaning 'pepper water', which is hardly an adequate description of this curry-flavoured soup of east Indian origin. It can be made clear or thick. It is traditionally made with chicken pieces and stock together with some chopped apple, cloves, and chopped onions browned with a spicy curry seasoning. Cream is stirred in at the last moment, and the soup is served with a separate bowl of boiled rice. There are many variations.

mulloway. Also known as jewfish, kingfish, and buttterfish, the mulloway is a medium to large silvery fish found around the southern half of Australia from Fraser Island in Queensland to Exmouth Gulf in Western Australia. It is available all year round, but mostly from September to February, and is sold whole and in fillets, cutlets, and steaks. The mulloway's flesh is white to pale pink and has a large flake and only a few large bones. It has a mild but distinctive flavour. Suitable for grilling and frying. Large fish can be rather dry and may need moist methods of cooking. (See also FISH.)

mung beans. See BEAN SPROUTS.

muscatel. A RAISIN made from a muscat grape.

mushrooms. While there are countless varieties of mushrooms and other edible fungus in all manner of shapes and colours, the most commonly cultivated for sale is the one appropriately known as the common or cultivated mushroom, which has a white skin and dark brown gills showing when open. It is sold at three stages of growth: button (small, tightly closed, cap still joined to stem), cup (medium size, open but still cup-shaped), and flat (large, fully open and mature). Button mushrooms are mild-flavoured and are used in salads and sauces and for pickling and as garnishes. Cup mushrooms are for general use, in pies, casseroles, and soups, stuffed, baked, barbecued, and so on. Flat mushrooms are richly flavoured and are the kind that are fried or grilled, with steak or bacon, or served on their own on toast.

Cultivated mushrooms are available all year round. Choose clean, dry, firm, undamaged specimens. Store them in the refrigerator in a brown paper bag—not in a plastic bag, which makes them sweat. Mushrooms dehydrate fairly quickly, so eat them fresh. They don't need peeling but may need to be brushed or wiped clean and the stalks trimmed before cooking.

Mushrooms are rich in B vitamins and iron ('the only vegetable that contains vitamin B12', the mushroom poster says) and low in kilojoules.

Field mushrooms, the ones that grow wild and spring up overnight in suitable conditions, are similar in appearance to cultivated mushrooms and are treated in the same way, though they may need peeling or washing if they are particularly dirty.

There are an estimated three thousand or more species of mushroom native to Australia. They are the last in the world to be commercially exploited. A number are being developed for commercial use. Among the exotic mushrooms available in Australia, fresh or dried (see also FUNGI), are:

Oyster mushrooms, which look like a grey-white fan rather than a cap and grow in clumps on trees. They can be tough and need careful cooking.

Shiitake mushrooms, with dark brown caps and a pungent smell, used in Chinese and Japanese cooking. Meaty and full of flavour. Also known as winter mushrooms.

Enoki mushrooms, which have tiny cream caps on long, slender, cream stems and grow in clusters. Delicately flavoured and crisp.

Shineji mushrooms, which have silvery-grey caps and grow in clusters. Similar in texture to oyster mushrooms but sweeter in flavour.

Morels, with crinkly, sponge-like pointed caps coloured brown, yellow, or cream, available fresh for only a brief period in September-October.

Boletus edulis. Known in France as *cèpes* and in Italy as *porcini* or *funghi porcini*, boletus mushrooms have a stout stalk and a smooth brown cap. They are available in Australia in dried form, imported from both France and Italy. When reconstituted by soaking, they may be cooked in omelettes, pasta sauces, and meat dishes. Cooked with fresh cultivated mushrooms, they add a strong, wild-mushroom flavour.

Dried mushrooms should be soaked in warm water for 10–30 minutes depending on the type. The soaking water may also be used.

mussels. The mussel is a bivalve mollusc, brown to purple-black in colour (or green in the case of the larger New Zealand green-lip mussel) which is typically found in clusters on rocks and wharf piles in the intertidal zone. They are grown commercially on ropes or poles. Though not as popular as oysters, mussels can be enjoyed in various ways.

Mussels should be firmly closed when you buy them; when open they are dead. Small mussels have a better flavour than larger ones. Store them in cold water or a wet hessian bag. Before cooking, scrub them thoroughly under running water to remove any dirt or slime, and remove the fibrous threads (the beard) attached to them. Soak them for a few hours in cold fresh water with a handful of oatmeal, which makes them disgorge any sand. They can be cooked in a COURT BOUILLON and served in a sauce of the cooking liquor, perhaps with added cream (see À LA POULETTE); or they can be stewed with other seafood. They can also be grilled, baked, or barbecued in their shells. Discard any mussels that don't open during cooking.

mustard. A condiment used since prehistoric times, mustard comes in three forms: whole seeds, powdered, and prepared. There are two main types of mustard seeds: yellow and black; the black is the hotter. (There is a third kind, the Indian brown mustard seed, which is used in chutneys, pickles, and curry powders.) The mustard of the Western World is made from a blend of ground yellow and black seeds mixed with certain other ingredients.

English mustard, made from blended mustard-seed flours and other spices, can be bought as a powder or ready mixed. The powdered mustard is prepared simply by adding cold water (hot water stops the enzyme action) and allowing it to stand for a while to develop its flavour. It should be made fresh each time it is used. English mustard is hotter and sharper than French and German mustards; it is ideal for roast beef.

French mustard is made from mustard flour mixed with grape must (hence the name *mustard*), vinegar, or VERJUICE, and aromatic herbs and spices. Dijon, the mustard centre of the world, is synonymous with French mustard, although famous mustards are also made in Bordeaux (blended with unfermented claret, and brown in colour) and Meaux (a coarse-grained mixture of ground and half-ground seeds).

German mustard, made from a strong mustard-flour mixture and vinegar, is hotter than French but not usually as hot as English. It is used extensively on frankfurt-type sausages.

When using mustard in cookery, add it towards the end of cooking, as it loses its aroma when subjected to heat.

mutton is meat from a sheep more than thirty months old—that is, too old to be classified as lamb or hogget (see LAMB). Mutton has a darker colour and stronger flavour than lamb, and is not as tender.

N

naan. A traditional Indian bread, slightly leavened, flattish and shaped like a teardrop. Naan is made from a rich dough of plain wheat flour with eggs, milk, and sugar, leavened with baking powder or yeast. The dough is divided into individual-size pieces and formed into teardrop-shape leaves, which are traditionally slapped onto the sides of a TANDOOR oven and cooked quickly. Naan can also be cooked in an ordinary oven and then put under the griller for a minute or two to brown lightly on top. The bread is served hot or at room temperature

nachos. Corn chips served with a spicy sauce and melted cheese topping. The Moosewood People, who created the Moosewood Restaurant in Ithaca, New York, have a recipe for nachos sauce in their *Moosewood Cookbook* which is made from onions, garlic, tomatoes, capsicums, and spices with beer and grated cheese. They say this rich sauce is 'delicious enough to dip plain, steamed tortillas in—and call it lunch'.

nam kati. Thai for coconut milk (see COCONUT).

nam pla. A fish sauce used extensively as a seasoning in Thai cuisine, being for the Thais what soy sauce is for the Chinese and Japanese. It is also used widely in Vietnam (where it is known as *nuoc mam*) and other parts of South-East Asia. Nam pla is a thin, watery, clear amber-coloured liquid made from salted and fermented dried fish, shrimps, or other seafood. It has a strong, salty, fishy flavour. Its odour of rotten fish is fortunately not usually transferred to a prepared dish. Nam pla is available from supermarkets and Asian food stores and will keep indefinitely unrefrigerated, though it is best kept in a cool place and well sealed.

nam prik. Thai chilli sauce, for which there are countless recipes.

nam prik pao. See CHILLI PASTE.

nannygai. See REDFISH.

napoleon. A small oblong cake consisting of a top and bottom of thin puff pastry, a centre of vanilla-flavoured plain cake joined to the pastry with apricot jam, and the top iced with royal icing sprinkled with chopped almonds or lightly browned coconut. In US terms a napoleon is a MILLEFEUILLE.

nashi fruit. An Asian member of the pear family, the nashi fruit has the taste of a pear and the appearance of an apple. The flesh is crisp and crunchy. Most of the nashis cultivated in Australia are the greenish-yellow Nijisseiki variety. Another two varieties, Hosui and Kosui, have a russeted green-brown skin. Nashis are available from late summer to early winter. Picked ripe, they will remain crisp for up to a fortnight if kept in a cool place out of the sunlight. Eat them as you would an apple or a pear. Slices of nashi go well with cheese.

nasi goreng means fried rice in Bahasa Indonesia, and there are probably as many recipes for nasi goreng as there are Indonesian cooks (and Dutch cooks, who call it *rijsttafel*). Usually, cooked rice is fried in seasoned oil with such ingredients as onions, garlic, shredded chicken or beef, prawns, chillies, coconut milk, and BLACHAN. The dish is often garnished with strips of omelette, prawn crisps, and fried banana.

navarin. A French mutton stew or ragoût, said to have been created to commemorate the victory of the combined French, British, and Russian fleets over the Turkish and Egyptian fleet at the Battle of Navarino in 1827.

A **navarin printanier** is made with small spring vegetables—button onions, new potatoes the size of a pigeon's egg, baby carrots, tiny white turnips or small pieces of turnip, and fresh green peas and beans. The meat is browned first with flour and a little sugar and allowed to stew in stock with tomato and garlic for some time before the vegetables are added.

nectarines. The nectarine is a fuzzless peach. Botanists have changed their minds over the years about whether the nectarine is a separate species or not, but it seems to be regarded now as simply a variety of the peach, *Prunus persica* var. *nectarina*. There are stories of nectarines growing from peach seeds and peaches growing from nectarine seeds, and the two fruits have been known to grow on the one tree. All very mysterious.

Nectarines are generally smaller than peaches. Their skin is not only smooth but also thinner than the peach's and is predominantly red. The flesh may be white or yellow. Like peaches, nectarines can be either clingstone or freestone depending on how strongly the flesh adheres to the stone.

Nectarines are available from late spring to early autumn, with heaviest supplies in January–February. Choose smooth, plump, well-coloured fruit that yield to gentle pressure. As they are quite perishable, eat them soon after purchase. Washed, they can be eaten out of the hand or cut up and eaten with ice-cream or with breakfast cereal. They can be stewed and treated in much the same way as peaches.

Neufchâtel cheese. A soft, fresh, unripened cheese that takes its name from the town of Neufchâtel in the rich dairying Bray region of North-eastern France (not to be confused with Neuchâtel, with no *f,* in Switzerland). An Australian version of the cheese is also available. A low-fat CREAM CHEESE, Neufchâtel has a delicate, refreshing taste. It is used and treated in the same way as other cream cheeses.

nga choi. Chinese BEAN SPROUTS.

Niçoise is a term meaning the way they do things in Nice, and when it comes to food they do things with tomatoes, garlic, olive oil, and black olives. At least that is what the designation *Niçoise* usually implies. Salade Niçoise, always served as an hors d'oeuvre, is prepared with lettuce, tomatoes, hard-boiled eggs, black olives, anchovy fillets, and a garlic-flavoured VIN-AIGRETTE as pretty much essential elements; other ingredients, such as tuna, artichoke hearts, sliced capsicums, potatoes, etc., can be added if you have them and if they would go with the next course.

nockerln. An Austro-Hungarian version of GNOCCHI. Nockerln are small DUMP-LINGS made by dropping teaspoonfuls of dough into boiling salted water. After cooking them for a few minutes, they are rinsed under cold water, drained, and then heated in a little melted butter. Nockerln are served with GOULASH and other stews.

noisette. A small, round piece of lamb, veal, or pork. Lamb noisettes may be prepared from the boned mid-loin, including the fillet, rolled up and tied at intervals, then cut between the ties into rounds about 3 centimetres thick. Noisettes are usually sautéed in butter but may be cooked in other ways.

noodles could be described as non-Italian PASTA. (Or should that be pasta is the Italian version of noodles?) Like pasta, noodles are made from a flour and water paste; the dough is generally rolled into a thin sheet and cut into strips. European noodles are made from wheat flour, often with eggs and milk included in the dough. The flour used to make Asian noodles may be rice flour, soya or mung bean flour, pea starch, ground seaweed or the starchy roots of plants as well as buckwheat and the usual wheat.

European noodles are usually fresh and home-made. They may be like dumplings, with a variety of fillings. Some German cooks make *Knöpfle* noodles by tilting a bowl of batter over a pot of boiling water and quickly running a knife repeatedly along the edge of the bowl to cut off thin strips. Asian noodles are sometimes made at home but are usually bought fresh or dried. Among the Asian varieties are:

Wheat noodles. The common Asian noodle, made from wheat flour, in various widths but always in long strips. They are sold fresh, dried, parboiled, or, very often, steamed and fried.

Egg noodles. Made from a dough of wheat flour and eggs. Available fresh or dried in single-serve bundles or larger hanks.

Rice noodles. Made from ground rice and water. Various widths and thicknesses, the finest being known as rice vermicelli. Available fresh or dried.

Cellophane noodles. Made from soya or mung bean flour. Shiny, thin, and translucent. Must be soaked (30 minutes in cold water or 10 minutes in hot) to soften before frying.

Soba noodles. Made from buckwheat flour. Eaten by the Japanese in soups or as snacks.

Udon. Thick, white, wheat noodles, also eaten in soups.

nori. Dried laver (see SEAWEED).

nougat can mean several things, but it usually refers to a chewy confection made from sugar and / or honey, egg-whites, and nuts, usually almonds. Other ingredients are often added—glucose, butter, vanilla or rose water or orange flower water, glacé cherries or pieces of Turkish delight. The blocks of prepared nougat are sometimes covered in edible rice paper.

To make nougat, boiled SUGAR SYRUP is poured over and mixed into beaten egg-whites, then the other ingredients are added and the mixture turned into a pan and cooled. When set, the nougat is cut into cubes or blocks.

nouvelle cuisine. The object of nouvelle cuisine—'new cooking', or new as it was in the 1970s—was to get away from the over-rich complicated dishes of traditional French cooking in favour of something lighter and simpler, incorporating, among other things, light sauces, fresh, crisp vegetables, airy mousses, purées of vegetables and fruits, and rapid cooking without fat. Often, however, what it seemed to be was a chaste morsel delicately arranged on a large plate.

nutmeg. The kernel of the fruit of a tall evergreen tree that grows in the Moluccas and other parts of the East Indies. The fruit itself looks something like a peach. The seed is covered with a net-like red membrane known as MACE, which is removed to be used separately. The seed is allowed to dry out in the shell until the kernel rattles about in it, at which time it is extracted. Nutmegs are available whole or ground. Freshly ground nutmeg is preferable because it is more aromatic and has a much fresher flavour than the ready-ground. Special nutmeg graters are available for this purpose. Buy unbroken nutmegs with no borer holes, and store them in airtight jars.

nuts. The kernels of dry, hard-shelled fruits. The common edible nuts are dealt with in this book under their individual names. Nuts in the shell should be clean and free of cracks and holes. As a rule the kernels should not rattle if shaken, as rattling indicates a dried-out kernel. Nuts keep longer when stored in their shells. To prevent them from going rancid, they should be stored in an airtight container in a cool place and not kept for long before eating. Most nuts can be frozen for longer storage, and because of their low moisture content can be refrozen successfully. Once jars or cans of nuts have been opened, refrigerate or freeze them depending on how long you intend to keep them. Nuts are rich in fats and high in kilojoules.

To roast nuts, spread them in one layer on a baking tray and put them in the oven at 180°C for 10–15 minutes. Give them a shake every now and then. For information on blanching nuts, see under ALMOND.

O

oats. Though a highly nutritious cereal grain, oats have been regarded as weeds or no more than horse fodder in times past. Dr Johnson in his famous dictionary defines oats as 'a grain, which in England is generally given to horses, but in Scotland supports the people'. Even today the most common use for oats in the kitchen is for making breakfast PORRIDGE or MUESLI.

Only the outer husk or hull of the oat grain is removed in the milling process. With rolled oats, or oat flakes, the hulled grain is steamed and flattened between rollers, a process that makes the oats quicker to cook. Rolled oats may also be used in making chewy biscuits such as Anzac biscuits. For finer biscuits, oatcakes, and scones, a fine grade of **oatmeal** is used. Oatmeal is also used to make muffins, for thickening soups and stews, and in the national dish of Scotland, HAGGIS. **Oat bran**, the fibre-rich layer of cells under the husk, was promoted for a while as a miraculous substance for reducing blood cholesterol, though why oatmeal and rolled oats, which contain the bran, were not equally effective was not explained.

ocean perch. Not to be confused with sea perch or deep-sea perch, which the ORANGE ROUGHY is sometimes called, the ocean perch (properly red gurnard perch) is found in deep, offshore waters of southern Australia and on coastal reefs adjacent to deep water. It grows to about 47 centimetres in length and has three reddish-brown bands across its body. It is good eating and is usually sold in fillets.

ocean trout. A common name for several kinds of fish, including Australian SALMON and farmed rainbow trout that have been transferred to sea cages to rear.

octopus. See SQUID, CUTTLEFISH, OCTOPUS.

offal. The *Macquarie Dictionary* defines offal as 'the inedible parts of a meat carcass after slaughter, excluding the skin' but directs the reader to an alternative term, *fancy meat,* which it defines as 'the internal organs of animals used for food, including brains, heart, kidney, liver, tripe, sweetbreads, tongue, cheek, tail or spleen'. These organs are what are generally regarded as offal, also known as variety meats.

oil. Cooking and salad oils are extracted from a variety of seeds, nuts, and, of course, the fruit of the olive tree. The oil is extracted by pressure, and it can be classified as either refined or unrefined. Unrefined oil is cold-pressed—that is, the raw material (seeds, nuts, or fruit pulp) is simply crushed and the oil runs out and is collected. Refined oil is extracted by pressure under heat and undergoes other refinements such as steam-deodorising, 'winterising' to prevent cloudiness, and treating with artificial preservatives.

Oil is 100 per cent fat. With most vegetable oils, the fat is predominantly polyunsaturated or mono-unsaturated (see FAT). The important exceptions are coconut oil and palm oil, which are predominantly saturated fat. All vegetable oils, being plant material, are free of cholesterol.

Oil should be stored in a sealed container at room temperature out of direct sunlight. Refrigerating tends to cause cloudiness and solids to form in the oil.

The various oils have different 'smoke points' when heated. Oil may be heated until a blue haze rises from it, but it should not be allowed to smoke. When oil smokes, it begins to decompose, discolour, and develop off flavours and harmful toxins. Oil that has been overheated should not be reused. Oil used for DEEP-FRYING and STIR-FRYING, which has to be heated to a fairly high temperature, should have a high smoke point. Peanut oil and maize oil have high smoke points and are suitable for these purposes. In general, oil can be reused for frying up to five times if it has not been overheated and has been strained after use.

Vegetable oils in common use are OLIVE OIL, PEANUT OIL, maize oil (see under CORN), SUNFLOWER OIL, safflower oil, and, more recently, CANOLA OIL, made from rape seed. These can all be used for cooking and in salads and mayonnaise. SESAME OIL should be used with discretion, as the dark-coloured Chinese sesame oil is very aromatic and its flavour can be over-powering if used with a heavy hand.

okra. A green, curved, ridged and tapering pod of a plant belonging to the hibiscus family originally from tropical Africa. The okra plant was taken with African slaves to America, where the pods became a feature of Creole and Cajun cooking, especially in soups and stews such as chicken and shrimp GUMBO (okra is also called gumbo, and lady's fingers). It has a glutinous texture and is a natural thickening agent.

Okra is available (not widely) during summer and autumn. Choose small, young pods; they are eaten when immature and should snap easily when fresh. Stored in the refrigerator crisper, they will keep for up to a fortnight. Okra is also available in cans.

As well as being used in soups and stews, okra can be cooked as a vegetable in boiling salted water or fried. The Arabs are particularly fond of frying okra with tomatoes and onions. Before cooking, wash the pods and trim the stalk end. To reduce the glueyness of okra, soak the pods in white vinegar for 30 minutes, then rinse and dry.

olive oil. In my childhood, olive oil was something you bought in small, thin bottles at the chemist's shop and used for treating earache and for other medicinal purposes. How times have changed! Now it is an essential kitchen requirement and available in a multitude of grades and pressings, with their regional differences of colour, flavour, and fragrance.

Most of the olive oil available is produced in Spain and Italy. However, olive plantations have existed in South Australia and western Victoria for many years, and good quality olive oil is produced from these plantations, though it has never been widely marketed. With increasing production and better distribution, the situation should gradually improve.

The best quality olive oil is cold pressed (see OIL). 'Virgin' means that the oil comes from the first cold pressing. 'Extra virgin' is the first cold pressing from specially selected olives. The most desirable of the virgin oils have traditionally been those from Tuscany (especially from Lucca) and Provence. Subsequent pressings of the olive pulp produce oil of a progressively lesser quality with a blander, less fruity taste and paler colour. Olive oil may also be refined, which means pressing with heat as well as filtering and other treatments. 'Light' olive oil is refined oil to which a little extra virgin oil has been added, then further filtered. The lesser quality oils and the light oils are good for sautéing and regular cooking. Extra virgin should be saved for salads and as a special flavouring.

olives. Olive trees grow wild in South Australia and central-western Victoria. Olives have in fact been cultivated in Australia on and off for over 150 years—South Australian olive oil gained an Honorable Mention at the Great Exhibition in London in 1851. But competition from the highly organised European olive trade made commercial olive growing in Australia uneconomic. Although the Greek and Italian communities picked wild olives from trees in Adelaide parks and the Clare and Barossa valleys, and small-scale growers provided for some local requirements, the olives sold in Australia have mostly been imported from Spain, Italy, and Greece. However, Australian olives are gradually becoming more widely available.

Green olives are immature, picked when they are hard and very bitter. To reduce the bitterness and make them more succulent, they are soaked first in caustic soda, then in several changes of water, after which they are pickled in brine flavoured with herbs and garlic. Cracked green olives, which are picked earlier still, have a crack cut in them to help leach out the oleuropein, which is responsible for the bitterness. There are many varieties of green olive, from the popular large Spanish olive known as the Queen, which is mild flavoured because the Spanish soak their olives in water for a longer period, to the small Manzanillas, which are often stoned and stuffed with strips of red capsicum, and the Caterian from Italy, which is green when ripe and has a white flesh.

Black olives are mature, picked at various stages of ripeness. They may be pickled in brine, packed in dry salt, bottled in oil, or sun-dried. Among the black varieties is the Kalamata, from Greece, which is pale when picked but black when sold, after being cured in red-wine vinegar and marinated in olive oil, herbs, chillies, garlic, or whatever the delicatessen thinks appropriate.

Olives are eaten as a savoury nibble or palate cleanser, in salads, and in pizza toppings. Black olives can be made into an olive paste (see TAPÉNADE), cooked in olive bread, and mixed in with stuffings.

Store jars of olives in a cool, dark place. After opening, keep them in the refrigerator. A film sometimes forms on the top of the liquid in an opened jar. It is harmless and doesn't affect the olives. Olives bought loose may be stored in olive oil or a mixture of oil, water, and vinegar, in the refrigerator.

omelettes. Every culture seems to have a version of the omelette, which is essentially a dish of beaten eggs cooked by frying, often folded round or incorporating a filling of some kind. There are French omelettes, Spanish omelettes, Chinese omelettes, Indian omelettes, Indonesian omelettes which are cut up into strips to go in NASI GORENG, the firm, flat Italian FRITTATA, the Middle Eastern EGGAH, and so on. But when we refer to an omelette, we usually mean the savoury French omelette: 'a soft bright golden roll plump and spilling out a little at the edges', as Elizabeth David writes in *An Omelette and a Glass of Wine.*

'As everyone knows,' Mrs David says elsewhere (in her *French Provincial Cookery*), 'there is only one infallible recipe for the perfect omelette: your own.' Nevertheless, there is a general procedure and a few general rules. You need a good pan with a heavy base and a smooth, preferably non-stick, surface. Some cooks never wash an omelette pan, but simply wipe it out with paper towels after use. The eggs should be at room temperature, and they should be beaten with a fork only lightly, until the yolks and whites are blended. Elizabeth David believes they should not be beaten at all, but stirred. Some cooks add a teaspoon of water, and of course season with salt and pepper. The pan should be placed over the highest heat, some butter melted in it, and when the butter has foamed and begins to brown, the beaten eggs are tipped in. The pan is given a shake so that the eggs are distributed evenly.

Omelettes cook very quickly. When the eggs have coagulated but are still a bit runny in the centre, add whatever filling you're using, if any, in the centre. Tilt the pan, and with a spatula fold the high side over the centre, then tilt the opposite way and fold the other side over the centre so that you have a plump oval shape that is lightly browned on the outside. Lift the pan off the stove, tilt it over a warmed plate, and gently slide the omelette out of the pan and onto the plate.

To make the traditional *omelette aux fines herbes*, add finely chopped parsley, tarragon, chives, and chervil to the beaten egg. Other fillings, such as grated cheese, chopped bacon, cooked sliced mushrooms or onions, and cooked asparagus tips, may be added to the beaten egg if fine enough, otherwise when the eggs have coagulated.

(See also 'soufflé omelette' under SOUFFLÉS.)

onions. The onion is said to be the most widely used vegetable in the world. Certainly countless savoury dishes in most cuisines would be tasteless without it. The onion and its close relatives in the *Allium* genus—GARLIC, SHALLOTS, LEEKS, and CHIVES—are indispensable flavouring agents.

There are many varieties of onion. Those commonly available are usually sold by colour rather than variety: white, brown, yellow, and red. White onions are milder than brown. The yellow and red (often known as Spanish) are very sweet. There are also small white and brown pickling onions. Onions are marketed at three stages of maturity: as green onions, spring onions, and fully mature globe or dry-skin onions.

Green onions, which are confusingly called SHALLOTS by greengrocers and are known in other parts of the world as scallions, are harvested at an early stage of development, before any bulb has formed. The tops are green and the bottoms are slender, white, and cylindrical. Green onions are used raw in salads and on cheese plates, chopped as garnishes or added to cooked dishes where mature onions would be too strong.

Spring onions are harvested when the tops are still green and a white bulb has started to form—they are pulled when the onion bed needs thinning out. They can be cooked whole (roots and tips trimmed) like asparagus or a delicate vegetable, and also chopped and added to salads or cooked in Chinese recipes.

Dry-skin onions are those left in the ground until fully mature. These are what we refer to simply as onions. They are available all year round, but are best in summer and autumn. Look for firm, well-shaped onions that have dry, papery skins, small necks, and no signs of sprouting. Store them in a cool dry, dark place, in an open-weave bag or open tray. Red Spanish onions should be stored in the refrigerator crisper. A cut onion can be kept wrapped in plastic in the refrigerator.

To peel and chop an onion. Cut off the top and bottom cleanly, then peel off the skin with a paring knife. Some cooks peel the onion under water to prevent their eyes from watering. Others find holding a match between their teeth effective. Spring onions, with filmy skin, can be blanched in boiling water for a minute or two; the skins will then slip off easily. To chop an onion into dice, peel it without cutting off the roots, then slice it in half from top to bottom. Lay a half on a chopping board cut-side down, and cut vertical slices from one end to the other, but not through the root. Then make horizontal slices (knife blade parallel to the chopping board) from the crown to the root, leaving the root still attached. Holding it together with one hand, cut across the onion at right angles to the other cuts, starting from the crown and working down to the root, and you will have dice.

Recipes often tell you to sauté onions in butter until golden brown. To do this without burning them, you must stir continuously. A safe method is to just cover the onion with water, add the butter, and cook until the water evaporates and the onion takes on the required colour.

Onions may be baked in their skins, which intensifies their sweetness and retains their food value.

To make crisp onion rings for salads, let the rings stand in iced water for an hour or so, then drain them and pat them dry with paper towels.

orange flower water. An essence made by distilling the blossoms of the bitter Seville orange. Orange flower water is an important culinary flavouring in the countries bordering the Mediterranean from Morocco to Turkey and east to Afghanistan. Although it is used mainly in pastries, puddings, syrups, and drinks, it is sometimes added to savoury lamb and chicken dishes.

orange roughy. Previously known as sea perch or deep-sea perch, the quaintly named orange roughy is a deep-sea fish of medium size with a thick skin. Living as they do at great depths, orange roughies were only discovered in the 1980s, and their huge numbers were exploited energetically by commercial fishermen. What was not realised at the time was that the orange roughy took twenty-five years to mature and lived to the age of a hundred and fifty or so. Stocks are now believed to be dangerously low. Chilled and frozen fillets are imported from New Zealand.

The orange roughy is always sold in fillet form, with the skin removed. The fillets must be skinned before cooking because the black lining under the skin can cause severe diarrhoea if eaten. The pearly-white boneless fillets can be cooked in all ways, but they have a rather bland taste. (See also FISH.)

oranges. With the two main varieties of orange in season at opposite times of the year, there are always fresh oranges available. **Valencias** can be bought in spring and summer. **Navels**, regarded as a winter orange, are in fact available from autumn through to spring. The bitter Seville orange, which is used for making marmalade, and the red-fleshed blood orange are also winter oranges.

Navels are seedless and have a deep orange coloured, pebbly textured skin with a navel shape at the blossom end. The skin and pith are thick and easy to peel. Valencias have a smoother, thinner skin. Sometimes the skin turns partly green, although the fruit is ripe. This is just a natural protection against sunburn. Valencias have a high juice content, which makes them ideal for squeezing. If navels are used for juice, it should be drunk within five minutes of squeezing, as it tends to turn bitter if left.

When buying oranges, choose firm fruit heavy for their size. Store them in a cool, dry place or in the refrigerator.

For information on grating, squeezing, segmenting, etc., see CITRUS FRUIT.

oregano / origano. 'The herb that launched a zillion pizzas,' as Helen McCully describes it in her book *Nobody Ever Tells You These Things*. Oregano is wild MARJORAM, the parent of sweet marjoram but more robust than its offspring. It is widely used in Italian and Greek cooking. It goes well with tomatoes, eggplant, zucchini, beans, cheese, fish, lamb (Greek kebabs), beef (the Mexicans use it in CHILLI CON CARNE), in pasta sauce, and of course on pizzas. Greeks use the flower tops as well as the leaves. Because of its strong flavour, oregano should be used sparingly. (See also HERBS.)

oreo. Known also as smooth dory, spotted dory, deepwater dory, and oreo dory, this medium-size, dark blue, big-eyed fish is found in very deep open water around the southern and western coast of Australia but is caught mainly off the south coast of Tasmania. It is available whole and in round fillets. The white flesh is moist and delicately flavoured, similar to that of the DORY, and may be cooked in a similar fashion. The skin is very tough and must be removed before grilling or frying. It may be left on if the fish is to be baked whole (stuffed with rice, herbs, and nuts) and removed before serving.

Osso Buco. A Milanese dish of veal shanks braised in white wine and stock with tomatoes and other vegetables, herbs, and seasonings. *Osso buco* means 'bone with a hole' in Italian. The dish is traditionally served on a bed of Risotto alla Milanese (see RISOTTO) or plain buttered pasta, and sprinkled with gremolata, a piquant garnish of grated lemon rind, chopped garlic, and chopped parsley mixed together.

Get your butcher to cut the shanks into pieces about 5 centimetres thick. The hind shanks are meatier and more tender than the front ones. Some cooks tie each piece with string to hold the meat on the bone. Elizabeth David recommends using a wide, shallow pan so that you can stand the pieces upright and the marrow in the bone will not fall out while the meat cooks. There is a special spoon for removing the marrow, which some people consider the best part.

ovens. Unless you are reheating food, always preheat an oven. Allow 15–20 minutes for the oven to heat to the required temperature before putting the food in.

The following table gives approximate metric and Fahrenheit equivalents of the descriptive terms for the heat of the oven.

Description	Thermostat setting	
Cool	100°C	200°F
Very slow	120°C	250°F
Slow	150°C	300°F
Moderately slow	160°C	325°F
Moderate	180°C	350°F
Moderately hot	190°C	375°F
Hot	200°C	400°F
Very hot	230°C	450°F

With a conventional 'zoned heat' oven, the temperature of the thermostat setting applies to the centre of the oven. A shelf higher than centre would be exposed to a slightly higher temperature; a shelf set lower than centre would receive a slightly lower temperature. Food should be placed in the middle of the shelf.

With a fan-forced oven, the temperature is evenly distributed vertically in the oven. Food may be cooked on any shelf, and two things may be cooked at the one time in the knowledge that each will be cooking at the same temperature. Sometimes it means that the food can be cooked either at a lower temperature or for a shorter time. Shelves should be positioned so that there is plenty of space above and below, and if possible dishes should be staggered so that one is not directly above the other.

Stove thermostats are notoriously unreliable, however, and it is up to the individual cook to work out the stove's temperature variation by experience and adjust recipe temperatures accordingly, or use a separate oven thermometer.

oxtail. The skinned tail of the ox is used mainly for making soup and stew. (A favourite dish of chef Stephanie Alexander's is oxtail braised in red wine with black olives and served with mashed potatoes.) Oxtails are usually trimmed of excess fat and jointed into 5-centimetre pieces, then washed or soaked in water and dried before long, slow cooking. If the cooking is done the day before the dish is wanted, the fat can be skimmed off when it is cool.

oysters. The **rock oyster** of the Australian east coast, usually referred to as the Sydney rock oyster, has been highly prized as a food delicacy for thousands of years, as the heaps of shells in Aboriginal middens testify. It is farmed by more than a thousand lease-holders in estuaries along the coast of New South Wales. As a result of poisoning caused by polluted water in 1978 and 1990, all oysters sold in New South Wales must undergo a cleansing process after harvesting, being left in a tank for 36 hours with purified salt water passing through. The rock oyster will remain alive out of water for up to three weeks in winter and ten days to a fortnight in summer. Unopened oysters should be kept in a bucket with a wet hessian bag over them.

On the southern Australian coast the flat **'mud' oyster**, larger and coarser than the rock oyster, can be found on the seabed in certain areas. It has never been widely marketed or very popular. The introduced **Pacific** or **Japanese oyster** is farmed in South Australia and Tasmania. It is large and fast growing, but can be tough. The native **Tasmanian oyster**, known as the belon because of its resemblance to the highly prized flat oyster of that name from Brittany, is also farmed.

P

paella. The ingredients for this famous Spanish dish are fairly flexible, but they always include rice seasoned and coloured with saffron and usually include shellfish and perhaps other seafood, chicken, CHORIZO sausage, garlic, tomatoes, capsicums, peas and perhaps other vegetables, and chicken stock. Some recipes, however, contain no seafood. Paella is a substantial dish, and because of this it is traditionally cooked in a large, heavy-gauge metal pan shaped like an ordinary shallow frying pan but with two curved metal handles instead of one long one. This pan is known as a *paëllera* or simply a *paella*. The cooked dish is usually served in the pan.

pak choi. See BOK CHOY / BOK CHOI / PAK CHOI.

panada / panade. A panada is a kind of LIAISON, a binding agent for stuffings, QUENELLES, and the like. It may be made with bread (the *pan* in *panada*) and milk, or with flour, potatoes, or other starches mixed with milk, butter, or egg yolks. A type of bread-and-milk soup is also known as a panada.

pancakes. See CRÊPES, PANCAKES.

pancetta. Cured belly of pork. The pork belly is cured in salt and spices and

165

tightly rolled up in a salami shape. It may be cut in thin slices and eaten as it is, like PROSCIUTTO, or used as a flavouring in pasta sauces, risotto, stuffings, meat loaves, and as a BARDING for veal. It adds a delicious flavour to veal rolls.

panettone. A light Italian fruit cake made with yeast. It is really more like bread than cake—the name is said to have originally been *pan de Tonio*, 'Tony's bread'. It is baked in a tall mould and has a domed top. The light yellow cake is studded with sultanas and candied peel. While panettone has strong associations with Milan and is traditionally given as a Christmas gift, it is eaten far and wide at any time of the year. According to the American food writer and gastronome Waverley Root, it is 'just about the best possible accompaniment for breakfast coffee'.

panforte. A rich, spicy nut and fruit cake from Siena in Italy, 'oddly reminiscent of plum pudding', according to Elizabeth David. Panforte is made from almonds and hazelnuts, mixed dried fruits and peel, sugar and honey melted into a syrup, and flour, baked into a flat cake and sprinkled with icing sugar.

pan-frying. See FRY, PAN-FRY, SAUTÉ.

papaya. See PAWPAW / PAPAW, PAPAYA.

papillote. A paper frill used to decorate the bone end of a chop or cutlet. The term is also used for the oiled paper in which certain foods are baked (see EN PAPILLOTE).

pappadam / pappadum / poppadum / poppadam / papadam, etc. A thin, crisp wafer made from spiced lentil, potato, or rice flour, eaten with curries and other Indian foods. Pappadams are available from Asian food shops. To prepare them for eating, deep-fry them in oil until they swell and become straw-coloured and crunchy, then drain them on paper towels. Small quantities can also be cooked quickly in a microwave oven. Pappadams may be served warm or at room temperature.

paprika. Not to be confused with (or substituted for) CAYENNE, which it resembles in appearance but not in pungency, paprika is made from a sweet, non-pungent member of the CAPSICUM family and is used as much for its red colour as for its sweet, mild flavour. There are grades of flavour, however, and it can be bought as 'hot' as well as 'sweet'. The bright red powder is obtained by grinding the dried pods of the particular capsicum, which originally came from Central America but is now cultivated in various places around the world. Hungarian paprika is traditionally regarded as the best, and it is paprika that gives the distinctive colour and flavour to Hungarian GOULASH. Paprika is also used as a garnish for light-coloured dishes such as eggs, poultry, fish, potatoes, cream sauces, and dips such as HUMMUS BI TAHINA.

parboil. See BLANCH, PARBOIL.

parfait. Another term that has changed meaning over the years, parfait (French for 'perfect') originally referred to a coffee ice-cream frozen in a plain mould. It then came to mean a rich frozen dessert, something like a BOMBE but without the outer coating of ice-cream, made from eggs, whipped cream, and sugar syrup, with lemon juice or a flavouring such as brandy or rum. American culture has converted it into layers of ice-cream interspersed with syrups, nuts, jelly, fruit, etc., served in a tall stemmed glass.

paring. To pare is to cut off the outer layer of skin with a knife or vegetable peeler. Paring and peeling mean much the same thing, although paring usually applies only to fruit, whereas peeling applies to both fruit and vegetables.

Parma ham. Another name for PROSCIUTTO.

Parmentier. A designation meaning 'with potatoes'. It is in homage to Antoine-Auguste Parmentier, who introduced potatoes to France in the eighteenth century. Potage Parmentier is a soup made from potatoes and leeks, puréed when cooked, then reheated and lightened with cream.

Parmesan cheese. Parmesan is a generic name for a kind of hard, dry cheese (*grana* in Italian, because cheeses of this kind are closely grained) originally produced around Parma in northern Italy. Parmesan cheeses are made in various countries, including Australia, but the genuine cheese from Parma is known as *parmigiano reggiano,* and it is produced under strict regulations from milk given by cows between 1 April and 11 November. It is straw-coloured and brittle, with pinpoint holes. For centuries it was made from the milk of Reggiana cattle, but by 1993 there were only 1024 Reggiana cows in existence according to the World Watch list of endangered species, so the *parmigiano reggiano* of today is made from the milk of other breeds of cows. Nevertheless, it is still justifiably the world's most popular grating cheese. It may also be eaten as a table cheese.

The great advantage of Parmesan for grating is that it doesn't form elastic threads as it melts. It is salty and sharp and is commonly used, freshly grated, as a seasoning on soups and pasta, or spread on top of dishes to be served *au gratin.*

parsley. 'Parsley / is gharsley,' wrote Ogden Nash in what must be one of the shortest poems ever written. For many people, however, parsley is the most used and useful herb in the kitchen. It makes an excellent garnish; it adds flavour to white sauce, scrambled eggs and omelettes, mashed potatoes, soups, stuffings, and many other savoury dishes; it forms the basis of TABBOULEH salad, FINES HERBES, and BOUQUET GARNI; deep-fried, it goes well with fish. It is the herb for all seasons (or seasonings).

Parsley has been grown for thousands of years around the world, although Sardinia claims to be its place of origin (parsley was depicted on the coinage of Sardinia during its independence). There are two main kinds in culinary use, the curly-leafed variety and the flat-leafed, stronger-flavoured Italian variety. It is available all year round.

Parsley can be stored in the refrigerator for up to a week. First, wash it thoroughly, shake off the water, and remove any long stems. Use a paper-towel-lined plastic bag or a wide-mouthed jar with a screw top to store it in. The leaves can also be frozen or dried; however, dried parsley loses much of its flavour and nutritional value.

Parsley's deep-green leaves are a good source of vitamins A, C, and E and various minerals. It is good for the digestive system and the kidneys.

Tea made from parsley acts as a diuretic. Chew a little raw parsley to sweeten the breath.

parsnip. A root vegetable looking like a cream-coloured carrot, the parsnip is not everyone's favourite, perhaps because its slightly spongy texture is not like the firm carrot. Yet it has a sweet, nutty flavour and can be satisfyingly boiled, steamed, baked, fried, mashed or puréed, and used in soups, stews, and casseroles. Parsnips are available all year round. When buying them, choose smooth, firm, well-shaped roots; avoid any that are soft or shrivelled. Small to medium size are best—large ones have a woody core. Store them in the refrigerator crisper; they will keep for a week or two. Before cooking them, trim off tops and root ends, wash or peel them, and cut them up according to the recipe.

parson's nose. The piece of fatty flesh at the rump of a cooked fowl. Alternatively known as the pope's nose.

passionfruit. When sixteenth-century Spanish missionaries in South America came across the flower of a certain native vine, they felt that its structure represented the Passion of Jesus Christ. The five petals and five sepals represented the ten Apostles, the five anthers Christ's five wounds, the three stigmas the three nails in the Cross, the filaments the Crown of Thorns, and so on. The flower became known as the passionflower, and the vine's thick-skinned, globular fruit with its sweet pulp containing many small edible seeds consequently became known as the passionfruit.

Passionfruits are cultivated extensively in Australia and are available all year round, with heaviest supplies in summer and autumn. Though the skin colour varies according to the variety, the common passionfruit is dark purple. Choose fruit heavy for their size. Avoid withered fruit; however, the skin wrinkles as the fruit ripens. Store smooth-skinned fruit at room temperature, and refrigerate when the skin is wrinkled.

Use passionfruit pulp in fruit salad or as a sauce for ice-cream and pavlovas. Eat the pulp out of halved fruit with a spoon.

The **banana passionfruit** is an egg-shaped yellow-coloured fruit with a soft skin and a flavour reminiscent of banana. Its orange-coloured pulp has a drier texture than the pulp of other passionfruit.

pasta. Although pasta is a generic name covering a range of foods made from a basic mixture of flour and water, the term is generally used to refer to Italian-style pasta; Asian and other European versions are usually called NOODLES. This distinction is observed here.

Pasta may be divided into two kinds: home-made (fresh and soft) and factory-made (dry and hard). Home-made pasta is usually made with ordinary plain flour and eggs instead of water. The best-quality factory pastas are made with hard, durum wheat SEMOLINA. The dough for home-made pasta is kneaded and rolled and cut into strips or shapes. Home pasta machines, which roll the dough to the precise thickness required and then cut it into even strips, make the work a lot easier. Fresh pasta is also sold in some specialty shops. It will keep in the refrigerator for three or four days.

Pasta is made in countless shapes, but they fall basically into four groups:

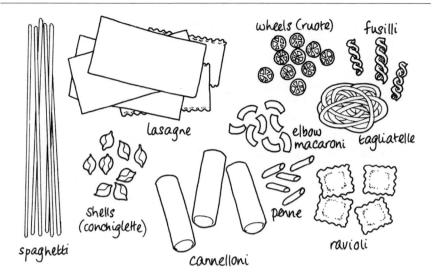

wheels (ruote) fusilli

lasagne elbow macaroni tagliatelle

shells (conchiglette) penne

spaghetti cannelloni ravioli

pasta for soup, pasta to be boiled, pasta for baking, and pasta to be stuffed. Soup pasta comes in small shapes like rings, shells, rice-like seeds, etc. Pasta for boiling is mainly long and cylindrical like SPAGHETTI or corkscrew-shaped like fusilli. Pasta for baking comes in flat or curly sheets such as LASAGNE or short, curved, and ribbed tubes, spirals, wheels, shells, etc, which trap sauces within the shapes. Pastas for stuffing are large tubes such as CANNELLONI and flat sheets folded and crimped round the stuffing, such as RAVIOLI. Many of the shapes, however, may be used interchangeably. Some of the common forms are dealt with under their individual names elsewhere in the book.

To cook pasta. Allow 100–125 grams of pasta for each person. Bring a large saucepan of salted water (about 1 litre per 100 grams of pasta) to a rolling boil and drop in the pasta all at once. Long pasta such as spaghetti should not be broken; wait for the ends in the water to soften and bend, then push the strands under. Make sure all the pasta is under water. Boil fairly briskly until the pasta is *al dente,* or firm to the bite. Start testing after about 4 minutes. As soon as it is cooked, take the pot off the heat and drain the pasta in a colander, then transfer it to a warm bowl without delay. If grated Parmesan is being used, add some now so that it will melt in the heat of the pasta. Then add the sauce and toss with two forks.

Some cooks add a little olive oil or butter to the water during the last minutes of cooking to stop the pasta from sticking together, but if you are quick to stop the cooking and waste no time in draining and saucing, it should not be necessary.

pasteurisation. The process of exposing milk, beer, etc., to heat in order to destroy certain micro-organisms and limit fermentation (see MILK).

pasticcio. Literally a mess or a pastiche, a culinary pasticcio is, as Marcella Hazan explains in *The Second Classic Italian Cookbook,* 'a mixture of cheese and vegetables, meat or cooked pasta, bound by eggs or béchamel, or both. It is baked, usually but not invariably, without a pastry crust.'

169

pastrami. In Romania, where pastrami originated, lamb, beef, pork, or goose breast is used to make this highly seasoned preserved meat, which is first heavily salted and then smoked. The Romanians eat it grilled. In Australia, by way of the United States, pastrami is made solely from cuts of lean beef, dry-cured and rubbed with spices and coated with crushed black peppercorns. It is sold cooked and ready to eat, usually in wafer-thin slices on rye bread or as part of a cold meat selection.

pastry is a dough made with flour, fat (butter, margarine, lard, suet, oil, etc.), and a little liquid (usually water, but also milk), with or without sugar, salt, and egg yolks, used for the crusts of pies, tarts and the like. The word *pastry* also means the baked food made with dough of this kind. Simple **shortcrust** (or short) pastry is made with flour, fat, and water, with a pinch of salt. There are various other pastry mixtures, some with additional ingredients, used for different purposes. Some of the familiar pastry doughs are:

Rich shortcrust pastry (*pâte brisée*). Shortcrust pastry with the addition of egg yolk and a little sugar. Used for tarts and pies.

Sweet shortcrust pastry (*pâte sucrée*). A rich shortcrust with extra sugar and a little more butter. Used for open tarts, flan cases, and tartlets.

Puff pastry (*pâte feuilletée*). Also known as **flaky pastry**, this is made with no other fat but unsalted butter and usually a little lemon juice. The dough is rolled out into a square which is folded around a piece of flattened softened butter. This parcel of butter wrapped in dough is rolled out into a long oblong, the bottom third of which is folded up and the top third folded back over it to make a square of three layers, which is given a quarter turn and rolled out again into an oblong. The rolling and folding is repeated until there are hundreds of layers which, when baked, rise to more than twice the size of the uncooked pastry. Used for light tarts, meat pies, vol-au-vents, etc.

Choux pastry (*pâte à choux*) is made with additional eggs, and the flour-and-butter mixture is cooked in a saucepan before the eggs are beaten in. Used for cream puffs, ÉCLAIRS, and PROFITEROLES.

In making pastry there are a few rules to observe:

- Work quickly, with a light hand.
- Use a cool working surface; a marble slab is ideal.
- Make sure the fat is cool and the water chilled.
- Rub the fat into the flour with your fingertips. Avoid contact with the palms of the hands, which are warm.
- Add only as much water as necessary. Too much will make the crust hard.
- Mix in liquids and egg yolks with a knife, metal spatula, or fork to avoid heating.
- Chill pastry for at least half an hour before rolling it out. This allows it to lose its elasticity.
- Roll pastry away from you. Lift and turn it around when necessary, but never turn it over.

(See also BAKE BLIND; FILO / FILLO / PHYLLO PASTRY; PIE, TART, FLAN; and ROLLING PINS.)

170

pasty. See CORNISH PASTY.

pâte. Although pâte and pâté (see below) come from the same Old French word meaning paste, they should not be confused. Pâte in culinary parlance means pastry dough. In French there are a number of terms to distinguish the various PASTRY doughs. Those sometimes referred to in English are *pâte brisée* (rich shortcrust pastry), *pâte sucrée* (sweet shortcrust pastry), *pâte à choux* (choux pastry), and *pâte feuilletée* (puff pastry).

pâté, terrine. A pâté is a savoury mixture of chopped and / or minced meat—pork, veal, game, bacon, livers, etc.—and wine or cognac, herbs and seasonings cooked in an earthenware baking dish known as a terrine. The word *terrine* has come to mean the food cooked in the dish as well as the dish itself. Some people make a distinction between pâtés and terrines, but they are essentially the same thing. The terrine (dish) is usually lined with strips of pork fat or bacon rashers. It is placed in a BAIN-MARIE and cooked slowly in the oven. A pâté is sometimes baked in a casing of pastry rather than in a terrine; it is then known as *pâté en croûte*. It may be served either hot or cold, whereas *pâté en terrine* is always served cold.

Another kind of pâté is the rich paste or spread made from finely minced cooked liver, meat, or fish, which is served as an hors d'oeuvre.

pâté de foie gras. A paste made from fatted goose liver, usually studded with truffles. In France, geese are traditionally force-fed so that their livers are enlarged and fattened.

paupiettes are thin slices of meat (usually veal) which are stuffed with a savoury filling, rolled, and wrapped in a bacon rasher, then braised or grilled. Fillets of fish may also be cooked *en paupiette;* they are baked in the oven.

pavlova. One of Australia's few claims to international gastronomic fame, the pavlova was created in 1935 by Bert Sachse, chef at Perth's long-demolished Esplanade Hotel. Chef Sachse was unsatisfied with the ordinary meringue cake, which was 'invariably too hard and crusty,' he said in an interview before he died in 1974. 'So I set out to create something that would have a crunchy top and would cut like a marshmallow.' He achieved this by simply mixing some vinegar into the meringue mixture of beaten egg-whites and castor sugar. The mixture is piled in a circle on a piece of greaseproof paper and baked in a slow oven. Pavlovas are traditionally topped with whipped cream and passionfruit, but strawberries and / or kiwi fruit are often used instead.

pawpaw / papaw, papaya. A native of tropical America, the pawpaw is cultivated in tropical areas around the world, including Australia. It grows quickly, and the fruit is available most of the year, with heaviest supplies in autumn and spring. There are two kinds grown in Australia. The Fijian variety has salmon-pink flesh and is slimmer, firmer, and less juicy than the South American variety, which is larger and has orange-yellow flesh. Both have black seeds and green to yellow skin.

When buying a pawpaw, choose one that is more yellow than green, with smooth, unblemished skin and no soft spots. It should have a pleasant aroma.

If it is still fairly green, store it at room temperature until well coloured and soft to the touch; then it may be kept in the refrigerator for a short while.

Halved, seeded, peeled, and cut into slices or cubes, pawpaw is delicious with a squeeze of lemon and some yoghurt and / or ice-cream. Add pawpaw to fruit salads or eat as an accompaniment to curry, or with pork.

Pawpaws contain the enzyme papain, which acts as a meat tenderiser, so pawpaw is good to use in marinades for tough meat.

Papaya is the species name of the pawpaw (*Carica papaya*). Papaya and pawpaw are alternative names for the one fruit. However, there are a number of varieties of pawpaw grown in different parts of the world, and sometimes one imported from, say, Hawaii, which is different in shape and colour from the common variety, is sold under the name papaya.

Peach Melba / Pêches Melba. In the words of Auguste Escoffier, the famous French chef who created this dessert for the equally famous Australian soprano Nellie Melba, 'Poach [peeled] peaches in vanilla-flavoured syrup. Dish them in a timbale upon a layer of vanilla ice-cream, and coat them with a raspberry purée.' Escoffier's timbale is a drum-shaped silver bowl which could have a false bottom, the lower compartment containing crushed ice.

peaches. The peach originated in China. It made its way by the Silk Road to Persia (its botanical name is *Prunus persica*) and then reached Greece and Rome through the agency of Alexander the Great. It was brought to Australia by early white settlers.

There are many varieties of peach cultivated, some having white flesh and some yellow. All can be classified as either clingstone (the flesh clings tenaciously to the stone) and freestone or slipstone (the flesh comes away cleanly and easily). Peaches are available in Australia from October to April, with heaviest supplies in December–January. Some of the popular varieties are Suncrest (yellow flesh, freestone), O'Henry (yellow flesh, freestone), Fragar (white flesh, clingstone), and Golden Queen (yellow flesh, clingstone), a major canning variety.

As peaches do not ripen further after being picked, select fruit with a good colour and peachy aroma which yield to gentle pressure. They deteriorate rapidly, so treat them gently and keep them in an unsealed plastic bag in the refrigerator.

peanut butter. It is better to buy peanut butter from a health food shop where the peanuts are freshly ground and the peanut butter consists solely of ground peanuts. In commercially produced peanut butter the peanut oil is sometimes replaced with an inferior vegetable oil. You can make your own peanut butter by grinding shelled and skinned roasted peanuts in a food processor or blender with a little peanut oil and salt. Don't keep home-made peanut butter too long, as it is inclined to go rancid after a while.

peanuts are not true nuts but the pods of a leguminous plant whose flower stems bend over and bury their tips in the soil, where their seed, the peanuts, form underground. Originally from tropical South America, the peanut is farmed in tropical areas around the world, including Queensland. Being legumes, peanuts are a good source of protein. Like other nuts, they have a high oil content, but it is 85 per cent unsaturated (52 per cent mono; 33 per cent poly). They provide many kilojoules.

Peanuts are available all year round, roasted, in the shell, shelled, with or without their skins on, salted, or ground into PEANUT BUTTER. Peanut oil, extracted from the nut, is an excellent cooking and salad oil (see OIL). Beware of mouldy peanuts, as the toxic substance aflatoxin may be present. (See NUTS for storage and other information.)

pearl barley. See BARLEY.

pearl perch. Two species of this warm-water, deep-bodied finfish are found in relatively small areas off the eastern and western coasts of Australia. The eastern pearl perch is caught from about the Tropic of Capricorn down to Cape Byron in New South Wales. The northern pearl perch is caught off the northern coast of Western Australia from Cape Bougainville to Port Hedland. They are similar fish, although the northern species does not have the pearly-lustred scapular bone which accounts for the fish's common name. Caught all year round but mainly in autumn and winter, pearl perch have never been abundant, but they are exceptionally good eating and thus expensive. They are usually sold in fillets. The white flesh is moist, tender, and fine, with a delicate, sweet flavour. Pearl perch can be cooked in most ways. (See also FISH.)

pears. The Packham pear, like the Granny Smith apple, is an Australian horticultural success story. Bred in 1896 by Charles Packham at Molong, New South Wales, Packham's Triumph, as it is properly called, became the world's best-selling variety. It is one of the forty or more varieties available in Australia, of which the following are common:

Beurre Bosc: medium to large, slim, long-necked; tan skin turning brown when fully ripe; firm white flesh with an aromatic flavour; good for cooking.

Comice: large, rounded; greenish-yellow turning yellow with russet spots and fawn splashings; yellow-white flesh with sweet, spicy flavour; good for everything.

Corella: small; green skin with pink blush, turns light green-gold when ripe; juicy white flesh and very little core.

Josephine: medium size, conical shape; light green turning yellow with pink blush; juicy yellow flesh, aromatic.

Packham: medium to large, rounded with short neck; green turning green gold; juicy, white flesh with sweet flavour.

Sensation: Bell-shaped, green turning burgundy.

Williams (WBC, Bartlett): medium to large, regular bell shape; light green turning yellow; smooth, musky-flavoured white flesh; good for cooking, and canning. Very perishable. **Red Williams**, also known as **Red Sensation**, is dark red to maroon when picked, ripening to bright red.

Winter Cole: small to medium, rounded; green-bronze; firm, sweet-flavoured flesh.

Winter Nelis: small; russet skin; yellowish flesh; early ripening.

Pears are available for most of the year, with heaviest supplies in autumn. They are picked before they are fully ripe, but they ripen well at room temperature. They soften as they ripen. When buying pears, select ones that are firm, plump, and have the characteristic colour of their variety, with unblemished skin and stem attached. When they have changed to their ripe colouring, store them in the refrigerator, as they deteriorate quickly.

As virtually no one is allergic to peeled pears, they are an important part of the diet when testing for food sensitivities, and they are ideal for infants starting on solid food.

All pears may be eaten out of the hand or with cheese, though some varieties are softer and juicier than others. Some of the firmer varieties are better for cooking; however, most can be poached. A simple but impressive dessert can be made by poaching whole peeled pears, still with their stems attached, in spiced red wine, which dyes them an attractive red. Poires Belle Heléne is a dessert of pears poached in vanilla-flavoured SUGAR SYRUP, served on vanilla ice-cream with a topping of hot chocolate sauce.

peas. How many people still shell peas? Will the technique of pressing just the right spot on the rounded edge of the pod to make it open, and running your thumb down to send the peas tumbling into the pot (and onto the floor), be passed on to later generations? Perhaps not. Frozen peas are much more convenient and would have been snap-frozen when freshly picked; those on the greengrocer's shelves might have been there for a long time. Best of all is to pick peas from your own garden just before cooking them.

Wild peas were eaten by humans in prehistoric times. The smooth, green, tender pea we know today was developed by the French in the sixteenth century. They also produced a miniature variety which they aptly named *petit pois.* Meanwhile, the Chinese had long been cultivating the broad, flattish **snow peas**, with their small, immature seeds and edible pods. Later the Americans developed the **sugar snap pea**, another kind with edible pods but more like the garden pea in appearance.

These three kinds are available fresh in Australia for most of the year. Choose shiny, crisp, bright green pods. Open one and taste before you buy; if peas are sweet when raw, they will be sweet when cooked. Allow about 250 grams of peas in the pod per serving—after shelling, peas weigh about half their original weight. Store them in a plastic bag in the refrigerator; when peas are kept at room temperature, enzymes turn their sugar into starch and they lose their sweetness.

Steam or boil peas with some mint, or cook them the French way with lettuce, tiny onions or shallots, some butter, and a little stock or water. Snow peas and sugar snap peas may be stir-fried as well as boiled. They need to be topped and tailed before cooking.

pecan. The smooth, thin-shelled, oval pecan, with its ridged kernel similar in structure to the walnut, grows on a tree native to the southern United States. It is now cultivated in Australia. The nuts are harvested in autumn and are available all year round. As well as being eaten as a snack, they are used whole or chopped in pies, cakes, and biscuits, and ground in stuffings, pastry, and confectionery. Like most nuts, pecans have a high fat (oil) content, but it is 92 per cent unsaturated (66 per cent mono, 26 per cent poly). They are also high in kilojoules. (See also NUTS.)

pecorino is Italian cheese made from ewe's milk (*pecora* is Italian for sheep). In Italy it may be soft or hard, fresh or matured, mild or sharp. The pecorino sold in Australia is mainly pecorino romano, which is a hard, pungent grating cheese like Parmesan. Pecorino pepato has black peppercorns in it. Pecorino-style cheeses are made in Australia from both cow's and ewe's milk.

pectin is the substance in fruit which combines with sugar and acid to form a jelly (see JAM and JELLY). It is found mostly in the skin and seeds of fruit, and it varies in amount according to the kind of fruit. Citrus fruits, grapes, plums, cooking apples, and quinces are high in pectin. Fruits such as apricots, peaches, pears, cherries, various berries, pineapple, and passionfruit are low in pectin and need additional pectin, usually in the form of citrus juice, to make a well-set jam. Commercial pectin is available in liquid or powder form. It is an approved food additive, with the code number 440.

peel, candied. See CANDIED / CRYSTALLISED / GLACÉ FRUIT.

peel, rind, zest. *Peel* and *rind* have much the same general meaning: the outer covering of certain fruits and vegetables. Dictionaries usually define peel as 'skin or rind' or give rind as a synonym of peel. Both words are used, pretty much interchangeably, with reference to citrus fruits. However, *rind* has a sense of toughness and is used to refer also to the firm outside layer of cheese and bacon and to the bark of certain plants.

Zest is the outermost part of citrus peel, the coloured part which is used as flavouring. It has to be pared carefully or scraped off with a special zester so as not to include any pith. Older cooks who grew up before *zest* came into vogue used *rind* in this sense.

Peking cabbage. See CHINESE CABBAGE.

Peking Duck. A famous Chinese method of cooking and serving duck. The duck is prepared in a complicated way. First air is blown between the skin and the flesh to produce crisp skin; then the bird is basted with a mixture of hot water and molasses and hung in the sun for four hours. After the duck is roasted, it is carved into thin, small slices of flesh and skin which are arranged on a platter. Diners place a piece of duck in the centre of a Chinese pancake together with a spring onion and some sauce made of sweet paste and sesame oil, wrap the pancake around the filling and eat it while it is warm.

penne are short pieces of tubular PASTA cut diagonally at both ends (the word *penne* is Italian for 'quills'). The pasta is usually smooth, but a ridged variety, *penne rigate,* is also available. Penne can be eaten with almost any sauce and also used in baked pasta dishes and even in soup.

pepino. The little-known pepino, also called tree melon or mellowfruit, is a small, melon-shaped fruit with a smooth, greenish-yellow skin, sometimes with purple stripes. Its pale yellow flesh has an acid but refreshing taste that is described as being like lemon, pineapple, and melon. Its seeds are edible. The plant is a native of Peru and is cultivated in Queensland and on the northern coast of New South Wales. The fruit is available from March to May and again from September to November.

Allow pepinos to ripen at room temperature away from direct sunlight—they lose their green tint and turn creamy yellow when ripe—then store them in the refrigerator. Peeled and sliced or cubed, they can be eaten, like a rockmelon or honeydew, on their own or as part of a fruit salad or cheese platter. They may also be puréed.

pepper is a word sometimes used for CAPSICUM and CHILLI as well as for the common pungent spice with which we season our food (or allow ingratiating waiters with oversized pepper mills to do for us). To avoid confusion, it seems sensible to confine the word *pepper* to the latter meaning, and use *capsicum* rather than *sweet pepper* or *bell pepper,* and *chilli* rather than *hot pepper* or *chilli pepper.*

Black and white peppercorns (and, for that matter, green and pink peppercorns) come from the same woody vine, *Piper nigrum,* which originated in India and is now cultivated throughout tropical Asia and America. Black peppercorns are harvested when the berries are immature and green. They are left to dry, shrivel, and turn black. White peppercorns are harvested when fully mature, at which stage they are greenish-yellow. The hull is removed and they are dried, turning a creamy white. Black pepper is more suitable for general use because it has a more aromatic scent and flavour than white, although not as hot. White pepper is used in white sauces and pale dishes where black specks would spoil the appearance.

Because ground pepper quickly loses its aroma and savour, it is best used freshly ground, both in cooking and at the table. A pepper mill is therefore an essential piece of kitchen equipment. Black and white peppercorns are sometimes mixed in the mill, the result being referred to as **mignonette pepper**. Some recipes call for cracked pepper, which is very coarsely ground or crushed with the back of a spoon.

Green peppercorns, also known as **poivre vert**, are immature berries canned in their soft, undried state. They have a vibrant flavour and can be mashed in sauces or used instead of cracked black peppercorns in pepper steak.

Pink peppercorns, which are the fully ripe berries preserved in brine, have a more subtle flavour than green. They have none of the pungency associated with pepper.

pepperoni. A hot, sweet, Italian salami-type sausage made from pork and beef with added fat and flavoured with pepper. It is used extensively in pizzas.

perch. A number of fish of different species found in Australian waters go under the name of perch. Some are freshwater fish, others are found in the sea; some migrate from one environment to the other. Among them are the freshwater perch (Australian bass), sea perch (MORWONG and several Barrier Reef fish, including the RED EMPEROR), deep-sea perch (ORANGE ROUGHY), OCEAN PERCH (RED GURNARD PERCH), golden perch (Murray perch, yellow-belly, callop), silver perch (grunter or Murray bream, also morwong), PEARL PERCH, and the giant perch (BARRAMUNDI). (See also FISH.)

persimmons. There are two kinds of persimmon available: the traditional heart-shaped variety, which is edible only when fully ripe and very soft (the astringent taste of the unripe fruit is as mouth-puckering as that of a green olive off the tree), and the newer, tomato-shaped Fuji variety, which is not astringent and can be eaten slightly soft or even crisp like an apple.

Persimmons are native to China, Japan, and the northern United States. They are strikingly coloured when ripe, usually a glossy orange-red.

The flesh of the traditional kind becomes a sweet, translucent jelly when fully ripe. They are in season during autumn and early winter. Select plump, unblemished, uniformly coloured fruit, with stem and cap attached, which are just beginning to soften. Let them ripen at room temperature, then eat them as soon as they are fully ripe. You can cut them in half and scoop out the flesh, or peel the skin back and eat them out of the hand (with a napkin at the ready). They can be puréed for sauce, sorbets, and ices. Their flavour goes well with grapefruit or pineapple.

pesto, pistou. Pesto is the famous Genoese basil sauce used with pasta and potato gnocchi and in soup. Pistou is the Niçois version of pesto, and it is almost always used as a flavouring addition to vegetable soup, which is known in all its variations as *soupe au pistou*.

The ingredients of pesto are fresh basil leaves, garlic, a mixture of Parmesan and pecorino romano cheese, pine nuts or walnuts, salt and olive oil. The Genoese insist that to crush and mix the ingredients properly you must use a pestle (hence *pesto*) and a marble mortar, but elsewhere nowadays a food processor or electric blender is acceptable. The finished product should have the consistency of a smooth paste, like mayonnaise. When using pesto, don't add any more grated cheese to the dish, or you will upset the balance of flavour.

Pistou, which Nice and the surrounding region of Provence borrowed from neighbouring Genoa and adapted to their taste, is made with basil, garlic, and grated cheese crushed together with oil, but also includes skinned and seeded tomatoes (sometimes grilled). The vegetable soup to which this sauce is added also contains tomatoes as well as haricot beans and some vermicelli.

petits fours. Small, dainty cakes or fancy biscuits, often iced or decorated. The term *petit four* means 'little oven', said to refer to the slow oven in which the little cakes were cooked after the higher temperature for the big cakes.

pheasant. Regarded as the tastiest of the game birds, pheasants are available from specialist poultry shops. Although the cock pheasant is bigger than the hen, the hen is plumper and juicier. However, the flesh of the pheasant is dry, so it should be 'supplied with a tightly fitting waistcoat of bacon fat before cooking', according to Andre Simon, 'and, if roasted, it must be basted abundantly.' Maggie Beer of the Pheasant Farm in the Barossa Valley recommends roasting a young, farm-raised pheasant at a very high temperature for a relatively short time and then letting it rest for at least the equivalent of the cooking time. Birds of an indeterminate age caught in the wild are best pot-roasted, she says. An average size pheasant will provide three servings.

pho. A Vietnamese soup made from beef stock (when it is called *pho bo*) or chicken stock (*pho ga*) with ginger and spices and served with rice noodles. Pho is a popular breakfast dish in Vietnam.

pickles. While various kinds of vegetables, fruit, nuts, fish, and meat can be pickled—that is, preserved in brine, vinegar, or some other preserving liquid—by 'pickles' we usually mean something like bread and butter pickles or piccalilli. Bread and butter pickles are thinly sliced cucumber and onions in white wine vinegar with sugar and such flavourings as celery seeds, mustard seeds, and turmeric. Piccalilli, or mustard pickle, is a mixture of vegetables such as cauliflower, onions, cucumbers, green tomatoes, and chopped apples, with such other ingredients as chillies, cloves, ginger, mustard, turmeric, and cornflour in with the sugar and vinegar. There are many other pickles, both sweet and sour, made with individual vegetables or fruit, or mixtures. Almost any fruit or vegetable can be pickled.

In making pickles, best-quality, just ripe, vegetables or fruit, and best-quality vinegar should be used. The chopped vegetables are salted and allowed to stand for some time, then rinsed, placed in sterilised jars, and covered with the spiced vinegar. Make sure the liquid covers the vegetables and comes to within 2 centimetres of the top of the jar. Dispel any air bubbles, which may encourage bacteria. Seal the jars with cellophane or plastic screw tops, or pour melted paraffin wax on the top. Never use bare metal covers. Pickles should be allowed to mature for two to three months before being eaten.

pie, tart, flan. A **pie** could be described simply as a dish of meat, fish, fowl, fruit, or vegetables baked in a pastry crust—that is, having a pastry case and a pastry lid. However, some pies have a top of pastry but no bottom crust (deep-dish apple pie, for example). Others are baked in a pastry case but instead of a pastry lid have a topping of mashed potato or scone dough.

A **tart** could be described as a pie without a lid. However, it may be topped with a lattice of pastry or a glaze. It usually has a filling of fruit or jam or something sweet and is often baked in a saucer-shaped pie dish.

A **flan** is a free-standing tart with a savoury or sweet filling. It is baked in a metal flan ring or tin which often has fluted sides and may have a loose base to facilitate removal of the cooked flan. The pastry case may be cooked with the filling, or it may be baked blind and the filling added afterwards and either baked further or, if filled with cooked or fresh soft fruit, eaten as it is.

All that having been said, the terms *pie, tart,* and *flan* mean different things in different parts of the world and are at times used interchangeably.

A few tips about making pies, tarts, and flans (see also BAKE BLIND and PASTRY):

- To transfer the pastry to the pie tin, roll it up on the rolling pin and unroll it over the pie tin.
- Don't pull and stretch the pastry to fit the tin, or it will shrink back when baked; lightly press it into place. Trim off excess with a knife, or run the rolling pin over the top of a flan ring or tin to remove the surplus cleanly.
- Prick the base of the pastry case with a fork to prevent the pastry from buckling or shrinking.
- Chill the pastry case before baking.
- To prevent the bottom from going soggy when the filling is inclined to be moist, brush the base with raw egg or melted and strained apricot jam or redcurrant jelly.

- Slash the top crust of a pie before baking, to let the steam escape and prevent a soggy crust.
- To remove a cooked flan from a loose-based tin, stand it on a jam jar or something similar, and gently ease the outer ring down. The flan may be left on the metal base or transferred to a serving dish.

pigeon. See SQUAB.

pikelet. A small, thick, sweet pancake, also known as a drop scone. Pikelet batter is made with self-raising flour, bicarbonate of soda, milk, butter, eggs, and sugar. Spoonfuls of the batter are dropped onto a hot, greased surface such as a griddle or frying pan, and the circles of batter are browned on both sides.

pilaf / pilaff / pilau / pilaw. A Central Asian and Middle Eastern rice dish with many variations. The rice, preferably long-grain Basmati rice, is often precooked and then added to other cooked ingredients—meat, chicken, chicken livers, vegetables, etc.—to finish off cooking. Pilau rice is usually fried in butter or oil, with onions, then cooked in seasoned stock until the stock is absorbed by the rice. Raisins and almonds are sometimes added.

pilchards. See SARDINES.

pimento, pimiento. Pimento is another name for ALLSPICE; pimiento is another name for CAPSICUM. To add to the understandable confusion this creates, a mild, spicy variety of capsicum which is skinned, cored, and pickled in brine and vinegar is sold in jars and cans inevitably labelled 'pimento'. Red when ripe but packed also in its green and yellow state, this 'pimento' pimiento is used in salads or with cold meats.

pine nuts. The small, cream-coloured 'nuts' are in fact the seeds shed by the mature cones of various species of pine tree, notably the Stone or Parasol pine which grows around the Mediterranean, where pine nuts have been eaten since prehistoric times. They are also obtained from pine species in America and China, where much of the product imported into Australia comes from. Pine nuts are used in meat and rice dishes and dried-fruit salads in Middle Eastern cookery. They are also used in stuffing for vegetables and poultry and are an important ingredient in PESTO.

pineapples. A native of tropical South America, the pineapple is actually a composite made up of the fruit of many flowers fused together. It gets its name from its resemblance to a pine cone. Pineapples are cultivated extensively in Queensland and are available all year round, though winter pineapples are a bit of a gamble. There are two main kinds. The most readily available is the large, smooth-leafed variety with juicy, pale-yellow flesh. The smaller variety with saw-toothed leaves has golden flesh which is not so juicy but is very sweet.

Pineapples are harvested when ripe. There is some difference of opinion about whether they ripen further after harvest, but they do deteriorate fairly quickly, so they should be eaten soon after purchase. Colour is not a reliable indication of ripeness: winter pineapples may be only one-third yellow when ripe; summer ones three-quarters yellow. A good guide to ripeness is a fragrant aroma. A central leaf should pull out easily. Once a pineapple is skinned and cut up, it should be stored in an airtight container in the refrigerator.

An enzyme in pineapple reacts with milk products and tends to give them an off flavour, so it is better not to combine pineapple with dairy products. This enzyme also affects the setting of gelatine. As the enzyme is destroyed by heat, cook chopped pineapple in juice or sugar syrup for about 5 minutes when making jelly.

pinto beans. Like black and red kidney beans, borlotti beans, cannellini beans, and haricot beans, pinto beans are the dried, kidney-shaped seeds of a variety of the green bean plant, *Phaseolus vulgaris*. They are plump and beige-coloured, speckled with brown. Information on preparation, storage, etc., is given under BEANS, DRIED.

To cook pinto beans, boil them gently until tender (1½–2 hours), or pressure cook them for 20–30 minutes. They are used in making CHILLI CON CARNE and other chilli-spiced bean dishes.

pipérade. One of the best-known Basque dishes, a pipérade is a mixture of capsicums, tomatoes, and onions cooked together in a frying pan, with beaten eggs stirred in at the end, which produces a kind of scrambled eggs with vegetables. Pipérade can also mean a mixture of red and green capsicum, onion, and garlic lightly sautéed in olive oil with herbs and seasonings which is used as a hot or cold garnish on omelettes and pizzas or to simmer with fish fillets or chicken breasts.

pipis. Smooth-shelled bivalve molluscs, also known as Goolwa cockles, found burrowed in the sand of ocean beaches around the southern Australian coast. Though traditionally used as a fishing bait, pipis can be cooked and eaten in the same way as mussels.

piroshki / pirozhki. Small Russian pies or turnovers made with a yeast pastry and either baked or deep-fried. Fillings include beef and onions, smoked salmon and hard-boiled eggs, carrots and hard-boiled eggs, mushrooms and sour cream, cabbage and rice, potatoes, mixed vegetables, cotttage cheese, berry fruit, among many others.

pissaladière. The French version of the PIZZA, a specialty of the Nice region. In Elizabeth David's words, 'the *pissaladière* is a substantial dish of bread dough spread with onions, anchovies, black olives, and sometimes tomatoes, baked in the oven on large heavy baking trays, and sold by the slice in bakers' shops or straight from the baking trays by street vendors.' The onions are fried gently until they are soft (and the tomatoes, if they are being used, cooked with them until amalgamated). This sauce is spread on the bread dough, and the anchovies and olives are arranged on top.

pistachio nuts. The pistachio tree is a native of Asia Minor and the Middle East, where the nuts are used extensively, particularly in sweet pastries. The fruit of the tree grows in clusters, like grapes, and is coloured yellow-green with pink flecks. Pistachios in this form are available in specialist fruit shops for a brief period in autumn. Within the fruit is a beige-coloured brittle shell, conveniently half-open, which encloses the nut itself, a pale green kernel encased in a pinkish wrinkled skin. The skin can be scraped off or blanched (see under ALMONDS). Pistachios in their shells or shelled are available all year round. The kernels are used in meat, poultry, and fish cookery, in stuffings, terrines, pastries, cakes, confectionery, and ice-cream. Like most nuts, pistachios have a high fat (oil) content, but it is 87 per cent unsaturated (71 per cent mono; 16 per cent poly). (See also NUTS.)

pistou. See PESTO, PISTOU.

pitta / pita is the round, flat, soft bread of Greece and the Middle East. It is only slightly leavened and has a hollow like a pocket running through it which is ideal for filling with salad or chopped meat. The bread is also torn into pieces to dip into HUMMUS BI TAHINA and TARAMASALATA. Pitta may also be used as a base for a pizza.

pizza. The Neapolitans claim to have invented the pizza, and in Marcella Hazan's opinion there is no way to improve on the taste of the genuine Neapolitan product. In the first place it is never baked in a pan but on a hot brick or stone surface (an unglazed terracotta floor tile, or quarry tile, heated in the oven is a good substitute for the baker's brick oven). The dough, made with yeast and olive oil, should be elastic and tender when kneaded, and crisp on the outside and firm throughout when cooked. It should be no more than 9 millimetres thick. The topping should be simple.

The most traditional of Neapolitan pizzas, *pizza alla marinara,* has just tomatoes (peeled, seeded, and cut up), garlic, olive oil, and oregano. Others have tomato, mozzarella cheese, olive oil, and Parmesan, or mozzarella and anchovies with no tomatoes. Outside Naples the toppings vary with the region: onions and oil; onions, black olives, and anchovies; and others that include mushrooms, mussels, capsicums, capers, salami, peperoni, prosciutto, and so on.

In Australia, since the arrival of the *pizzeria* and especially the ubiquitous chains of pizza houses, anything and everything goes into a pizza topping: king prawns, smoked salmon, scallops, chillies, lentils, pesto, mango, curried chicken, artichokes, fried eggs, and tinned pineapple, sometimes on a dough so sweet it would be more appropriate with ice-cream. Home-made pizzas sometimes have a pastry base rather than bread dough, or a round of pitta or similar flat bread.

plantain. A member of the BANANA family used for cooking, as it is regarded as being indigestible eaten raw. Plantains are plumper, longer, and more angular than regular bananas. They can be boiled, baked, barbecued, grilled, or fried and added to curries and casseroles.

plums. Stone fruits, which don't keep in cold storage (or controlled atmosphere, as they like to say nowadays), are available only during their season. For plums the season may stretch from late spring to early autumn, but summer is their best time, and each variety is usually available for only a brief period. There are many varieties to choose from, and these represent only a small proportion of the thousands of varieties and several species grown round the world. Those available in Australia generally belong to either the Japanese or the European species, and they can be classified as dessert plums (large, juicy, high sugar content) or cooking plums (smaller, drier, more acid), though all can be eaten out of the hand. The small, sweet sugar plums are dried to produce prunes.

Choose firm to slightly soft plums with a pleasant aroma. Store them in a cool place or in a plastic bag in the refrigerator, but eat or cook them soon after purchase. Bake them in pies and tarts; stew them to go on your breakfast cereal; use them to make jams, jellies, and sauce—but not in plum puddings; raisins are the 'plums' in that recipe.

po' boy. The name in New Orleans for a bread roll with filling, in other words something even a poor boy can afford for a meal. New Orleans' most famous poor boy, Louis Armstrong (whose nickname, Satchmo', was short for Satchelmouth) would have been able to fit a whole po' boy in his satchmo'.

poaching. To poach is to cook food in simmering liquid. You might say the ingredients of a stew were being poached, but that is not what is usually meant. An egg cooked in simmering water (out of its shell, the yolk cooking in a *poche,* or pocket, of albumen) is the origin of poaching. Fish are traditionally poached in a COURT BOUILLON. A whole chicken may be poached in stock or wine, the liquid coming halfway up the bird so that the dark meat simmers and the light meat steams. Eggs may be poached in olive oil, which cooks the eggs gently at 100°C without boiling, or in red wine, as the Burgundians are wont to do.

polenta. The staff of life in much of northern Italy, polenta is corn meal that is cooked in simmering water to make a kind of porridge. It may be eaten in this porridge-textured form with butter and cheese or as an accompaniment to braised, stewed, or roasted meat or fowl (Napoleon liked it with roasted thrushes, their beaks and feet intact). Or it may be left to cool and harden, when it is cut into squares and fried in oil, toasted on a grill, or layered like lasagne with sauce or Gorgonzola cheese and baked in the oven. The uses of polenta are infinite.

Cooking polenta is very time consuming. The corn meal must be added to simmering salted water in a fine stream while stirring so that it does not stick together, and when it is all added you must keep stirring continuously for 20 minutes, until it is the consistency of mashed potato. A large saucepan and a long wooden spoon are recommended, as the polenta spits when it thickens. It is then turned out onto a platter, board, or marble slab, or onto a greased baking tray if it is to be dried out in the oven.

pomegranate. One of the theories about the origin of the word *pommy* is that it derives from *pomegranate* and is an 'allusion to the pink and white complexions of the English in contrast to [the Australians'] own tanned countenances'. So says *Brewer's Dictionary of Phrase and Fable,* anyway. It is just one of the many myths and legends that are associated with this unusual fruit from western Asia.

The pomegranate is a round fruit the size of an apple or orange with tough, reddish-golden skin. Inside are many white, edible seeds, each enclosed in a sac of juicy crimson pulp with a spicy taste. The fruit is available in autumn, and when fully ripe the skin splits. To eat one, break it open at the split (or cut it in half) and scoop out the seed sacs with a spoon; the pithy dividing walls are not eaten. The seed sacs can also be used in salads and rice dishes and cooked with chicken. The juice can be used in drinks and sweet soup and to make jelly. Extract the juice by squeezing the halved fruit on a reamer or by warming the whole fruit, rubbing it between the hands to break the sacs, and letting the juice run out through a hole made in the bottom.

Pomegranates are rich in vitamin C and fibre.

pomelo. Also known as the shaddock, the pomelo is a large citrus fruit with thick skin and juicy, yellow-pink flesh. It is thought to have originated in Indo-China and was crossed with a sweet orange in America to produce the GRAPEFRUIT. Pomelos are available in Australia between June and November. Store them at room temperature or in the refrigerator, where they will keep for up to two months. Peel and eat them as you would an orange, or use them as a substitute for grapefruit.

popcorn. The Americans have been eating popcorn since pre-Columbian times. Ancient corn poppers have been found in various parts of the continent. Legend has it that the aboriginal Americans introduced popcorn to the Plymouth Colonists at their first Thanksgiving feast. Since then there has been no stopping the popping. Sales of commercial popcorn began in the United States around 1885.

Popping corn is a variety of maize with hard kernels that burst when heated to form white, irregularly shaped puffs. It can be bought at supermarkets and specialty shops.

To make the corn pop, heat a little oil in a frying pan and add the corn. Put a lid on the pan, or the exploding kernels will fly all over the kitchen. Shake pan occasionally until all popping ceases. Popcorn can also be popped, without oil, in a microwave oven.

popover. Made from a batter of eggs, milk, and flour and baked in a small, flowerpot-shaped mould, a popover is a sort of individual Yorkshire pudding and is served, like Yorkshire pudding, with roast beef. It gets its name from its habit of popping up over the rim of the baking mould. They should be eaten as soon as they come out of the oven.

poppy seeds. Although opium comes from a species of poppy, there is no opium in poppy seeds, and an addiction to poppy-seed loaves is not a notifiable drug offence. (However, people have been known to eat excessive amounts of poppy seeds to give them a feeling of euphoria.) The tiny, round, blue-black seeds are widely used in Jewish cookery and throughout Central Europe. As well as being sprinkled on bread rolls and biscuits, they can be used in potato salad and as a seasoning for hot poultry and meat dishes. The white poppy seeds used in Indian cookery come from another plant of the poppy family and have a different flavour, so the two kinds should not be used interchangeably. White seeds are ground to add to curry pastes and powders.

Poppy seeds should be stored in an airtight glass container in a cool, dry place.

porcini. European mushrooms of the species *Boletus edulis* (see under MUSH-ROOMS).

pork. The composition of pork, as Harold McGee points out in his informative book *On Food and Cooking,* is 45 per cent fat, 12 per cent protein, and 42 per cent water. Pork fat is, however, less saturated than beef fat, and fat keeps meat moist and adds flavour. For some time the Australian Pork Corporation has been promoting Lean New-Fashioned Pork, 'low in fat and cholesterol, now 50% leaner than it was even 8 years ago'. As well as being leaner, pork now comes in steaks, schnitzels, medallions, diced, and other lean cuts.

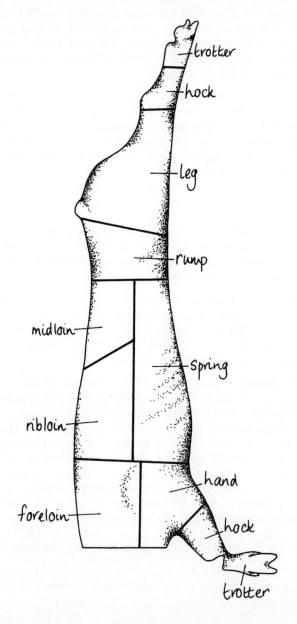

184

When you buy pork, look for pale pink, finely grained flesh, pearly-white fat, and thin, smooth skin. Store it in the coldest part of the refrigerator; it will keep for up to three days. When freezing pork, wrap it well in moisture-proof material, and separate each piece with freezer wrap. Small cuts will keep for up to three months, larger cuts up to six months. Allow frozen pork to thaw thoroughly before cooking, as pork juices coagulate when cooked frozen.

When roasting a leg or loin of pork, score the skin with a sharp knife, and rub it with salt; brush the flesh with oil. The Pork Corporation recommends roasting for 1 hour per kilogram at 170°C. If using a meat thermometer, the internal temperature should reach 76°C before you turn off the oven. Don't cook pork too quickly; but don't overcook it, which makes it tough and dry. Allow the cooked meat to rest for 10 minutes before carving, or juice will escape and the meat will lose its tenderness and flavour. Apple sauce is traditionally served with roast pork, but prunes also go well with it. Brussels sprouts, red cabbage, and other members of the *Brassica* family are good accompaniments.

porridge. Although porridge is regarded simply as a breakfast food in Australia—and an old-fashioned one at that—it is the staple food of many people in other parts of the world, particularly in Africa, and has been so for cultures in the past. Maize porridge was the staple food of the Amerindians in pre-Columbian times. The Ancient Romans ate *pulmentum,* a porridge made from millet or spelt, a primitive type of wheat, and later barley. (The present-day version of *pulmentum* is POLENTA, still a staple food in northern Italy.) Porridge was also made from pulses ('pease-porridge hot, pease-porridge cold . . .'), in fact from any cereal or pulse steeped in hot water or milk—or blood, for that matter; the Masai of East Africa mix millet flour with the blood of their cattle.

Today's breakfast porridge is usually made from rolled oats. With oatmeal porridge the water has to be boiling and the oatmeal added in a fine stream while stirring, as in cooking polenta. With rolled oats, which have been steamed and flattened to make them easier to cook, it is a simple matter to pour a measured quantity of boiling water over the oats in a saucepan, add salt to taste, let it stand for a few minutes (or while you have your morning shower) to allow the oats to absorb the water, then cook it for ten minutes or so, stirring from time to time, preferably with a spurtle, a wooden bat cunningly curved to reach into the corners of the pot. If you melt a little butter in the saucepan before making the porridge, the pan will be easier to clean.

Port-Salut. A smooth, whole-milk cheese with an orange rind, originally made by Trappist monks at their abbey in Brittany. Creamy-yellow and mild tasting, Port-Salut is a semi-firm cheese that can be used as a table cheese, in sandwiches and savouries, and in cheese pastries. The rind may be eaten. (See also CHEESE.)

potage. French for 'soup'. The word usually is applied to thick soup, as opposed to the thinner CONSOMMÉ or BOUILLON. The French word *soupe* originally referred to the piece of bread (the 'sop') over which the liquid from the pot, or *potage,* was poured.

Potage Bonne Femme is a chunky soup made from potatoes and leeks, which, when puréed, becomes **Potage Parmentier**; chill this purée, add a cup of cream and some chopped chives, and you have **vichyssoise**.

potato flour. When potatoes are dried, they can be ground into a starchy powder which is used as a thickening agent and as flour or flour additive for making bread, cakes, and biscuits. Store potato flour in an airtight container. It should keep for months.

potatoes. Although potato consumption is declining in Australia, with pasta and rice becoming increasingly more attractive to the young, potatoes are still eaten in larger quantities than any other vegetable. And understandably so; they are nutritious, with plenty of high-quality protein and vitamin C, they are filling, and they can be cooked in many different ways.

Potatoes are tubers, underground swellings of the root-like stems of *Solanum tuberosum,* a plant native to the high plateau in the Andean regions of Peru and Bolivia. There are many varieties, only a small porportion of which are cultivated for sale in Australia. However, the number of named varieties available in vegetable markets has increased considerably over recent years. A selection is described below. Each variety has its own characteristics. Those with waxy flesh are good for chips but not for mashing, as they are too glutinous. The floury or mealy kinds are ideal for mashing and baking but break up if boiled or made into chips. Some are all-purpose varieties with a firm texture that is good for any kind of cooking.

Besides different varieties, there are new potatoes and old potatoes. New potatoes are dug when they are still immature and usually small. Known as chats or cocktails in the trade, they do not keep as well as old potatoes and should be eaten soon after purchase. They can be scrubbed or scraped, cooked and eaten in their skins. Old potatoes are harvested when they are fully mature, and they can be stored for months in a cool, dark place. (Don't store them with onions, which will make them go bad quickly.) When exposed to light they may develop green patches which contain the poisonous alkaloid solanine. Any green bits should be cut off or the potato discarded entirely. Potatoes should be peeled thinly, as vitamins are concentrated just under the skin. That is why cooking potatoes in their jackets is recommended.

Bintje. Oblong to long. Smooth, creamy-white skin and pale yellow flesh. Good flavour. All-rounder, excellent for potato salad and good for chip making.

Coliban. Round and slightly flat. Smooth white skin and white flesh. For boiling, mashing, dry baking, and roasting. Not for chips. Flesh tends to break up when overcooked.

Crystal. Oblong to round. Smooth thin white skin and waxy white flesh. All-rounder, excellent for baking. Doesn't need peeling.

Desirée. Long, oval shape. Smooth pinkish-red skin with yellow waxy flesh. Good for roasting and potato salad; can be mashed and dry baked.

Exton. Round. White skin and white flesh. Good for dry baking, roasting, mashing, and salad.

Kennebec. Oblong. White skin and white flesh. Good for mashing, baking, and roasting; excellent for chip making. Not for salad.

Kipfler (Golden Crescent). Elongated crescent shape. Yellow skin and yellow waxy flesh with a nutty flavour. Good for roasting and can be mashed and dry baked; excellent for potato salad.

Patrones. Oblong. Cream skin and light yellow, slightly waxy flesh. An all-rounder, but best boiled or steamed for salad or for mashing.

Pink-Eye (Pink Lady, Southern Gold). Thin white skin with very deep, pink eyes; waxy flesh. Usually sold when immature. Good for boiling, steaming, and in potato salad.

Pink Fir Apple (French *ratte*). Elongated and flexible. Pink skin. Good for frying, boiling, and baking.

Pontiac. Round shape. Red skin and white flesh with firm, dry texture. All-rounder, although not recommended for chip making; excellent for mashing, and good for baking in jacket, roasting, and salad.

Purple Congo. Elongated. Purple skin and purple flesh. Floury. Good for mashing.

Russet Burbank. Long. Rough white skin and white flesh. Excellent for dry baking and chip making, and good for roasting. Grown mainly for McDonald's French fries.

Sebago. Large, oval shaped. Usually unwashed creamy-white skin and white dry flesh. All-rounder, excellent for mashing.

Sequoia. Round. Creamy-white skin. Moist white flesh. Good for boiling, roasting, and salads.

Spunta. Large and elongated. Thin, practically eyeless skin and yellow flesh. Good for chip making.

Toolangi Delight. Round. Thin purple skin and white flesh. Good flavour. All-rounder, excellent for mashing.

Winlock. Round. Light buff skin and white flesh. Good all-rounder.

pot-au-feu. Traditionally the pot-au-feu ('pot on the fire') has been the French provincial family's stand-by, providing a meal of soup, beef, and vegetables from the one pot. (**Poule-au-pot**, a version of pot-au-feu, is made with chicken instead of beef.) As well as the main piece of beef, other meats such as a knuckle of veal, beef marrow bone, chicken giblets, and oxtail may be added. The vegetables usually include onions, leeks, carrots, parsnips, turnips, and celery, together with a BOUQUET GARNI. The ingredients are put in a MARMITE or large covered pan with water and simmered gently for 3–4 hours. When cooked, the meat and vegetables are lifted out, the soup is strained and served first, and the meat and vegetables served as the second course.

pot-roasting. To pot-roast is to cook a piece of meat slowly in a covered pot. The meat is usually browned first. Some vegetables and herbs, browned separately, may also be added to the pot. Pot-roasting is a moist-heat form of cooking, as opposed to the dry heat of oven roasting. Some cooks say the only liquid you need in the pot is the juice from the meat. Others, and these seem to be in the majority, say to add stock and / or wine—enough to come about a quarter of the way up the side of the meat—which makes the pot-roast the same as a braise (see BRAISE, CASSEROLE, STEW). The pot-roast is usually cooked over low heat on top of the stove, although some recipes say to cook it in the oven, in which case it becomes a casserole. Perhaps the difference between a pot-roast and a braise or casserole is the size of the meat. With braises and casseroles the meat is usually in small pieces; with a pot-roast it is in one large piece.

pound cake. Pound cakes are really equal-weight cakes—that is, the flour, butter, sugar, and eggs all weigh the same, usually the weight of the eggs. 'A pound all round' was the phrase used back in the days of imperial measurement, with 8 eggs being about the equivalent of 1 lb of each of the other main ingredients. The cake itself varies according to the other ingredients—vanilla, lemon or orange zest, chopped nuts, caraway seeds, dried fruit—and the country in which it is made, but it turns into a tea or coffee cake with a fine buttery texture.

poussin. A very young CHICKEN.

praline, pralin. For some years after World War II, in a tiny shop on the ramp leading down to Sydney's Wynyard station, a refugee from Hitler's Europe could be seen stirring a large, round-bottomed copper pan in which he had placed some sugar and almond kernels. By the time the sugar had caramelised, the nuts were roasted. These delightful toffee-coated almonds sold as fast as the man made them. He was using a process invented in the seventeenth century by the cook of the Compte de Plessis-Praslin, a French field marshal. The candied nuts were called pralines.

When a mixture of hot toffee and almonds is turned out to set into a kind of almond brittle, then ground or pounded in a mortar, the powder produced is a delicious flavouring that can be used in French pastries, custards, creams, and mousses and for dredging over ice-cream. This powder is also known as praline or pralin.

prawns. Like many of the seafood species in Australian waters, prawns have been overfished. Fleets of trawlers range the seas, equipped with sonar to detect the schools of prawns, and with refrigeration and freezing equipment which allows them to spend long periods at sea. They are in radio contact with a central control room which disposes the fleet strategically. The beleaguered prawns have little chance of escape. Most of the prawns caught are exported. In return, we import prawns from New Caledonia, Thailand, and Indonesia.

To make up for the decline in wild prawns, a number of prawn farms have been set up in Queensland, northern New South Wales, and the Northern Territory. Much of this produce also is exported.

Apart from the common small school prawns and large king prawns, there are greasybacks, banana prawns, and tiger prawns (which the prawn farms concentrate on), among others (see also SCAMPI). They vary in colour when raw but assume a similar orange-red colour when cooked. When buying raw prawns, make sure they are firm and springy; avoid limp ones and those with black heads. Cooked prawns should be firm, with tight shells and a fresh smell.

To remove the dark intestinal tract, or vein, make a shallow cut down the back of the prawn and remove the vein with a toothpick or the tip of a paring knife. Or use your fingers with the help of a paring knife or a piece of paper towel.

pretzel. Although pretzels began as one of many kinds of sculptured and decorated breads traditional in Germany, they are now mainly crisp, dry biscuits with salt crystals stuck to the outside, baked in the shape of a loose knot or a stick. They are eaten as a snack with beer or other drinks.

prickly pear. See INDIAN FIG.

profiteroles are small balls of choux pastry which are baked and then filled with something sweet or savoury—cream (when they become cream puffs), custard, jam, cheese, meat or chicken purée, etc. Sweet profiteroles are used for making a CROQUEMBOUCHE. Savoury profiteroles are used as a garnish for soup.

prosciutto is ham that has been cured by salting and then drying in the air. It is known also as Parma ham, because the finest prosciutto is cured in the Parma region of northern Italy, at the town of Langhirano, where the air is said to be the most suitable for air curing. Prosciutto needs no cooking. It is traditionally cut in thin slices and eaten as an ANTIPASTO with rockmelon, honeydew melon, or figs. It is also used extensively in Italian cooking, diced or shredded, as a flavouring. Australian-made prosciutto is available. So too is a kind of prosciutto made from kangaroo leg; the manufacturer suggests dressing it with a fruity olive oil, lemon juice, a little balsamic vinegar, and some cracked pepper.

prove. To prove dough is to get it to rise by leaving it in a warm place before baking.

Provençale. A term used to denote a dish that is flavoured with a mixture of tomato and garlic, or sometimes garlic alone, characteristic of traditional food in Provence, France.

provolone. An Italian cheese, golden yellow in colour, with a glossy rind, often moulded into the shape of a pear, melon, pig, cylinder, or something equally fanciful and hung by a cord to mature. While it is young, provolone is a delicate and mild table cheese. It becomes sharper as it matures, and the aged cheese can be used for grating. It is sometimes smoked.

prunes are dried plums, d'Agen or sugar plums for preference. They are harvested when fully ripe, washed, and then dried in hot air, which gives them their wrinkled appearance. Prunes usually need to be soaked in water to plump them up before cooking, the length of soaking time depending on their dryness. Some packaged prunes already have water added and need little or no soaking. Stewed prunes are served as a dessert or on breakfast cereal. Stoned prunes can be stuffed with marzipan or nuts for sweetmeats, or wrapped in bacon and grilled (see DEVILS ON HORSEBACK). Prunes are also cooked with pork and rabbit or hare and used in stuffings for pork and game.

puddings. Some people call any dessert course a pudding. To others a pudding is a dessert containing flour or a cereal which has been baked, boiled, or steamed—for example, bread and butter pudding, rice pudding, plum pudding, and golden pudding. There are savoury puddings such as steak and kidney pudding and Yorkshire pudding. Black pudding is a large black sausage made of pig's blood. Puddings can in fact be dishes of many kinds, hot or cold, sweet or savoury, with a wide range of ingredients and made in many ways.

Steamed puddings can be cooked either in the top half of a steamer over simmering water or standing in a large saucepan of simmering water with the water coming halfway up the side of the basin. If you haven't got one of those old metal pudding basins with a clip-on lid, use a pottery or metal basin and cover it with a piece of buttered foil (buttered-side down, of course) held in place with string. Butter the inside of the basin well before you put in the pudding mixture. Keep an eye on the water level as the pudding slowly steams; you will probably have to add some more hot water before the pudding is cooked.

Summer Pudding was created to use up some of the glut of summer soft fruits on the farm. Raspberries and redcurrants are two of the fruits traditionally used, but strawberries, blueberries and other berry fruits, redcurrants and blackcurrants, and cherries may also be included in the mixture, which is cooked for a few minutes with some sugar and sometimes a little Kirsch, until the juices begin to flow and the sugar has dissolved. The cooled fruit is spooned into a basin lined with overlapping slices of crustless bread and covered with another slice of bread. A small plate is placed on top with a weight on it to compress the pudding, which is refrigerated overnight. The bowl is upturned on a plate to unmould the pudding. Serve with whipped cream.

puftaloon / puftalooner / puff de looney. A fried scone. Like DAMPER and JOHNNY CAKES, puftaloons are the bushwhacker's simple substitute for bread. Rounds of plain damper dough are fried in fat until they are golden brown and crisp. Puftaloons are eaten spread with jam, golden syrup, honey, or sugar.

pulses. The edible seeds of certain pod-bearing plants, such as peas, beans, lentils, and chickpeas.

pumpernickel. A dark, slightly sour German bread made from coarsely ground whole rye. The dough is left to rise for many hours and then baked slowly in a shallow, rectangular tin for an equally long time. This results in a dense bread with a strong flavour which goes well with strong cheese, raw smoked Westphalian ham, and a glass of schnapps. Pumpernickel has a reputation for being hard to digest—at least if the etymology of the word is any guide [*Pumpern*, a fart; *Nickel*, 'devil']. Fart like the devil?

pumpkins. Although pumpkin is regarded in some parts of the world as only fit for cattle fodder, in Australia it has always been a popular vegetable. And rightly so; there is nothing sweeter than a piece of pumpkin that has been roasted with a leg of lamb or a chicken (except perhaps a left-over piece eaten as a cold snack next day). Pumpkin soup is a perennial favourite, and freshly baked pumpkin scones are likely to produce a request for the recipe. Pumpkin may also be boiled, steamed, and mashed.

A member of the gourd family, the pumpkin originated in South America. There are many varieties, and pumpkins of one variety or another are

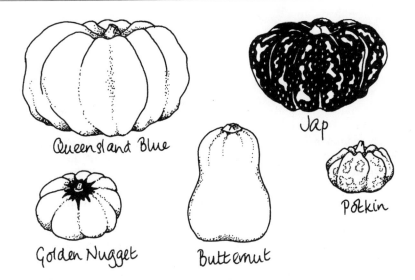

Queensland Blue

Jap

Golden Nugget

Butternut

Potkin

available in Australia all year round, with heaviest supplies in late summer and autumn.

Queensland Blue. Medium size, with flattened ends; thick, slate-blue skin, deeply ribbed; yellow-orange flesh.

Baby Blue. Small, spherical; thick blue-grey skin; pale orange flesh.

Jap. Tapered, flattened; dark green skin with yellow flecks, deeply ribbed; deep orange flesh.

Jarrahdale. Large, round; hard, slate-blue to grey skin; yellow-orange flesh.

Crown Prince. Flattened drum shape; thin, creamy-grey skin; red-orange flesh.

Golden Nugget. Small, round; orange-red, slightly ridged skin; bright orange flesh.

Butternut. Pear or bell shape; smooth, hard, yellow-brown skin; deep orange flesh.

Choose firm pumpkins that are heavy for their size; if cut, look for bright, well-coloured flesh with a sweet, nutty aroma. Store whole pumpkins in a cool, dark, well-ventilated place for up to two months; wrap cut pumpkin in plastic wrap and store in the refrigerator. Before cooking, remove the seeds and stringy bits and cut the pumpkin into appropriately sized pieces; cut off the skin if you like. Pumpkin seeds can be roasted and eaten as a snack.

purée. To purée is to reduce solid food to a smooth, fluid consistency by mashing, forcing through a sieve or food mill, or processing in a blender or food processor. The food is often cooked first. Vegetables and fruit are the usual foods puréed, but meat and fish may also be reduced to a purée. Some foods may need the addition of liquid to produce the desired consistency. Watery vegetables may need thickening with a cereal or starchy vegetable or a sauce. Purées are used for soups, garnishes, pastry fillings, etc.

191

Q

quail. The common quail is a migrating bird that breeds in Europe and spends the winter in Africa or India—if it gets there; millions of quails have been trapped in Italy and other parts of the Mediterranean region during the quails' immemorial migratory flights. Although there are quail species found in Australia, the quails sold for consumption are bred on farms. They are available from specialist poultry shops. As they are very small birds, at least two are needed for each person. They may be roasted (often wrapped in bacon, as they are inclined to dry out), braised, and casseroled. Sydney food writer Suzanne Gibbs wraps quails in pancetta and grape leaves and cooks them with muscat grapes. Elizabeth David has a recipe for braised capsicums stuffed with boned quails stuffed with FOIE GRAS.

quark. A kind of cottage cheese made with skim milk and without salt. *Quark* is German for 'curds' and has nothing to do with sub-atomic particles or James Joyce's 'three quarks for Muster Mark'.

quatre-épices. A mixture of four spices—peppercorns, cloves, nutmeg, and ginger—used by the French to flavour sausages, pâtés, and ham and pork dishes. Mixed with olive oil and lemon juice, it can be used to marinate barbecued meats, poultry, and vegetables. *Quatre-épices* can also mean allspice, which has a fragrance resembling nutmeg, cloves, pepper, and cinnamon.

quenelles are delicate dumplings made of finely chopped fish, meat, or poultry bound together with flour, breadcrumbs, butter, eggs, etc., and moulded into various large and small shapes. They are poached in salted water and served with an appropriate sauce or, if small, used as a garnish.

quesadillas. A quesadilla is a Spanish cheesecake. Mexican quesadillas, however, are pancakes or TORTILLAS rolled round a savoury filling and deep-fried, then baked in a dish with a topping of, say, avocado, sour cream, and grated cheese.

quiches. The quiche originated in the French province of Lorraine. The name is a French corruption of the Alsatian dialect word *küche,* a diminutive of the German *Kuchen,* 'cake', although the quiche is not a cake but a savoury custard tart. Quiches are made with shortcrust pastry and baked in a fluted flan ring (see PIE, TART, FLAN). The fillings are many and varied. Even in Lorraine, each town is said to have its own closely guarded secret recipe. However, the universal quiche Lorraine has a filling of lightly fried bacon (sometimes ham) covered with a mixture of beaten eggs and cream or milk. Some add grated cheese to this. Other popular additions to the basic custard filling are onions, spinach, herbs, leeks, asparagus, and even various seafoods.

Quiches should be served warm, about 10–15 minutes after being taken out of the oven. They are also good cold, especially for picnics.

quince. A pome fruit related to the apple and pear, the quince is too bitter to be eaten raw. However, it may be stewed, poached in syrup, made into jams, jellies, and marmalade, cooked in pies, and turned into a paste to eat as a sweet or an accompaniment to cheese. Quinces are available in autumn, and they have a golden yellow colour and a strong perfume reminiscent of autumn. Choose firm, well-coloured, aromatic fruit. Handle them carefully, as they bruise easily. Some have a furry bloom on them, which should be washed off before cooking if they are not peeled. Usually they are peeled, cored, and cut into slices or chunks to cook. The cut flesh, like that of the apple, turns brown when exposed to the air. This can be avoided by putting the cut fruit into ACIDULATED WATER. The flesh turns a beautiful deep pink when cooked in liquid.

Quinces are high in vitamin C. They also contain an abundance of pectin, which makes them ideal for setting jams and jellies.

R

rabbit. Before chicken became widely available and relatively cheap through battery raising, rabbit, or 'underground chook', was the common inexpensive source of animal protein. Itinerant street vendors with rows of rabbits hanging from their horse-drawn carts roamed the suburbs calling 'rabbit-oh', and when stopped for a sale would rip the skin off a rabbit with one deft tug.

Nowadays rabbits are not so freely available or so cheap, but they can be bought, skinned and cleaned, from some butchers and delicatessens. They are also available divided into portions. Farmed rabbits are plumper and more tender than wild ones, which can still be bought. A skinned rabbit may have a bluish sheen, which is nothing to worry about. Before cooking, wash the rabbit in cold water (wild rabbits used to be soaked for hours in salted water). Rabbits may be roasted, but they are better stewed, or braised with bacon, onions, and carrots, or cooked in wine, or fricasseed and served with parsley sauce. As rabbit tastes much like chicken, recipes for chicken may be used for cooking rabbit, though rabbit may take longer to cook.

radicchio. An Italian member of the CHICORY family, radicchio looks like a miniature lettuce with wine-red leaves and white ribs. Sometimes the leaves are marbled red, pink, and white, or cream splashed with red. They make an attractive colour contrast in a green salad. They have a slightly bitter taste, and the ribs are tougher than those of lettuce.

radishes are thought to have originated in China, though they were cultivated in Egypt two thousand years ago and are grown in temperate climates around the world. There are many varieties, from the giant white radish and the DAIKON extensively cultivated in China and Japan, where they are prepared as a vegetable in many ways, to the small, round, red radish popular in the West as an hors d'oeuvre or sandwich filling and for adding to salads. Red radishes have a hot and peppery white flesh. They are often cut into decorative rose or fan shapes and refrigerated in a bowl of ice water to make them fan out and set their shape. (See also HORSERADISH.)

ragoût, ragù. A ragoût is a French stew. It is made with poultry or meat and vegetables. The pieces of poultry or meat are usually browned first, and the ragoût is often flavoured with tomatoes, mushrooms, garlic, and wine and thickened with BEURRE MANIÉ.

Ragù (*ragù bolognese*) is Bologna's famous meat sauce used for seasoning its home-made pasta. It is made with minced beef, sautéed vegetables (see SOFFRITTO), wine, milk or cream and nutmeg, and chopped tomatoes or tomato paste, and simmered for a long time in an earthenware pot. A dish designated as *alla bolognese* on a menu means that it is served with ragù, or bolognaise sauce.

raisins are dried grapes. Various sweet varieties are dried, Thompson Seedless (Sultana) being the main drying variety, which produces the lighter-coloured and smaller raisins known as sultanas. Black Muscat grapes, often left with seeds in and stalks on, produce muscatels. Although sultanas and muscatels are raisins, in Australia they are regarded as separate dried fruits and the term *raisin* is used solely for the larger, dark-skinned fruit produced usually from Waltham Cross grapes. However, raisins may be packed together with sultanas and CURRANTS as dried-fruit mixture. Some packaged raisins are sold washed and ready for use; others need to be rinsed in warm water, drained, and dried with a tea-towel. Raisins are used in cakes and biscuits, home-made muesli, pilafs and savoury rice, and salads. When adding raisins to a cake mixture, a coating of flour will prevent them from sinking to the bottom of the cake during baking.

raitas / raytas are refreshing yoghurt mixtures frequently served with Indian meals, especially as a mouth-cooling complement to spicy curries. The basic ingredient of a raita is always yoghurt, into which is mixed chopped fruit or vegetables—banana and cucumber are popular—with perhaps some coriander, cumin, mint, or other spices and seasonings. Raitas are usually refrigerated for an hour or so before serving.

rambutan. A hairy cousin of the LYCHEE, the rambutan is indigenous to Malaysia and is grown commercially in Queensland. The oval fruit has a yellow to red skin covered with soft spines and juicy, translucent flesh which separates from a single flattened seed. Like the lychee, the rambutan has a flavour that resembles a grape but is slightly sharper in taste than the lychee.

Rambutans are harvested ripe and are available from February to August. Choose firm, dry, brightly coloured fruit. Store them in a sealed container in the refrigerator; they will keep for seven to ten days. To remove the skin, cut a slit around the middle and give a twist. Eat the fruit out of the hand or use the peeled and stoned fruit in fruit salad and green salad, on fruit platters and cheese boards, or cooked in Asian pork or duck dishes.

ramekin. Which came first, the ramekin or the egg? Or to put it another way, is a ramekin a small dish or a dish baked in a small dish? It seems that a ramekin was originally a small, separately cooked individual portion of food (especially a cheese preparation made with eggs, breadcrumbs, or unsweetened puff pastry), and the dish in which is was baked was called a ramekin dish. Now, it would seem the word is generally used to refer to the small ovenproof dish. All sorts of savoury foods are cooked in ramekins, from a single baked egg to custards, pâtés, gratins, soufflés, etc.

raspberries. Wild raspberries grow throughout Europe. They are a cool-climate fruit and in Australia are mainly cultivated in Victoria, Tasmania, and South Australia. There are yellow varieties as well as the traditional red. Not so long ago they were available only for a few weeks in December and January and were fairly expensive. New varieties produce a second crop in March, and Tasmania's colder climate allows the season to extend from November to May. They are more affordable now.

Raspberries are usually sold hulled. They are soft and deteriorate rapidly, so should be eaten soon after purchase. Meanwhile, store them, well covered, in the refrigerator. They have an intense flavour and are delicious eaten with whipped cream or ice-cream. Raspberries are also used in tarts and Summer Pudding (see under PUDDINGS), made into jam, and crushed into a purée which is used for making sorbets and a sauce to accompany ice-cream, custard, soufflés, and the famous PEACH MELBA.

ratafias. A ratafia may be a biscuit or a drink. The biscuit is a kind of bitter almond MACAROON. The drink is properly a liqueur or cordial flavoured with almonds or the kernels and juices of fruits such as cherries, apricots, and peaches, with added spices. But any home-made liqueurs made from fruit, sugar, and brandy or eau-de-vie are commonly referred to as ratafias.

ratatouille. A Provençal vegetable casserole with many versions. The main ingredients, however, are always the same: eggplant, zucchini, capsicums, tomatoes, and onions, with garlic, herbs, and seasonings and olive oil as the cooking medium. The variations are mainly in the quantities and how the vegetables are prepared. According to Julia Child, the best of the recipes require the vegetables to be cooked separately at first and then finished off with a short communal simmer. Ratatouille can be served hot or cold, as a separate dish or as an accompaniment to roast lamb or beef, grilled steak or fish, or with cold meats and as a salad.

ravigote. A ravigote may be a hot sauce or a cold sauce, and they are quite different. There are many versions of them, too. According to Escoffier's recipe, the hot sauce is made by reducing some white wine and vinegar, mixing in some VELOUTÉ SAUCE and cooking gently for a while, then adding some shallot butter and a little chervil, tarragon, and chopped chives. The cold sauce is a VINAIGRETTE to which are added capers, chopped onions, parsley, chervil, tarragon, and chives. Elizabeth David's recipe for cold ravigote includes anchovy fillets and gherkins or pickled cucumbers, with tarragon vinegar and lemon juice as the vinaigrette. The sauce is served with boiled beef and chicken, as well as fish.

ravioli. Legend has it that Ligurian sailors on long voyages conserved their scanty provisions by chopping up any leftovers (*rabiole,* or things of little value, in their dialect) and stuffing them into little envelopes of PASTA to eat for the next meal. Far from containing leftovers, the classic Genoese stuffing includes escarole, borage, lean veal, sweetbreads, calf's teats, lamb's brains, egg yolks, soft cheese, breadcrumbs, and grated Parmesan. Not all the stuffings nowadays are as complex; some of the most popular are spinach and cream cheese or pork and veal. The pasta may or may not be made with eggs. Ravioli are cooked in boiling salted water and served either in a clear consommé or tossed in butter and cheese or a light tomato sauce.

réchauffé. A réchauffé (from the French word meaning reheated) is a warmed-up dish of food or warmed leftovers. BUBBLE AND SQUEAK, an example of a réchauffé, also fits the figurative meaning of the word: a rehash.

red emperor. A deep-bodied fish with spectacular red or pink colouring, the red emperor—previously known as government bream—is one of the sea perches and grows to a weight of more than 18 kilograms, although the average size is 2.5 kilograms. It is found around the northern coast of Australia from northern New South Wales to Shark Bay in Western Australia. It is also imported from Thailand, Vietnam, Singapore, and Burma. Red emperor is an excellent eating fish, with moist, medium-textured flesh. It may be cooked in all ways. Serve hot or cold. (See also FISH.)

red kidney beans. Like borlotti beans, cannellini beans, haricot beans, and pinto beans, red kidney beans are the dried, kidney-shaped seeds of a variety of the green bean plant, *Phaseolus vulgaris.* They can be plump or elongated and range in colour from pink to dark red. For information on preparation, storage, etc., see BEANS, DRIED.

To cook red kidney beans. Boil them gently for 1–1½ hours, with 10 minutes of rapid boiling at the end, or pressure cook them for 20–30 minutes. They may be used in making CHILLI CON CARNE and in place of borlotti and pinto beans. They are also used in the cuisine of India, where they are known as *raajma.*

redcurrant. See CURRANTS.

redfish. Also known as nannygai and red snapper, the redfish is a relatively small, orange-red finfish with heavy, tightly knit scales which is caught off the coast of New South Wales. It is available all year round, but mainly in spring, and is usually sold skinned and filleted. The pale pink flesh is moist and fine-textured, with large flakes. Redfish fillets are best pan-fried or battered and deep-fried. They can also be grilled and baked. Good for sweet and sour fish and for making fish cakes, QUENELLES, or croquettes. (See also FISH.)

reduce, reduction. A recipe sometimes requires you to reduce a liquid—say, by half. Or it may tell you to thicken a liquid by reduction, especially when making a sauce. What you are being asked to do is to boil down the liquid so that some of its water content evaporates and its volume reduces, which concentrates the flavour and colour of the liquid and often thickens it. Take care not to burn the liquid or reduce it to the extent that it becomes unpalatable.

refresh. In culinary parlance, to refresh usually means to plunge blanched or partially cooked vegetables or other food items in cold water to stop them cooking further and to make them retain their colour and freshness.

refrigerating. Storage instructions for perishable food often say to store in the coldest part of the refrigerator. In a 'refrigerator only' unit, the coldest part is at the bottom, because cold air falls. In a combined refrigerator and freezer, the coldest part is that nearest the freezer.

refritos. See FRIJOLES REFRITOS.

relish. A kind of CHUTNEY, generally with finely cut ingredients, which means that relishes don't take as long to cook as other chutneys.

rémoulade is a sauce with a MAYONNAISE base, but how the mayonnaise is modified depends on which cookery writer you consult. Even the mayonnaise itself is made with hard-boiled egg yolks in some recipes. Chopped herbs are usually mixed in; tarragon, chervil, parsley, and chives are generally mentioned, but not all in every recipe that calls for herbs. Chopped capers are pretty much essential in these recipes, as is mustard. Spring onions sometimes get a run, and so do gherkins. What is puzzling, however, is that anchovy, an ingredient with a strong and distinctive flavour, is included in some recipes and not in others. One even describes rémoulade simply as mayonnaise with crushed anchovies added. Rémoulade is served with egg salads, cold meat, poultry, prawns, and lobster.

render. To render means to extract fat from meat trimmings by melting them down. It also means to clarify fat by melting it slowly into a liquid and then straining it to get rid of any residue.

rennet is the name given to the preparation used to coagulate milk so that it forms a CURD, as when making CHEESE or JUNKET. Originally rennet was extracted from the stomach lining of an unweaned calf. Vegetable rennet, made from fungi and certain plants, is now also used. Junket tablets are virtually compressed rennet.

rhubarb. An important thing to remember about rhubarb is not to eat the leaves. They contain a toxic substance that could kill you, though some authorities seem to ignore this piece of information. While rhubarb is not a fruit, the rosy, celery-like stalks are best treated as a fruit, a tart fruit that needs cooking and sweetening, usually stewed in water with sugar or baked in a pie or tart. It can be used in a marinade or chutney to counteract the richness of duck or pork.

Rhubarb comes originally from China or Siberia or, as the Greeks thought, from where the barbarians beyond the Rha (Volga) lived. It is available all year round. Choose crisp, firm, red stalks; greenish tinges indicate that it will be more sour than usual. Flamingo-pink stalks, on the other hand, can indicate that the rhubarb has been grown under special pots that exclude the sun and make it sweet. Store in a plastic bag in the refrigerator.

Rhubarb is high in calcium and low in kilojoules.

rice. There are more than two thousand varieties of rice, each with its own special qualities, but they may be all grouped in two general categories: Indian (long-grained) and Japanese (short-grained). Long-grained rice tends to be dry and easily separated when cooked; short-grained rice becomes moist and glutinous or sticky. In Australia, both long-grained and short-grained varieties are cultivated and sold. Special varieties such as the Indian Basmati rice and the Italian Arborio rice are imported.

Stored in a cool, dry place and out of the way of vermin, rice will keep almost indefinitely. Once cooked, rice should be kept for no longer than two or three days in the refrigerator.

Brown rice is rice that has had just the inedible husk removed, leaving the intact kernel covered with layers of bran. It has thus more nutrients than **white rice**, from which the bran and the thin aleurone layer containing a high level of oil, minerals, vitamins, and protein, has been rubbed off in the polishing process. Brown rice takes longer to cook and needs more water than white rice.

Converted rice is produced by an age-old Indian method. The unhusked rice is parboiled before milling. This not only makes husking easier but also causes the B vitamins in the bran to be diffused into the rest of the rice and allows the aleurone layer to remain attached. 'Sunbrown Quick' and 'Sungold' are two brands of Australian rice that are prepared in this way.

Arborio is the generic name for the kind of short-grained plump rice imported from Italy. It is ideal for making RISOTTO, as the grains can absorb a lot of liquid while still retaining their firmness yet adhering together creamily.

Basmati rice is a long-grained white rice cultivated in the hills of India and Bangladesh. It is aromatic and firm in texture, which makes it suitable for pilafs and as an accompaniment for Indian vegetable and meat dishes.

Calrose is an Australian variety of rice, medium-grained but best used as a short-grained rice in puddings, risotto, etc., and to accompany Japanese food.

Jasmine rice, also known as Thai rice, is a long-grained variety with a distinctive taste and fragrance and is used in many South-East Asian dishes. Jasmine rice is also grown in Australia.

Wild rice is not a true rice but the seed of a grass that grows in the shallows of the Great Lakes of North America. The long, thin grains are brown to black in colour and chewy in texture, with a nutty flavour. Cook wild rice in boiling salted water; it takes longer to cook than common rice. It goes well with poultry and game.

To cook rice. Rice can be cooked like pasta in plenty of rapidly boiling salted water and drained in a colander. It can also be cooked by the absorption method, which is efficient and nutritious, as nutrients are not discarded with the cooking water. To cook plain boiled rice this way, the Ricegrowers Co-operative Limited says to bring 1½ cups of water to the boil, slowly add 1 cup of rice, with optional salt to taste, give it a few stirs, then cover the saucepan, lower the heat, and simmer for 18–20 minutes. All you need to do then is to fluff the rice with a fork and let it stand for a few minutes before serving. Other absorption recipes tell you to boil the rice with the lid off until the water has been absorbed or evaporated, then put the lid on and turn the heat down very low or off, and leave for 5–10 minutes. Always fluff the rice up before serving.

rice flour. Flour made from pulverised rice. When it is made from milled or polished grains, the flour is white; when made from brown rice, it is a creamy colour. Rice flour is used mainly as a thickening agent but may also be mixed into other flours for cakes and biscuits.

ricer. A ricer is an implement used to convert boiled potatoes into a kind of dry purée, lighter and fluffier than mashed potato. The ricer may comprise a V-shaped or cylindrical sieve with a hinged pusher, or it may be a conical sieve on a stand used with a pestle. The potato is forced through the fine holes and emerges like little grains of soft rice. Cooked apples and other fruit, and cooked root vegetables such as carrots, parsnips, and turnips, may also be processed in this way.

ricotta should not really be called cheese, because cheese is made from the CURD of milk, whereas ricotta is made from WHEY, the watery part that separates from the curd. It was originally made out of poverty by poor Italians using the whey left over when cheese was made. However, ricotta looks like fresh cheese, and the locally made product is usually enriched with whole milk or cream, so it seems no great crime to refer to ricotta cheese. White and sweetish-bland in flavour, ricotta is used in cheesecakes and certain pasta fillings and as a dessert cheese with fresh or dried fruits. It is a high-moisture, delicate cheese which is extremely perishable. Keep it in the refrigerator and use it within a day or two.

rillettes. An hors d'oeuvre or sandwich spread, common throughout France, made from lean and fat pork cut in small pieces, cooked, and pounded or mashed into a coarse pâté mixture. The mixture is placed in an earthenware pot and covered with pork fat to keep it moist. Rillettes can also be made from a combination of pork and goose or rabbit.

rind. See PEEL, RIND, ZEST.

risotto is the antithesis of fast food. To cook this much-loved dish of northern Italy takes time and care. You also need good stock and an absorbent, short-grained rice, preferably the Arborio rice grown in northern Italy and available in Australia. The idea is to get the rice to absorb the stock, little by little, until it swells and forms a creamy mixture of tender yet firm grains.

To make a basic risotto. Sauté some finely chopped onion in butter or oil (or a combination of both) until it is pale golden, then add the rice and cook for a minute or two while stirring, so that the grains are coated with fat. Passionate cooks insist that the rice should be almost crying out for liquid before you add the first ladleful of stock, which has been gently simmering in a pot on the stove. The rice will give a huge sigh of relief. You will keep stirring as it ingests the stock. When the stock has been absorbed and the rice is thirsting for more, you add another ladleful. And so it goes, teasing the rice with a little liquid every so often, stirring all the while, until the rice is tender but still *al dente* and the mixture is creamy but not sticky.

Almost any ingredient can be added to risotto—poultry, shellfish, sausage, vegetables, herbs, fungi, chicken livers, etc.—or it can be served plain with butter and grated Parmesan cheese. Risotto alla Milanese has diced beef marrow sautéed with the onion, and saffron is added to the rice.

rissole. Rissoles have been round for centuries (if you'll pardon the pun). While they have been made for more than three hundred years, they may be shaped like a sausage, cork, cake, or ball. The original French rissoles were made of forcemeat encased in pastry and deep-fried. What we know as a rissole nowadays is much the same as a CROQUETTE or a QUENELLE: minced meat or fish, sometimes mixed with rice or vegetables and bound with egg, sometimes spiced, coated with egg and breadcrumbs and fried until golden brown.

roasting. Oven-roasting is a dry-heat form of cooking suited to large pieces of meat that need a fair amount of time to cook through. It is a relatively slow cooking method, but timing is important, because overcooked meat becomes dry and tough. Temperature is also important; different cuts and sizes of roasts require different temperatures as well as different cooking times. Some cooks recommend a high initial temperature to sear the outside and seal in the juices, then reduce the heat to moderate for the remainder of the cooking time.

The trick is to ensure the inside is cooked to your liking (and at a sufficiently high temperature to kill any bacteria) and the outside is not charred or dried up. A meat thermometer inserted in the thickest part of a joint of beef or lamb will indicate when it is cooked—an internal temperature of 60°C for rare, 70°C for medium, and 75°C for well done. Otherwise you need a sensitive touch (soft and springy for rare, fairly firm for medium, firm for well done), a practised eye, and a cook's intuition to know just when to take the roast out of the oven. With poultry, you can test if the bird is cooked adequately by pricking the skin of a thigh with a skewer; when the juice runs clear and not pink, the bird is done (see also CHICKEN).

There is some difference of opinion about the efficacy of basting. Though most cooks seem to advocate basting with the pan juices from time to time, to keep the meat or the breast of the fowl succulent, others feel that it has the reverse effect.

A few tips on roasting garnered from the experts:

- Preheat the oven to the required temperature.
- Cook all roasts on a wire rack in the roasting pan. Place meat with the fatty side uppermost. With poultry, start with the bird breast-side up, turn it onto one side and then the other during the cooking (conveniently when you baste), and finish breast-side up for the last 15 minutes or so.
- After you take the meat or poultry out of the oven, allow it to rest for 15–20 minutes. This lets the juices settle and makes the roast easier to carve.

rock-cods. Medium to large fish of several species of the *Epinephelus* and other genera, often having spotted skins, found near reefs around the eastern-northern-western coast of Australia. They are available all year round and are sold whole and in fillets, cutlets, and steaks. Flesh colour depends on the age of the fish and where it is caught. Flavour varies with size; the smaller fish have a sweeter flavour as well as a finer texture. Rock-cod fillets may be cooked in all ways. (See also FISH.)

rocket. This old-fashioned cottage-garden herb with thin stems and pointy or lobed green leaves has recently been revived, with much success, as a salad green. Rocket is a native of the Mediterranean region and is known variously as roquette, rucola, rucchetta, and arugula around the Mediterranean and in the United States. The leaves have a slightly bitter, peppery taste that adds a sharp bite to a green salad. Rocket blends well with Parmesan cheese and is often served on its own in a vinaigrette dressing with shavings of Parmesan arranged on top. It is also cooked in pasta dishes, with prosciutto, anchovies, or sun-dried tomatoes.

rockmelon. The rough-textured, sandy-grey rind of this distant cousin of the cucumber accounts for its common name. Its other name, cantaloupe (wrongly attributed, it seems), derives from Cantalupo, a former country seat of the Pope, near Rome, where the cantaloupe was first cultivated in Europe. Rockmelons are available all year round these days, although they used to be seen only in late summer, which is still the best time for them. Melons don't ripen further after they are picked—that is, they don't get any sweeter, although they do get softer—so choose a rockmelon that has a strong, sweet aroma and a smooth and shallow stem end, which shows that it separated from the stem readily. Keep it in a cool, dry place until it gives a little to the touch, which indicates the texture will be good for eating. Once it is cut, keep it in the refrigerator—wrapped in plastic, or other food may pick up its flavour.

Rockmelons can be served halved and seeded or cut into segments, cubes, or melon balls and served with ice-cream. Served with prosciutto, it makes an admirable snack or starter to a meal, and it can be thinly sliced to go on a savoury platter with prawns, ham, and cheese.

Rockmelon is an excellent source of vitamins A and C and is low in kilojoules.

roe. There are two kinds of roe: hard and soft. Hard roe—what we usually mean by roe—is the mass of eggs enclosed in a female fish's ovarian membrane. Soft roe is the milt, or sperm, of the male fish. The 'coral' on a scallop is its roe, and lobsters also have a coral-coloured roe. The most famous roe is CAVIAR, the eggs of three species of sturgeon. Caviar is produced only in countries bordering the Caspian Sea, but since Atlantic salmon have been successfully farmed in Tasmania, we have been producing salmon roe, fresh, salted, and chilled. It is eaten in the same way as caviar—indeed, salmon roe is sold as red caviar. Because it is perishable when fresh, it must be eaten soon after it is taken out of the fish.

Roes from fish such as snapper, tuna, mackerel, and mullet are also eaten. The best TARAMASALATA is made from mullet roe, which is considered second only to caviar. Mullet roe is also produced and processed in Australia. Prepared mullet roes—brined and either dried or smoked—come in pairs of amber-coloured elongated sausage shapes joined at one end. They have a slightly grainy texture and a mildly fishy flavour. Dried and smoked roes are eaten on bread, toast or biscuits as a snack or hors d'oeuvre.

rolling boil. See BOILING.

rolling pins. Some cooks make do with a bottle for rolling out pastry. Others have rolling pins of different lengths and diameters for specific purposes (thick and heavy for shortcrust and puff pastry, long and thin for pasta, etc.), pins with loose handles, and 'cool' pins made of marble or china; there are even one-handed rolling pins. Professional chefs, however, use pins made from one straight piece of unpolished hardwood, sanded and rubbed smooth, about 50 centimetres long and 5 centimetres in diameter, with no handles (which allows them to 'feel' the pastry). Having a weight of about 600 grams, these pins need only a light touch. If a precisely even thickness of pastry is called for, chefs use a pair of spacers—square-sectioned plastic rods about 6 millimetres square placed at right angles to the rolling pin near each end—to keep the pin at an even height.

Rolling pins should always be floured before using to prevent sticking. They are used for rolling icing and marzipan as well as pastry. You can also make breadcrumbs by running the roller over some baked dry bread, or use it to crush cornflakes or biscuits.

(See also PASTRY and PIE, TART, FLAN.)

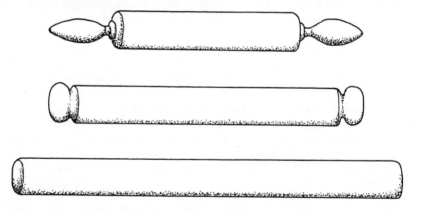

rollmop. A pickled herring fillet rolled around dill-pickled cucumber or gherkin and onion. Rollmops are a popular snack in Germany and other parts of northern Europe and are also highly regarded as a pick-me-up after a heavy night.

To make you own rollmop. Rinse and drain some salted herring fillets, spread with German mustard and scatter with capers and onion rings. Place a wedge of pickled cucumber at the narrow end of each fillet, roll it up, and secure with a toothpick. Soak the rolls for a few days in a marinade of vinegar and water flavoured with juniper berries, cloves, peppercorns, and bay leaf. Serve with beer or schnapps.

romano cheese. See PECORINO.

romaine. Another name for cos LETTUCE.

Roquefort cheese. A veined cheese made from ewe's milk and ripened in the limestone caves at Roquefort in southern France. Creamy-coloured with blue-green veining (procured by layering the curds with mouldy breadcrumbs), Roquefort has a rich, heady flavour and distinctive aroma. It is a versatile cheese that can be used in salad dressing (sieved into VINAIGRETTE) and in cooked dishes and served with fruit, on a cheese platter, or on its own with crusty French bread.

rose water. A flavouring agent made by distilling scented rose petals. It is used in cakes, pastries, puddings, custards, jellies, and even in savoury croquettes and some meat dishes. It is especially favoured by Egyptians, Turks (it is a traditional flavouring of Turkish delight), and Lebanese. You can make a simple version yourself. Put two handfuls of rose petals in a jug with 1 litre of water and 200 grams of sugar. Let them steep for an hour, then pour the water and rose petals back and forth from one jug to another. Strain the water and keep it in a cool place. Rose water can also be used in finger bowls.

rosella. The fruit of a species of hibiscus which consists of a green seed surrounded by dark red fleshy leaves. Used for making jam.

rosemary. A hardy evergreen shrub with spiky leaves and pale blue flowers native to the Mediterranean region. Rosemary grows wild in Turkey, and after the Gallipoli campaign many an Anzac could not eat food cooked with rosemary, as its scent was for ever associated for them with the smell of death.

Rosemary is an extremely fragrant herb which blends well with lamb, pork, and chicken. It is also used in soups, stews, and stuffings and is excellent with tomatoes and vegetables. But because of the powerful oil in its leaves, rosemary should be used sparingly.

rôti / roti. *Rôti* is French for 'roasted' or a meat roast. Roti is a round, saucer-size wholewheat flatbread which is served with Indian, Sri Lankan, and Malaysian curries and sambals.

rouille. A sauce made with capsicums, garlic, and olive oil which is served with BOUILLABAISE or fish stew. There are variations to the recipe and its ingredients. Canned 'pimento' (see PIMENTO, PIMIENTO) is generally used together with or in place of the capsicums; egg yolks and dry breadcrumbs may be mixed in; and a small amount of saffron, chilli powder, or Tabasco may be added to give it extra colour and flavour. The ingredients are either mashed in a mortar and mixed by hand or put through a food processor.

roulade. A preparation in the form of a roll. A savoury roulade is usually a piece of meat (veal or pork, sometimes beef) spread with a stuffing of some kind and rolled up into a sausage shape. There are German versions of this (*Rouladen*) as well as French. But it may also be a roll of pastry with a stuffing of cheese, or a GALANTINE of chicken pressed into a roll shape, or a rolled soufflé omelette (*soufflé roulade*). Cakes of the SWISS ROLL sort are also known as roulades.

roux. A mixture of fat (usually butter) and flour cooked over low heat to make the basis for a savoury sauce. Roughly equal quantities of fat and flour are gently heated in a pan and stirred so that the mixture doesn't stick to the bottom of the pan. For a white or pale roux, which is used to make sauces such as BÉCHAMEL and VELOUTÉ, the mixture is not allowed to colour more than a buttery-yellow. A brown roux, used to make BROWN SAUCE, is cooked until it turns a rich nut-brown. Although the white roux does not brown, it must be cooked until it loses the odour (and thus the taste) of raw flour. When the roux is cooked and coloured to the required degree, milk or stock and any other ingredients are added and the sauce is simmered until done.

rub in. Pastry recipes usually tell you to rub the butter or other fat into the flour. The idea is to mix the two ingredients together using the fingertips so that little warmth is transferred, 'until the mixture resembles breadcrumbs', as the recipes often say, in other words until the texture is crumbly rather than smooth.

rye. A very hardy grain originally from central Asia but cultivated for thousands of years in northern Europe, where bread made from rye flour is still widely eaten. Rye flour is greyer and contains less gluten than wheat flour, and it makes a darker, heavier loaf that takes longer to digest. However, it keeps well, especially the very dense breads such as PUMPERNICKEL. Lighter rye loaves are made with a mixture of rye and wheat flour. They are often flavoured with caraway seeds. Rye flour is also used to make crispbreads.

S

sabayon. A French adaptation of the Italian ZABAGLIONE. Made from egg yolks, sugar, and Marsala (or white wine and a liqueur of some kind), it is cooked over hot water, being beaten all the while with a wire whisk until the mixture thickens. The difference between sabayon and zabaglione, it seems, is that sabayon is served as a sauce—on fruit compote, ice-cream, or some other dessert—whereas zabaglione is served as a dessert on its own. There is also a sabayon sauce that is served with poached fish. It is made by whisking egg yolks into an equal amount of FUMET over hot water, sometimes adding pieces of butter for thickening

Sachertorte. Vienna's most famous cake, a chocolate-rich sponge filled or spread with apricot jam and given a thin coating of chocolate icing. The Sachertorte was created by chef Franz Sacher in 1832 to please his employer, Prince Metternich, who was always asking him for something new. Later it was the subject of a seven-year-long court case to decide which Viennese organisation had the right to call its product the 'original' Sachertorte. The decision went to the Hotel Sacher, in whose coffee room it was a permanent feature, eaten by the sweet-toothed with a side serving of whipped cream.

saffron is the most expensive of all spices. It consists of the stigmas—the female flower parts that catch the pollen—of a mauve, autumn-flowering crocus, and it takes about half a million of these fine, orange-red filaments to make up a kilogram of saffron. Each stigma has to be picked by hand, and there are only three on each plant. Fortunately only a tiny amount of saffron is needed to impart the gold colour and warm, aromatic flavour to dishes such as BOUILLABAISE, PAELLA, and ARROZ con Pollo, in which it is used. Too much gives a pungent, bitterish flavour. The required number of saffron threads are usually soaked in warm water, stock, or milk until the characteristic colour and aroma are produced, and the liquid is strained into the partially cooked dish when required by the recipe (for rice, when it is about two-thirds cooked). As saffron powder can be easily adulterated, it is better to buy the whole saffron threads.

sage. A perennial herb with long, pointed, grey-green, rough-textured leaves. By tradition a medicinal herb, sage is used to counter the richness of pork, duck, goose, rabbit, and sausage dishes. Sage and onion stuffing is customary for duck. The herb has a powerful flavour and should be used with discretion. Fresh sage is far preferable to dried, which has an even stronger flavour and should be used at only one-third the amount of fresh sage.

sago is a starchy extract from the inner trunk of various kinds of palm tree that grow in South-East Asia. It is usually available in pearl form, produced by pressing the starch paste through a screen and drying the granules thus formed. Sago is used as a thickener for soups and is also made into sago pudding. Sago and TAPIOCA are similar and may be used interchangeably.

salad burnet. A perennial herb with rounded and serrated green leaves which have a cucumber flavour. Salad burnet is not well known or readily available, but it is easily grown in the garden. Young leaves can be tossed in green salads, added to drinks, or used as a sandwich filling with cream cheese. Fresh or dried leaves can be used to make a herb vinegar, dried leaves to make a herb tea.

salad dryers. Implements to extract the water from washed lettuce and other salad greens. There are wire baskets with handles, some completely collaps-ible, that are whirled around on the end of a flailing arm so that the water flies off by centrifugal force. These are for outdoor use. A more sophisticated model, suitable for use indoors, has a plastic basket within a container. The basket is twirled by some mechanical means, and the water is spun out of the basket into the outer bowl.

salads. 'Don't give me any of that rabbit food,' my father-in-law used to say when he was offered salad. His reaction was not uncommon, especially among Australian males. But the preparation of salads and the variety of ingredients that go into them have improved markedly in Australia over recent years, and their popularity has increased correspondingly, even though salad still does not rate very highly as 'bloke food'.

A salad can be made out of almost any raw or cooked food with a savoury dressing. It may consist simply of lettuce or be a combination of several ingredients, including raw and cooked vegetables, herbs, cooked or cured meats, seafood, hard-boiled eggs, cheese, olives, fruit, nuts, cold cooked pasta or rice, croûtons, even flowers. The dressing may be a simple VINAI-GRETTE or one with added garlic or mustard, or it may be MAYONNAISE or one of its variations. Once a salad could be described as a cold dish, but now there are warm salads. A salad may be served as an hors d'oeuvre, as a side dish with the main course, after the main course, or as a light meal in itself.

A simple green salad—plain lettuce or other salad green with a dressing of oil, vinegar, salt, and pepper—is served either as an accompaniment to the main course or afterwards. Any of the various kinds of LETTUCE can be used, as well as endives, cresses, and herbs. The leaves should be fresh and crisp. Wash them in cold water and dry them in a SALAD DRYER or with a clean tea-towel. (Any water will dilute the flavour of the dressing and prevent the dressing from clinging to the leaves.) If the leaves are not used whole, they should be torn rather than cut. The dressing should be added just before serving, so that the leaves do not have time to sit in the dressing and wilt, and the salad tossed at the table. Some people mix the dressing beforehand; others, Italians especially, pour the oil and vinegar on separately. The vinegar should be added before the oil and used with discretion; it should never be overpowering.

Salads such as Salade Niçoise (see under NIÇOISE) and Greek salad—a mixture of lettuce, tomatoes, sliced onions, fetta cheese, and black olives—are always served as an hors d'oeuvre. A fruit salad, on the other hand, is a dessert. Salads offer unlimited possibilities.

salami. The generic name for many kinds of highly seasoned dried sausage. Originally Italian, the salami has been made for centuries in Central European countries such as Hungary and Poland, as well as in Germany, Denmark, and other countries. Some salamis are known by their place of origin (e.g., Polish salami, Danish salami, Milano, Calabrese, etc.); others by names such as cacciatore, pepperoni, gyulai, csabai, mettwurst, and chorizo. Salamis of various kinds are made in Australia. The ingredients are usually lean pork and pork fat, sometimes with beef or veal, and they are flavoured with such things as garlic, peppercorns, paprika and other spices, and wine. Some salamis are smoked, but they are generally cured by air drying.

Buy salamis that are fresh looking and red or pink rather than brown. They will keep for two to three months in a cool, dry place, but may need wiping occasionally with a damp cloth to remove a harmless mould. Once cut, they should be kept in the refrigerator. Serve salami, cut thinly, as an hors d'oeuvre, sandwich filling, in salads, or on a cold-meat platter. Salami is also used in pizza toppings.

salmon. The Australian salmon (*Arripis trutta*), also known as salmon trout, is not a true salmon but a species of perch. It is a school fish found in the waters of the southern half of the Australian coast, where it is caught by sport fishermen in the surf. The flesh is coarse and dark and not considered very good eating.

The Atlantic salmon, on the other hand, is considered very good eating indeed, both fresh and smoked. It is also canned in great quantities. Once imported from Scotland, Canada, and Alaska, Atlantic salmon are now farmed very successfully in sea cages in Tasmania and in fresh water on the Rubicon River near Lake Eildon in Victoria. Locally produced fresh salmon is available from August to June, frozen and smoked salmon all year round. More than half the fish Australia produces are exported.

'Atlantic salmon is best eaten rare after barely sealing it on a very hot grill,' says the *Australian Seafood Catering Manual*. Fresh salmon steaks may be poached in white wine or COURT BOUILLON and served with a butter sauce or HOLLANDAISE, or wrapped in foil or pastry and baked. Fresh salmon can also be served raw cut in very thin slices or cured in a mixture of salt, sugar, and dill (see GRAVLAX). Smoked salmon is usually eaten in paper-thin slices on rye bread, sometimes with sour cream or CRÉME FRAÎCHE, or in Jewish style with cream cheese and bagels.

(For king salmon and Cooktown salmon, see THREADFIN.)

salsa means 'sauce' in both Italian and Spanish. Hence there is an Italian *salsa verde,* or green sauce, which is made with finely chopped parsley, capers, and garlic, mashed anchovies, oil, and vinegar; a Spanish *salsa verde,* which is made with minced parsley and celery, bread, garlic, oil, and vinegar; and a Mexican *salsa verde,* which is made with chopped tomatillos (Mexican green tomatoes; see TOMATILLO), onions, coriander, and chilli. The salsa as we know it in Australia seems to be mainly of the Mexican, or New Mexican, persuasion. There are numerous versions, but they are all composed of chopped vegetables, often including tomatoes, onions, and coriander and always chilli, to form something between a sauce and a salad. These salsas are served with TACOS, ENCHILADAS, QUESADILLAS, and TOSTADAS, as well as with grilled meat and fish. Italian *salsa verde* is served with boiled meats and fish, Spanish *salsa verde* with cold vegetables.

salt. Although too much salt (sodium chloride) in the diet can raise blood pressure, and people with hypertension should therefore eat less salt, it seems excessive for people not at risk to banish salt completely from their diet. Since time immemorial salt has been highly prized as a seasoning and a food preservative. It is a concentrated source of two important mineral elements that are a biological necessity for our existence. Unfortunately, many processed foods contain far more salt than we need.

As no deposits of rock salt have been found in Australia, our salt is derived from the evaporation of sea water or from dry salt lakes and is produced mainly in South Australia. It is available in coarse-grained form for kitchen use and in a refined form—mixed with an anti-caking agent such as sodium aluminosilicate (approved food additive 554) to make it flow freely—for the table and salt shaker.

Salt has the effect of drawing moisture out of food. This is the principle by which salt is used to preserve foods. It is also used by cooks to extract much of the moisture from slices of EGGPLANT and cucumber (see DEGORGE DISGORGE and EGGPLANT). The moisture-extracting property of salt should be borne in mind when cooking. Meat, for example, should not be salted before frying, grilling, or barbecuing. The juices will be drawn out, making the meat tough. The moisture drawn to the surface also prevents the meat from browning properly. Dried beans are also toughened by salt, which is why it is not added to the cooking water until towards the end of cooking time.

Iodised salt is ordinary salt to which the essential trace element iodine has been added, for the benefit of those people with a malfunctioning thyroid gland and for those regions where the water and soil lack iodine.

Maldon salt is a sea salt imported from Essex in England. It has a clean flavour and flaky texture. It may be ground in a mill or sprinkled on food as it is. Available from specialist food shops and delicatessens.

Rock salt. The local product sold as rock salt is sea salt in large crystals. It is used for grinding in a salt mill but may be sprinkled on top of FOCACCIA before it is baked.

Seasoned salt. Garlic, celery, and other flavouring agents are added to salt for those who want their common salt to be sophisticated.

Spicy salt is salt mixed with Chinese FIVE-SPICE POWDER and tossed in a hot, dry wok until a toasty aroma is produced.

saltimbocca. An Italian dish which will 'jump into the mouth', if the name can be taken literally. Thin slices of veal are each overlaid with a slice of ham and a leaf of fresh sage, rolled up, and secured with a toothpick. The rolls are browned gently in butter, then simmered in Marsala or white wine until the meat is tender. Serve with fried CROÛTONS.

sambol, sambal. Sambols and sambals are side dishes served with Indian, Indonesian, and Malay food. Indian and Sri Lankan sambols may be simple or elaborate, sharp, pungent, sweet, salty, or tart. They are made from raw vegetables and fruit, seafood, etc., with spices, usually chilli, garlic, ginger, coconut milk, etc. In Indonesia a sambal is any sauce or paste made with chillies, used either as a condiment or a cooking ingredient. **Sambal oelek / ulek** consists of finely minced red chillies mixed with salt and soy sauce. Malaysian sambals can be dishes of meat or fish fried with chillies, as well as condiments made with chillies.

samosa / samousa. A small, triangular, Indian pastry filled with a spicy meat or vegetable mixture and deep-fried in oil or ghee. Samosas may be served as savouries with drinks or as an hors d'oeuvre with a fresh CHUTNEY.

sandwiches. The fourth Earl of Sandwich (1718–92) started something when he called for a piece of ham between two slices of bread so that he could keep gambling without stopping to eat. 'We owe him so much,' wrote Woody Allen in *Getting Even*. 'He freed mankind from the hot lunch.' Or did he? For generations workmen and travellers had been taking a slab of meat between two slabs of bread to keep them going during the day. But whether Lord Sandwich was entitled to the distinction or not, his name has been perpetuated in this portable and convenient item of takeaway food.

The sandwich is nothing if not adaptable. Any kind of bread can be used, and the filling may consist of almost any cooked or raw food, from the thin slices of cucumber favoured by Lady Bracknell in *The Importance of Being Earnest* to the contents of the refrigerator, which Dagwood Bumstead of the comic strip 'Blondie' often tried to include, sometimes between more than two slices of bread. Crusts may be cut off or left on. The bread may be toasted. The sandwiches may be cut in triangles or rectangles or finger shapes. Open sandwiches (something of a contradiction in terms), with the slices of bread separated and the filling divided between them, have to be eaten with a knife and fork. There are some famous sandwiches, among them New York's BLT (bacon, lettuce, and tomato), France's CROQUE-MONSIEUR, the New Orleans PO' BOY, and the club sandwich (three slices of toast enclosing various meats, lettuce, and dressing). When asked to name a single complete health food, the Professor of Nutrition and Dietetics at Newcastle University insisted that there was no such thing but offered as a compromise a sandwich made from two slices of wholemeal bread with lean roast beef, chickpeas, and salad.

sapodilla. The sapodilla tree has a shady past to live down. It was the dried sap of the sapodilla, a native of tropical America, that the likes of William Wrigley turned into the quintessentially American confection, chewing gum, and thereby created an international refuse problem. However, for some years the tree has been free of guilt; today's chewing gum is made mostly from synthetic polymers.

The sapodilla is now cultivated for its fruit, which has a rough, brownish, thin skin and honey-coloured translucent flesh with inedible black seeds. The flesh is sweet and fragrant but sometimes gritty. Sapodillas, which are grown in Australia, are available from early winter to late summer. The fruit is soft when ripe. Allow sapodillas to ripen at room temperature away from direct sunlight, and refrigerate when ripe. Peel and slice or cube them, removing the seeds. Serve with ice-cream or add to fruit salads. The flesh may be puréed.

sapote. See BLACK SAPOTE.

sardines. A sardine is a young pilchard, and a pilchard is a small member of the herring family. Sardines are slim fish with silvery sides and dark on top. For centuries they had been caught in large quantities along the Atlantic seaboard of France, Portugal, and Spain, as well as in the Mediterranean. In the 1960s, for some reason (a change in the course of the current, lowering of the temperature, overfishing?), they deserted the French and Iberian seaboard and emigrated to the coast of Africa, although they remained in the Mediterranean. The Norwegian 'sild' sardine is actually a sprat, another relative of the herring.

Since the development of canning in the nineteenth century, sardines have been canned in oil and exported to many countries, including Australia. The canned fish are first brined, dried, and cooked in oil. The cans should be kept in a cupboard and not in the refrigerator, which would cause the oil to solidify and the fish to dry out. Canned sardines may be eaten bones and all (gut too in the case of Norwegian sardines).

The Australian species of sardine or pilchard is found in abundance around the eastern, southern, and western coasts of Australia below the Tropic of Capricorn. Although they are used to a great extent as bait for bigger fish, fresh sardines are good eating and can be fried, grilled, barbecued, or breadcrumbed and sprinkled with oil and baked or fried. A sardine-processing factory began operating in Fremantle in the late 1980s.

sashimi. Japanese-style raw fish. Fresh, good-quality fish (tuna, salmon, mackerel, etc.) are sliced in bite-sized pieces, shaped in various ways, garnished with pickles, soy sauce, WASABI (Japanese green horseradish paste), or DAIKON, and served in an aesthetically pleasing arrangement.

satay / sate. A Malay and Indonesian version of the shish kebab (see KEBAB / KEBOB / KABOB). Cubes of meat, fish, or poultry are marinated in a spicy paste, then threaded onto bamboo skewers and grilled over a charcoal fire. Satays are often served with a peanut sauce and *Sambal Oelek* (see *sambol / sambal*).

sauce-boat / gravy-boat. A small, often boat-shaped vessel in which sauce or gravy is served at table. There is a double-spouted version which is also useful in the kitchen; it pours the separated fat that has risen to the top from a shallow spout on one side and lean gravy from a funnel-shaped spout on the other side.

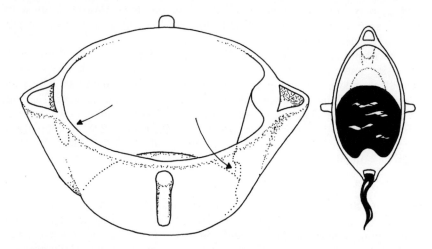

saucepans. It is better to choose saucepans of sizes and shapes that suit the kinds of food you cook and the number of people you usually cook for than to buy a matched set. You may also need to have pans made of different materials to do different jobs, for there is no perfect material from which to make a saucepan.

Copper, for example, is by far the best conductor of heat, an important attribute of a saucepan, but copper reacts with some foods, so copper pots are usually lined with tin or stainless steel.

Stainless steel is extremely durable, retains its polish, and does not react with food, but it is a poor conductor of heat and develops hot spots which catch and burn foods, especially sweet, sticky sauces. Stainless steel pans therefore often have a copper or aluminium base or a core of mild steel sandwiched between the layers of stainless steel.

Aluminium is a good, all-round saucepan material provided it is of heavy gauge. It is second only to copper as a conductor of heat. It is light in weight and easy to handle. But it does react with acid foods, turning some a greyish colour and changing their taste. Food should not be left in aluminium saucepans after it is cooked, as it could pit the metal and taint the food. Clean the saucepans soon after use.

Cast-iron conducts heat slowly but evenly and is ideal for long, slow cooking. The saucepans are heavy to handle and, if not enamelled, will rust unless carefully looked after. 'Seasoning' an iron pan by heating oil in it for several hours helps to prevent rusting, and drying quickly over high heat after washing is also recommended.

Enamelled saucepans should be treated carefully so that the enamel does not chip. Steel wool or harsh abrasive cleaners should not be used to clean them.

In general, saucepans should be made from thick, heavy-gauge metal, especially the base, so that heat is distributed evenly and the metal does not buckle. They should have lids that fit tightly and allow the condensed steam to run back into the pot. The handles should be strong and firmly attached, with rivets rather than screws. Plastic handles are cool to hold but are inclined to get burnt. Metal handles, however, need a cloth or mitt to hold them.

sauces. A sauce is a liquid or semi-solid preparation that adds relish to food or makes it more appetising. There are very many sauces, sweet as well as savoury, some served hot and others cold. They may be as simple as melted butter or so complicated that to make them in the way of the celebrated nineteenth-century French *saucier* Antonin Carême requires days of preparation. If sauces are no longer the works of art that Carême created, they can be tricky to make, as the chemical processes involved, the nature of emulsions, the quality of the ingredients, the effect of heat, and so on test the cook's skill. Many sauces can of course be bought ready-made. Some of the better known sauces are listed in this book under their individual names. See, for example, AÏOLI; BÉARNAISE SAUCE; BÉCHAMEL SAUCE; BEURRE BLANC; BROWN SAUCE; CUMBERLAND SAUCE; CUSTARD; GRAVY; HARD SAUCE; HORSERADISH; MAÎTRE D'HÔTEL; MAYONNAISE; MORNAY SAUCE; ROUILLE; SABAYON; TARTARE SAUCE; VELOUTÉ SAUCE; and VINAI-GRETTE.

sauerbraten. A traditional German dish of marinated beef claimed as their own by several German regions and consequently prepared in slightly different ways. A piece of boneless beef (topside, silverside, or rolled brisket) is marinated for two or three days in wine, vinegar, buttermilk, or beer, depending on the region, with chopped carrots, onions, and celery, herbs, and spices, then browned all over, and finally cooked slowly in some of the marinade in a covered casserole dish. Sauerbraten is traditionally served with dumplings or boiled potatoes and red cabbage and a sauce made from the thickened pot juices, sometimes with added crushed ginger-snaps or honey-cake crumbs or raisins.

sauerkraut. The principle of pickling cabbage originated in China and was probably brought to Europe by the Tartars in the thirteenth century. The cabbage is fermented in brine strong enough to kill the unwanted bacteria but weak enough to allow other bacteria to grow and produce the lactic acid that pickles the cabbage and turns it appealingly sour. Sauerkraut (*choucroute* in French) can be made at home—if you can stand the smell of fermenting cabbage. Put a layer of shredded cabbage in a sterilised crock or barrel, cover it with a layer of salt and some juniper berries, and repeat the process until the crock is full. Cover with a board or plate with a weight on top and leave the cabbage to ferment for a few weeks in a cool, airy place. But unless you eat it often, it is probably better to buy it canned.

Sauerkraut is served in various ways: for example, cold, as a salad or relish; hot with frankfurts or SPARE-RIBS; or cooked in chicken or bacon fat with chopped onion, sliced apple and grated potato, then simmered with salted and smoked loin of pork. First rinse and soak sauerkraut in cold water to remove the excess salt and sourness, then squeeze out the water.

sausages. There are many kinds of sausages, and they may be grouped into several categories:

Fresh sausages are made from minced pork, beef, veal, or a mixture of meats, usually bound by a starchy agent such as breadcrumbs, flour, or rice, with water, and stuffed in a casing of pig or sheep gut or an artificial, edible casing made from beef hide. They contain both lean meat and fat and may be thick or thin. They are seasoned with salt and pepper as well as any herbs, spices, etc. that the butcher may include as a special flavouring. Fresh sausages should be eaten within two days of purchase, after keeping them in the coldest part of the refrigerator. They can be frozen for up to two months. Fresh sausages can be fried, grilled, barbecued, baked, or curried.

Frankfurt-type sausages are fully cooked or smoked but are usually reheated in boiling water, grilled, or added to other foods to cook further. Other sausages of this type are saveloys (thicker than frankfurts, spicy, some skinless), knackwurst (pork and beef, highly seasoned, contains garlic), and cotechino (large, pork, with white wine and spices).

Pâté-type sausages such as LIVERWURST and Teewurst (finely minced pork and beef) are soft and meant to be eaten as a spread on bread or biscuits.

Pudding-type sausages such as black pudding and blood sausage, which are made from pig's fat and blood with cereal of some kind, and white pudding (veal or pale pork, with cereal and cream) are grilled or fried.

Semi-dry sausages. Also referred to as slicing sausages, they include DEVON, MORTADELLA, Mettwurst, and similar sausages which are cooked or smoked and meant to be sliced and served on sandwiches, in salads, or as part of a light lunch.

Dry sausages. These are the SALAMI sausages, which are highly seasoned and made from pork and pork fat, sometimes smoked, and usually quite hard and dry. They are used on sandwiches, cold meat platters, in salads and cooked dishes

sautéing. See FRY, PAN-FRY, SAUTÉ.

savarin. A variation of the BABA created by a Parisian pastry chef in honour of the gastronome Anthelme Brillat-Savarin. The cake is made with a yeast-leavened dough and cooked in a ring mould with a central funnel. When cooked, the savarin is doused with liqueur-flavoured syrup (traditionally Kirsch) and coated with apricot-jam glaze. The central hole may be filled with CHANTILLY cream, CRÈME PATISSIÈRE, or fresh soft fruits.

Savarin is also the name of a soup made from white bean purée.

savory. Summer savory is an annual; winter savory a perennial. They are closely related species of the same herb genus, and both resemble thyme but have longer, narrower leaves. Summer savory has a milder flavour than winter savory. Savory is known as the 'bean herb', because it goes well boiled with beans in the way mint does with peas. It also goes well with fish and in stuffings.

scalding. To scald is to heat a liquid, usually milk or cream, almost to boiling point, so that small bubbles begin to form around the edge of the pan and a film shines or wrinkles over the surface of the liquid. Some cooks heat the milk over boiling water to make sure it does not catch on the bottom of the pan. Rinsing the saucepan first with cold water will make the pan easier to clean afterwards.

To scald can also mean to blanch—that is, to immerse fruit or vegetables briefly in boiling water so as to make their skin easier to remove.

scallions. The American term for young green onions, commonly known as shallots (see ONIONS and SHALLOTS).

scallops / scollops. Scallops used to be referred to as Tasmanian scallops, not only because most of them were caught in Tasmanian waters but also because if you asked for just 'scollops' in a fish shop you would be given thin slices of potato dipped in batter and deep-fried. Potato scallops were better known and more widely eaten than the bivalve mollusc in those days. Oysters were the only molluscs most Australians would bother to eat. Nowadays, mussels, abalone, squid, octopus, cuttlefish, even pipis, as well as scallops, are eaten enthusiastically. But with the old scallop fisheries in Tasmania's D'Entrecasteaux Channel and Victoria's Port Phillip Bay closed through over-fishing, the scallops in the markets may come from Coffin Bay on Eyre Peninsula in South Australia (small, magenta-shelled queen scallops, with purple coral), Carnarvon in Western Australia (huge deep-sea, pure-white scallops), Jervis Bay in New South Wales or from scallop farms in Tasmania. They are also imported from New Zealand, Asia, and North America.

Wherever they come from, the scallops will often have been frozen and thawed out on the fishmonger's tray, which means that some of the juices and flavour will have been leached out and they may become tough when fried or grilled. Some will have been soaked, to bulk them up, rather than dry-shucked and sold on the half-shell, which retains flavour and texture. Unopened scallops are sometimes available, but it is not an easy job to insert a knife between the shells and sever the muscle at the straight-edged part which holds the shells together. The white aductor muscle and the pink coral are then separated from the other parts, which are not usually eaten.

Scallops should be cooked very quickly—a minute or so in a hot frying pan or on a hot ribbed grill. The coral cooks more quickly than the white part. They should be washed and patted dry before cooking. They can be marinated and grilled on a skewer with bacon or with vegetables, poached, baked (see COQUILLES SAINT JACQUES), deep-fried in TEMPURA batter, and made into soup.

scaloppine. The Italian equivalent of the French ESCALOPE and the German SCHNITZEL, scaloppine are small slices of veal, usually cut off the leg across the grain, which are pounded thin and then cooked in various ways. They are often dredged in seasoned flour, browned on both sides, and simmered in a sauce made with the pan juices and Marsala (*scaloppine al marsala*) or lemon juice (*scaloppine al limone*). They may also be rolled around a slice of ham and a sage leaf and cooked in wine (see SALTIMBOCCA).

scampi. Certain decapod crustaceans found in the Adriatic sea and which are used to great effect in Italian seafood cookery are known as scampi. They are like big prawns, but their two front legs are enlarged and have pincers. Similar crustaceans are known to the French as *langoustines* and to other nationalities as Dublin Bay prawns and Norwegian lobsters. Before the Australian fishing zone was extended from twelve miles to two hundred miles in 1978, Russian trawlers operating off the coast of Western Australia in what were then international waters had been catching a species of scampi (*Metanethrops australiensis*). In 1986 an Australian research vessel from Fremantle located the grounds of this species, and since then fresh and frozen scampi have been available in Australia.

Scampi can be boiled in their shell and eaten hot with butter or cold as you would eat prawns or lobster. They can also be fried, grilled, or stewed.

schnitzel. A schnitzel is an ESCALOPE, normally of veal, which is prepared in various ways in the cooking of Germany and Austria. Probably the most famous is the Viennese way—Wiener Schnitzel: a thin, well-flattened slice of veal which is floured, dipped in beaten egg and then in breadcrumbs, fried in lard or butter until golden brown, then drained well on absorbent paper before being served with mashed or sautéed potatoes and a salad.

Schnitzels may be of beef or pork as well as veal. They may be simply dipped in seasoned flour and fried (Naturschnitzel) or floured and coated with egg without breadcrumbs (Parisian Schnitzel). Some schnitzels are served with a cream sauce, others with mushrooms and sour cream, or cooked and served with bacon or tongue, or spread with a filling, wrapped in a pancake, sprinkled with grated cheese, and baked. (See also SCALOPPINE.)

scones. It takes only about 15 minutes to produce a batch of scones. They are simple light plain cakes made essentially from a dough of self-raising flour, salt, butter, and milk and baked for 10–15 minutes in a hot oven. Yet everyone who makes scones seems to do so with an individual ingredient or technique. Plain milk, milk and water, or powdered milk? Sugar or not? Castor sugar? Honey? Roll the dough out or pat it flat? Cut the rolled-out dough with a cutter, or form the scones with your hands? Or mould one squarish lump and slash it with a knife into squares? Then there are the variations: pumpkin scones (mashed boiled pumpkin added to the dough), date scones (dates added), and drop scones (cooked on a hotplate or griddle instead of in the oven).

Scones are usually split open and spread with butter or jam and cream (Devonshire tea). Scone dough can be used as a topping for a stew or casserole or as the base for a pizza.

scoring. To score is to make shallow cuts with a sharp knife over the surface of certain meats, particularly the rind of pork or ham and the fat on roast meat to prevent buckling and allow the melted fat to run out, and sometimes to tenderise steaks by cutting through their fine connecting tissues.

Scotch broth. See BROTH.

Scotch egg. A hard-boiled egg enclosed in sausage meat, coated with egg and breadcrumbs, and deep-fried.

sea urchin. Many an unwary wader in a rock pool has had the painful experience of being spiked by one of the spines of a sea urchin, or sea egg. (The word *urchin* in this sense probably derives from *hérisson*, the French word for 'hedgehog'; *egg* supposedly comes from the old Marseillaise custom of lightly boiling their much-prized *oursins* in sea water and eating them like an egg.) These close relatives of the starfishes, with rounded bodies of beautifully formed plates from which the spines protrude, are found throughout the world. Their roe is considered a delicacy in various countries. It is best eaten raw on bread or toast, with perhaps a squeeze of lemon. It is also made into a paste to flavour sauces, to accompany fish and seafood, and to use as a spread. The Italians cook sea urchin roe in olive oil with garlic, parsley and wine and serve it as a sauce with LINGUINE. In Japan the roe is eaten in SUSHI.

There are many genera and species of sea urchin in Australian waters, and the export of sea urchin roe is a blossoming industry in Tasmania. The roe can be bought in fish markets and specialist shops, but if you happen to get a live sea urchin, cut it open in a circle around the mouth part (the opening at the base—you'll need gloves to hold the spines), and lift out the five coral-tinted strips of roe. Rinse them and discard the rest of the innards and shell.

seaweed. While seaweed is used in cooking in various ways in different parts of the world, in Australia it is eaten for the most part only in Japanese cuisine. Seaweed accounts for a significant proportion of the food intake of the Japanese. The main kinds of Japanese edible seaweed are:

Nori (dried laver), which comes in thin, greenish-black sheets. When warmed, it becomes crisper and purplish in colour. It is wrapped around balls of rice to form one kind of SUSHI and is crumbled over rice as a salty garnish.

Kombu (dried kelp), which comes in hard, greyish-black strips and is used mainly to flavour the Japanese stock DASHI. It is also used as a garnish for rice and as a seasoning for root vegetables.

Wakame, long, curled, dark-green dried seaweed which must be soaked before using. It is used mainly in salads and soups.

Hijiki, another dried seaweed that must be restored by soaking; also used in salads and soups.

Aonoriko, powdered green laver, which is used as a seasoning.

(See also AGAR-AGAR.)

semolina is the coarse product obtained from the first milling of hard wheat. When wheat is milled, the bran and germ are separated from the endosperm, and then the endosperm is progressively ground into flour particles of the desired size. Semolina is the coarsest grade of these particles (actually semolina itself can be coarse, medium, or fine). It is used for making certain puddings, cakes, and dumplings. Finely ground semolina is used to make Roman-style GNOCCHI. The best commercial PASTA is made from semolina produced from durum wheat, the hardest wheat grown. COUSCOUS is flour-coated semolina.

sesame oil. There are two main kinds of sesame oil. The most common in Australia is the heavy, reddish-brown, intensely fragrant oil that is extracted from roasted sesame seeds. Known also as oriental sesame oil, it is used extensively in the cooking of northern China, Japan, and Korea, mainly for seasoning. A few drops, often added to another oil, is enough to suffuse a dish with its powerful flavour.

The other kind, not readily available, is pressed from raw sesame seeds. It is fine-textured and pale yellow in colour, lightly scented, with a light, slightly sweet flavour. It has a fairly high smoke point and is used as a cooking oil in southern India (where it is known as gingelly oil), Sri Lanka, and parts of the Middle East. It may also be used as a salad oil. These two oils should not be substituted for each other in a recipe.

sesame seeds. Sesame is an annual herb grown in many parts of the world for its oil-bearing seeds. Where it originally came from is uncertain—East Africa, Indonesia, Afghanistan, and Turkey have been suggested—but there is evidence of its cultivation in the Middle East as far back as 3000 B.C., and it is mentioned in Sanskrit and Egyptian scripts. Marco Polo, while travelling through Persia, raved about the taste of sesame oil, while Cleopatra thought it made a good cosmetic. Ali Baba's magic words 'Open, Sesame!' in the *Arabian Nights* (whose origins go back to the first century AD) probably arose from the tendency of the mature pods of the sesame plant to pop open at the merest touch and send the small, flat, cream-coloured seeds flying.

Sesame seeds can be eaten raw or toasted (heat them in a small pan over low heat, shaking them frequently, until they are a light golden colour). They may be added to salads, sprinkled on cooked chicken, fish, and vegetables, and used to top bread, cakes, biscuits, scones, etc. before baking. Finely ground, they become the oily paste TAHINA, which is used in many ways. The crushed seeds are mixed with honey to make the confection HALVA. Sesame meal is used by vegetarians in various ways as a source of protein. SESAME OIL is extracted from the seeds. Store sesame seeds in an airtight glass container in a cool, dry place.

seviche / ceviche. A Peruvian dish of thinly sliced raw fish marinated in a mixture of lime and / or lemon juice, pounded chilli, onion rings, chopped garlic, salt, and pepper. The fish is left in the marinade overnight and served cold with toast or in lettuce cups with sliced boiled sweet potato and rounds of cooked corn.

shaddock. Another name for POMELO. (See also GRAPEFRUIT.)

shallots. Ask for shallots in an Australian greengrocer's shop and you'll probably be given immature onion plants with long green leaves and unformed bulbs. These are known in other parts of the world as green onions, scallions, or spring onions, although a spring onion should have a partly formed white bulb (see under ONIONS). A proper shallot (*Allium ascalonicum*), sometimes referred to as an eschalot, is something like a brown garlic bulb, which, like garlic, often separates into cloves. It has a delicate flavour with the slightest hint of garlic and is used in sauces, soups, stews, in fact in any dish that calls for a mild onion taste. The confusion in the use of the term *shallot* means that you often can't be sure what is required when shallots are listed in a recipe. (Some recipes, however, specify green shallots and golden shallots or bulb shallots to distinguish them.) Fortunately, one can be substituted for the other without any damage being done.

shaoxing / shao hsing. A straw-coloured rice wine which is used a great deal in Chinese cooking. It tastes something like dry sherry, which can be substituted for shaoxing in Chinese recipes if you haven't any of the real thing.

shark. 'Every now and then a shark eats an Australian,' Cyril Pearl wrote in *So You Want to Be an Australian.* 'But every day Australians eat enormous numbers of sharks. The trade balance is very much in our favour.' In Victoria, shark, known as flake, is the standard fish used in suburban fish-and-chip shops. It is white and boneless (it is also sold as 'boneless fillets') and quite good eating. Occasionally there is a scare about the quantity of mercury and other heavy metals that can accumulate in big fish such as sharks, but you would need to eat it often over a long period to have cause for concern. In any case, the mercury content is monitored by all states processing sharks to determine whether the flesh is safe to eat. Imported shark (from New Zealand, Chile, Taiwan, and Korea) is similarly monitored.

shark's fin. The dried cartilage from the fin of a shark, preferably a large shark, is a delicacy in Chinese cuisine. It is the main ingredient of the famous shark's fin soup and generally regarded as banquet food. At the biennial Hong Kong Food Competition, there is a category devoted to shark's fin recipes. There is no substitute for it in recipes where it is called for. Before cooking shark's fin, the long, dried threads must be soaked in many changes of water over several hours until they become jelly-like. In its dried state, shark's fin will keep indefinitely.

shashlik is the Russian name for shish kebab (see KEBAB / KEBOB / KABOB). *Shash* and *shish* come from the Turkish word meaning skewer, on which cubes of marinated lamb (*kebab*) are grilled.

shepherd's pie. Also known as cottage pie, shepherd's pie is a dish of seasoned minced or chopped cooked meat with a layer of browned mashed potato on top. Some people say a cottage pie is made with beef and a shepherd's pie with lamb, but dictionaries don't usually make this distinction.

sherbet / sorbet. Perhaps because *sherbet* means variously (*a*) a powder made from bicarbonate of soda, tartaric acid, sugar, and artificial flavouring which, when mixed with water, makes an effervescent drink, (*b*) a cooling drink of sweetened diluted fruit juices popular in Arab countries, and (*c*, colloquially), beer, its other meaning—a kind of water ice—has been assigned to the more fashionable term *sorbet*. And *sorbet* has come to be pronounced 'sorbay' more often than rhyming with *orbit,* although both *sherbet* and *sorbet* come, by way of Turkish and Persian, from the same Arabic word for drink. (Why not pronounce *sherbet* 'sherbay'?)

A sorbet can be made by mixing puréed fruit and / or fruit juice with SUGAR SYRUP, freezing the mixture in an ice-cream maker (*sorbetière*) or freezer tray until it is a frozen slush, then transferring it to a food processor to whip into a fine snow. Stiffly beaten egg-whites and some liqueur or sweet wine may be added at this last stage. The whipped sorbet is kept in a bowl in the freezer until needed.

Sorbets are often served as a dessert, but their original purpose was to act as a palate cleanser and digestive between rich savoury courses of a meal.

shish kebab. See KEBAB / KEBOB / KABOB and SHASHLIK.

short soup. A Chinese soup also known as won ton soup. The soup itself is simply a basic chicken stock or broth with perhaps some light SOY SAUCE and a few drops of SESAME OIL added. The stock is poured over a bowl of WON TON (balls of seasoned minced pork wrapped in squares of noodle pastry) and sprinkled with finely chopped spring onions or leeks. With **long soup**, plain egg noodles are substituted for the won ton dumplings.

shortbread. A thick, crisp, crumbly (i.e., short) biscuit made with butter (a generous amount), flour, and castor sugar. For Scotch shortbread the dough is kneaded until smooth and buttery, then baked in one round piece with frilled edges and cut or broken into pieces when cool. English shortbread biscuits may be piped into rosettes.

shortcake. An American specialty, particularly strawberry shortcake. There are variations, but it is traditionally made with a rich scone dough which is baked in a round and when cooked and cooled is split into two layers. The bottom layer is spread with butter and then covered with crushed and sliced strawberries mixed with sugar and Kirsch. The top layer is buttered underneath and placed on top of the filling, and it in turn is covered with whipped cream and decorated with whole strawberries.

shortening may be butter, margarine, lard, solidified vegetable oil, or other fat used to make pastry and other baked goods 'short', in other words to make them break or crumble readily. The fat reduces gluten development in the flour and breaks up the gluten sheets so that the pastry is a mass of alternate fat and gluten layers.

shredding. To shred is to cut or tear food into fine, narrow pieces. Cabbage is shredded with a knife or coarse grater to make coleslaw, lettuce to make lettuce soup and sometimes for salad. Cooked chicken and cooked pork are shredded with two forks for certain dishes.

shrimp paste. See BLACHAN / BLACAN.

sifting. See under FLOUR.

silver beet. See SPINACH, SILVER BEET.

silver dory. See DORY.

silverside. See under BEEF.

simmering. See BOILING.

sippets are small pieces of bread served with soup. The word *sippet* is apparently a diminutive of *sop*, which suggests that sippets were to sop up soup (*soup* itself originally being the piece of bread over which the *potage*, or liquid from the pot, was poured). Sippets may also be small cubes of toast or crisp, deep-fried bread (see CROÛTONS, CROÛTES), which are used in salads as well as soups.

sirloin. See under BEEF.

skate. Another name for STINGRAY.

skimming. To skim is to remove scum or foam from the top of a liquid—for example, when boiling meat, making soup, or cooking jam. There are specially made slotted or perforated spoons and scoops made from wire or wire mesh with which to do this, and these implements can also be used to retrieve dumplings or gnocchi from broth or boiling water, and to lift fritters or chips out of a saucepan of hot oil (wire skimmers are best for this). (For skimming off fat, see DEGREASING.)

skipjack. Another name for TAILOR. See also skipjack TUNA.

skordalia. A Greek garlic sauce. There are two ways to make it, one with mashed potatoes, the other with breadcrumbs and ground almonds or walnuts. These ingredients are pounded with garlic in a mortar, egg yolks are mixed in, and olive oil added drop by drop until you have a smooth, blended sauce like mayonnaise, only thicker. Lemon juice, salt, and pepper are also mixed in. Skordalia is traditionally served with fried or grilled fish, fried eggplant or zucchini, cold sliced beetroot, or cold halved hard-boiled eggs.

smorgasbord. In its adoption and imitation around the world, Sweden's *smörgäsbord* has lost its diacritical marks together with some of its integrity. In Sweden it is a carefully arranged feast comprising many of Sweden's finest traditional delicacies—a score or so of herring dishes (pickled, marinated, jellied, smoked, fried, baked, and so on), which usually occupy one end of the table, smoked salmon, gravlax, caviar, smoked eel, smoked reindeer, cold meats and pâtés, various breads and cheeses, pickled onions and gherkins, cucumber salad, boiled potatoes, and other cold foods, and at the other end of the table hot dishes such as Swedish meat balls, croquettes, mushroom omelette, deep-fried parsley, and anchovy and potato casserole.

In Australia and other places a smorgasbord may offer anything and everything in the way of cold and buffet foods. What the Swedes recommend, and everyone should bear in mind, is to make as many visits to the table as you like but not to overload your plate with too many dishes at the one time. It doesn't do justice to the food or to your appetite.

snapper. A pink-coloured, deep-bodied fish with a hump on its head when fully mature, the snapper is found in the waters of all Australian states. It is known to fishermen by different names at different stages of its development: cockney or cockney bream at the youngest stage, then red bream, squire, and finally snapper, although when the transition occurs is an arbitrary decision of the fishermen. The red snapper of South Australia and Western Australia is a different fish altogether, related to the REDFISH. King snapper is another name for the RED EMPEROR.

The flesh of the snapper is firm, white, and fine tasting. Small snapper are excellent grilled whole, larger ones cut into steaks or fillets and grilled or poached, or baked whole. They can also be prepared as a SEVICHE or for SASHIMI (snapper is exported from Western Australia to Japan for this purpose). (See also FISH.)

snow peas. See PEAS.

sodium bicarbonate, or bicarbonate of soda (approved additive no. 500), is a white, crystalline compound which is one of the two main ingredients of BAKING POWDER. It is also added separately to certain cakes and bread-like cake mixtures when the mixture contains an acidic ingredient such as sour milk, in which case the acid ingredient of baking powder, cream of tartar, is not required. Sodium bicarbonate is sometimes added to boiled green vegetables to give them a bright colour, but it reduces both flavour and vitamin content and is not recommended.

soffritto. A mixture of chopped vegetables, basically onion, carrot, and celery, sometimes with chopped bacon or ham, cooked in oil for a few minutes and used as a foundation for Italian soups, stews, and bolognaise sauce (see RAGOÛT, RAGÙ). In its uncooked state the mixture is known as a *battuto.*

There is a Spanish version, spelt sofrito, which is more of a sauce, although it too is used as something in which other foods are cooked. Its basic ingredients are olive oil, chopped onions and garlic, peeled and chopped tomatoes, and salt and pepper. The onions and garlic are cooked in the oil until soft, then the tomatoes are added and the sauce cooked gently until it is fairly thick. Additional ingredients such as capsicums, parsley and other herbs, and wine may also be included in a sofrito.

soissons. See HARICOT BEANS.

soles and flounders are known collectively as flatfish, although they don't begin life that way. When young they swim vertically and have an eye on each side of the head, but while still quite small the fish turns on its side and moves to the sandy bottom; meanwhile the eye on the lower side gradually moves across to be adjacent to the other eye on top, and the lower side of the fish becomes almost white.

Flatfish are not abundant in Australian waters, which is a pity because they are exceptionally good eating. However, imported New Zealand soles and flounders are available in the eastern states. Flatfish may be cooked in most ways—fried in butter, grilled, poached, served À LA MEUNIÈRE, etc. (there are more than ten pages of recipes in *Larousse Gastronomique* for the European or Dover sole, which is considered by many to be the best-flavoured of all sea fish).

sorbet. See SHERBET, SORBET.

sorrel. French sorrel, the kind generally cultivated, is a hardy perennial with broad, oval leaves on reddish stems. It tastes something like spinach but with an acid lemon flavour. And like spinach, the leaves contain oxalic acid, which is good for you in small amounts but can be a problem if you have too much of it. Sorrel goes well in soups, especially with potato, and sauces to accompany fish or veal. It is also cooked in omelettes, and the French braise it with a cooked leg of lamb. A few leaves of sorrel give a sharp tang to a salad.

Never cook sorrel in an iron pan, as it will take on a metallic taste and turn the pot black.

soubise indicates that strained or puréed onions are used in the dish. **Sauce soubise** is made from a purée of cooked onions mixed with reduced BÉCHAMEL SAUCE and some butter, nutmeg, and seasoning. It is served with eggs and with roast pork, chicken, or lamb.

soufflés. A soufflé is a light, spongy baked dish made with a savoury or sweet mixture containing stiffly beaten egg-whites which cause the mixture to puff up when baked in the oven. The basic savoury soufflé mixture is a BÉCHAMEL SAUCE augmented with beaten egg yolks and grated cheese, chopped or puréed vegetables, fish, etc. The beaten egg-whites are lightly folded in with a knife or spatula, and the mixture is baked in a buttered soufflé dish (or several small dishes). A dessert soufflé is made either with the béchamel and egg yolk base sweetened and flavoured, or just with beaten yolks, sugar, and flavouring.

Making a successful soufflé is not hard, the experts say, provided you have confidence and follow a few strict rules:

- When you separate the eggs, make sure not a scrap of yolk gets into the whites, or else they won't whip satisfactorily.
- Make sure the bowl in which you beat the egg-whites (an unlined copper bowl is best) and the beating implement (a balloon wire whisk is recommended) are scrupulously clean, with no trace of grease.
- Have the right ratio of yolks to whites: one more white than the number of yolks, some say; others say 5 yolks to 7 whites, or more or less depending on the size of the eggs. When in doubt, add an extra white.
- Preheat the oven.
- Whip the whites until they will hold a stiff, shiny peak when the whisk is dipped in and held straight up (see 'Beating egg-whites' under EGGS).
- Stir about a quarter of the beaten whites into the basic mixture so that the rest will fold in easily. Then fold in the rest very lightly but quickly (see FOLDING IN).
- Turn the mixture into the buttered soufflé dish without delay, and put this into the preheated oven on a preheated baking tray so that the cooking will begin, from bottom as well as top, before the mixture loses its sponginess.
- Don't open the oven door until you think the soufflé is cooked (about 25–30 minutes.

A **cold soufflé** is like a MOUSSE and is made with gelatine. It is made to look high and puffy like a hot soufflé (which rises above the dish but sets as it rises) by placing a collar of foil or oiled paper around the dish to allow the mixture to come above the rim. The collar is removed before the soufflé is served.

A **soufflé omelette,** is a sweet omelette for which the yolks and the whites are beaten separately as for a soufflé. The yolks are beaten gently with the other ingredients (sugar, flour, cream, lemon rind, etc.), the whites whipped stiffly and then folded into the seasoned yolks. The soufflé omelette is cooked in an ovenproof frying pan in the oven. It may be spread with jam or other filling, folded over, and dusted with icing sugar.

sourdough. A fermented dough used as a leavening agent in making bread. The principle of using some left-over dough to start a new fermentation goes back thousands of years to the Egyptians, but it was revived by the 'sourdough' miners of the Alaskan and Californian gold rushes who had no access to fresh supplies of yeast. Each time they made bread they would save some of the dough, known as a starter, to mix in with the next batch to get it working. As a starter ages—and some in use in California, renowned for its sourdough bread, are decades old—it picks up airborne yeasts of the local area and develops its own particular characteristics and flavour. According to some people, the older a starter the better.

soursop. Sometimes called prickly custard apple (to which it is closely related), the soursop is a large, heart-shaped, green-skinned fruit with rows of soft spines. It is a native of tropical America and is now cultivated in tropical Queensland. The name probably comes from the sour-smelling skin and the slightly acid, fibrous white pulp, which has been described as resembling cotton soaked in an aromatic liquid. Some people find this texture unappealing, so the flesh is often puréed and served with ice-cream or made into jellies, sorbets, mousses, soufflés, and drinks. If the texture doesn't bother you, cut the fruit in half and eat the flesh with a spoon, or cut it up into chunks. The numerous black seeds should not be eaten. The fruit may also be stewed.

Soursops are available all year round. Ripen them at room temperature away from direct sunlight, then refrigerate. Use within two days.

souse. To souse is to put food in a pickling liquid. The food is usually an oily fish such as herring or mullet, and the pickling liquid is usually brine and / or vinegar.

soy sauce. There are two methods of making soy sauce. One involves fermenting and brining a mixture of roasted soy meal and crushed wheat for six months to a year before filtering and pasteurising it. The other method uses a chemical fermentation and takes a matter of hours. The naturally fermented kind has more flavour and vegetable protein. It will form a frothy head if you shake it. Various grades of soy sauce are produced. They are generally grouped in light and dark categories. Light soy sauce is the general-purpose kind, used for all-round Chinese cooking and at table as seasoning. Dark soy sauce is used for long, slow cooking and to impart a dark colouring to a dish. Soy sauce is used by the Japanese as well as the Chinese, as a dip, as a seasoning for cooking liquids, and as an ingredient in marinades.

soya beans / soybeans. For thousands of years the thousands of varieties of soya bean have been cultivated in China (where the plant originated) and in other parts of Asia. Soya beans are eaten as green beans, as dried beans, and sprouted like mung beans, but they are better known for their products: soya milk and cheese, flour and meal, bean curd (TOFU), soya bean paste (MISO), and SOY SAUCE. The soya plant is also important industrially and agriculturally, being used for making paint, stock food, cardboard, glue, pet food, and oil, among other things.

Only two main varieties of soya bean are grown in Western countries, one for commercial use and the other for eating fresh or dried. In its dried form the soya bean is small, hard, oval, and beige coloured. Information on preparation, storage, etc., is given under BEANS, DRIED.

To cook soya beans. Soya beans take a long time to cook, 3½–4 hours gentle boiling (make sure they don't boil dry) or 1–1 / 2 hours in a pressure cooker. They are used in soups, casseroles, and vegetarian dishes, or in place of haricot, cannellini, and red kidney beans (increasing cooking time accordingly).

There is also a soya bean variety sold as black beans. These beans, which are black with a white seam, are also available canned in brine. They are used in Chinese cooking, in soups and sauces, and to make soya bean paste.

Soya beans are very nutritious. They contain more protein than any other legume, are an excellent source of thiamin, and provide fibre and other vitamins and minerals. They are high in kilojoules.

spaghetti is probably the most familiar of all the many varieties of PASTA. The thin solid cylinders are made from durum wheat semolina and come in strands too long to fit unbroken in the pot of boiling water (you must not break them but wait until the end in the water softens enough to bend and allow the rest to be pushed under). Spaghetti is the pasta associated with Naples, where the traditional way of preparing it, *alla napolitana*, is tossed in oil and topped with tomato sauce. However, it is eaten throughout Italy, with olive oil based sauces such as those with eggplant or zucchini, clams, mussels, and other seafood, and sautéed garlic; and with butter and cheese sauces with or without tomato. While it is sometimes served with PANCETTA, spaghetti is rarely if ever served in Italy with a meat sauce such as the bolognaise sauce popular in Australia, nor with meatballs.

spare-ribs. Pork spare-ribs are ribs cut from the fore end of the carcase, near the breastbone, where there is little meat on the bones. Beef spare-ribs are cut off the bottom, or belly end, of the ribs (see 'Rib' under BEEF).

American spare ribs have most of the meat trimmed off and are usually marinated in a thick, sweet marinade and barbecued.

spatchcock. A very young chicken, also known as a poussin, is often referred to as a spatchcock. But properly a spatchcock is a game bird or chicken (usually a small one) that has been split open and flattened, then grilled.

To split and flatten a chicken, cut it along the backbone and open it out, cracking the breastbone so that it lies flat.

spatulas of various kinds are essential tools in the kitchen. A wooden spatula is used for stirring hot foods. The wooden handle doesn't get hot, and the blade is usually shaped to fit snugly against the side of the pot and angled to scrape corners clean. Flexible spatulas with a rubber or plastic blade, similarly shaped with one side flat and sharply angled at the end, the other side curved at the corner, are designed to extract every vestige of cake or pudding mixture from a bowl. They are essential for scraping clean non-stick pans without fear of scratching the surface, and they are also used for folding

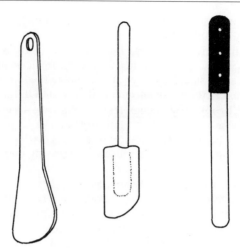

egg-whites into a soufflé base or cake mixture (see FOLDING IN). A metal spatula, or palette knife, with its long, narrow, flexible blade, is used mainly for smoothing out the icing on a cake to give it a professional look. It can also be used for folding, lifting a slice of pie or quiche, or turning pancakes.

speck is German-style smoked pork from the top of the pig's leg, which has a high proportion of fat to lean meat. It is sold in the piece or in slices and is used to add flavour to soups and cooked dishes such as beef or veal rolls, or served in the slice as an hors d'oeuvre with drinks. Speck will keep in the refrigerator for up to a fortnight in the piece, a week when sliced.

spices. The original purpose of spices in cooking is believed by some to have been to disguise half-rotten fresh food or to give salted and dried food a bit of a lift. But people probably also just liked the taste of spices and enjoyed highly seasoned food. Whatever it was, the market for spices was such that wars were fought over access to supplies, and lives and fortunes were risked in voyages of exploration to discover new spices and new sources of known ones. The history of the world has been greatly influenced by the spice trade.

Individual spices are dealt with separately in their alphabetical order. As a general rule, spices should be bought in small quantities, as their flavour and pungency diminish over the course of time and only small amounts are used in cooking. It is also better to buy whole spices where practicable, and grind or crush them freshly when needed. Although **mixed spice** powder (probably a compound of CINNAMON, CLOVES, NUTMEG, ALLSPICE, CORIANDER, and GINGER, or a selection of these) is obtainable and useful, you can grind and mix up a fresher and more satisfying mixture of your own.

spinach, silver beet. What greengrocers in Australia generally refer to as spinach is silver beet. (Gardeners know it by this name, even if shopkeepers don't.) Although some varieties of spinach have a crinkly leaf, the kind of spinach generally marketed in Australia, known as English spinach, has soft, delicate leaves on slender stems, whereas silver beet has big, firm, crinkled leaves with broad white midribs and well-defined white veins. Spinach is a native of south-western Asia and is an annual. Silver beet comes from the

Mediterranean coast of Spain and Portugal and the islands near by; it is a biennial. Silver beet is also known as Swiss chard.

Both spinach and silver beet are available all year round, though spinach is best and cheapest in winter. Choose leaves that are bright and fresh-looking, with no signs of limpness. Use them on the day of purchase, if possible, or store them in a plastic bag in the refrigerator (cut off the roots of spinach first). Wash the leaves thoroughly before using, and drain well, shaking off excess water.

Trimmed off the midrib, silver beet leaves are cooked in the same way as spinach and may be used interchangeably with spinach in many recipes.

To prepare and cook spinach. Put the chopped or torn leaves in a saucepan with only the water that clings to them after rinsing. Cook over low heat, with the lid on, just long enough for the leaves to soften. Squeeze dry after cooking. The white midribs of silver beet may be cooked separately and served with a white sauce, au gratin, or just with melted butter.

spoon measurements. A graduated set of metric measuring spoons takes the hit-or-miss element out of measuring small quantities of liquid or fine dry ingredients. The set comprises tablespoon, teaspoon, half-teaspoon, and quarter-teaspoon. In Australia the standard tablespoon contains 20 millilitres. (In Britain and the United States the tablespoon is equivalent to ½ fluid ounce, which is about 14 millilitres in imperial measurement and about 15 millilitres in US customary measurement. So four British or American tablespoons are equivalent to three Australian tablespoons.)

There are four metric teaspoons to the metric tablespoon (but only three teaspoons to the tablespoon in Britain and America, so all three countries have the same teaspoon measurement, about 5 millilitres). Most recipes expect spoon measurements to be level; that is, for dry ingredients such as flour, salt, sugar, or baking powder, the spoon should be overfilled and then levelled off with the straight edge of a knife or spatula.

spring onions. See ONIONS.

spring roll. A Cantonese delicacy consisting of a savoury mixture which may include minced pork or chicken, chopped prawns, mushrooms, bamboo shoots, shredded cabbage, spring onions, soy sauce, sesame oil, etc., wrapped in a thin dough or pancake and deep-fried. Spring rolls are usually served at breakfast in China or as a snack.

spumone / spumoni. An Italian frozen dessert of very fine, smooth, rich ice-cream containing fruits and nuts.

squab. A young pigeon raised for the table. At four to five weeks old, a squab is the perfect size for a single serving. Most of the squabs sold in Australia are produced in the Mallee area of Victoria. They may be roasted, braised with bacon, onions, and mushrooms, and made into a pigeon pie. Squabs should be roasted for only a short time and rested before serving. They go well with green peas and root vegetables. Italians serve them with POLENTA.

squashes are any of several species of the *Cucurbita* genus, which belong to the gourd family and include ZUCCHINI, MARROW, VEGETABLE SPAGHETTI, and PUMPKIN, among others. Summer squashes grow quickly and are eaten immature, before the skin and seeds have become hard. Winter squashes are left to mature before harvesting, when their skin is hard and they can be stored for months. Those generally sold in Australia as squash are the small, round, flattish summer squashes known as pattypan squash or baby squash. They range in colour from cream and yellow to various shades of green and have a topknot and scalloped edge. They may be boiled or steamed, hollowed out and stuffed and baked, grilled, or sautéed.

squid, cuttlefish, octopus. Only the fleshy body pouch and the tentacles of these cephalopods are eaten.

To prepare a squid, hold the body pouch with one hand and the tentacles with the other, and pull them apart. The innards should come away with the tentacles. Cut the tentacles off below the eyes, and discard the eyes with the rest of the head and the viscera (keep the ink sac if you want to use the ink). Squeeze out the bony, beak-like mouth from the base of the tentacles and discard it. Pull the transparent 'pen' out of the body pouch. Wash the pouch under running water, and peel or rub off the skin. The edible flaps may be removed to cook separately.

Squid may be stuffed and baked in a sauce, stewed in its own ink, cut into rings, strips, or squares and fried in oil together with the chopped tentacles, or cooked according to the many other recipes for squid. To be tender, squid must be cooked very quickly or very slowly; in between produces a tough, rubbery texture.

To prepare cuttlefish. Cuttlefish can be prepared in the same way as squid. However, if the ink sac is to be used, you may have to make a slit down the back of the body from head to tail, fold back the flesh on both sides, and lift out the oval white cuttlebone. This exposes the ink sac among the rest of the viscera. Carefully detach the ink sac and discard the rest of the viscera. Cuttlefish may be cooked in the same way as squid, although it is not so tender.

To prepare octopus, cut off the tentacles, then turn the body pouch, or hood, inside out to remove the innards. As the skin of an octopus is firmly attached, you may need to parboil the octopus before stripping off the skin. Octopus is tougher than both cuttlefish and squid. It is usually stewed for up to four hours. You can tenderise it by bashing it with a mallet (or beating it against the rocks if you catch it yourself).

star anise. Also known as Chinese anise and badiane, star anise is the dried, eight-pointed, star-shaped fruit of an aromatic tree from eastern Asia. It has a liquorice taste and is used in Asian cooking to impart a subtle, slightly sweet flavour to slowly stewed and steamed dishes. The dried stars, which are about 2 centimetres across, can be kept indefinitely in a tightly closed container.

star apple. A tropical American fruit related to the SAPODILLA, the star apple is 5–10 centimetres in diameter, apple-shaped, and green, yellow, or purple in colour. It gets its name from the star-shaped calyx. The segmented white flesh is soft and sweet when ripe. Available from June to November, star apples should be allowed to ripen at room temperature, away from direct sunlight, then stored in the refrigerator. Eat them out of the hand, or cut them open and scoop out the flesh. They go well with citrus fruits and may be puréed for drinks.

star fruit. See CARAMBOLA.

steak. Some time ago a couple dining in a Sydney restaurant refused to accept, or to pay for, a grilled steak they had ordered 'medium to well done'. They considered it was undercooked. The chef was adamant that it was not. The police were called in, and so were the journalists. The ensuing debate showed that there was little agreement on what constitutes medium to well done, especially whether there should be any pinkness in the middle. What everybody agreed upon was that a lot depends on the thickness of the steak, the cut and its age, whether or not it comes straight out of the refrigerator, and the cooking temperature.

A few general hints gleaned from the experts on cooking steak, which apply whether it is pan-fried, grilled, or barbecued (see also FRY, PAN-FRY, SAUTÉ; GRILLING; and BARBECUING):

• Dry the steak with a cloth or paper towel before cooking. Damp meat will not brown satisfactorily.
• Nick the fatty edges of the steak to prevent it from buckling while it is cooking.
• Start cooking on high heat to seal in juices. The temperature can be reduced once the steak is seared on both sides.
• Don't turn the steak too often: once only for rare, twice for medium, three times at the most for well done.
• Cook 2–3 minutes on each side for rare, 4–6 minutes on each side for medium, and 6–9 minutes on each side for well done.
• Test the meat by pressing it with blunt tongs. Rare will feel springy to touch, medium firmer to touch, well done very firm to touch. Never test a steak by cutting it, as juices will escape and the meat will become dry and tough.

The various cuts of beef are dealt with under BEEF. Some of the named steaks and methods of preparation are:

Carpetbag steak. A thick steak with a pocket cut in it and oysters inserted, which is then grilled or pan-fried.

Fillet steak. Steaks cut from the fillet, or tenderloin, are the tenderest though not necessarily the tastiest. Those from the thin end are used for FILET MIGNON, the slightly larger ones for TOURNEDOS, and the thick butt end for CHATEAUBRIAND.

Minute steak. A thinly cut steak from no particular part of the carcase, usually beaten to tenderise it further so that it will cook very quickly; hence the name. Pan-fry, grill, or barbecue.

New York steak. Boneless sirloin, with very little fat. Grill or pan-fry.

Oyster blade. The choicest part of the meat cut from the shoulder blade. Pan-fry, grill, or barbecue.

Pepper steak (*steak au poivre*). Press a generous amount of cracked black peppercorns, or green peppercorns, into both sides of a piece of steak with the heel of the hand. The steak may be brushed with olive oil and allowed to stand for a while. Pan-fry or cook it on a ribbed grill. Sometimes the steak is blazed with brandy or the pan juices deglazed with brandy (see DEGLAZING.).

Porterhouse steak. A thick steak cut from the rump end of the sirloin, having a T-bone and a sizeable piece of fillet. The name comes from the chophouses in London where the market porters drank their favourite dark beer, named porter in their honour, and ate what was then, according to tradition, an offcut from the rib area of the carcase. Grill or pan-fry.

Rib steak is cut from the first few ribs and has the bone left in. **Rib eye**, or Scotch fillet, is rib steak with the bone removed. They can both be grilled, pan-fried, or barbecued.

Rump steak. A tender, juicy cut. Pan-fry, grill, or barbecue.

Sirloin steak. Generally the most sought-after cut, excellent for grilling, pan-frying, or barbecuing.

Skirt steak. A lean cut from the flank of the sirloin and rump section. It is used mainly in casseroles, braises, and stews. For roasting, it should be lightly scored with a knife on both sides, spread with a stuffing mixture, then rolled and tied with string.

Steak Diane. Fillet steaks pounded thin, quickly pan-fried on both sides in butter with parsley, garlic, and Worcestershire sauce. Sometimes cream is stirred in, sometimes the steaks are flamed.

Steak Tartare. A mound of raw finely minced fillet or rump steak with a well in the middle into which an egg yolk is dropped. This is mixed at table with salt, pepper, capers, chopped onions, and anchovy fillets to individual taste. Served with black bread and butter.

T-bone steak. Cut from the rib end of the loin, T-bone comprises sirloin and fillet on either side of a T-shaped bone. Grill, pan-fry, or barbecue.

Topside steak. Cut from the inside of the top of the leg, topside is usually recommended for frying or grilling only if it is marinated first to tenderise it. However, the first slice of topside, next to the rump, is almost as tender as rump itself and far tastier.

steak and kidney pie, steak and kidney pudding. Both these dishes are made with boneless sirloin or topside and calf's or sheep's kidneys cut into cubes, mushrooms, onions, parsley, and seasonings. With the pie, the meat mixture is floured and browned, the mushrooms and onions sautéed, and all the ingredients placed in a casserole dish, then covered with a lid of rough puff pastry, and baked in the oven. With the pudding, a pudding basin is lined with suet pastry, the uncooked ingredients are put in, and the top is covered with more pastry. A floured and dampened cloth is tied over the basin, and the pudding is cooked standing in a large saucepan of boiling water or steamed.

steaming. To steam usually means to cook food in a perforated container above boiling water. The steamer may be a saucepan with a perforated bottom that fits neatly over a regular saucepan. It may be three-tiered, the middle part being the steamer and the top acting as a double boiler. It may be a deck of woven bamboo baskets set one above the other to cook or heat various Chinese delicacies for DIM SUM. It may be an expanding metal basket made of interleaved perforated panels that fits saucepans of various sizes and stands above the water on little legs. But you can also steam food in water rather than above it. Rice or vegetables cooked in a little hot water with the saucepan tightly covered are also steamed.

steamboat. The Mongolian hot pot, or *huo kuo,* is familiarly known as a steamboat because of the chimney containing glowing charcoal in the centre of the metal cooking pot. As the charcoal burns, broth in the circular basin surrounding the chimney heats up to boiling point. The pot stands in the centre of the table, and diners select wafer-thin slices of raw meat, fish, and vegetables from bowls on the table and dip them into the simmering liquid to cook quickly. Alternatively, a variety of precooked foods in bite-size pieces may be placed in the simmering broth to heat up or finish cooking. Guests select what they fancy from the steamboat.

steep. See INFUSE, STEEP.

stewing. To stew is to cook slowly, by simmering or slow boiling. For the difference between a stew and a braise or casserole, see BRAISE, CASSEROLE, STEW. See also BLANQUETTE; FRICASSEE; HOTPOT; IRISH STEW; POT-ROAST-ING; and RAGOÛT, RAGÙ.

Stilton is one of the great blue cheeses, to England what Roquefort is to France. Made from the richest milk with more cream added, it is off-white in colour with green-blue veining. The rind is dark, crusty, and wrinkled. Stilton has a mellow rather than pungent flavour and a velvety texture. Serve it with plain water biscuits and a glass of port.

stingray has never been a popular choice of edible fish, although many people have no doubt eaten it unknowingly as a piece of fish-shop flake. It is commonly known as skate. The pectoral fins, or wings, of the ray are considered a delicacy by those who fancy the rather gelatinous flesh. Food writer Diane Holuigue suggests cooking it in COURT BOUILLON or salted water and serving it with BEURRE NOIR or a sauce made with tomatoes, garlic, and oregano.

stir-frying is an energy-efficient method of cooking used by Asians to conserve fuel. Finely chopped or sliced ingredients are quickly cooked, usually in a WOK, while being stirred and tossed in a little oil over high heat. The fast cooking retains the colour and crispness of the ingredients as well as the nutrients.

The food to be stir-fried must be prepared before you start to heat the oil in the wok. Vegetables should be cut into pieces of about the same size. Meat and poultry should be cut into evenly sized strips across the grain to ensure they don't become tough during cooking. (Partially frozen meat is easier to slice.) Sauces to be used should be readily to hand. The wok should be hot before the oil is added. Any edible oil can be used. The Chinese traditionally use peanut oil, which has a high smoke point. Swirl it around to cover the whole inside of the wok, and let it get hot before adding the food. If spices or flavourings such as garlic, chilli, or ginger are being used, they are quickly stir-fried before the other ingredients are added. Once the cooking has begun, it should be continued quickly at high heat.

Chinese chefs use a specially shaped, wooden-handled metal turner, like a flat scoop with a gently curved front, and a shallow ladle that suits the

contours of the wok, to keep the ingredients on the move and in contact
with the hot surface of the wok during the cooking.

stock, broth, bouillon. Essentially, stock, BROTH, and bouillon are the same
thing—the clear, savoury liquid obtained from beef, veal, poultry, or fish,
together with vegetables, herbs, and seasonings, simmered in water to
concentrate their flavours. The only difference is that stock never goes to
the dinner table, whereas broth and bouillon (the French word for stock or
broth) sometimes do. Stock remains in the kitchen to provide its essential
service as the base for soups, sauces, stews, and aspics.

To make a good, tasty stock you should use fresh, good-quality ingredients, although vegetable tops and skins, bones from roast joints, chicken
feet, fish heads and backbones, and seafood shells, which would normally
be discarded, may be added to the stockpot. Stock can also be made out of
vegetables alone. Avoid using potato or parsnip, which cloud a stock, and
cabbage, which gives it a sour flavour. **Brown stock** is produced by
browning beef or veal bones and meat first; **white stock** can be made from
chicken, veal, or beef which is not browned.

Begin with cold water so that the flavours are extracted as the water
heats. Bring to the boil slowly, then simmer gently with the lid on the
saucepan. Beef and veal stocks are usually simmered for several hours
(restaurant chefs may keep them simmering for days), chicken stock for
about 3 hours, and fish stock for about 30 minutes (longer cooking makes
it bitter). Skim off the scum that forms on top, especially during the first
half-hour. Strain the stock through a fine sieve. Allow it to cool, and then
refrigerate it. Beef, chicken, and vegetable stock will keep for up to a week
in the refrigerator; fish stock for 2–3 days. Stocks also freeze well, and they
are very useful to have in the freezer to turn quickly into soup. Remove any
fat before using the stock (see DEGREASING).

To clarify stock. First, make sure the stock is free of fat. Beat 1 egg-white
for every 2 cups of stock, and add the beaten whites (some cooks include
the eggshells) to the cold stock in a saucepan. Over gentle heat bring the
stock slowly to the boil, stirring continuously with a wire whisk, then reduce
the heat to a simmer and stop whisking. The tiny floating particles that cloud
stock will have attached themselves to the egg-whites, which rise to the
surface. Leave the saucepan on very low heat, below a simmer, for 15
minutes to allow the egg-whites to coagulate firmly. Line a colander or sieve
with three layers of washed cheesecloth or muslin and place it over a bowl,
making sure the bottom of the colander will remain above the surface of
the strained liquid. Then ladle the stock carefully into the colander and allow
the clear liquid to drain through. Do not squeeze the cheesecloth or disturb
the egg-whites unduly.

stollen. A German yeast loaf or cake made with dried fruits, nuts, and candied
peel. The most famous is the Dresdner Weihnachtsstollen, the Dresden
Christmas cake or sweet bread, baked in an oval shape to represent the Holy
Child in swadling clothes, which is exchanged throughout Germany as a
holiday gift. It is traditionally made well in advance of Christmas and eaten
during Advent. The loaf has a dryish yellow crumb liberally studded with
raisins, currants, slivered almonds, candied lemon or orange peel, and

perhaps glacé cherries and angelica, with some rum as added flavouring. When baked, it is brushed with butter and dusted with icing sugar.

strawberries. 'Doubtless God could have made a better berry, but doubtless God never did,' said Dr William Butler, the sixteenth-century food writer whose other much-quoted observation was: 'It is unseasonable and unwholesome in all months that have not an *r* in their name to eat an oyster.' The berry referred to by the good doctor was the strawberry. In Butler's time it was a much smaller fruit than the large specimens of today, which are descended from a Chilean-Virginian hybrid; European wild strawberries were much smaller than those of the Americas. Actually the strawberry is not botanically a berry (see BERRIES) or indeed a true fruit but a 'false fruit'; the actual fruits of the plant are the tiny seed-like achenes carried on the outside of the red, fleshy receptacle.

Several varieties of strawberry are cultivated commercially in Australia, including the Tioga (medium-sized, tart), Shasta (deep-coloured, soft, juicy), Hecca (large, perfumed, juicy), Silvan and Pajero (sweet), Parker (large, longer-lasting, less flavoursome). The best are grown in Victoria, near the Dandenongs. They are available all year round, with best supplies in spring. Choose strawberries that are brightly coloured, with no soft spots or mould, and have their green stem caps intact. Avoid those with white or green patches. Eat them soon after purchase; meanwhile, store them in a covered container in the refrigerator. Wash them just before eating, not before storing, and leave the stem caps on until after washing them or they will lose juice and absorb water. Eat stawberries out of the hand or as a dessert with cream, ice-cream, yoghurt, liqueurs, etc; in fruit salad; puréed for fruit sauce, FOOL, or COULIS; as a cake filling or decoration; in jams, preserves, tarts, strawberry SHORTCAKE, etc.

Strawberries are high in vitamin C and low in kilojoules.

strudel. The Austro-Hungarian strudel derives from the Turkish BAKLAVA. It is made with a large sheet of pastry as thin as onion skin (you should be able to read a newspaper through it, the Viennese say), which is brushed with butter and spread with a filling such as diced apples mixed with sugar, cinnamon, lemon peel, sultanas, and almonds (for the famous Apple Strudel), or stoned sour cherries, cottage cheese, or any of a multitude of fillings. It is then carefully rolled up, brushed with butter and sprinkled with breadcrumbs, cut into sections to fit on a baking tray, and baked until crisp and brown. Strudel is eaten hot or cold, often with whipped cream.

stuffing may be anything from seasoned breadcrumbs or a mixture of sage and onion to a complex blend of minced meats, vegetables, herbs, fruit, eggs, bread or breadcrumbs, rice, cream, melted butter or cheese, and wine. Various mixtures are used to stuff poultry or game, and often the same mixtures can be used to stuff meat, fish, eggs, and vegetables such as zucchini, squash, tomatoes, onions, whole cabbage, and cabbage leaves or vine leaves. Meat-based stuffings, also known as FARCE or forcemeat, may also be made into a PÂTÉ or terrine.

Stuffed poultry takes a little longer to roast than poultry without stuffing. Allow extra time for the stuffing to cook through.

Don't stuff poultry until you are about to cook it; stuffing goes off quickly at room temperature and could spoil the poultry if it is not cooked straight away. For the same reason, don't stuff poultry and then freeze it, because bacteria could breed in the stuffing while the poultry is thawing.

suet is the hard, white, crumbly fat from around the kidneys and loins of an ox or sheep (beef suet is most commonly available). It is used for making pastry, especially for enclosing steamed puddings such as steak and kidney pudding and Christmas pudding.

sugar. Many kinds of sugars are found in nature. The one known as sugar in the kitchen is sucrose, which is a combination of two other natural sugars, glucose and fructose. Although sugar can be refined from beet and other plants, the sugar used in Australia is made from the juice of crushed sugarcane, a tall perennial grass of the genus *Saccharum* which originated somewhere in tropical Asia, probably in the Ganges Delta.

The technology of sugar refining was developed in India about 500 B.C. and remained much the same for centuries. The cane was crushed and the extracted juice clarified with lime and other substances, then boiled into a concentrated syrup and poured into conical moulds to crystallise into 'loaves' (their distinctive shape gave rise to many a 'Sugarloaf' mountain or other topographical feature), while the left-over syrup, molasses, drained off through a small hole in the tip of the cone. Today the molasses is extracted by centrifuges, and the raw sugar is further refined into colourless crystals of uniform size rather than a solid, brownish loaf.

White sugar is over 99 per cent pure sucrose. It has no nutrients but provides foods with sweetness and the body with a concentrated source of energy. Sugar is available in several forms under various names for use in different ways (see also CARAMEL):

Brown sugar is essentially a white sugar with a thin film of molasses coating each crystal, which makes it moist.

Castor sugar is finely ground white sugar which is used in making cakes, meringues, custards, or where the sugar is required to dissolve more readily.

Coffee crystals. Raw sugar in larger crystal form for serving with coffee.

Confectioner's sugar. The US term for ICING SUGAR.

Cubed sugar. White granulated sugar pressed into small cubes for serving with tea or coffee.

Demerara sugar was originally raw cane sugar produced in the Demerara region of Guyana. A product marketed by the CSR as demerara sugar is imported from Mauritius. It is moister and more richly flavoured than ordinary raw sugar.

Icing sugar. See separate entry.

Raw sugar is the amber-coloured crystals remaining after the molasses is extracted from the clarified and concentrated juice of the sugarcane.

Superfine sugar. The US term for castor sugar.

Vanilla sugar is white sugar, usually castor sugar, lightly flavoured with vanilla (see under VANILLA).

sugar syrup is sugar dissolved in water and boiled until it reaches the desired concentration for its purpose. A simple syrup of 1 cup of sugar to ½ cup of water heated until the sugar has merely dissolved may be used to poach fruit or to glaze bread. Stronger concentrations are used for making such things as MARSHMALLOWS, NOUGAT, TURKISH DELIGHT, toffee, and CARA-MEL. As the water evaporates, the syrup reaches various stages of concentration. The easiest way to test the concentration is with a sugar thermometer, because the boiling point of a sugar solution increases as the concentration of sugar increases. But if you haven't got a sugar thermometer, some time-honoured practical tests can be carried out on the behaviour of the syrup at certain concentrations: **thread** is when a drop of syrup falling from a spoon forms a thread in the air (107–110°C on a sugar thermometer); **soft ball**, when a small amount dropped in cold water forms a soft mass that can be rolled between your fingers (113–118°C); **hard ball**, when the ball resists pressure (118–130°C); **soft crack,** when the syrup dropped in water will crack but the piece will stick to the teeth if you bite it (132–143°C); **hard crack,** when it breaks like glass and no longer sticks to the teeth (149–154°C). (The temperatures given are a compromise, as few authorities seem to agree on the temperatures for the various stages, and some give alternative names and intermediate stages. The best advice is to follow the recipe.)

sukiyaki. A dish of beef and vegetables prepared in the Japanese 'one pot' style of cooking at the dinner table. Prime rump or fillet of beef cut in thin slices is fried briefly on both sides in fat and then pushed to one side of the pan. Sliced or chopped vegetables such as onions, spring onions, mushrooms, bean sprouts, and bamboo shoots are added, perhaps with some TOFU and cooked noodles, and cooked briefly, then the lot is simmered for a few minutes in a mixture of soy sauce, sugar, and sake. Guests take morsels from the pan, sometimes dipping them in a side dish of raw egg before eating.

sultanas. See RAISINS.

Summer Pudding. See under PUDDINGS.

sundae. 'Orig. uncert.,' says *The Macquarie Dictionary* regarding the etymology of *sundae*. I recalled Marion Halligan saying in *Eat My Words* that it was 'an American word from the beginning of the century supposed to mean the ice-cream left over from Sunday'. Following that lead, I consulted H. L. Mencken in *The American Language*. In the early 1890s, says Mencken, in what he considers the most plausible theory, a man named George Hallauer called into an ice-cream parlour in Two Rivers, Wisconsin, and ordered a dish of ice-cream. 'Being in an experimental mood, he asked for chocolate syrup on his ice-cream, and the *sundae* was born. News of the novelty spread to nearby Manitowoc, where the thrifty George Giffy sold it on Sundays only, but the public—epitomised in the traditional little girl—demanded it every day, so that it acquired the name. How and when the spelling shifted from *Sunday* to *sundae* is still a mystery.' Nowadays the ice-cream sundae may have either chocolate or fruit syrup poured over it, together with toppings of chopped nuts, fruit, and whipped cream.

sunflower seeds and oil. The sunflower is a native of the Americas, where the Amerindians cultivated and made extensive use of the plant for thousands of years. They used the dried leaves as a tobacco substitute and the stems as bean poles, and ground the seeds into a nutritious flour. (Actually the 'seed' is botanically a complete fruit, or achene, like the pips on the outside of a strawberry.) Sunflower seeds may be eaten raw, roasted as a snack, tossed in salads, or added to cooked vegetables. They can also be sprouted and used as a salad green. But they are mainly cultivated commercially for the oil that is extracted from them. Sunflower oil is an excellent light cooking oil and may also be used for salads, though the flavour is fairly bland. Oil now available from a new strain of sunflower seeds is said to be higher in cholesterol-lowering mono-unsaturates than olive and canola oil and to have a high smoke point, allowing repeated deep-frying re-use.

suprême / supreme. There is some disagreement about what constitutes a suprême of chicken. *Larousse Gastronomique* says that a suprême is 'the breast and wing of chicken or game'. And *The Macquarie Dictionary* defines *suprême* as the breast and wings (plural). However, Escoffier says *suprême* is synonymous with *fillet:* 'They are the names given to the breast of the fowl, divided into two along the sternum, and cleared of all skin. Each fillet or *suprême* comprises the large and the minion fillets.' Australian usage, despite the *Macquarie Dictionary*'s definition, seems to agree with Escoffier: a suprême (or supreme) is a skinless, boneless half-breast. One breast contains two supremes, which are also known as fillets.

The designation *suprême* in the name of a dish means that it is served in a rich cream sauce. This sauce, known as **suprême sauce**, is chicken VELOUTÉ with cream mixed in just before serving.

sushi. Sometimes referred to as the sandwich of Japan, sushi consists of vinegar-flavoured rice with a wide variety of toppings and fillings, often wrapped in dried seaweed (see 'Nori' under SEAWEED). The rice is cooked with some kombu seaweed, and then a dressing of rice vinegar, sugar, salt, and MIRIN is mixed in. When cool, the rice may be formed into oblongs and topped with a dab of WASABI (Japanese green horseradish) and a slice of tuna, squid, or other fish, a butterflied prawn, or a strip of omelette or sliced vegetable; or the rice may be spread on a sheet of nori, covered with delicately seasoned ingredients—fish, vegetables, mushrooms, omelette strips, etc.—rolled up, and cut into thick slices. Sushi is usually accompanied by soy sauce for dipping and slices of pickled ginger.

sweating. To sweat is to soften vegetables, particularly members of the onion family, by cooking them gently in butter or oil until they release their juices but do not brown. To sweat leeks, which may be served as a separate vegetable, slice one leek for each person, toss the leeks in a little butter, then cover them with buttered paper and cook on a very low heat with the saucepan lid on.

swede / swede turnip. See TURNIPS, SWEDES.

sweet corn. Although all types of CORN (maize) can be eaten when young, the type known as sweet corn, which has had sweetness, tenderness, and high water content bred into it, is the one cultivated and marketed for this purpose. (Other types are used for stock feed, rolling into cornflakes or grinding into POLENTA, milling into flour, and turning into popcorn.)

Sweet corn is available most of the year but is best in summer. Choose cobs with fresh, green husks, moist stems, silk tassels free of decay or matting, and plump yellow kernels (no dry or white ones). Eat as soon as possible after purchase; meanwhile, store in a plastic bag in the refrigerator.

To prepare and cook sweet corn. Before cooking corn on the cob, strip off the husks and remove the corn silk. Cook in boiling water for 3–5 minutes, until the milky juice in the kernels is set. Don't add salt to the water—it makes the corn tough. Some people say boil the water and not the corn; that is, turn off the heat when you put the corn in and let the cobs sit in the hot water for 10 minutes. You can also steam corn. Serve with butter and freshly ground pepper. You can also bake or barbecue corn in its husk, or you can cut or scrape the kernels off the cob and cook them in a little butter in a covered pot.

sweet potatoes are the tuberous roots of a tropical vine of the morning glory family originally from Central America but also cultivated since prehistoric times in Polynesia. Maoris call them *kumara*. Columbus brought sweet potatoes to Europe. There are many varieties with a range of colours from light yellow to dark purple, some with dry and mealy flesh and others with moist flesh. Those available in shops mostly have a light brown skin and dry white flesh that cooks to an unlovely grey. The variety often known as kumara, which has an orange-brown skin and bright orange flesh, is very sweet and moist and has a high vitamin A content. All sweet potatoes are a good source of vitamin C and fibre.

Choose firm tubers with no cracks or blemishes. Store them unwashed in a cool, dark, well-ventilated place. Scrub them or peel them before cooking. They can be boiled, steamed, baked, mashed, or fried as chips. They are also used in soups and stews.

sweetbreads. No, they are not testicles but another gland that comes in pairs, or at least two parts, the thymus gland from a lamb or calf. These are called the neck sweetbreads and are more of a delicacy than the stomach sweetbread, which is the pancreas.

To prepare and cook sweetbreads. Sweetbreads must be very fresh and need to be soaked in cold water, frequently changed, for about three hours to remove any blood. Then they should be brought slowly to the boil and simmered for a couple of minutes before refreshing in cold water and removing any membrane. They may then be fried in butter, perhaps coated with egg and breadcrumbs. Veal sweetbreads prepared in this way and then simmered in cream with sautéed mushrooms and some nutmeg become the famous Ris de Veau à la Crème aux Champignons.

sweetlip emperor. Four fish of the *Lethrinus* genus, known as spangled emperor, red-spot emperor, red-throat emperor, and blue-spotted emperor, are referred to collectively as sweetlip emperor. These brightly coloured and patterned fish are caught near reefs and on rocky bottoms around the eastern, northern, and western coast of Australia. Available all year round but mainly from November to February, they are sold whole and in fillets. The white flesh is firm and moist and has a mild, sweet flavour. The sweetlip emperor may be baked, steamed, grilled, or deep-fried whole (score larger fish when grilling and deep-frying); fillets may be fried, grilled, barbecued, or steamed. 'Teriyaki complements this species superbly,' says the *Australian Seafood*

Catering Manual, 'and emperor can be marinated in other similar mild flavours.' (See also RED EMPEROR and FISH.)

Swiss cheese does not necessarily mean cheese made in Switzerland, although it generally refers to EMMENTAL, the quintessential Swiss cheese with the large, shiny holes, or one of the innumerable copies of Emmental that have been produced by virtually every country that makes cheese.

Swiss roll. Perhaps if the Swiss roll had the jazz and sexual connotations of the American term for the cake—jelly roll—it wouldn't seem quite so mundane. Nevertheless, this cylindrical cake with the spiral cross-section is a perennial favourite. It is made from a thin, flat piece of sponge cake spread with jam, whipped cream, or butter-cream filling, rolled up, and sprinkled with icing sugar. To prevent the sponge from cracking when you roll it up, bake it until it feels springy to touch, then turn it out onto a piece of greaseproof paper dusted with icing sugar, trim the crisp edges with a sharp knife, and roll it up while it is still warm, using the paper as an aid. When cool, unroll it, spread it with filling, and roll it up again.

syllabub. Back in the seventeenth century there were three kinds of syllabub, says Elizabeth David in *An Omelette and a Glass of Wine.* One was made by milking a cow into a bowl of sweetened and spiced cider or ale (or both). The liquid was allowed to stand for an hour or so until curds formed on top and an alcoholic whey remained underneath. This kind of syllabub was served as a drink at rustic festivals. Another kind was made with wine or spirits mixed with a lot of whipped cream. You ate the main part with a spoon and afterwards drank the winy whey that separated out. The third kind was an 'everlasting syllabub', also made with wine and whipped cream, which remained thick without separating.

Today's syllabub is the everlasting kind. It is made by marinating some grated lemon peel overnight in some white wine or sherry and brandy, straining off the liquid the next day into a large bowl with some castor sugar to sweeten it, then stirring in some cream. The mixture is whipped until it stands in soft peaks—but not any longer, or it will separate. Syllabubs are served in small glasses, often with RATAFIA biscuits.

syrup. See GOLDEN SYRUP and SUGAR SYRUP.

T

Tabasco. John McNulty once wrote an article for the *New Yorker* called 'A Dash of Tabasco', which he began by musing about the label on the bottle. As it gave a forthright description of the product which has been superseded by more flowery prose, it seemed worth reproducing here: 'Tabasco is the pepper sauce manufactured since 1868 by McIlhenny, New Iberia, La. Tabasco is made of vinegar, red pepper, and salt. A few drops mixed with soup or gravy, with breakfast eggs or glass of milk give a piquant and delicious flavor. No sea food should be eaten without tabasco. There is only one tabasco, McIlhenny's. THIS IS THE GENUINE ARTICLE. Made in U.S.A.'

Tabasco is still made only by McIlhenny's in New Iberia—actually on nearby Avery Island, which is not technically an island but an area bounded on three sides by a meandering Louisiana bayou and on the other by a cypress swamp. And the ingredients are still the same: red tabasco chillies grown in the area, salt from Avery Island's own salt mine, and vinegar. Tabasco is very hot and peppery, and if you don't fancy it with your breakfast eggs or glass of milk, you can still add a few drops to fish soup, prawns and other seafood, or wherever a hot sauce is called for. It's used a lot in Creole cooking. And it adds zip to a Bloody Mary, they say.

tabbouleh / tabouli. A Lebanese salad made out of BURGHUL (cracked wheat), soaked and squeezed, mixed with chopped onions, plenty of parsley, some mint, olive oil, lemon juice, salt, and pepper. Sometimes finely chopped tomatoes are added. The salad is traditionally served with lettuce leaves to scoop it up with.

table d'hôte. A lunch or dinner consisting of a set menu of several courses served at a fixed price, especially in a hotel. Also known as 'prix fixe'. It refers to the 'table of the host' a communal table for all guests at a hotel or restaurant.

taco. A Mexican version of the sandwich: some minced meat, cheese, or other filling in a folded or rolled TORTILLA, often fried.

tagine. A North African dish named after the pot with a tall, conical lid in which it is cooked. In Morocco a tagine is a lamb stew, but in Tunisia it is first prepared as a stew and then covered with a mixture of beaten eggs, breadcrumbs, and grated cheese and baked into a kind of custard pie. The stew is sometimes made with added dates, prunes, or fresh fruits.

tagliatelle. Just as the standard metre in the form of a platinum bar is enshrined at the International Bureau of Weights and Measures in Paris, the standard piece of tagliatelle in the form of a solid gold noodle is held in Bologna, the uncontested centre for this long, narrow, flat pasta. (FETTUCCINE, very similar in shape, belong to Rome.) The correct dimensions of tagliatelle, according to the Italian Academy of Cookery, are 1 millimetre thick and 6 millimetres wide. But if you are making your own, without a machine, you just roll out some egg pasta as thin as you can, roll it up into a long, cylindrical shape, then cut it into 6-millimetre slices and quickly unroll them. Tagliatelle are traditionally served with bolognaise sauce (see 'Ragù' under RAGOÛT, RAGÙ; see also PASTA).

tahina / tahini. An oily paste made from ground sesame seeds. Tahina cream salad is made by mixing the paste with crushed garlic, salt, lemon juice, and enough cold water to make a thick sauce. This is served sprinkled with chopped parsley as an appetiser with Arab bread and as an accompaniment to many cold main dishes and some hot ones. When tahina cream salad is mixed with puréed chickpeas it becomes HUMMUS; when mixed with puréed eggplant it becomes BABA GHANOUSH.

tailor / tailer. Also known as skipjack and bluefish, the tailor is a medium to large silvery fish, blue-green on top, found around the southern half of Australia from south Queensland to Western Australia. Fast-swimming and a voracious feeder on other fish, including its own kind, it gets its name (depending on how you spell it) from its ability to shear through a fishing net or another fish as cleanly as tailors' shears, or from the way it 'tails' unsuspecting prey. Tailor are available mainly from July to September and are sold whole and in fillets, cutlets, and steaks. The dark flesh is moist and rather soft, although bleeding and gutting as soon as it is caught prevents the flesh from further softening. It has a strong 'fishy' flavour. Being an oily fish, tailor is best grilled, barbecued, or baked. It is excellent smoked. (See also FISH.)

tamale / tamal. A Mexican dish made of chopped or minced meat (beef, pork, chicken, or turkey), highly seasoned with red chillies, etc., and mixed with masa harina (CORN MEAL), the mixture being wrapped in corn husks to make small packages, which are then steamed.

tamarillo. Also known as the tree tomato, the tamarillo is a smooth-skinned, egg-shaped, red fruit that grows on a treelike shrub native to South America. The flesh has a tart flavour—a cross between tomato and passionfruit, some say. The skin is particularly bitter and should be removed before you eat or cook the fruit. If you pour boiling water over the fruit and let it stand for 2–3 minutes, the skin will peel off easily.

Buy tamarillos that are firm and well-coloured with the stems firmly attached. They will keep for a long time in the refrigerator. Eat them peeled, sliced, and sprinkled with sugar or cut up in salads. They can also be baked or poached in SUGAR SYRUP or wine, or made into a sauce to go with game, pork, or lamb.

tamarind. The tamarind tree is native to Asia. It bears pods shaped like long pea pods which are brown and brittle on the outside and have a doughy pulp inside. This pulp is steeped in water, squeezed, and strained to obtain a brown juice which is used instead of limes or lemons to give a sharp, acid flavour to curries, chutneys, fish and other Indian and Thai dishes. The pulp is available dried in packets and also as a liquid or concentrate in jars. Citrus juice or a mixture of 6 parts vinegar and 1 part sugar can be substituted for tamarind in recipes.

tandoor, tandoori. A tandoor is an Indian clay oven, barrel-shaped and heated from the base by a charcoal fire. Tandoori is a designation given to dishes traditionally cooked in a tandoor—for example, tandoori chicken, which is marinated in a mixture of yoghurt, crushed garlic, grated ginger, lemon juice, and GARAM MASALA and cooked on a spit lowered over the coals.

tangelo. In attempting to produce a grapefruit that could be eaten out of the hand, Californian orchardists developed over the years a number of hybrids of grapefruit and mandarin (tangerine) which they grouped under the name of tangelo. The one grown commercially in the Riverland and Sunrasia districts of Australia is the Minneola tangelo, a cross between the Duncan grapefruit and the Dancy mandarin. It is orange-red in colour, round with a 'sexy little nipple on top', as food writer Leo Schofield puts it, and about the size of an orange. Tangelos are available from August to October. They are sweet and juicy, with a flavour that combines the sweetness of the mandarin with the tang of the grapefruit. The skin peels off easily, and the segments are easily separated. The fruit is technically seedless, but the odd seed may still be found. Tangelos contain more vitamin A than other citrus, but less vitamin C. Eat and use them as you would oranges.

tangerine. See MANDARIN / MANDARINE, TANGERINE.

tansy can be a plant or a dish. The plant is a hardy perennial with fernlike green foliage and tiny yellow flowers. It was widely used in Europe in the Middle Ages as a culinary and medicinal herb but is now grown mainly as a garden border subject.

The dish has had a long and varied history. 'From the tenth to the fourteenth century,' writes Marion Halligan in *Eat My Words,* 'tansies were 'a hot purgative porridge', made of rough grain, probably barley or bran, fats, suet or marrow perhaps, and worts, the tansy part.' By the sixteenth century the tansy had outgrown its purgative past and by the eighteenth had become what Marion Halligan describes as 'an eggy pancake or cakey omelette'. Apples seem to be a popular ingredient in a tansy. Slices of apple are fried in butter, then beaten eggs and cream flavoured with sugar and nutmeg are poured over them and the mixture is cooked on both sides.

tapas are appetising little dishes offered with a glass of wine in the bars and tavernas of Spain. They may be a simple slice of CHORIZO, some fried bread cubes, stuffed olives, grilled prawns or anchovies, fried calamari rings, meat balls, or little spicy stews made from tripe or offal. Tapas are mainly eaten in the late afternoon, between the siesta following lunch and the evening meal, which does not appear until nine o'clock at the earliest and usually much later. The word *tapa* means 'top' or 'lid' in Spanish, and one explanation of the origin of the name is that when a customer bought a drink in a bar, it was served with a small slice of bread on top to keep the flies out. The slice of bread was later replaced by a small plate, and a titbit was added to encourage trade.

tapénade. A paste or solid sauce made from black olives, anchovies, capers, olive oil, and lemon juice. It originated in Provence, the name coming from *tapéna,* the Provençal word for capers. Tapénade can be spread on toast, spooned over home-made pizza, or used as a sauce with hard-boiled eggs, boiled potatoes, cold fish, or cold boiled beef.

tapioca. A starch derived from the tuberous roots of the tropical plant manioc, also known as cassava. The moist starch is formed into granules, or pearls, by shaking drops onto a hot plate to dry out. Like SAGO, which it resembles, tapioca is used mostly in milk puddings or as a soup thickener.

taramasalata. A Greek and Turkish specialty, taramasalata is a pale pink cream salad made from the dried, salted and pressed roe of the grey MULLET (or other fish ROE) mixed with crushed garlic, lemon juice, olive oil, and bread soaked in water or milk, then squeezed dry. Other ingredients such as mashed potato, egg yolk, and grated onion are sometimes included. Taramasalata is served as a dip, often garnished with black olives, or spread on thin toast.

taro is the tropical equivalent of the potato and provides much of the starchy food for people of the western Pacific. The Polynesian word *taro* is a generic name for any of a number of plants of the arum or 'elephant's ear' family native to tropical Asia. While the leaves and young shoots of some kinds of taro are eaten, the fleshy rhizomes constitute the main edible part. They are more starchy than potatoes and have a similar taste. All parts of the taro should be cooked before being eaten, as they may contain calcium oxalate 'needles' which cause intense pain if they penetrate the soft tissues of the mouth or throat. Cooking eliminates the needles.

tarragon. French or Russian? The French variety is considered far superior in flavour; the Russian more vigorous and easier to grow, as it sets seeds (French tarragon must be propagated by root division). French tarragon is one of the great culinary herbs, renowned for its distinctive aromatic flavour. It is an essential ingredient of FINES HERBES and sauces such as BÉARNAISE and RAVIGOTE. It goes well with poultry, pâtés, fish, shellfish, and vegetables. Tarragon vinegar, delicious with green salads, can be made by steeping a few leaves of tarragon in white wine vinegar for a couple of weeks, then straining. Tarragon should not be overcooked or it will become bitter. Dried tarragon loses the fine flavour.

tart. See PIE, TART, FLAN.

tartare sauce. How do you pronounce it—like 'Tartar' (from which the name derives) or 'tart*air*'? *The Macquarie Dictionary* gives the 'tart*air*' pronunciation (or the equivalent in the International Phonetic Alphabet) as its first choice, with 'Tartar' as an alternative. *The Australian Concise Oxford* gives only the '*air*' pronunciation. However, people who like to display their knowledge of French or gastronomy say 'Tartar'.

The sauce itself is usually MAYONNAISE with other ingredients mixed in. The other ingredients, all finely chopped, are parsley and perhaps tarragon, onion or shallot, gherkins, and capers. Some people add French mustard to the mayonnaise; some add chopped hard-boiled eggs, while others make the mayonnaise with hard-boiled egg yolks instead of raw ones. Tartare sauce is supposed to attack the tastebuds as the Tartars attacked just about everyone. It is usually served with fish. (See also 'Steak Tartare' under STEAK.)

tarwhine. See BREAM.

tasty cheese. Matured cheese, usually of the Cheddar kind.

tea. Apart from water, tea is the most popular drink in the world. It was popular in China for a thousand years before it replaced beer as the preferred drink at English breakfast tables. Australians have always been enthusiastic tea drinkers, and when the early settlers couldn't get the real thing they used leaves of the false sarsaparilla vine and the tea-tree to make substitute tea.

The real thing is an evergreen bush of the camellia family native to South-East Asia. Although it is cultivated only in tropical and sub-tropical regions (including plantations in Queensland and northern New South Wales), the best tea comes from plants grown at high altitudes, which produce fewer leaves but of finer quality. The choice 'pluck' is the terminal shoot and the first two leaves of each branch. Darjeeling tea, grown in the Himalayan foothills, is considered the champagne of teas.

There are many varieties of tea plant but three main kinds of tea: **black,** the rich, aromatic, and full-flavoured teas which account for most of the tea consumed internationally; **green,** which come mainly from China, Japan, and Taiwan and have a more mellow, subtle flavour; and **oolong,** the best of which come from Taiwan and are known as Formosa oolongs.

For **black tea**, the leaves are first rolled, to mix up the chemical components and give the leaves a characteristic twist, then allowed to ferment, which makes them turn coppery-brown and develop astringent tannins. Finally they are dried. **Green tea** does not undergo fermentation but is steamed before it is rolled and dried. **Oolong tea** is a compromise between black and green, being fermented briefly before and after rolling.

The names under which black tea is sold often do not indicate the variety or the quality but the size and shape of the leaves. **Orange pekoe**, for example, means long, thin, closely twisted leaves (the terminal shoot has a yellow-orange down on it); **pekoe** means more open leaves without the downy bud; **souchong** large, coarse leaves. The term *broken* with these names indicates smaller, broken leaves. The larger the leaf, the longer the tea takes to brew. The smallest leaves, known as 'dust' in the trade, are put into tea bags because they suffuse almost instantly. (Incidentally, the tea bag came into being in 1904 when Thomas Sullivan, a New York tea merchant, distributed samples in silk bags.) **Gunpowder,** an old China tea, has large greyish-green leaves rolled into pellets resembling lead shot.

To make a pot of tea. Empty the kettle and fill it with fresh water from the tap—reheated water contains less dissolved air and makes flat-tasting tea. Just before the water comes to the boil, pour some into the teapot (glazed china for preference) and swirl it around to heat the pot. This is to prevent the pot from cooling the boiling water too much when it is poured over the tea leaves. Discard the rinsing water and put 1 teaspoon of tea for each cup and 1 more 'for the pot' into the warmed teapot. When the water in the kettle begins to boil—don't let it boil for long, or you'll lose that dissolved air—pour it over the tea. Let it brew for 3–5 minutes depending on the tea; remember, larger-leafed tea takes longer to infuse than small or broken-leafed tea. Then give the tea a stir and pour it out, using a strainer to catch the leaves. If the tea is too strong for your liking after letting it brew for as long as this, use less tea rather than pour it out sooner; the full flavour of the tea takes time to be extracted.

tempura. If you were a traditionalist, you would eat tempura only during Ember Weeks, which occur four times a year, once in each season. The Wednesday, Friday, and Saturday of Ember Weeks used to be observed as days of religious fasting and abstinence, and the Portuguese traders and missionaries in Japan in the sixteenth century, being good Catholics, refrained from eating meat on these days in Ember Weeks, which they called by the Latin name Quatuor Tempora ('four times'). They asked instead for seafood, usually prawns, and in the course of time the Latin word for *times*, adapted to local pronunciation, became the Japanese word for prawns fried in batter.

Nowadays, prawns are not the only food given the tempura treatment. Chicken, fish, and most vegetables are also used. The food is coated with a very thin batter made from flour, egg, ice water, and any special ingredients the Japanese chef may choose to include, and deep-fried in oil of the chef's own particular blend. The batter must be cold so that it puffs up as soon as it hits the hot oil, and the food partly fries and partly cooks in the steam trapped within the batter. Tempura is served straight from the pan and is accompanied with dipping sauces, including soy sauce combined with slivered ginger, and a mixture of soy sauce, MIRIN, and DASHI.

teriyaki. The Japanese word *teriyaki* means 'shining grill' or 'grilled with a glaze', which aptly describes the cooked food. Meat, fish, or poultry is marinated in a mixture of soy sauce and MIRIN in more or less equal proportions, and then cooked on a HIBACHI or under a grill, the food being basted with, or redipped in, the teriyaki sauce while it is quickly cooking. The sauce is also used as a dipping sauce to accompany the cooked food.

terrine. See PÂTÉ, TERRINE.

threadfin. King threadfin and blue threadfin are tropical finfish found around the northern coast of Australia from southern Queensland to Exmouth Gulf in Western Australia. Also known as king salmon and Cooktown salmon, they are medium to large silvery fish with a darker top and whiskery pectoral fins that act as organs of touch. Threadfin are caught all year round, but mainly from May to September. They are sold whole and in fillets, cutlets, and steaks. Some threadfin fillets are imported from Indonesia. The flesh of the threadfin is firm and moist with large flakes that separate into bite-size pieces. It can be cooked in most ways and is particularly suited to grilling and barbecuing.

thyme. Of the many varieties of thyme, the common or garden variety, *Thymus vulgaris,* is the one most used in the kitchen. Thyme grows wild throughout Europe, and it is an easily grown hardy perennial in the herb garden. It has tiny leaves and pretty little creamy-pink flowers. Thyme is powerfully aromatic and is one of the important culinary herbs. It is used widely in stews, braises, and casseroles and also in soups and stuffings. It is an essential ingredient in BOUQUET GARNI. It also goes well with vegetables such as zucchini and eggplant and adds interest to food that would otherwise seem bland.

Lemon thyme, as the name implies, is a citrus-flavoured variety. It goes well with fish.

tian. An oval GRATIN dish famous in Provence. The name is also given to the food cooked in dishes of this kind.

timbale. Another of those names that can mean a cooking utensil or the dish cooked in that utensil. The word *timbale* means 'kettledrum', and the cooking utensil is a mould shaped rather like a drum—round with straight or slightly sloping sides, sometimes fluted—made of tinned copper, earthenware, or fireproof china. Some timbale moulds have a central funnel like a GUGELHUPF mould. The mould may be lined with pastry and then filled with a sweet or savoury filling, covered with a pastry top, and, when baked, turned out on a serving plate. The pastry may also be BAKED BLIND and then filled. A timbale may also be a moulded dish of minced meat, fish, vegetables, pasta, rice, or mousse, sweet or savoury, hot or cold. If it is made in a mould with a central funnel, a suitable sauce, purée, or cream can be poured into the centre.

tisane. An infusion or decoction of dried or fresh herbs, flowers, seeds, or roots drunk as tea. Tisanes may be calming, stimulating, or tonic, depending on what they are made from. Camomile, mint, lemon thyme, lemon balm, bergamot, and sage are some of the herbs used; lime flowers, orange flowers, camomile flowers, rose hips, and ginseng root are among other things tisanes can be made from. Tisanes are often drunk before going to bed or after meals to aid digestion.

Dried herbs or flowers can be made into a tisane by pouring boiling water over them in a teapot or cup and letting them infuse for a few minutes; fresh herbs are usually crushed, chopped, or bruised to extract their therapeutic properties; seeds and roots may need to be boiled and then left to infuse. Tisanes with a bitter flavour may be sweetened with honey. Herb teas and tisanes are available in packages or tea bags.

tofu. Originally a Chinese creation, this white curd made from mashed soya beans was introduced into Japan with Buddhism in the seventh century. It is now widely eaten in Japan as well as in China. Although tofu has a bland taste and the consistency of firm custard, it can be prepared and used in many ways. With its capacity to soak up other flavours, it is used as a substitute for meat, fish, and chicken and is often included in soups and braises. It can be sautéed, boiled, or grilled; rolled in cornflour and deep-fried; scrambled with eggs and other ingredients; and used in many other dishes both savoury and sweet.

tomatillo

Fresh tofu may be stored for a few days in the refrigerator if kept in fresh water and the water changed each day. Tofu is high in protein and low in kilojoules.

tomatillo. Also known as the Mexican green tomato (*tomatito verde, pelado,* or *tomatillo entero*), this small green and purple variety of the CAPE GOOSEBERRY is a vital ingredient of the Mexican version of salsa verde (see SALSA). Tomatillos are about the size of cherry tomatoes and have a distinctive flavour. They are full of vitamin C. Fresh ones are occasionally available.

tomatoes. Some people like to argue about whether the tomato is a fruit or a vegetable. It is, of course, both, botanically a fruit ('the developed ovary of a seed plant with its contents and accessory parts', in *The Macquarie Dictionary*'s definition) and broadly a vegetable ('any herbaceous plant . . . whose fruits, seeds, roots, tubers, bulbs, stems, leaves or flower parts are used as food'). However, it is generally used as a vegetable, as are peas, beans, capsicums, cucumbers, and pumpkins, which are also, botanically, fruits.

The tomato is a native of South America and was brought to Europe in the sixteenth century, though it was treated as a decorative plant rather than a food plant in most places. Being a member of the nightshade family, it was suspected of bearing fruit that was poisonous; its leaves are.

Tomatoes come in various shapes—globular, oval, banana-shaped, smooth or ridged—in sizes from large to cherry-size, and coloured yellow as well as red. There are innumerable varieties. Those grown commercially are mostly hybrids bred for their keeping and travelling qualities, not for their flavour, as many consumers have noted and deplored. Commercial tomatoes are also generally picked green or at 'quarter-coloured', 'half-coloured', or three-quarter-coloured' stages of ripening, although it is possible to buy them vine-ripened. Tomatoes are available all year round, with heaviest supplies in summer.

Choose smooth, firm, well-formed tomatoes that are heavy for their size. Buy bright red ones for immediate use and green to pink ones for later use. (One advantage of selecting obviously unripe tomatoes is that they are unlikely to have been squeezed by previous shoppers.) Allow them to ripen at room temperature, stem down, out of direct sunlight and preferably in a brown paper bag. When ripe, refrigerate if you must, but take them out of the refrigerator an hour before eating, as the flavour is best at room temperature.

As well as being prized salad ingredients and an essential part of countless cooked dishes, tomatoes themselves can be stewed, baked, sautéed, or stuffed. Stuffings may be mixtures of mushrooms, meat, ham, fish or prawns bound with some breadcrumbs or cooked rice. In Provence they use a simple stuffing of breadcrumbs, parsley, and lots of crushed garlic and olive oil. Cut off the top of the tomato, scoop out some of the inside and replace it with the stuffing, then bake. With fillings such as canned tuna, sliced olives, or chopped hard-boiled eggs, the stuffed tomato can be eaten raw.

Slice a tomato from top to bottom for use on sandwiches; in this way the juice is prevented from leaking out and making the bread soggy.

To skin and seed a tomato. Recipes sometimes require tomatoes to be peeled and seeded. To make a tomato easy to peel, plunge it into boiling water for about 10 seconds, then refresh it under cold water; cut out the top at the stem end and peel off the skin from the top down. To extract seeds and juice, cut the tomato in half crosswise and gently squeeze in the palm of the hand over a bowl to catch the seeds and juice. Give it a shake, and dislodge any residue with your little finger.

Sun-dried tomatoes are halved and allowed to dry on a wire frame in the sun, though they may also be oven dried. Some are then packed in oil, others packed dry in halves, dice, or julienne strips. Locally produced as well as imported sun-dried tomatoes are available.

tongue. Although calf's and sheep's tongues can be bought, ox tongues are the kind generally eaten. They are available fresh, salted, or smoked. Fresh and salted tongues are usually soaked in water for a few hours before cooking.

To cook a tongue, put it in a saucepan of water with flavourings such as peppercorns, bay leaf, BOUQUET GARNI, onion, carrot, celery, and cloves, and slowly bring it to the boil. Simmer for 3–4 hours until tender. Skim off any scum that forms on top while it is cooking. When the tongue is cool enough to handle, trim off any fat at the root end and remove the bone-like parts, then peel off the skin (slit the underside and push your thumb in). If you want to press the tongue into a compact mass for carving, curl it into a bowl small enough to make a tight fit, put a plate on top and weigh it down with something heavy such as a tin of fruit. Leave it in the refrigerator overnight. Serve tongue cut in slices, hot with mashed potatoes or cold with pickles or mustard.

torshi. Middle Eastern style pickled vegetables.

torte. 'A *Torte* is a round cake, but not every round cake is a *Torte*,' they say in Vienna. Like the GATEAU, the torte is for festive occasions, an elaborate, highly decorated cake, often built up in layers, containing cream and other rich ingredients and flavoured with a liqueur or a spirit. Among the well-known tortes are the SACHERTORTE and the LINZERTORTE.

tortellini, tortelloni. Home-made stuffed pasta. Tortellini are small and ring-shaped, made from discs of egg pasta folded over any of a variety of stuffings into a half-circle and then bent around a finger into a coil joined at the two points of the half-circle. A specialty of Bologna, tortellini are often served in hot broth but may also be served with butter, cream, or other sauce. Tortelloni are larger, square dumplings, like RAVIOLI, which are usually stuffed with spinach.

tortilla. The Mexican staff of life, the tortilla is a thin, round, unleavened pancake made traditionally from *masa harina* (see 'Corn meal' under CORN) but also from wholewheat flour, then baked on a griddle. Tortillas are eaten as bread and often used as a spoon to scoop up food. Folded or rolled around various fillings, fried or baked as snacks or substantial dishes, they become such things as BURRITOS, ENCHILADAS, TACOS, and TOSTADAS. The dough is also baked as corn chips.

tostadas are tortillas that have been fried until crisp and covered with fried beans, chopped meat, capsicums, onions, tomatoes, cheese, etc.

tournedos. A MEDALLION of beef weighing about 100 grams cut from the middle part of the FILLET and quickly fried in butter (so quickly the chef hasn't time to turn his back, as the word *tournedos* implies). Tournedos are sometimes served on a fried CROÛTON of the same size, and they are garnished and presented in many ways. Tournedos Rossini, for example, is served on a croûton and topped with PÂTÉ DE FOIE GRAS and a slice of truffle simmered in port.

treacle is a dark, heavy syrup obtained as a by-product from the refining of sugar (see GOLDEN SYRUP).

tree tomato. See TAMARILLO.

trevalla. See BLUE EYE / BLUE-EYE COD and WAREHOU.

trevally. There are a number of fish grouped in the trevally family, but those sold as trevally are two similar deep-bodied fish—the silver trevally, found in the northern half of Australia, and the golden trevally, found around the southern half—sleek, silvery or golden with a blue-green back. They have a strong flavour and make good eating when freshly caught, the cooked flesh being white and tender, but they do not keep well. Trevally should be gutted as soon as they are caught. Small specimens may be pan-fried whole; larger ones should be filleted and deep-fried in batter or baked whole with a stuffing of breadcrumbs and crabmeat. Trevally are also good in a casserole. (See also WAREHOU and FISH.)

trifle. Originally a trifle was thick cream heated with spices—usually ginger, sugar, and rose water—until lukewarm. By the middle of the eighteenth century it had acquired a solid base made of crushed biscuits or macaroons soaked in wine and a central layer of custard, with a SYLLABUB on top. The present-day trifle usually has a base of sponge cake soaked in sherry and sprinkled with slivered almonds or macaroons, then a layer of custard; the syllabub top has been replaced by a layer of whipped cream decorated with such things as blanched almonds, glacé cherries, crystallised fruits, and fresh strawberries or raspberries. Trifles are traditionally made in the cook's prettiest cut-glass bowl.

tripe is the stomach of a ruminant, usually an ox, prepared as food. The first division of the stomach is smooth or plain, the second honeycombed; both are eaten. Tripe is almost always sold in Australia ready prepared and partially cooked; if it weren't, much preliminary scrubbing, soaking, and blanching would have to be done and hours of cooking would be needed to make it tender. In the famous Tripes à la Mode de Caen of northern France, for example, the tripe is simmered in cider and Calvados with aromatic herbs and vegetables for more than 10 hours. Whichever way you cook tripe, cut it into strips or squares to make it easy to handle on the plate. Tripe and onions are traditional companions; the tripe is simmered in milk, then cooked with some sautéed onions and a ROUX made with some of the milk in which the tripe was simmered.

trout. Brown trout were first hatched in Tasmania in 1864 from ova imported from England at great expense in a specially made ice-house. They were released in Victoria during that decade and in New South Wales in the 1880s. American rainbow trout, brook trout, and golden trout were introduced in later years. All are available, though farmed rainbow trout are the most commonly encountered. Tasmanian trout farmers transfer young rainbow trout to sea cages to rear; these are often known as ocean trout or sea-run trout.

    To cook trout. Trout may be steamed, poached, fried, grilled, or baked. They are perhaps best poached in a COURT BOUILLON. As the flesh is oily, trout cooked with nuts is excessive for some stomachs. Even frying in butter is too much for some tastes, although trout cooked à la MEUNIÈRE is a popular dish. Smoked trout, with head and skin removed and the flesh lifted off the bone, makes a fine entrée with bread and butter and horseradish sauce.

truffles. As truffles cannot be cultivated, they are one of the few valuable foods that are still in the domain of the hunter-gatherer. You could say they were hunted as well as gathered because dogs (in the past, pigs) are used to sniff out these small, aromatic, ball-shaped fungi that grow under the ground in the root systems of trees. There are many varieties, the most esteemed being the black truffles that grow beneath oak trees in the vicinity of Périgueux in south-western France and the white ones of the Piedmont region in Italy. However, the world's largest truffle field is said to be the Kalahari Desert in southern Africa, where an orange-ochre truffle grows amid the roots of the scrubby desert bush.

    In the past, truffles were available in Australia only in cans and fully sterilised, but in recent years, during the brief harvesting seasons of the different varieties, cryovac-packed, ice-chilled, or snap-frozen fresh truffles have been air-freighted from France and Italy, and also from Namibia, for the degustation of those who can afford them ($3200 a kilo has been charged for fresh Piedmont truffles in Sydney). They are also available dried, canned in their juice, and in paste form.

    With their rich, earthy flavour, truffles are eaten to a large extent as taste provokers and used in small quantities in stuffings, sauces, pâtés, omelettes, and the like, or shaved in thin slices over special dishes.

    A certain chocolate confection made in the shape of a truffle is also known as a truffle.

trussing. See under CHICKEN.

tuile. A thin biscuit which is shaped into a curve resembling a French roof tile (*tuile* is the French word for 'tile'). Tuiles are often made with ground almonds or decorated with flaked almonds. The biscuits are bent over a rolling pin while still warm to give them the curved shape.

tuna. In past years, tuna was something that came in cans. Canned tuna was popular in the United States, and the American style of mixing together canned and other prepared and packaged ingredients was followed here to some extent by magazine cookery writers trying to find ways of making use of it. Then we learned from the Japanese that tuna was good eaten fresh, even raw. While much of the tuna catch is still canned (in oil or brine), fresh tuna is now available most of the year, although the winter catch is considered the best quality, and only the best quality is used to cut into thin slices to eat raw as SASHIMI.

The main species of tuna caught in Australian waters are southern bluefin, yellowfin, big-eye, albacore, and skipjack. Most are caught in the wild, but with tuna having been overfished, some are farmed. Southern bluefin, yellowfin, and big-eye tuna are big fish, and their flesh is firm, coarse-grained, and reddish with dark bands along the side but creamy-white when cooked. They are excellent for sashimi and SUSHI. Albacore is a smaller fish, and its flesh is lighter coloured and softer in texture. Skipjack tuna is mostly canned.

Tuna is sold in cutlets or steaks. They can be grilled or barbecued and are best seared and left fairly rare inside; overcooking makes the flesh very dry. Marinating in citrus juice, oil, and herbs or baking in a herbed crust prevents tuna from drying out. Thin slices may be dusted with flour and fried; they may also be briefly poached in COURT BOUILLON or dipped and simmered in a STEAMBOAT.

turkey. Wild turkeys originated in America and were brought to Europe by the Spanish conquistadors, together with the turkey's main food, maize.

In Australia, most turkeys are eaten at Christmas or other festive occasions. They tend to be rather dry, so cooking methods are aimed at keeping the flesh moist. Some turkeys are sold with herbed oil injected into them, but this is not to everyone's liking. There are more traditional methods of preventing a turkey from drying out during roasting: tie large pieces of pork belly fat over the breast and thighs; wrap the bird in buttered greaseproof paper (opening it at the breast towards the end of cooking to allow the breast to brown); stuff the turkey with a stuffing rich in butter or one from which steam will rise and keep the bird moist from the inside; or put a little water in the baking dish and stand the turkey on a wire rack above the water.

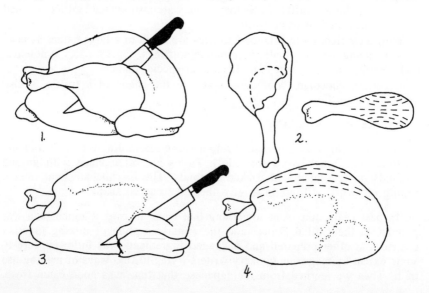

When cooking a frozen turkey, make sure it is completely thawed out before putting it in the oven. It will take about 48 hours to thaw in the refrigerator.

To carve a turkey. Holding the turkey firmly with a carving fork, cut down between the thigh and the body on one side, then pull the leg away and cut it off at the joint. Separate the drumstick from the thigh, and carve the meat off both pieces into attractive slices. Cut off the wing by pressing it down and severing it at the joint. Carve the breast downwards, at a bit of an angle, into thin slices. If it is a large turkey, when you reach the widest part of the breast you can carve the front and back alternately to make the slices a suitable size. Carve the other side of the turkey in the same way. Serve light and dark meat to each person.

Turkish delight. The Turks and the Greeks argue about who created this chewy, gelatinous confection, as they do about many things. However, Turkish delight is what it has come to be known as in English; in Turkish it is *lokum*. Although home-made Turkish delight is usually made with gelatine, corn-flour is the proper gelling agent. The sugary jelly mixture is flavoured with rose water, orange flower water, oil of peppermint, and the like, and coloured accordingly. Pistachios or other nuts are often incorporated in the jelly, which is cut into cubes when set and coated with a mixture of icing sugar and cornflour.

turmeric. Often misspelt *tumeric* and correspondingly mispronounced, turmeric is a yellow powder obtained by grinding the dried rhizomes of a tropical plant of the ginger family (*Curcuma domestica*) native to southern Asia. It is turmeric that gives curry mixtures their characteristic colour and some of their flavour. Turmeric is also used in pickles and chutneys and to colour and flavour rice, chicken and egg dishes. (Approved additive no. 100.)

turnips, swedes. The turnip and the swede (also called swede turnip and, in the United States, rutabaga) are both members of the brassica or cabbage family. Turnip tops may in fact be boiled and eaten as a green vegetable. However, they are grown essentially for their roots. Turnip roots are globe-shaped and white with a purple top and have white flesh. They are usually sold when small (their flesh coarsens in taste and texture as they get bigger), in bunches with their tops on. Swedes are yellow with a darker, purplish top, and are usually sold with the base and sides sharply trimmed of whisker roots. Their yellow flesh has a dense texture. They grow to a bigger size without a coarsening of texture and flavour. Both are available all year round, with heaviest supplies from April to September.

Choose roots that are firm, with no blemishes or moist spots. Store them in a cool, dry place or, for long periods, in the refrigerator. Turnips and swedes are used in stews and soups. They are also boiled and eaten as a vegetable. Baby turnips are sometimes glazed. Pickled turnips, coloured pink or red by adding beetroot, are a Middle Eastern favourite. Swedes may be mashed, eaten on their own or mixed with mashed potatoes.

turnover. Like a pasty, a turnover is made by putting a filling of some kind (cooked apple or a spoonful of jam, for example) on one half of a round piece of pastry, folding the other half over, and baking it. Various sweet and savoury fillings can be used, and you can use a square of pastry and turn it over to make a triangle. In Tunisia they make a savoury turnover known as a *brik,* which is made with paper-thin pastry filled with minced lamb, chicken, or anchovies mixed with onions, herbs, and seasonings with an egg broken onto it, and the turnover is fried in oil.

tzatziki / cacik. A cool, refreshing salad popular throughout the Middle East (*tzatziki* is the Greek name, *cacik* the Turkish), made from drained yoghurt, chopped cucumber, and minced garlic. Often served with fried fish, fried slices of zucchini and eggplant, or with bread and black olives.

V

vacherin. A crown-shaped dessert which is a specialty of Alsace. It may be made with meringue rings placed one on top of the other on a pastry base to form a bowl, which is filled with whipped cream or ice-cream, fruit or fruit purée. It can also be made with two solid circles of meringue with the filling in between and icing sugar dusted on top.

vanilla comes from the dried seed-pod of a tropical vine of the orchid family native to Central America. (The pod is also known as a vanilla bean, but pod is a more precise term.) An extract, vanilla essence, is obtained from the pod, and this is used as a flavouring for cakes, custards, ice-cream, and other sweet dishes. (There are also synthetic essences made from such things as oil of cloves and wood wastes, and while these may be cheaper than genuine vanilla, they don't have the same rich flavour.) Many cooks prefer to use the pod itself for flavouring.

When making custards and other sweet sauces, the pod is scalded in milk or cream and allowed to infuse while the milk cools. A vanilla pod can be used again and again if it is washed and dried and put away (in the freezer, some recommend). It will gradually lose its flavour, so you will have to replace it eventually, but it will last for a long time, nevertheless.

Vanilla sugar is made by placing a vanilla pod in a screw-top jar of sugar, usually castor sugar. The vanilla perfume permeates the sugar, and regular topping up of the jar with sugar allows you to have some always on hand. Vanilla sugar is used for making biscuits, cakes, meringues, etc.

veal is meat from an unweaned or recently weaned calf. In the dairy industry, female calves go into the herd, and male calves end up as veal. The meat should be light pink in colour, finely grained, with only a thin covering of satiny fat and little marbling. The flavour of veal is fairly bland, so it can take a strongly flavoured garnish, and as it has little fat to lubricate it when cooking, it tends to dry out unless cooked in a way to retain moisture.

Roasted veal should be barded with strips of pork fat or cooked on a rack in a pan with some water in it.

Because of calves' size, there are fewer cuts of veal than there are of beef. The hind leg can be roasted bone in or boned and rolled or stuffed; it can also be sliced into steaks and SCHNITZELS (ESCALOPES, SCALOPPINE). The loin provides short loin chops (some containing a prized section of kidney) and rib chops (CUTLETS), which can be left together and roasted as a rack. The forequarter provides forequarter chops. The shoulder may be roasted bone in or boned and rolled or stuffed, or cut into cubes for stewing. Veal shanks, or knuckles, are celebrated for their use in OSSO BUCO.

velouté sauce is a simple white sauce made from white STOCK (veal or chicken) or FUMET thickened with a pale ROUX and simmered for 20–25 minutes (chefs simmer it for hours). Sometimes milk and / or cream are added. Velouté (the name means 'velvety') is the basis of many sauces and cream soups. When cream is added to velouté sauce, it becomes sauce SUPRÊME; when egg yolks are added, it becomes sauce ALLEMANDE.

venison. Although much of the venison sold in Australia is imported from New Zealand, deer farming is a growing industry in places such as Gippsland in Victoria and Mudgee in New South Wales. Nevertheless, venison is still not widely available and is sold mainly in specialist game outlets. It is a dark red, tender meat with little fat, low in cholesterol and high in iron, and not gamy as one would expect. It is sold mostly as steaks, but larger cuts for roasting are sometimes to be had. Melbourne chief and author Stephanie Alexander writes approvingly of 'a small venison steak turned a few times in rich meat juices with some braised cabbage and lovingly peeled chestnuts'. *Sydney Morning Herald* food writer Meryl Constance recommends a butterflied silverside of venison marinated in a cumin-flavoured marinade and roasted with parboiled asparagus and cobs of sweet corn.

verjuice / verjus. The unfermented, acid juice of unripe grapes. It is used in the same way as vinegar or lemon juice, but its flavour has, in the words of South Australian food writer and chef Maggie Beer, 'the tartness of lemon and the acidity of vinegar without the harshness of either'. Verjuice is used in place of vinegar in the manufacture of Dijon mustard.

vermicelli. Pasta in the form of long, slender, solid threads, like fine spaghetti ('little worms' is the literal translation of the Italian). A dish of rice and vermicelli (*roz bil shagria* in Arabic), cooked with chickpeas and chopped onion, is eaten in many countries of the Middle East on the second night of the New Year.

vichyssoise. Properly known as Crème Vichyssoise Glacé, vichyssoise is a chilled version of Potage PARMENTIER, which is itself a puréed version of Potage BONNE FEMME. French chef Louis Diat, who probably wouldn't have dared present such an outlandish adaptation back in Vichy, introduced the soup to New York society at the old Ritz-Carlton in the summer of 1917. It is made with sliced leeks and diced potatoes, lightly sautéed in butter with some chopped onions, simmered in water or stock and wine, then puréed and cooled. Some cream is mixed in and the soup is chilled until needed. It is served with a blob of cream on top and sprinkled with chopped chives.

vinaigrette. The most commonly made and basic salad dressing or sauce, vinaigrette is essentially a mixture of oil and vinegar. The traditional proportions are 3 parts of oil to 1 part of vinegar. Salt and pepper are usually added according to taste. The mixture is whisked together or shaken in a bottle or screw-topped jar and poured over the salad.

Vinaigrette can be varied in many ways. Although olive oil—best-quality extra-virgin olive oil—is recommended, any good salad oil can be used. Lemon juice, lime juice, or VERJUICE may be substituted for vinegar (which should be wine vinegar). And the proportions of oil to vinegar may be varied to suit one's taste. Some French mustard is often mixed in; this not only adds flavour but helps the mixture to form an emulsion. Garlic is another frequent addition; it may be crushed to a paste with salt or chopped and mixed in with the other ingredients, or steeped in the vinegar beforehand. Chopped herbs may be either added to the vinaigrette or sprinkled over the salad.

Make sure that lettuce is dry before pouring vinaigrette over it. Moisture on the lettuce dilutes the dressing and repels the oil.

Some people prefer to put the oil and vinegar on their salad separately. When doing this, remember that the vinegar should go on first. If the oil goes on first, it puts a coating on the salad that the vinegar can't adhere to.

vindaloo is an intensely hot, sour, Goanese dish of meat, poultry, or game flavoured with a paste made from hot Indian spices in a vinegar base.

vinegar. The word *vinegar* comes from the French *vin aigre,* meaning 'sour wine'. Vinegar is made by letting various alcoholic liquids—not only wine, but cider, fermented malt (crude beer), rice wine, and distilled alcohol such as ethanol—become infected with bacteria that turn the alcohol into acetic acid. Vinegar has long been used for pickling and preserving food. The acid in the vinegar discourages the growth of most microbes. In marinades, the acid acts as a tenderiser.

While all vinegars are a dilute solution of acetic acid and have a sour taste and pungent aroma, the liquid from which they are made can give a characteristic flavour to each. Some vinegars are made richer by ageing in barrels; others are flavoured with herbs and fruits.

Wine vinegar is made from both white and red wine of various kinds and grape varieties. White wine vinegar is called for in most recipes requiring vinegar these days. Red wine vinegar is traditionally used as an aromatic in sauces and marinades for game.

Sherry vinegar, made from sherry, has a mellow, smooth taste. It may be used in vinaigrette (sometimes in combination with lemon juice) or to deglaze a roasting pan to make a rich gravy for beef or to add extra flavour to a casserole.

Balsamic vinegar is a reddish-brown, rich, strong-flavoured vinegar made in Modena, Italy, and aged in barrels for at least five years and often for a much longer time. Because of its pervasive flavour, it is used in small amounts.

Cider vinegar has something of a reputation as a cure for all ills, especially in combination with honey. It has a milder flavour than other vinegars.

Malt vinegar. No one seems to recommend using malt vinegar in cooking. However, it is excellent for pickling. It can be white as well as brown.

Rice wine vinegar is made by both the Chinese and the Japanese. The Chinese make black, red, and white vinegars, varying from very strong (black) to the delicately flavoured white. Japanese rice vinegar (*su*) is pale yellow and mild in flavour.

Fruit-flavoured vinegars. Certain soft fruits, especially raspberries, can be steeped in white wine vinegar for a few days. The liquid may be used as vinegar and also as a syrup to add to sweet sauces and cool drinks. A tablespoon of raspberry vinegar in a cup of iced water used to be a tipple of ladies in the Victorian era.

Herb-flavoured vinegars. Sprigs of herbs such as tarragon, rosemary, basil, mint, and thyme are often placed in an attractive bottle of vinegar—for show, it seems, as much as for use. But these herb-flavoured vinegars are suitable for use in sauces, gravies, and salad dressing if consideration is given to the appropriateness of the individual herb to the dish to be garnished.

vine leaves. When 'vine leaves' are called for in a recipe, you are expected to know that the vine should belong to the genus *Vitis*—in other words, the grapevine. Don't just go out into the backyard and grab a few leaves off the bougainvillea or the purple trumpet vine—while you may create a new culinary delicacy, you may also cook up a new way of poisoning your guests. The leaves of the grapevine, however, have long been used in countries around the Mediterranean, where the grapevine originated, as an edible wrapping for savoury titbits (see DOLMADES / DOLMAS), or around small game birds or fish before braising or baking them. They may also be used for lining a pot in which mushrooms are cooked, or as decorations for cheese plates and fruit bowls. The leaves, which should be young and tender, are first blanched in boiling water, then drained and dried. Vine leaves preserved in brine are available in cans.

vol-au-vent, or 'flight in the wind', obviously refers to the lightness of the puff pastry used to make this small, usually round, pastry case in which a morsel of meat, chicken, or fish in a sauce or some other savoury mixture is contained. Vol-au-vents are useful as 'finger food' at social gatherings, but beware of taking a bite of one without first assessing the temperature of the filling. A piece of small talk can be made even more unbearable by the sensation of red-hot sauce stuck to the roof of your mouth. Ready-cooked vol-au-vent cases can be bought in cake shops and supermarkets if you can't be bothered making your own.

W

waffle. A light, crisp cake with deep indentations made by baking BATTER in a waffle iron. The waffle iron consists of two hinged metal plates with grid-pattern indentations. The plates are greased with oil and the batter is poured onto the bottom plate, the top one folded over to seal in the batter and spread it to fill the iron, then the iron is heated briefly on each side to cook the waffle until it is puffed and brown. Waffles are usually served with a syrup and whipped cream or ice-cream

wakame. See SEAWEED.

Waldorf salad. Any fan of the television series *Fawlty Towers* will know what goes to make a Waldorf salad: 'Celery! Apples! Walnuts! Grapes! In a mayonnaise sauce! And tell your chef,' the irate American guest warned Basil, 'if he doesn't get on the ball you'll bust his ass!' As Sybil explained to Basil when he grumbled, 'What's a waldorf, anyway—a walnut that's gone orf?', it is the Waldorf Astoria hotel in New York, where the salad was first served. Dictionary definitions don't include grapes in the ingredients, and they mention that the ingredients are diced.

walnuts. Although there are various kinds of walnut tree native to Europe, Asia, and America, it is the Persian walnut, which found its way to Italy before the Christian era and was taken to Britain by the Romans, which provides the nuts that are second only to almonds in popularity and consumption. Walnuts are grown commercially in south-eastern Australia, particularly in the Ovens Valley of Victoria and, more recently, on a large scale in Tasmania.

Like other nuts, walnuts have a high oil content, but it is 90 per cent unsaturated (24 per cent mono; 68 per cent poly) and rich in linoleic acid, a beneficial fatty acid. Walnuts are used in cakes, breads, and biscuits, in stuffings and salads. They can be ground and added to pastry and used to make tarts and confections. Whole nuts can of course be eaten on their own or with a glass of port. Pickled walnuts, a favourite of the British, are made from immature, green walnuts with soft shells. They are cooked and pickled in spiced vinegar.

wampi. Originally from southern China and described in Andre Simon's *Encyclopaedia of Gastronomy* as 'the finest fruit in Thailand', the wampi is a small, round, yellow or brown fruit that has a lychee-like flesh with a slightly chewy texture and a taste that some people find to be like ripe grapes and others like a gooseberry.

warehou. Although its name is often pronounced 'wahoo', the warehou is not the large, tropical sporting fish called wahoo which Ernest Hemingway described as 'the best-eating of all game-fish'. The blue warehou and the silver warehou, formerly known as the Tasmanian trevally, spotted trevally, and snotty nose trevally or trevalla, among other names, are deep-water fish caught around the south-eastern coast of Australia and usually sold as fillets in fish shops. The flesh is white to off-white, often with dark meat along the sides, which is removed, of medium texture and fairly oily. It may be grilled, fried, baked, and barbecued and is suitable for smoking and for use in fishcakes. The *Australian Seafood Catering Manual* says that the warehou, 'being a slightly dry finfish, will marinate wonderfully in citrus or rice wine flavours . . . It is delicious when marinated and then either grilled and served with chilli jam or deep-fried and served with chips.'

warrigal greens. Also known as New Zealand spinach, Botany Bay spinach, and warrigal cabbage, the leafy prostrate plant *Tetragonia expansa* is native to southern Australia as well as New Zealand, South America, Polynesia, and Japan. Captain Cook was pleased to find it growing wild in the sandy environs of Botany Bay and fed it to his crew to prevent scurvy. His botanist shipmate Joseph Banks noted in his journal: 'We dind to day upon the sting-ray and his tripe . . . We had with it a dish of the leaves of *tetragonia cornuta* [since renamed] boild, which eat as well as spinach or very near it.' Warrigal greens are easy to grow and can be cooked like spinach. Young leaves can be eaten raw in salads; however, blanching is recommended to dissolve any oxalates that might be present.

wasabi. Japanese green horseradish. Wasabi is made from the root of a plant native to Japan and is eaten either freshly grated or as a paste. It is also sold as a green powder which can be made up into a paste by mixing it with water. Much of the imported paste and powder sold in Australia, however, contains little or no true wasabi, as a reading of the list of ingredients on the container will confirm. The plant is now being grown commercially in Tasmania.

Wasabi is a very hot condiment and is used to liven up the fairly bland taste of raw fish in SASHIMI and SUSHI. For sashimi it is often mixed with soy sauce in a dipping bowl. For sushi a blob of wasabi is placed on top of some vinegared rice and covered with a thin slice of fish or other topping. *Wasabi zuke* are vegetables, such as miniature eggplants, pickled in wasabi and mustard.

water chestnuts. The Chinese water chestnut is the corm (a swollen stem base) of an aquatic plant of the sedge family native to Asia and cultivated in China and Japan. The walnut-size corm has a tough, dark brown skin and crisp white flesh. Water chestnuts can be bought fresh in some Asian food stores during their brief season in spring; otherwise they are available peeled in cans. Fresh ones will keep for at least two weeks in the refrigerator. Peel them just before using, and trim root and stem flat. Canned water chestnuts, once opened and drained, can be kept for up to a week in a covered jar of water in the refrigerator if the water is changed daily. The Chinese eat water chestnuts raw as a snack or cooked in sweet dishes. They also use them to provide a crunchy texture in minced meat dishes. In Australia, water chestnuts are often included in stir-fry dishes.

water spinach (ong choi) is not related to English SPINACH or silver beet, but

255

is an aquatic member of the *Ipomoea* genus, which includes the morning glory vine and the sweet potato. Water spinach is grown and eaten throughout South-East Asia. The heart-shaped leaves and the top part of the stems are eaten, either cooked like spinach or stir-fried with something spicy, pungent, or fermented to complement the vegetable's mild flavour.

watercress. There are a number of plants known as cress. Watercress (*Nasturtium officinale*) is an aquatic variety that grows best in running streams but will also grow in ponds and boggy ground. It has fleshy green leaves which have a pleasant, pungent peppery flavour. Other cresses—garden cress, land cress, upland cress, winter cress—are similar in appearance and flavour although they are plants of different genera and species.

When buying watercress, choose a bunch that has bright, fresh leaves with no sign of limpness. Use it as soon as possible, but you can store it for a few days in the refrigerator wrapped in a damp paper towel in a plastic bag or standing in a jar of water (change the water daily). Watercress is a popular salad green and is also eaten raw on sandwiches. It is used in soups and sauces and in egg and meat dishes. It may also be cooked like spinach.

watermelon. Originally from southern Africa, the watermelon was taken to India and Egypt in prehistoric times and is now cultivated all over the world. Watermelons are available in Australia most of the year, certainly from September to May, with heaviest supplies in January-March. As melons don't get any sweeter once they have been picked, choose one that is heavy for its size and has a rich green colour (with a yellow underside where it has stood on the ground). A clean break at the stem end rather than a cut in the stem is another indication of ripeness. Store watermelons in a cool place, and, once cut, keep them in the refrigerator with plastic wrap over the cut surface.

weevils. Although there are nearly four thousand species of weevils native to Australia, it is the introduced ones that you may find in grain products, pulses, and nuts, especially in the autumn, when they hatch out. The eggs are usually not noticeable. If you think there may be weevils in the packets of food you buy, put them in the freezer for forty-eight hours to kill the eggs, then transfer the food to glass jars and store them, labelled and dated, in the pantry. Storing packets of flour and the like in the refrigerator will usually prevent weevil eggs from hatching.

Welsh rabbit / Welsh rarebit. Like Bombay duck (actually a fish), Balmain bug (a crustacean), Murrumbidgee jam (brown sugar and cold tea), or Bundaberg honey (golden syrup), the name Welsh rabbit is a culinary joke. The *rarebit* variant probably came about because it sounded more refined. *Fowler's Modern English Usage* gets quite heated about it: '*Welsh rabbit* is amusing and right, and *Welsh rarebit* stupid and wrong.' Whatever you call it, the dish consists of melted cheese, sometimes mixed with such things as butter, milk, beer, Worcestershire sauce, and seasonings, spread on toast and browned under the grill.

Westralian jewfish. Closely related to the pearl perch, which it resembles in appearance, the Westralian jewfish (or dhufish) is a cold-water finfish found off the southern coast of Western Australia from about Exmouth Gulf round to King George Sound. Caught all year round, but mainly in summer, it is sold whole and in fillets, cutlets, and steaks. It is an excellent eating fish with a full, sweet flavour. Its white flesh is moist, tender, and fine. Westralian jewfish can be cooked in most ways and is highly regarded for eating raw as SASHIMI. (See also FISH.)

wheat is one of the oldest cultivated food plants, its cultivation going back to about 10 000 B.C.. There are about 30 000 known varieties of wheat, which can be loosely grouped as hard (strong) and soft (weak). Hard wheat is grown in hot, dry areas. The flour has a high GLUTEN content and is used to make bread and pasta—durum wheat, the hardest of all, is generally used in the manufacture of commercial pasta. Soft wheat, grown in temperate areas, produces general-purpose flour. (See FLOUR.)

A grain of wheat consists essentially of an outer coat (BRAN); the embryo (wheat germ); and the endosperm, the floury part, which takes up most of the volume of the grain. In the milling of wheat, the endosperm is progressively ground into finer particles. When it is simply cracked, it is known as kibbled wheat; this can be cooked as porridge. BURGHUL is wheat that is cracked after being boiled or steamed. SEMOLINA is a coarse grinding of the endosperm (see also COUSCOUS). The wheat germ is removed in the milling process mainly to improve the flour's keeping quality, as wheat germ contains oil that quickly turns rancid.

whey. The watery liquid that separates from the CURD when milk coagulates, as in CHEESE making. Whey itself can also be made into cheese (see RICOTTA). It also makes an acceptable energy drink.

whisks. The object of whisking is to beat air into an ingredient or a fluid mixture to lighten or thicken it, or to disperse one liquid into another to form an emulsion. The looped-wire whisk, or *fouet*, is the simplest and most popular implement for these tasks. Fouets are used for beating egg-whites (see under EGGS), whipping cream, whisking sauces, and other beating and whisking operations. They come in various sizes, weights, and designs to suit each purpose. Egg whisks are springy and balloon-shaped, whereas

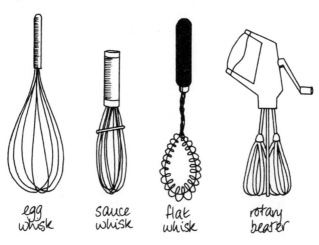

egg whisk   sauce whisk   flat whisk   rotary beater

sauce whisks are rigid and elongated. To get the best out of a whisk, make sure you use a bowl of a size to suit the size of the whisk—the diameter of the bowl should be just a little less than the total length of the whisk. If the bowl it too small, the mixture won't have room to expand and the whisk will be cramped for space; if it is too big, you will have to work harder.

white sauce. See BÉCHAMEL SAUCE.

whitebait are tiny silver fish of various kinds which are cooked and eaten whole without being cleaned. They used to be available in cans, but the canning industry declined and now they are sold fresh or frozen. Wash them thoroughly and drain them before cooking. They are usually coated in flour and deep-fried, but they can also be added to batter and cooked in spoonfuls as FRITTERS.

whiting. Various kinds of whiting are found around the southern half of Australia. They belong to the *Sillago* genus and are not related to the North Sea whiting imported from Europe or the southern blue whiting imported from New Zealand and Singapore, which are not as good eating as the local kind. Small to medium size long-bodied fish, mainly silvery in colour, Australian whiting of one kind or another are caught all year round and are sold whole and in fillets and butterflied fillets. The flesh is moist and delicate, with very little oil, and very white when cooked. It has a delicate, sweet flavour. There are many fine rib bones, but they are easily removed. Whiting are delicious floured and fried, either whole or as fillets. They can also be steamed, baked, and grilled. Fillets are sometimes rolled round a stuffing and poached in wine. (See also FISH.)

witloof / witlof, or Belgian endive, is the blanched, tightly furled, underdeveloped leaves of a type of CHICORY. The leaves are kept from turning green by growing the plant in the dark or by heaping damp sand or soil over the crowns. Witloof is available from August to October. Choose firm heads that are creamy-white to light yellow with no brown discoloration. Use as soon as possible; meanwhile, store in the vegetable crisper of the refrigerator. Witloof can be eaten raw in salads, sliced across or with the leaves separated. It can also be steamed, sautéed, stuffed and braised, stewed in butter, or made into a creamed soup. First cut off the tough part of the root end and remove any wilted outside leaves.

wok. The wok, which originated in China, is the main cooking utensil in several Asian countries. A versatile piece of equipment, it can be used for stir-frying, deep-frying, steaming, and braising. With its large surface area that distributes heat evenly, it is ideal for quick, even cooking (see STIR-FRYING). A specially shaped turner and ladle are used to turn, stir, and blend the food as it rapidly cooks.

Before using a new iron wok, it should be seasoned. First clean off any coating that may be on the metal, then place the wok over moderate heat, put enough oil in to coat the whole interior surface, and stir-fry some chopped spring onions and garlic for 2–3 minutes. Discard the cooked ingredients, wash the wok in warm water, and wipe it dry with paper towels. Rub a fine film of oil over the inside of the wok whenever it is not in use.

The traditional wok with a curved bottom, designed to fit Chinese stoves, is unsuitable for use on a gas stove without a metal ring to sit it on.

won ton. A ball of minced pork and / or prawns mixed with chopped spring onions and seasonings and wrapped in a square of thin noodle dough. Won tons are usually boiled and served in broth, which is variously called SHORT SOUP or won ton soup.

Worcestershire sauce. As the story has it, in 1837 a retired governor of Bengal asked the Worcester chemists Lea and Perrins to make him a barrel of sauce to his personal recipe. The sauce didn't come up to his expectations, and he refused delivery of it. The barrel was left in storage, and three years later, before throwing it out, Mr Lea and Mr Perrins tasted the contents and found the matured sauce to their liking. They dug out the recipe, and the sauce has been made to that recipe ever since. Manufacturers around the world now make it under licence. In Sydney it is made by the Aeroplane Jelly company. The recipe is a secret, they say, but the ingredients as listed on the label are vinegar, molasses, sugar, salt, anchovies, tamarinds, shallots, garlic, spices, and flavourings.

yabby. See CRAYFISH.

yakitori. A Japanese version of the shish KEBAB—food grilled on skewers over a charcoal fire. Pieces of chicken, chicken liver, and spring onions brushed with TERIYAKI sauce are the usual morsels impaled on the slim bamboo skewers, but they may include quail eggs, gingko nuts, pieces of capsicum, even tiny sparrows.

yams are the edible tubers of climbing plants of the genus *Dioscorea,* which occur naturally in tropical and subtropical areas round the world. Yams are staple food items in China, parts of southern Asia, and Melanesia. Three or four species are native to Australia and formed part of the diet of the Aborigines. The rough-skinned tubers vary in colour, size, and shape. The common variety has brown skin and white flesh. Like tubers generally, it grows underground. However, there is a species that bears purple-fleshed aerial tubers that grow from the leaf axils. Yams can be prepared and eaten like potatoes or sweet potatoes—boiled, mashed, baked, or fried as chips.

yeast. For thousands of years before Louis Pasteur discovered what yeasts were and how they worked, people baking bread had been making use of beer froth and other fermenting substances to get their dough to rise. Yeasts, as Pasteur established, are single-celled microscopic fungi responsible for fermentation, converting sugar into alcohol and carbon dioxide. It is the carbon dioxide that is useful in baking. Little bubbles of the gas are trapped in the dough, making the bread or bun light and appetising.

Baker's yeast is available in a compressed or fresh form, from health food stores, and in a granulated dry form, usually in packets of five 7-gram foil sachets, from the supermarket. Compressed yeast, which is partly dried and pressed into a block, should be cream to pale grey in colour and have a clean, pleasant smell; it will keep for up to two weeks in a sealed container in the refrigerator. Dry yeast will keep for up to a year in the pantry; it will have a use-by date on the packet.

Use yeast according to directions in the recipe. Don't use more than required, or your bread will soon go dry and stale. Normally you need only half as much dry yeast by weight as compressed yeast. The yeast is usually dissolved in a lukewarm liquid. If the liquid is too hot, it will kill the yeast; if it is too cool, the yeast will not be activated.

yellowtail kingfish. Known simply as yellowtail or kingfish, the yellowtail kingfish is a popular sport fish found around the southern Australian coast from Queensland to Western Australia. It is a fairly large, streamlined fish, silver with a purple-blue top and yellow tail. Its pink flesh is fairly firm and dry and can be coarse if the fish is a big one. It is not highly regarded for eating cooked, although it is popular eaten raw as SASHIMI.

yoghurt / yogurt. Unlike cheese, which is made from milk treated with rennet to curdle it, yoghurt is milk curdled by the action of acid-producing bacteria. A 'culture' of *Lactobacillus bulgaricus* and *Streptococcus thermophilus* introduced into whole or skim milk converts the lactose (milk sugar) into lactic acid, which produces a soft curd with a fresh, tangy flavour. *Lactobacillus acidophilus* and *L. bifidus,* two forms of beneficial bacteria that naturally inhabit the intestines, are also included in some yoghurts. These bacteria are believed to improve the body's immunological response and decrease the levels of toxic by-products formed in the digestion of certain foods. Yoghurt containing these cultures is thought to restore the healthy balance of bacteria in the gut when it has been disturbed by too much alcohol, too much protein and refined foods, high levels of stress, and the effects of broad-spectrum antibiotics on friendly as well as harmful bacteria.

Skim-milk yoghurt, which contains a negligible amount of fat, usually is reinforced with added skim milk powder, making it an excellent source of calcium and high-quality protein, and because the lactose has been used up as fuel by the fermenting bacteria, it is easier to digest than milk. Some commercial flavoured yoghurts, however, contain up to 16 per cent sugar.

Yoghurt can be eaten as it is as a snack or used instead of cream on fresh or stewed fruit. Ice-cream and yoghurt go well together on fruit. Yoghurt is also used as a substitute for cream, sour cream, and mayonnaise in sauces, marinades, salads, and dips. Season it with salt and pepper and mix it with one or more of the following: chopped spring onions, garlic, chives, parsley, dill, or mint, grated cucumber, tahina and lemon juice, even chopped tomatoes, olives, gherkins, and chillies.

When used in hot dishes and hot sauces, yoghurt will curdle unless it is first stabilised by adding cornflour or a mixture of cornflour and beaten egg-whites.

If it is beaten rapidly, yoghurt liquefies and can be used to make refreshing drinks (see, for example, LASSI).

Yorkshire pudding. This is not a pudding in the accepted sense but a kind of light, puffy pancake that the English eat with roast beef. (Traditionally they eat it *before* the roast beef, just with gravy, to fill them up so they don't eat too much meat.) Yorkshire pudding is made with flour, eggs, and milk baked in a shallow baking tin greased with beef dripping and, if practicable, placed under the beef to catch the dripping juices. Nowadays, the pudding is usually cut into squares to serve with the beef.

yum cha. A Chinese meal consisting of a wide range of savoury and sweet DIM SUM style dishes served in small baskets on trolleys wheeled from table to table. Diners select what they fancy from the trolley. Yum cha is taken at any time from breakfast to early afternoon.

Z

zabaglione / zabaione. An Italian custard flavoured with Marsala. It is made by beating together egg yolks and castor sugar until they are pale yellow and fluffy, then adding the Marsala and beating the mixture in a pot over gently simmering water until it swells into a light, soft mass. Zabaglione is served hot in glass goblets. (See also SABAYON.)

zest. See PEEL, RIND, ZEST.

zucchini are marrows picked when immature. *Cucurbita pepo,* the species of marrow, or summer SQUASH, that produces the zucchini, was brought back from America (where all the Cucurbitae originated) by Columbus. It was cultivated in Italy and other countries around the Mediterranean as well as back in Mexico, where it is still important in Mexican cooking. The rest of the world got to know about zucchini only relatively recently.

Zucchini are available all year round, with heaviest supplies in summer. Choose firm, smallish vegetables without any wrinkles or softness. They will keep fairly well in a plastic bag in the refrigerator. There are several varieties. The common one is dark green, but there are also yellow ones. The Lebanese variety is striped, pale green, and bottle-shaped, which makes it good for stuffing. Zucchini can also be boiled, steamed, baked, fried, or eaten raw. The flowers too are a delicacy—stuffed, dipped in light batter, and deep-fried. Before cooking zucchini, all you need to do is wash them and trim off the stem and the hard spot at the other end. Then cook them whole, halved, or cut up as the recipe requires.

References

Alexander, Stephanie *Stephanie's Australia* Sydney: Allen & Unwin, 1991

Asher, Jane *Jane Asher's Party Book* London: Pelham Books, 1982

Australian Concise Oxford Dictionary, The 2nd edn., eds. J.M. Hughes, P.A. Michell, and W.S. Ramson, Melbourne: OUP, 1992

Australian Seafood Catering Manual Brisbane: Queensland Department of Primary Industries and Fisheries Research and Development Corporation, 1994

Ayto, John *The Diner's Dictionary* Oxford: OUP, 1993

Baker, Janice *Herbs for Better Living* Sydney: Bay Books, n.d.

Beckett, Barbara *Chutneys and Pickles* Sydney: Weldon, 1992

—— *The Harvest Pantry* Sydney: Allen & Unwin, 1993

—— *Jams and Marmalades* Sydney: Weldon, 1992

—— *Salad Greens* Sydney: Barbara Beckett Publishing, 1995

—— *Step by Step Poultry* London: Bloomsbury Books, 1994

—— *Tropical Fruits* Sydney: Barbara Beckett Publishing 1995

Bourne, Ursula *Portuguese Cookery* Harmondsworth, Mddx: Penguin, 1973

Brazel, Susan *Step by Step Wok* London: Bloomsbury Books, 1994

Brown, Dale, and the Editors of Time-Life Books *The Cooking of Scandinavia* Time-Life International, 1969

Campbell, Susan *The Cook's Companion* London: Chancellor Press, 1985

Chapman, Anne *Herbs* Sydney: Weldon, 1992

Child, Julia *The Way to Cook* New York: Knopf, 1989

Cribb, A.B. and J.W. *Wild Food in Australia* Sydney: Fontana, 1976

David, Elizabeth *A Book of Mediterranean Food* Harmondsworth, Mddx: Penguin, 1955

—— *English Bread and Yeast Cookery* Harmondsworth, Mddx: Penguin, 1979

—— *French Country Cooking* Harmondsworth, Mddx: Penguin, 1959

—— *French Provincial Cooking* Harmondsworth, Mddx: Penguin, 1964

—— *Italian Cooking* Harmondsworth, Mddx: Penguin, 1963

—— *An Omelette and a Glass of Wine* Boronia, Vic.: Dent, 1984

—— *Spices, Salt and Aromatics in the English Kitchen* Harmondsworth; Mddx: Penguin, 1970

—— *Summer Cooking* Harmondsworth, Mddx: Penguin, 1965

Deighton, Len *Len Deighton's Action Cook Book* Harmondsworth, Mddx: Penguin, 1968

—— *Où est le Garlic?* Harmondsworth, Mddx: Penguin, 1965

Escoffier, A[uguste] *A Guide to Modern Cooking* London: Heinemann, 1907

Fanton, Michel and Jude *The Seed Savers' Handbook* Byron Bay: Seed Savers Network, 1993

Field, Michael and Frances, and the Editors of Time-Life Books *A Quintet of Cuisines* Time-Life International, 1971

Fisher, M.F.K., and the Editors of Time-Life Books *The Cooking of Provincial France* Time-Life International, 1968

Floyd, Keith *Floyd on Fish* London: BBC, 1985

Fulton, Margaret *Encyclopedia of Food and Cookery* Sydney: Octopus Books, 1983

—— *The Margaret Fulton Cookbook* Sydney: Paul Hamlyn, 1968

—— *Margaret Fulton's New Cookbook* Sydney: Angus & Robertson, 1993

Gibbs, Suzanne *Sweet Things* Sydney: Angus & Robertson, 1994

Halligan, Marion *Eat My Words* Sydney: Angus & Robertson IMPRINT, 1990

Hazan, Marcella *The Classic Italian Cookbook* New York: Knopf, 1987

—— *The Second Classic Italian Cookbook* London: Macmillan PAPERMAC, 1983

Hazelton, Nika Standen, and the Editors of Time-Life Books *The Cooking of Germany* Time-Life International, 1970

Hemphill, Rosemary *Fragrance and Flavour* Sydney: Angus & Robertson, 1959

—— Spice and Savour Sydney: Angus & Robertson, 1967

Heritage Illustrated Dictionary of the English Language, The, ed. William Morris, New York: American Heritage Publishing Co., 1969

Katzen, Mollie *The Moosewood Cookbook* Berkeley, Cal.: Ten Speed Press, 1977

Kitchen Handbook, The Sydney: Reader's Digest, 1982

Larousse Gastronomique London: Hamlyn, 1984

Lo Mei Hing, Giulia Marzotto Caotorta, and Sun Tzi Hsi *Chinese Cooking* Sydney: Mead & Beckett, 1983

McCully, Helen *Nobody Ever Tells You These Things* London: Angus & Robertson, 1968

McGee, Harold *On Food and Cooking* New York: Scribner, 1984

MacMiadhachain, Anna *Spanish Regional Cookery* Harmondsworth, Mddx: Penguin, 1976

McNulty, John *The World of John McNulty* New York: Dolphin Books, 1961

Macquarie Dictionary, The Sydney: Macquarie Library, 1981

Maher, Barbara *Cakes* Harmondsworth, Mddx: Penguin, 1984

Mencken, H.L. *The American Language*, 1 vol. abridged ed., New York: Knopf, 1967

Maree, Aaron *Cookies, Biscuits and Slices* Sydney: Angus & Robertson 1992

Miller, Somi Ananta, and Patricia Lake *Thai Cooking Class*. Sydney: Bay Books, n.d.

Nelson-Henrick, Shaun *The Complete Book of Yoghurt* New York: Collier Macmillan, 1980

Nickles, Harry G., and the Editors of Time-Life Books *The Cooking of the Middle East* Time-Life International, 1970

Papashvily, Helen and George, and the Editors of Time-Life Books *Russian Cooking* New York: Time-Life Books, 1975

Pascoe, Elise *Elise Pascoe's Cooking Class* Sydney: Bay Books, 1993

Paston-Williams, Sarah *The National Trust Book of Traditional Puddings* Harmondsworth, Mddx: Penguin, 1986

Rodale, J.I. *How to Grow Vegetables and Fruits by the Organic Method* Emmaus, Pa.: Rodale Press, 1961

Roden, Claudia *A Book of Middle Eastern Food* Harmondsworth, Mddx: Penguin, 1970

Rogers, Sheridan *The Cook's Garden* Sydney: Angus & Robertson, 1992

Root, Waverley, and the Editors of Time-Life Books *The Cooking of Italy* Time-Life International, 1969

Rosten, Leo *The Joys of Yiddish* Harmondsworth, Mddx: Penguin, 1972

Roughley, T.C. *Fish and Fisheries of Australia*, rev. edn. Sydney: Angus & Robertson, 1966

Santin, Gino, and Anthony Blake *La Cucina Veneziana* New York: Prentice Hall, 1988

Sawyer, Jessie, and Sara Moore-Sims (comps.) *The Coronation Cookery Book*, 10th edn., revised, Country Women's Association of NSW, 1970

Simon, Andre *A Concise Encyclopaedia of Gastronomy* London: Collins, 1952

Simpson, Helen *The London Ritz Book of Afternoon Tea* London: Ebury Press, 1986

Skull, John *Key Terms in Cuisine* Brighton, SA: Elbrook Press, 1991

Steinberg, Rafael, and the Editors of Time-Life Books *The Cooking of Japan* Time-Life International, 1970

Stobart, Tom *The Cook's Encyclopaedia* London: Batsford, 1980

Tipping, Jill *Iced Follies* London: Macdonald Orbis, 1988

Toussaint-Samat, Maguelonne *History of Food* trans. Althea Bell, Cambridge: Blackwell, 1992

Wechsberg, Joseph, and the Editors of Time-Life Books *The Cooking of Vienna's Empire* Time-Life International, 1969

References

Wells, Troth *The World in Your Kitchen* Oxford: New Internationalist Publications, 1993
What Food Is That? Jo Rogers, chief nutritionist, Sydney: Weldon, 1990
Wolfert, Paula *Mediterranean Cooking* New York: Quadrangle / The New York Times Book Co., 1977
Wong, Ella-Mei *Chinese Cookery* Sydney: Angus & Robertson, 1961